Music and the New Global Culture

BIG ISSUES IN MUSIC

A project of the Chicago Studies in Ethnomusicology Series
Edited by Philip V. Bohlman and Ronald M. Radano

ALSO IN THIS SERIES

MUSIC and
THE NEW GLOBAL CULTURE

From the Great Exhibitions to the Jazz Age

HARRY LIEBERSOHN

The University of Chicago Press

Chicago and London

Publication of this book has been supported by the Joseph Kerman Endowment of the American Musicological Society, funded in part by the National Endowment for the Humanities and the Andrew W. Mellon Foundation.

The University of Chicago Press, Chicago 60637
The University of Chicago Press, Ltd., London
© 2019 by The University of Chicago
Published 2019
Printed in the United States of America

28 27 26 25 24 23 22 21 20 19   1 2 3 4 5

ISBN-13: 978-0-226-62126-5 (cloth)
ISBN-13: 978-0-226-64927-6 (paper)
ISBN-13: 978-0-226-64930-6 (e-book)
DOI: https://doi.org/10.7208/chicago/9780226649306.001.0001

Library of Congress Cataloging-in-Publication Data

Names: Liebersohn, Harry, author.
Title: Music and the new global culture : from the great exhibitions to the
    jazz age / Harry Liebersohn.
Other titles: Big issues in music.
Description: Chicago ; London : The University of Chicago Press, 2019. |
    Series: Big issues in music
Identifiers: LCCN 2019008605 | ISBN 9780226621265 (cloth : alk. paper) |
    ISBN 9780226649276 (pbk. : alk. paper) | ISBN 9780226649306 (ebook)
Subjects: LCSH: Music and globalization—History. | World music—History and
    criticism. | Ethnomusicology—History. | Globalization—History. | Sound
    recording industry—History.
Classification: LCC ML3916 .L54 2019 | DDC 780.9—dc23
LC record available at https://lccn.loc.gov/2019008605

♾ This paper meets the requirements of ANSI/NISO Z39.48-1992 (Permanence of Paper).

For Dorothee

CONTENTS

Introduction

Anyone who has heard of Ravi Shankar will probably associate his name with some of the most marvelous moments of the 1960s. There is the image of him at Woodstock: the world-famous sitar player amid the galaxy of rock stars, becoming a kind of rock star himself in the giddy days of summer '69. Fans around the world heard the sounds of his instrument, the sitar, in the albums of the Beatles, first toyed with as an exotic prop, then played with greater seriousness by George Harrison after the group spent time with Shankar in India. At the time, the master reacted with private impatience to the adulation of his countercultural admirers. Yet in later years he could take a wider view. Some of the people who on first hearing Indian music treated it so casually, he wrote in his autobiography, went on to develop a serious relationship with it. In the end, he had made the right decision to take up the role of Indian music's emissary to the West.[1]

Shankar's experiences in the 1960s were but one chapter in a lifetime of cultural encounters. They began in Paris in the 1930s, when he was still a boy. A film clip shows him with the dance troupe of his older brother, Uday Shankar.[2] Uday brought Indian dance and music to European and American audiences. Ravi not only played and danced in his brother's ensemble but also got a French education, reading novels, cultivating himself widely, and girl-chasing in the French capital. Before this adventure, he had spent his first ten years with his mother and siblings in the sacred Hindu city of Varanasi along the banks of the Ganges. From his mother he absorbed folklore, and from his surroundings a nearness to the gods that made the stories of their lives everyday realities for him. After Paris, he went with his brother's dance company to Hollywood and lived for awhile among the stars. But eventually he followed the invitation of a master musician, Allauddin Khan, and returned to India to study with him in Maihar. Famous as a teacher to several of the great Indian musicians of the twentieth century, but also for his volcanic emotional outbursts, Allaudin Khan immersed him in a discipline that turned a gifted novice into an accomplished virtuoso. After finishing his training and working in Bombay, Ravi Shankar returned to the West for memorable musical encounters. Just a few years before Woodstock, Yehudi Menuhin, the celebrated violin prodigy and yoga devotee, collaborated with him on a record album. During the 1960s, John Coltrane, one of the most famous and adventurous jazz musicians, met him and absorbed his sitar music into the wandering ruminations of his saxophone. By the time of Shankar's encounters with the Beatles and other 1960s rock and roll musicians, the sound of his music had already crossed continents.[3]

Today, we may think that global culture is a product of our own time—to be exact, of the years since the 1980s. The fall of the Berlin Wall, the end of the Soviet empire, the creation of a Chinese market economy, the retreat of the nonaligned movement in India, and the electronic speed-up of communications around the world—these and other changes have created the impression of a radically new cultural moment. Traditional ways of thinking and feeling seem to have given way to an unprecedented flow of art without origin or end, an unending circulation of words, images, and sounds.[4] Yet there is more to the story: Ravi Shankar's career took place in the twentieth century, but it hints at a longer history. The new global culture began before World War I in an era of aristocrats and immigrants, overseas European empires and local crafts. Nowhere was the transformation of culture more sudden than in music.

Since the age of Columbus, visual artifacts and literary texts had sifted into Europe from around the world. It was not hard to transport fabrics, porcelain, or books from India or China to Portugal, Spain, Italy, Holland, France, or England. Difficult though it might be to interpret them, torn out of their contexts as they were, exotic commodities confronted Europeans as originals. But music was another matter. Missionaries and naturalists made an effort to include foreign music in their travel accounts. But their impressions generally amounted to a drastic Europeanization of what they observed. And music was evanescent, without the temporal continuity of material objects. At worst, the attempt to transcribe foreign music lopped off its distinctive qualities and turned it into a grotesque approximation of European music. Without original examples, without a readiness to be done with prejudices about one's own and foreign forms of music, without an understanding of unfamiliar musical instruments and pedagogy, Europeans could hardly begin to comprehend what they were hearing.

Suddenly there was music without walls.[5] From the mid-nineteenth century, musicians traveled in unprecedented numbers from foreign continents to European metropolises; anthropologists and a multitude of colonial, business, and private travelers went from Europe and North America to distant places; a flood of recordings washed over all continents; pianos were transported to Asia; and sitars entered European museums. By 1914 the culturally curious looked out on vastly expanded horizons. They did not stop at the bounds of Europe, with occasional exotic messages from afar. Instead, their ears opened up to sounds disseminated through global networks. Londoners could learn about the structure of Middle Eastern music or hear bands of visiting musicians from China or Thailand; Parisians and Chicagoans could hear exotic music at the world exhibitions staged in their cities; residents of Calcutta, Shanghai, Cairo, and Buenos Aires could play recordings in local languages or listen to the latest American popular music. While people in metropolises were best placed to enjoy this expansion of artistic offerings, shipments of phonographs went out to hundreds of smaller places across Asia, the Americas, the Middle East, and Europe. A startling influx of sounds could be heard around the world.

At the time and ever since, there has been debate about what took place. Was it the beginning of a great homogenization in which Western music drowned out traditions high and low, from the delicacy of the Chinese qin to the blare from the street? Or was it the start of a new era celebrated by world music fans today, in which musicians from Mali with a Cuban inflection, klezmer bands from Poland and Ireland, fado artists, preservers of folk tradition, and celebrants of fusion and rock perform at the music festivals that now seem to sprout up everywhere, joyfully reworking their homemade goods for mutual appreciation? Either way, music has occupied a noisy place in the new global culture.[6]

It would simplify the story to write it up as a narrative of either decline and fall or of exchange and appreciation—but it is too discontinuous for that, by turns a tale of commercialization, breakup of ancient crafts, and cracking of alien cultural codes. There is no uniform answer to the question of whether it added up to homogenization or diversity. There was also no steady progression from provinciality to global consciousness; changing economic conditions, world wars, and fluctuations of artistic taste narrowed and expanded aesthetic horizons.

Music in the History of Global Encounters

This book takes a historical approach to music and globalization. It recounts the social and economic history of globalization since the mid-nineteenth century; it recalls how that history took shape in the late-nineteenth-century era of European imperialism; it asks how artistic institutions and individuals responded to new technologies and political challenges.

The artistic responses to globalization formed numerous dramas over the past century and a half. To recapture these histories of global encounter in their local diversity—pitting large social forces against individual creativity—one must go to their specific time and place. A necessary approach, but also a treacherous one. Encounters are vivid; they tell stories. They may also seem to offer an easy starting point for understanding how cultural exchanges work; all one has to do is go to the place of encounter and record the history as it really was. But on closer examination, one comes up against riddles that only research and persistence can unravel. If European challenges and non-European responses marked the globalization of culture after the mid-nineteenth century, what actually did take place at the point where foreign cultures intersected—where individuals tried, despite their differences, to communicate? The paradox of the moment of encounter (and by extension, indirect communication through books and recordings) is that it is an illusion or a cipher when taken in isolation. To analyze travelers' tales is to learn that their record of a moment in time is often sparse and at first sight banal. One has to work outward from the isolated moment in different directions: backward in time, on both sides of the encounter, to each one's palimpsest of assumptions about foreigners, rituals of welcome, and correctives to misunderstandings; and forward beyond the moment to the recollections of the encounter, its propagation and reception, and the encapsulations of it—the slogans, anecdotes, and clichés—in public discourse. Clear and straightforward at first sight, encounters turn out to be many-sided, deceptive, and rewarding as one follows their sources and returns to them newly aware of their multiple dimensions. To work with the history of encounters is a historian's task that calls for an integration of macrohistory and microhistory, a recounting of local stories that links them to global transformations.

This book concentrates on music and globalization in Europe and North America and how local aesthetic horizons irregularly widened out to the rest of the world—and retreated from it. Yet one cannot understand this much without attention to *both* sides of musical encounters—an awareness, to mention only two examples, of the changes taking place in an aggressively modernizing Japan or a politically strife-ridden China in the early twentieth century. Beyond its European focus, this book follows the dialectical relationship between non-Western and Western cultures. Europeans and North Americans expanded outward in the late nineteenth and early twentieth centuries, intoxicated by the self-proclaimed greatness of their own civilization and confident in its triumph among all the peoples encountered on their journeys. Their impact was deep and many-sided. The prestige of European arts and sciences was almost irresistible, in particular to non-European elites demoralized by the disruption of their own inherited forms of cultural and social hegemony. Yet this turns out to have been only part of the story: subtler but significant was the impact of extra-European arts on Europe itself. By the early twentieth century, clusters of influential Europeans were intrigued by foreign ways of life; while many others were indifferent, the encounters impressed some of the era's more thoughtful artists and intellectuals.

By concentrating on the reverse impact of encounters on Europeans, this book takes up historical issues laid out by J. H. Elliott in *The Old World and the New, 1492–1650*. Elliott traces what he calls the uncertain impact of the discovery of the Americas, from Columbus to Alexander von Humboldt. He draws attention to the slow pace and limited quality of that impact, but also to its role in creating a more reflective, self-critical intellectual frame of mind by the time of Humboldt's voyage in the early nineteenth century. While Elliott's book ranges broadly across politics and economy as well as intellectual life, a second book, Bernard Smith's *European Vision and the South Pacific*, focuses more intensively on Elliott's endpoint, the late Enlightenment and early Romantic moment from around the 1770s to the 1820s, relating how difficult it was for European artists to capture on paper unfamiliar human societies and their environment in Oceania.⁷ Both books are cautionary tales; impact there was, but it was erring and uncertain. Similarly, the suddenness with which Europeans encountered non-European forms of music in the late nineteenth century should not lead to airy conclusions about the outcome, which was discernible but also limited by the deep hold of previously formed patterns of listening.

A useful constellation of metaphors for describing cultural encounters comes from the writings of Hans-Georg Gadamer. To describe the effect of education in a foreign culture, they speak of an expansion of mental horizons and a fusion of different worlds. *Truth and Method* develops this language of horizons and fusion as part of a plea for recovering Western tradition. While reaching across the temporal abyss of World War I and the Nazi era to reconnect his contemporaries to their literary and philosophical inheritance, Gadamer's vision does not extend in comparable manner across space to non-European cultures. One might argue that he was too much the pupil of classical philology, devoted to cultural exploration through texts, thereby excluding experiences of encounter and practices of cultural appropriation—too beholden to a post-1945 tendency in Western Europe and the United States to retreat from the wider world and regain one's cultural bearings at home. But Gadamer's text can have applications beyond his own foreshortened view. His limitations matter less than the usefulness of his vocabulary for discussions of cross-cultural interpretation. It remains a prescription for anti-dogmatic thinking and dialogue with other cultures.⁸ Gadamer's geographic vocabulary of widening horizons offers a way to discuss the pre-1914 history of people, artifacts, and ideas in movement around the world. His language becomes even more useful if one keeps in mind the opposite processes that it can describe, the narrowing of horizons and separation of worlds that have equally been a response to globalization.

The horizon of historical encounters is formed out of concepts. The experiences that widen, overlap, collide, scrape, or ignore one another are registered in concepts that capture collective historical experiences of different actors and how those experiences change over time. Reinhart Koselleck's historical writings and theoretical essays emphasized the specific historical experiences and sociopolitical presuppositions that inform historical concepts; with this emphasis on the specific and the experiential, he turned conceptual history from a collection of static terms into dynamic ways of imagining the world, with different parties vying for the power to define them. Conceptual history of this kind, imbued with the human responses to historical change, lends itself to the analysis of globalization as a defining force for cultural and intellectual life. Koselleck himself was fundamentally concerned with European society and politics; even though he wrote beginning in the early 1950s about the spread of European revolutions to the rest of the world, this was a gesture which did not in fact narrate extra-European histories or *their* actors' experience of sociopolitical transformation as the matrix of historical concepts.[9] Yet the clash of contesting conceptualizations was precisely the drama that took shape after 1850, with multiple, competing processes of globalization around the world and, in response, distinctive experiments in cultural innovation. Two of the most important historical concepts from the post-1850 era are suggested by the title of this book. The bounds of "music" changed within societies and through accelerating cultural transfers; it operated with an antipode, "noise," which was often Europeans' initial response to the alien musical systems they confronted. "Culture" itself is famously a contested concept whose meaning has steadily changed in the modern era, including and excluding different groups. At the center of dispute for music and globalization after 1850 was the assumption of cultural hierarchy as a fact of world history; hierarchical conceptions were widely taken for granted, but also disputed, in the decades before 1914. Colonial societies, at both elite and popular levels, confronted Western political hegemony and technological superiority by making a wide range of choices about how to change and still maintain their cultural independence. Critical opposition to cultural hierarchy came from a growing movement toward cultural democracy, which attained a new legitimacy after World War I. Through narratives from many different parts of the world, this book will trace how societies confronted alien forms of music and conceptually registered their responses.

Gadamer's and Koselleck's language can be brought into contemporary discussion with the aid of more recent works that have attempted to wrest the idea of culture away from the "thick description" of self-enclosed totalities, and which instead trace what a recent volume has called cultures in motion. In the long-standing tradition of cultural anthropology, it was often taken for granted that a holistic culture was the natural unit for study. Although Franz Boas, the most important founder of cultural anthropology in the United States, emphasized that cultures took shape through interaction with their neighbors, his scholarship compiled a mass of empirical details about every aspect of a distinct people and its way of life. His student Ruth Benedict brought to a wide public a notion of holistic tribal "patterns of culture" with a meaningfulness and beauty that was not only worthy of respect, but superior to the fragmented cultures of modern societies. Today, the paradigm of cultures as totalities has been replaced—nowhere more than in anthropology—by terms like "creolization" and "hybridization," which emphasize mixture and motion rather than internal cohesion and stability. Several works stand out for their attention to the cohesion that individual cultural formations *do* have, along with their openness to geographic contact and temporal change. Daniel Rodgers has pointed to the opportunities and hazards of capturing cultures in motion: historians are in the business of observing the peculiar and specific, and encounters between cultures are conditioned by the different historical trajectories that precede cultural contact. Stephen Greenblatt has defined mobility as intrinsic to the formation of any culture, but he also emphasizes that cultural identities, once formed, become sources of deeply felt loyalties. Rodgers and Greenblatt write as editors of respective essay volumes; their introductions lead not to aerial views of cultural mobility, but to on-the-ground examples of social practices and intellectual production. My book attempts in a similar way to avoid a formulaic reaction to earlier definitions of cultures as autonomous totalities. Without denying the integrity of cultures—which can actually be reinforced by accelerating cultural contact and a perceived threat of disintegration—it will relate how, since the mid-nineteenth century, cultures in motion have taken shape amid specific circumstances and unpredictable encounters.[10]

Building on Gadamer's insight that we start out as provincials and broaden our horizons through a process of education, we do well to approach foreign music with an awareness that initial aesthetic judgments are often another name for prejudice toward the foreign and the new. Anyone loyal to a local musical tradition will know that it does not have to be "great" in order to be precious; rather, it is felt to be *my* music, conveying an irreducible body of collective feeling and experience. Artless though it may be in its original form, it can become the stuff of art music. The challenges of globalization and responses of intellectuals and artists were a provocation to nineteenth-century observers; once again in our own day, they can either disturb or delight. This book leaves aesthetic judgment to the expertise of musicologists and musicians. Instead, it sticks to the historian's task of giving shape to an era and telling its story.

Empires

To capture the complexity of musical encounters is to go against the cliché of an imposition tout court of Western culture on the rest of the world, countered by the revolt of indigenous cultures.

It is not hard to understand the plausibility of this view. During the period from 1850 to 1914, European empires and the United States dominated most of the world as never before. Cultural plundering also marked adventures such as the British devastation of the Benin kingdom and the looting of the Tibetan capital, Lhasa. Less sensational but defining for the world order was the economic exploitation and authoritarian rule of European colonial regimes. As C. A. Bayly has written for the British Empire of the early nineteenth century, the freedoms and protections of home did not apply abroad; instead, absolutism and bureaucratic domination, long-standing inheritances of the European past, provided the model for colonial administration.[11] In the definition of culture, a distinct hardening took place after the mid-nineteenth century. Racial prejudice toward non-Europeans was already embedded in European thinking, but the meaning of "race" had been rather fluid. It was partially countered in the late Enlightenment by the assumption that "wild" peoples could be civilized just as the Romans had once civilized northern Europeans. European military and technological superiority was still limited in the late eighteenth and early nineteenth centuries; on location, many Europeans developed a respect for the warfare and social skills of Native Americans, the sophistication of South Asian courts, and the acumen of Chinese administrators.[12]

The resources of industrialized Western nation-states after 1850 were something else; they created chasms where there had once been divides, a sense of immutable superiority or at least a great gulf between northern Europeans and the rest of humanity. Racial theories entrenched this separation, with the vulgar and the vague reinforced by the authority of Charles Darwin, who declared that contact with Europeans naturally led to the extinction of indigenous peoples. Anyone who has read widely in the scientific literature of late nineteenth-century Europe will come away with the depressing knowledge that it was almost impossible for Europeans to be untouched by racism; it was taken for granted by even the most cosmopolitan, critical, and humane. Franz Boas stands out as one of the earliest exceptions—but he, too, had to struggle for decades before turning into an uncompromising critic of scientific racial theory. At first sight, then, it seems misplaced to imagine any kind of cultural exchange:

colonial subjects faced oppressive regimes, and Europeans were too smitten by their belief in their own superiority to take seriously any culture
different from their own.[13]

Without diminishing the severities and atrocities of colonial regimes,
recent scholarship has revealed a more complex cultural landscape than
the complete opposition of colonizer and colonized. The changing historical picture is especially striking among places and peoples who previously have been touted as helpless victims. Native Americans suffered
through a terrible period of land expropriation and violence beginning
in the late eighteenth century and building on earlier centuries of mal-
treatment; yet there were tribes that continued to thrive through trade,
and individuals who made careers as lawyers and intellectuals in the new
American republic. Polynesians endured biological, commercial, and
political invasion beginning in the late eighteenth century; yet in hard-
hit places like Tahiti and Hawaii they were also shrewd cultural brokers,
appropriating political symbols and forging alliances with captains, missionaries, and traders.[14] Larger, more populous places like China, Japan,
and India were better equipped to resist European incursions and made
selective use of European cultural institutions for their own ends. The
Meiji regime in Japan famously modernized on its own terms; Chinese intellectuals of the late nineteenth and early twentieth centuries hungrily
pursued knowledge of the wider world while the imperial regime traced
an erratic course of resistance and appropriation of Western models until
it was overthrown in 1911; Indian society accommodated British rule, but
also exported its own music, religion, and philosophical ideas. Despite the
asymmetries of economy and power, the high imperial era was a moment
in which non-Western societies laid out their own plans for autonomy.

The history of music in the age of imperialism exemplifies both the
havoc and the creative responses that resulted from exposure to European
culture. Only local stories reveal the details that make these responses
come alive. The image that builds up from a fine-grained view is a mixed
one. It includes a broad spectrum of outcomes that included the loss of
long-established musical traditions, rejection of foreign influences, and
innovation. No preordained evolution moved musical or any other artistic encounters toward a predictable end; the consequences of Western
hegemony differed from place to place and changed course over time.

A complete disavowal of continuities, however, would overstate the
case for historical haphazardness. In her survey of globalization from
1870 to 1945, Emily Rosenberg observes that despite the era's cataclysms,

it carried forward patterns of collective life that began to take shape at the beginning.¹⁵ Sharing her view of cultural persistence, this book unearths patterns that continue to have a hold on our tastes and habits. To be sure, the search for continuities has to proceed with caution. Great changes took place after 1914, including the rise of radio; the electrification of recording; the invention of successive audio media including tape, cassette, and electronic devices; and damage to some musical genres and repackaging of others. Yet even changes as large as these did not dislodge national musical traditions, pop genres, or classical canons that cultural contact had helped to shape before and after 1900. Overall, one can turn back to the pre–World War I era to check our perception today of globalization's radical novelty.

The Transatlantic Triad

The history of music and globalization during the past century and a half is too vast for any one book to re-create. It would have to take into account every record, every singer, every song, every salesman, and every listener in most parts of the world. This book is instead confined to a single chapter from this larger history. It circulates chiefly around three places: England, Germany, and the United States. The English revival of traditional arts and crafts encouraged the late-nineteenth-century fascination with non-Western music; Germany nurtured the modern discipline of global musical comparison; and the United States launched the phonograph industry. Each country, then, had a special affinity to one of this book's organizing terms: craft in England, science (in the broad German sense of organized higher learning) in Germany, and commerce in the United States. But to imagine these countries' response to globalization in national isolation distorts what was in fact a crisscross of exchanges around an Atlantic community. The resources for responding to globalization wandered freely around these three countries. England developed its curiosity about times and places outside modern Europe with a hefty dose of help from German immigrants. German scientists benefited from the example of English researchers who had greater access to extra-European instruments, musicians, and expertise. The American phonograph industry owed part of its success to German immigrants, and encompassed the world by cooperating with English and German partners. The expansion of cultural horizons happened differently in each place, but added up to a single cohesive story.

To recount the creation of the transatlantic network binding these three places does not lessen the importance of musical responses to globalization elsewhere in Europe. France had its own traditions of antiquarian and extra-European connoisseurship and scientific contributions to musicology, as well as commercial success in the modern phonograph industry. Annegret Fauser's study of music at the 1889 Paris World's Fair combines musicological and historical perspectives on a famous site of encounter. Debussy has received extensive attention for his uses of East and Southeast Asian music—a topic that leads to the larger subject of the Symbolist movement's appropriation of non-European arts.[16] Yet in some ways, what is remarkable is how little the French appropriation of extra-European cultures joined the steady traffic of communications around the German and Anglophone triangle. By contrast, British and American reception of German music, German migration to Britain and the United States, and Americans' study in and admiration of German universities shaped a common culture.

The Habsburg Empire furthered the comparative understanding of music amid its jostling of nationalities and high standards of university research. It is an anachronism in any case to make a neat separation between it and the German Empire, political rivals but parts of a common cultural landscape in nineteenth-century Central Europe. There is no reason to think of Austrian culture as less "German" than that of its northern rival; since the Middle Ages, Vienna had been the historic metropolis, and the Austrian monarchs had the better claim to Central European hegemony in their role as rulers of the Holy Roman Empire, while Prussia's claim to great power status dated only from the late eighteenth century. It was Austria's defeat in the Austro-Prussian War of 1866, not an intrinsic cultural logic, that led to its exclusion from the German nation-state. Despite their post-1866 political separation from the north, Austrians made central contributions to the widening of musical horizons in the German Empire. Erich von Hornbostel, as director of the Phonogram Archive in Berlin, was a crucial figure in the creation of modern ethnomusicology. Felix von Luschan furthered Hornbostel's work from his position as a high-ranking official in the Berlin Ethnological Museum. Under Luschan's tutelage, Richard Thurnwald became a prominent German anthropologist and made musical recordings for the Phonogram Archive's collection. All of these people came from comfortable, cultivated Viennese families; in Berlin, they formed a cluster of scholar-scientists who had grown up in a multicultural city. Yet it was Germany that became the economic, cultural, and political world power of the late nineteenth century, its economy rivaling those of Britain and the United States, its universities shining as the world center of science, its overseas empire and business expansion confronting it with the cultures of every region. As a result, it was Germany that became the louder conversation partner—sometimes friendly, sometimes quarrelsome—of the Anglophone countries. The Habsburg dimension enriches without altering the general outlines of our story.

Empires outside of Western and Central Europe, too, provided settings for cultural encounters. The career of Abraham Zvi Idelsohn illustrates how many places and cultures could overlap. Idelsohn was born in 1882 in Latvia, then part of the Russian Empire, and grew up in a culturally German Jewish household. After beginning cantorial studies in Libau, Latvia, he continued his education in German Königsberg and Berlin. His initial cantorial appointments were also in Germany, first in Leipzig and then in Regensburg. With the cooperation of the Academy of Sciences in Vienna, he went to Palestine in 1913 to begin years of fieldwork in what was then part of the Ottoman Empire. Later, he also spent time in Cincinnati and Johannesburg. Idelsohn somehow managed to live and work across the borders of multiple empires, gathering whatever he needed in the way of languages and material support for his recordings and multivolume studies.[17]

It would constrict historical horizons to imagine empires and nation-states as the only setting for cultural encounters, or Western nations as the only makers of music in response to globalization. Cities around the world—Shanghai, Hong Kong, Calcutta, Bombay, Buenos Aires, Mexico City, and Cairo, to name only a few of the most important—took advantage of cultures and technologies in motion to become makers of the new global culture. They played an important role in the development of the phonograph industry and of musical ideas that had discernible (and in the case of Latin American music, large) effects on European popular and art music. In addition it would be a mistake to imagine extra-European encounters as happening only outside the West; European and North American metropolises became gathering-places for non-European immigrants who set off bursts of fresh musical inspiration. Even as Europeans struggled to sustain their cosmopolitanism during the 1930s, African intellectuals gathered in London and enjoyed a rich club life, bringing together African and European musical genres and pulling in other African-inflected styles too, like rumba and calypso. During the same period of

European retreat from foreign cultures, Asian port cities like Rangoon, Penang, and Singapore became home to a heterogeneous public life that included modern styles of dance and music.[18]

The three countries at the center of this book, then, looked out on other worlds of musical experimentation. The triadic relations of Britain, Germany, and the United States were but a fragment of this larger collection of cosmopolitan encounters. A global history would fall short of its own aims if it attempted to recite all the things that happened in all of them. That would be not history but chronology: a succession of incidents, not a cohesive story shaped into a narrative. To try to encompass all the histories in one book would yield a numbing parade of exotic types without deepening our understanding of global culture; the aim of comprehensiveness would have the unintended effect of reverting to the world voyage accounts of the eighteenth century and their stereotypes. Defining this book around the Anglophone-German experience should instead invite dialogue with histories from other places, recounted by authors contributing their expertise from multiple points of view.[19]

World Culture, Global Culture

Global concepts of culture changed over the course of the nineteenth century, sometimes filling old words with new meaning, sometimes giving way to new terms. The great divide came at mid-century; it became a watershed moment defining older and newer settings for contact between Europeans and non-Europeans.[20] The 1851 Great Exhibition in London marked the beginning of the new era. It was the first large-scale public display of artifacts from around the world; afterward came a profusion of exhibitions, world's fairs, circuses, traveling troupes, and alongside them scientific events, sometimes held apart, sometimes overlapping with popular entertainment. Together they defined the period to 1914 as the age of the great exhibitions. Assembling participants and artifacts by the tens of thousands, they attracted visitors by the millions. Only the resources of nation-states and their overseas empires, only travel by railroad and steamship, made it possible to assemble the materials of the earth in microcosm and put them on display for mass audiences.

The great exhibitions were spectacles. The London Exhibition of 1851, the Paris Exposition of 1889, and the Chicago World's Fair of 1893—to name only three of the most famous—presented products of nature and artifice from around the world for the wonderment of their visitors. They also gathered together human beings who could provide spectators with entertainment and instruction. Exhibition handbooks taught visitors what and how to see: what the different peoples of the earth looked like and how to arrange them in a hierarchy leading from savagery to civilization.[21] Scholars have reconstructed how the spectacles shaped Europeans' belief that they were at the pinnacle of a racial hierarchy—an ideology with fateful consequences down to our own day. This was not all that visitors saw and heard, however. Artifacts from non-European countries could be objects of admiration, stimulating the fashion for Japanese crafts or appreciation of Indian textiles; some Europeans were impressed by the music onstage at exhibitions, and sought face-to-face communication with the musicians.

What else did visitors see and hear at the great exhibitions? It was a distinct moment in time, superficially resembling today's society, but on closer examination far removed from it. The world's fairs that once drew visitors by the millions have vanished. Two world wars diminished Europe's class divisions (which are still strong today, but not as stark as they were before 1914) and toppled its empires. Today's computer images, videos, films, and sounds have generated a whole new set of cultural conditions for the arts of the twenty-first century. It takes historical imagination to recapture the first global culture as it took shape in exhibitions and other encounters beginning in the mid-nineteenth century.[22]

The setting for the new global culture was comprehensive economic, social, and political change. *Globalization*, the general name for these changing conditions, is best understood as Michael Geyer and Charles Bright defined it in a classic article of the mid-1990s: as the linkage of different parts of the world into a single system of economics and communications that came together around the mid-nineteenth century. This is not to deny the importance of previous movements beyond local borders. It is, rather, to recognize a qualitative leap, an integration of economies, volume of production, and domination by the modern nation-state that by the 1850s reached ports on every continent.[23] This economic and political transformation in turn created the conditions for a new global culture.

The predecessors to the late nineteenth-century spectacles reach far back into European history. In the late eighteenth century, philosophes in France and elsewhere responded to a new wave of scientific voyages around the world by developing galleries in image and word of the different peoples they encountered as part of a single humanity. "Voyage around the world" was the standard title for voyage accounts since the beginning of the sixteenth century, but took on new meaning amid Enlightenment debates about how humanity did or did not share a common origin. The published accounts of Captain Cook's circumnavigations of the late 1760s and 1770s as well as other voyages were among the bestsellers of the eighteenth century; they sized up the travelers' hosts from Tahiti to Alaska, Capetown to Canton, sometimes arranging them into hierarchies from savage to civilized, sometimes citing them as evidence for human equality.[24] The term "gallery" may serve as a name for such a series of types. It could take the form of a literary, visual, or aural representation; it permitted the audience to assume a standpoint of detachment, and offered a mixture of entertainment and instruction.[25] Intellectuals made use of galleries to inventory cultures that they viewed with anything from revulsion to admiration. Philosophes across Europe attempted to expand their cultural knowledge by reading the works of travelers and incorporating their impressions into surveys of foreign characters. Such galleries were not necessarily ill-willed toward the peoples they presented. The writings of Johann Gottfried Herder—a Protestant minister, writer, and ethnographer—provide an especially appealing example of typologizing in a spirit of sympathetic curiosity about cultures across space and time. He repeatedly turned to music as a document of the diverse expressive capacities of the human spirit.[26]

Whereas Herder depended on travelers' reports, Sir William Jones could write from firsthand experience of extra-European music. From 1783 until his death in 1794, Jones was a judge on the supreme court at Fort William in Calcutta. While there, he belonged to the handful of employees of the East India Company (the chartered merchant company and ruler of Bengal) who took a serious interest in Indian culture. Jones was a linguistic virtuoso and culturally curious; he arrived in Calcutta with a good reading knowledge of Persian, learned Sanskrit, and promulgated the news of the affinity of Sanskrit with Greek and Latin. Jones's omnivorous appetite for Indian culture extended to music. He first drafted his essay "On the Musical Modes of the Hindoos" in 1784, presented it to the Asiatic Society of Bengal in 1790, and published it in 1792. While there had been curiosity about Indian music among European observers going back at least to the seventeenth century, Jones's essay is usually taken as the starting point for the modern Western understanding of Hindustani music. Musical contact back and forth between English and Indian elites was still rather free when he arrived, and it was not difficult for a British visitor to hear performances. Jones arrived at two general conclusions.

One was that Indian music was allegorical in character: that is, its ragas (the mood-tinged variations on melodies that structure the music) gave expression to time of day, season, mood, myth, and cosmology. The second was that the scales of different ragas used selections of notes that differed from one another and did not correspond to Western scales. As Bennett Zon's researches have shown, Jones's essay was a starting point for further scholarship down to the early twentieth century. Jones's method was designed to reach back to a primordial conception of Indian music in its most ancient form. Philologist that he was, Jones also sought direct contact with ancient Hindu written sources, waving away written Persian intermediaries as corruptions of the authentic tradition. Going beyond casual concertizing, he also conversed with musically erudite Indians. Jones's enquiries shaped a vision of Indian music as an embodiment of national character persisting over thousands of years, a counterpart to the typologies in travelers' visual atlases.[27] His conclusions belonged to a learned, respectful, but also static conception of national physiognomies that could remain constant over thousands of years, and indeed were only understood when grasped in their unchanging essence.

In the 1820s, drawing on the lessons to be learned from the Enlightenment and Romanticism, Herder's friend Goethe recognized the changing circumstances of incipient globalization when he coined the phrase "world literature." In recent years Hendrik Birus, Anne Bohnenkamp, and other German literary scholars have researched how Goethe came to this idea. His comments emerged from a dissatisfaction with the taxonomic thinking of the eighteenth century that arranged fixed types into orderly tables. The literary counterpart of this kind of ahistorical thinking would have been an imaginary republic of literary greats that placed the leading writers of modern Europe side by side and could always be supplemented by extra-European literary products such as Persian poetry and Chinese prose. This kind of assemblage of a literary gallery was the ancestor of the world literature courses (and their counterparts for art and music) that are a recurring favorite of American high school and college curricula. It was also the model for a wider typology across the arts of what may be called *world culture*, as fixed and unchanging as the eighteenth-century voyage atlases with their neat characterizations of unchanging facial types and folk costumes. Goethe looked beyond this kind of static taxonomy after the end of the Napoleonic Wars, when he became alive to the effects of a new age of accelerating commerce and communications. World literature referred not to objects or people, but to communication about them:

to the back-and-forth between cultures that would lead them to a new kind of relationship. He had in mind letters like the ones he exchanged with his French contemporaries and other correspondents across Europe, but he also valued translations and personal encounters like the conversations he had with a steady stream of visitors to Weimar. What could result from this intensifying communication was a heightened degree of intersubjective reflection. A party to these exchanges and encounters would learn to imagine the other person's subjective life; but more than just that, each person would learn how he or she appeared in the eyes of the other person or, more generally stated, in the perceptions of a foreign culture. In the years following an era of warfare, Goethe imagined a world culture that would create habits of mutual understanding. He did not seek a homogenization of different cultures through contact. Built into his conception of world culture was, instead, a persistence of difference that was the condition for mutual recognition. To distinguish this from Enlightenment conceptions of world culture, one may generalize from Goethe's ideas for literature and speak of an emerging *global culture*. Goethe worried privately about the homogenizing dangers of accelerating communication, but maintained a public confidence in humanity's capacity for mutual enrichment through literary exchange.[28]

After his time, how far did the new global culture go toward displacing the national and local cultures that preceded it? Globalization since the mid-nineteenth century has sometimes left the impression that everything solid melts into air under the sun of global capitalism, with all local products dispersed into the flow of commodity exchange without borders.[29] Yet in the late nineteenth century the crafting of local arts did not come to an end. Audiences did not simply capitulate to commodities for global distribution; rather, industrial production of standardized wares stimulated consumers' appetite for goods deemed homemade and authentic.[30] Simultaneously, over the course of the decades up to 1914, a departure from the static representations of eighteenth-century travel accounts began to take place among adventurous makers of music and their audiences: a mixing, a matching, an experimentation across continents.[31]

A fusion of music from widely different origins began before 1914. But classical European composers' use of exotic effects continued to be occasional experiments, while popular music like tango remained a splash of exotic novelty as long as the iron framework of social classes at home and empires abroad remained intact. World War I was the great earthquake that irreparably damaged both of those guarantors of order. Social divisions in European countries were disrupted, while overseas empires either collapsed or gave way to European demoralization and non-European self-confidence. New, democratic cultures came into existence around the world, whether borne by socialist revolution from the Soviet Union, capitalist expansion from the United States, or nationalist regimes within and beyond Europe. A widespread feature of these postwar societies was their emancipation from elite cultures, complemented by a willingness within elites to appropriate popular cultural genres. After 1918 came an unprecedented social breakthrough of new cultural forms, such as jazz and tango, that were democratic and cross-cultural. They clambered onto center stage as an unmistakable product and voice of globalization. Bounded cultures did not disappear. On the contrary, their adherents were sensitive to their fragility and clung to them more self-consciously than before. But they cultivated them with the self-consciousness of offering one choice among others, of vying for attention alongside the new artistic expressions of worlds in motion.

Intellectuals in a Global Age: Cosmopolitans, Nationalists, Transnationals, Localists

To enter the new global age was to seek a place amid paradox. Its entrepreneurs made a variety of choices that elude easy characterization.

A contemporary historical classic provided a first approximation in the familiar terms of its time. The German historian Friedrich Meinecke worked the alternatives of cosmopolitanism and nationalism into the title of his book *Cosmopolitanism and the Nation-State*.[32] It was published in 1907, at the moment when comparative musicology on a global scale and the spread of the phonograph across much of Asia, North Africa, and Latin America had reached a first stage of maturity. Not that Meinecke was paying attention: he was a Prussian conservative, a German nationalist, and, like many professors of his time and place, a devoted servant of the recently formed German nation-state, for whom everything beyond European boundaries was remote. How the cosmopolitanism of the Enlightenment gave way to the nationalism of the period after 1815 was the book's central theme. It repudiated cosmopolitanism in its late eighteenth-century form; continuing a long line of conservative critique, Meinecke portrayed intellectuals like Georg Forster, who traveled around the world with Captain Cook and later supported the French Revolution, as bloodless utopians cut off from the life of the nation. Yet Meinecke also acknowledged the universal idealism of Enlightenment cosmopolitanism as a valuable legacy in its own right. Far from being dismissive, he argued that the German nation-state subsumed the earlier era's embrace of all humanity. The balance of cosmopolitanism and nation-state in Meinecke's book was an uneasy one, perhaps too fine for the real world of politics; but it captured the inner tensions of its historical moment. By putting these two forces front and center in his history of nineteenth-century Germany, his book provided an initial conceptualization of the paradoxes of the arts and sciences in an age of globalization. The dichotomy persisted to the end of the twentieth century; as late as the 1990s, intellectuals took it for granted as they argued over whether larger human sympathies might lessen or even dissolve the hold of the nation-state.[33]

Exemplifying Meinecke's synthesis, the pre-1914 makers of music's global crossings could be simultaneously cosmopolitan and national. They crossed many kinds of borders. Educated non-Europeans visited Europe and North America, indigenous musicians toured metropolises, Westerners went on site to collect non-Western music, the phonograph played and sold in remote towns and villages, and a few Western connoisseurs and academics adjusted their ears to the tones and rhythms of alien musical systems. A hunger for new musical experiences motivated both Mexican villagers who paid to hear the tinny novelty of a phonograph recording in their marketplace, and urbane Germans made aware for the first time of the complexities of South Asian music. An uncaging of musical experience around the world took place, an exhilarating sense of flight that went along with one's ability to experience as never before the rhythms and tones of faraway places.

At the same time, the late nineteenth century was a moment for nurturing national loyalties. While they affirmed the superiority of Western technology—including its musical system—non-Western elites in Japan and elsewhere integrated melodies they called their own into their programs for national cultural revival and the creation of a modern nation-state. Their mixture of cosmopolitanism and nationalism continued a pattern going back to the eighteenth and early nineteenth centuries. Even before the French Revolution, the claims of French culture to be the universal culture provoked the resentment of the young Goethe (which later gave way to admiration for French artistic and intellectual life). The simultaneous cosmopolitanism of artists and intellectuals who were educated in the metropolises of Western Europe and their mobilization of music for national politics flourished throughout the nineteenth and early twentieth centuries, sometimes with productive results. Just as writers like the Brothers Grimm had used the written word in the early nineteenth century to preserve folktales, so Béla Bartók in the early twentieth century could use phonograph recordings to preserve folk music. In both cases, sophisticated intellectuals appealed to their contemporaries to respect the "pure" folk sources of culture—German for the Grimms, Magyar for Bartók—through a program of collecting and repackaging: for the Grimms in the artfully reworked fairy tale, and for Bartók in artful melody and song.[34] Cosmopolitanism and nationalism jostled in a variety of mixtures, often in the same individual. A reduction to one side or the other rarely took place; instead, the agents of musical globalization made their own choices about how to combine them.

As we look back a century after Meinecke, his terms remain current but contested, their aptness offset by others that have subsequently entered our field of vision. Since the eighteenth century, the term "cosmopolitan" has always stirred a certain sense of uneasiness. In Meinecke's book it connoted an *abstract* humanitarianism or, even worse, loyalty to a foreign power that turned it into synonym for the politically suspicious, a taunt to mark exclusion from the national community. By the 1920s, "cosmopolitan" was a code word in Germany for "Jew," a piece of the right-wing arsenal of fantasies about the ethnically pure nation and its imagined enemies.

Can the term be recovered for the nineteenth century and the social history of its music? George Eliot thought so when she introduced the figure of Julius Klesmer into her novel *Daniel Deronda*. He enters the story through his romance with Catherine Arrowpoint, the daughter and only child of gentry parents. They wish for the best for their daughter and have therefore supplied her with the best musician as her teacher, a pianist and composer of genius. During a year of piano lessons, teacher and pupil fall in love, though their social distance makes it impossible for either one to admit it. Their feelings burst into the open when a Mr. Bult enters the scene in courtship of Catherine—or rather, in courtship of her wealth. The "expectant peer" Mr. Bult is, as his name perhaps suggests, an ordinary John Bull who is about the business of rising in the political and social world, and who thinks of Catherine as his perfect catch. But Catherine is independent and Klesmer is frank. Without any of the three anticipating it, Bult, the crude contender, provokes a quarrel with Klesmer. The exchange pushes Catherine and Klesmer to recognize that they stand for qualities of artistic integrity and of love based on intellectual partnership that are incomprehensible to the Bults of this world.

The conflict between tender lovers and unfeeling outsiders eventuates in a plea for cosmopolitan idealism. Klesmer sets off the argument with Bult through "an after-dinner outburst . . . on the lack of idealism in English politics, which left all mutuality between distant races to be determined simply by the need of a market. . . ." Klesmer gesticulates, he goes on for too long, his words are "like stray fireworks accidentally ignited." Bult tries to imagine where this surprisingly eloquent and well-informed guest comes from; he is probably "a Pole, or a Czech, or something of that fermenting sort," or a political refugee who has to make his living from his music—a Panslavist, he further fancies. "'No; my name is Elijah. I am the Wandering Jew,' said Klesmer, flashing a smile at Miss Arrowpoint." Catherine, trying to keep things civil, throws in, "'Herr Klesmer has cosmopolitan ideas . . . he looks forward to a fusion of races.'" Klesmer's exact origins matter less than what he stands for: artistic genius, to be sure, but also a cosmopolitan embrace of all peoples—even fusion, a slap in the face of upholders of racial division. Catherine defends him, first to the unfortunate Mr. Bult and later to her mother, who is infuriated by the prospect of this *mésalliance*. Catherine and Klesmer marry and live happily in London, in a fictional rebuke to the purveyors of stifling social borders.[35]

Cosmopolitanism remains a useful category, but its idealistic component makes it also a specialized one. A more comprehensive term from our own time is transnationalism, which seems to have taken off as a term of scholarly discourse in the 1970s. Akira Iriye has observed that during this decade, new forms of political activity and economic organization began to operate outside the borders of the nation-state, including a growth in the number of nonpolitical organizations, a rising concern with human rights, and the emergence of international terrorism.[36] This initial stream of activities across state borders was followed by a larger movement of individuals who in many cases resettled with an advanced level of education and had the financial resources to seek professional work with high status in their new country. These immigrants, as well as their less prosperous counterparts, could move fluently across state borders, keeping up family and professional ties in their place of origin even as they developed loyalties in their new home. This recent description of transnationalism matches the movement of scientific and artistic innovators before 1914. Then as now, immigrants usually crossed state borders for pragmatic reasons, in search of economic or social advancement, but these motives could overlap with humanitarian idealism. Transnationalism and cosmopolitanism were distinct but could be complementary. Emile Berliner was not a "cosmopolitan" in the idealistic sense when he emigrated from Germany to the United States, but later he combined his professional success with generous philanthropy.

Transnational circulation formed part of the reality and legend of the interwar years. If we call it the Jazz Age, the phrase includes the ubiquity of American jazz musicians from Paris to Shanghai. In a different cultural register, classical composers like Henry Cowell and Aaron Copeland did stints in Paris and returned to the United States with newfound skills, worldliness, and prestige. Without displacing nationalist and older cosmopolitan cultural forms, interwar artists announced the heightened prominence of cultural mobility in an age of globalization.

Like cosmopolitanism, nationalism no longer serves as an adequate concept to describe cultural attitudes in the early twentieth century. For Meinecke, it seemed glorious and complete: the fulfillment of German political yearning, and in contrast to the abstractions of cosmopolitanism, the creation of a rich and vital community. He certainly captured part of the mood of the nineteenth century; nationalism had a large place in the globalization of music. Musicians and political actors might go abroad in order to strengthen their national music, as Meiji-era bureaucrats did; aesthetes might also react to foreign influence by asserting their national musical identity, as did members of the English Musical Renaissance, who were determined to topple the preeminence of German music and criticism. But others had a keener loyalty to musical life that was local. They admired the beauty of handcrafted instruments, recovered the fine gradations of difference in local and individual musicianship, and realized that large financial rewards might go to the record maker who knew how to tap nonnational linguistic markets. Contemporaries recognized this trend, but it did not crystallize into a descriptive category at a moment when local political autonomy was losing ground to nation-states. By contrast, localism in our own time has gathered strength and become an important form of resistance to national authority; movements like Catalan, Scottish, and regional English separatism are testimony to its seriousness and the earnestness with which national authorities (as in the Catalan case) may oppose it. Returning to the nineteenth century with this in mind, we may discern the early arrival of localism as a response to national and global challenges.

As we take a broad view of the time span from the mid-nineteenth century to the twenty-first, globalization and the responses to it look ever more complex; the older terms of nationalism and cosmopolitanism are indispensible, but transnationalism and localism take their place alongside them as constituents of the new global culture.

Craft, Science, Commerce

This book is structured to do justice to the complexity of global interactions and the arts. The reshaping of musical life in the age of exhibitions was not the product of a single cause; no one factor explains it in a way that leads to more than predictable inevitabilities. The organization of this book around three sources of global culture suggests how contingencies, experimentation, local variation, and individual ingenuity offset the structural conditions of change.

Globalization has historically involved a persistence of local patterns of culture as well as global flows. The first part of this book follows the assertion since the late eighteenth century of local *craft* traditions in response to the expansion of capitalist markets. The second part turns to the *scientific* analysis of extra-European music beginning in the mid-nineteenth century. After craft and science came the phonograph and *commerce* as an agent of globalization, the subject of part 3 of this book. All three factors shaped the globalization of music. The transformation was all the more pervasive, all the more deeply ineradicable, for coming from multiple directions. There was not an evolution from craft to science to commerce; the different factors combined in multiple ways in different times and places. The schematic succession of early, middle, and late nineteenth century does not do full justice to the manifestations of craft, science, and commerce as they mixed and matched over time. Craft comes first in this book, partly because of its historical priority within our story, but also because it is the least obvious and least appreciated of the impulses shaping the global age; it had no logical priority over the others. Beyond that, one should not exaggerate the formative power of all these factors combined; culture maintains a relative autonomy within its social and material setting. Musical life also grew from accidents of biography and creative inspiration.[37]

The globalization of music might at first seem to have been the product of applied science and capitalist marketing. The revolutionary technology within the modern history of music was Edison's invention of the phonograph in 1877, the realization of a dream that other inventors, too, had been pursuing. Busy with other projects, Edison only returned to the phonograph several decades later. By then he was joined by other successful innovators, including Emile Berliner, creator of the flat disc record that soon gained greater acceptance than Edison's cylinder. A multitude of technical improvements made mechanical recording in either medium more commercially viable until by 1900 the phonograph was beginning its rapid spread around the world. The revolution was astonishingly rapid; within a decade, the spread of recordings to remote villages of the equator and outposts of the extreme north, and mass sales in places like India, China, Mexico, and Brazil created a global network of sound. Officers, doctors, missionaries, adventurers, and ethnographers carried wax cylinders to European colonies and back to Western metropolises; phonograph companies sent sound engineers who recorded in dozens of local languages; immigrants in the United States became a market for foreign-language recordings. By the end of the decade, music was traveling through global networks. Preservers of tradition and emissaries of a bright middle-class future, cylinders and records were part of the modern culture industry's start-up; they redefined the work of any maker of music, from the most rarified advocate of l'art pour l'art to the most commercial.

Despite the noisy prominence of the new technology, the response of music to globalization did not start with the mechanical reproduction of sound. Before the phonograph and its engineers and marketers came the connoisseurs of craft. One such connoisseur, Carl Engel, was a pianist turned authority on world music and instruments; a second, A. J. Hipkins, started out as a piano tuner and became the next generation's leading expert on keyboard and string instruments. From the 1850s to the 1880s they earned the admiration of their contemporaries and merged their work with the scientific analysis of music. We turn first to this quiet expansion of horizons, and its beginnings in a liberal household of early nineteenth-century Germany.

PART I

CRAFT

1

A German Connoisseur in Cosmopolitan England

Provincial beginnings can widen out to global perspectives: so it was in the biography of Carl Engel, who taught his contemporaries to compare music across times and places.

German by upbringing and inclination, he moved to Victorian England as a young man and had to define his place in its society and cultural institutions. At first Engel supported himself with piano lessons in Manchester, but before long he married into an upper-class English family and moved to London. By then he had also made the transition from musical performance to scholarship. Through his writings, musical instrument collection, and museum activities, he turned into an early exponent of the idea of world music. With his historical writings and surveys of musical instruments, he asked his readers to put aside their local prejudices and become connoisseurs of musical offerings through time and across continents. His sweeping view of music around the world made him a founder of the comparative tradition that influenced the early music, folk music, and ethnomusicology movements of the twentieth century. His legacy of cosmopolitan scholarship shaped the work of younger contemporaries like A. J. Hipkins and Alexander Ellis.[1]

Engel's vision of world music was nurtured by the idealism of the post-Napoleonic era. After decades of violence beginning

in the French Revolution and engulfing large parts of Europe from Portugal to Russia, Europeans sought after 1815 to construct a peaceful political order. Visionary intellectuals recalled traditions dating back to the
late eighteenth century and imagined a continent, and indeed an entire
world, of nations that could cultivate their own arts at home and honor
the creations of their neighbors. As we have seen, in the 1820s Goethe
recommended the idea of world literature in part as a means to enhance
sympathetic understanding between peoples. A realization of this kind
of openness was the nineteenth-century English reception of continental and especially German music and musicians. Carl Engel became one
of the many Germans with musical expertise to become a beneficiary of
English cosmopolitanism; he used his welcome to widen English sympathies and encompass broad reaches of humanity.[2]

From Small-Town Germany to Cosmopolitan London

Engel's journey began in the hamlet of Thiedenwiese, near Hanover, where
he was born in 1818. The starting point is significant, for his later work
contained a deep appreciation of the local origins of musical styles within
the chorus of humanity. His early years belonged to a remote place—to an
older Germany not yet linked to the outside world by the railroad. It was
a north Germany of a kind whose musical life was recollected by Thomas
Mann in *Doctor Faustus*, where music as a form of entertainment and
source of spirituality pulsates from patterns formed in the Reformation.[3]
Engel left his own unpublished description of that provincial world in a
manuscript now housed at the Royal College of Music in London (where
one reads it in the right atmosphere, in a reading room with long dark
tables lit by old lamps while horn music or singing wafts in from elsewhere in the building). Engel composed the autobiography as a preface
to an unpublished essay collection. He recalled his childhood "fondness
for sweet sounds; my ear caught some of the beautiful national airs with
which the country abounds; I sang them, and soon learned to play them
on the piano, to the delight of affectionate aunts and puzzled peasants."
The nine children of the Engel family grew up in a large, squat country
house, to which the father added a smaller dwelling, rather stately in its
own right, which was used as a schoolhouse. The long winter evenings in
the isolated household were frequently filled with musical performances,
declamations of poetry, or readings of a translation from Shakespeare;

they often ended with everyone singing or a dance or two while Carl Engel accompanied his family on the piano. He recalled the beginnings of his interest in what we would today call folk music and salvage anthropology: "My leisure hours were mostly spent in composing music, collecting national songs, and pursuing national history in the neighboring forest," he wrote. "As the intellectual inclinations of the child are generally those which afterwards mould the man, these facts may account for my later fondness for the study of national music and ethnology." So began a musical career that otherwise followed an unexceptional path as he enjoyed the rich offerings of teachers in Hanover, Weimar, and Hamburg before accepting a position as tutor in an aristocratic household in Pomerania—still in the peaceful countryside, but linked by railroad to Berlin, which he could easily visit for concerts.[4] Engel also received an attractive offer to serve as family tutor to a Russian general whose regiment was stationed in Warsaw. "However, the unhappy condition of the oppressed Poland, for which every liberal German naturally felt deep sympathy, was not likely to render the life of a young artist in the family of a Russian General at Warsaw an enviable one." Even a visit by the general's wife to Thiedenwiese (she brought a special cake from Hanover) could not reconcile his mother to the thought of her son living amid the occupation. Engel's "national" and folkloristic interests were cast in the pre-1848 mold of liberal humanitarian sympathies.

After several years on the Pomeranian estate, Engel was restless to travel abroad. When a wealthy English gentleman whom he met in Berlin offered him a tutoring position in Manchester, he accepted, moving there in 1846. The Midland city was one of the bustling centers of British industrialization, rapidly growing with the attendant horrors and middle-class indifference that Friedrich Engels, two years younger than the musician, had just analyzed in The Condition of the Working Class in England.[5] There is no written record that Carl Engel paid any attention to the condition of Manchester's working class; as his communist countryman wrote, the city's bourgeoisie could easily ignore the misery that supported their wealth. What he did appreciate was a city that was "a musical Mecca," with a concert life going back to the eighteenth century and only growing more vibrant over time. During the first half of the nineteenth century a large number of Germans moved to Manchester in order to take advantage of its opportunities for business and industry; their support for music became so legendary that the author of today's Grove's dictionary entry on the town begins by disputing the notion that they were solely responsible for its brilliance. Engel's four-year stay overlapped with the arrival of the German-born musician Charles Hallé, who decisively elevated the quality of music making in Manchester. Well known in Paris in the 1830s and 1840s, after the Revolution of 1848 he moved to London and thence to Manchester, where he rapidly began organizing concerts that by the following year were playing to a wide public.[6] For Engel to leave the vicinity of Berlin for Manchester was not so much to leave a musical metropolis for the provinces as to enter a lively and open milieu.

Manchester was also where Engel made his entrance into English society. The gentleman who persuaded him to emigrate was an unnamed member of the Bowman family—possibly Henry Bowman, an architect in Manchester who wrote two books on medieval English architecture. Henry's brother William was one of the outstanding ophthalmologists of nineteenth-century Britain, and later personal eye doctor to Queen Victoria. Another family member who was close to Engel, his wife's nephew Herbert, became director of the Bank of England. The Bowmans were newly wealthy. Their grandfather was a tobacconist; their father had gone through business ups and downs before making a fortune as a banker in the 1820s, after which he retired and devoted himself to his naturalist interests. It may have been through the Bowman family that Engel met his future wife, Louisa Paget, who was William's sister-in-law. Members of the Paget family, originally Huguenot refugees who settled in Leicestershire, were well known for their innovations in sheep and cattle breeding as well as their hosiery and lacemaking firm. Louisa's father was an ophthalmic surgeon in Leicester who was also well known for his support of science and music. Together the two families fit the image of ambitious, hard-working, moralistic Victorians. Their Whiggish politics were a satisfactory fit with Carl Engel's German liberalism. The bits of surviving correspondence suggest that they had a warm relationship with Engel and took an active interest in his scholarship, while for his part Carl Engel took pride in his English family.[7] Engel somehow had enough money in the 1850s to build a new house for himself and his wife, though not to cover everyday expenses. In 1853 he reported to his mother that he was giving private lessons and teaching music in two schools. He also gave her an enthusiastic report on the surprisingly brisk sales of a manual he had published that year and was sending her, the *Pianist's Handbook*.[8] Nonetheless he was scrambling to keep up with the high cost of living in London.

Music around the World

After his arrival in the metropolis, Engel traded his composing and performing ambitions for the life of a scholar. A decade and a half later, he revealed the ambitious sweep of his research in his first major book, *The Music of the Most Ancient Nations* (1864). Within the compass of the ancient world, this work made a first attempt at a broadly comprehensive study of the music of the Assyrians, Egyptians, and Hebrews. But the introduction ranged more widely, announcing a historical program for what he called an ethnology of music. He had to combat a widespread public belief in the insignificance of non-European music:

> Besides the music of the ancients, we have become gradually more familiar with that of contemporary nations in every part of the globe;—at all events, more attention is paid now to national music than formerly, though this subject does not yet in my opinion receive that consideration which it deserves. Hitherto it has been almost entirely disregarded by musical *savants*. Sir John Hawkins, in the preface to his "History of Music," says: "The best music of barbarians is said to be hideous and astonishing sounds. Of what importance then can it be to inquire into a practice that has not its foundation in science or system, or to know what are the sounds that most delight a Hottentot, a wild American, or even a more refined Chinese?" I have transcribed Hawkins's own words, because he precisely expresses the prevailing opinion, not only of his own day, but also of the present time. I think, however, a few moments' reflection will convince the reader of its fallacy. The study of national music is especially useful to the musician, because it enlarges his musical conception and secures him from one-sidedness and an unwarranted predilection for any peculiar style or any particular composer. [9]

Engel's belief that he was combating a deep-seated public prejudice received some confirmation with the reprinting of Hawkins's five-volume history of music eleven years after Engel published his book. Engel's critique was a continuation of an eighteenth-century debate, since Hawkins for his part was responding to Enlightenment cosmopolitanism, and in particular his contemporaries' admiration for China. The hardening of upper-class attitudes came later. After the relatively open moment of the late Enlightenment, Europeans lost sympathetic interest in non-European cultures as their own expansion seemed to set them apart and the Evangelical movement added to prejudice toward non-European cultures. While one can variously date this decline of cosmopolitanism, the mid-nineteenth century was arguably a low point.[10]

It was not hard for Engel to point out the ignorance behind remarks like those of Hawkins when it came to the well-developed science of music of the Chinese, "since they, as well as the Hindoos, Persians, Arabs, and several other nations, all of which are entirely ignored by him, actually possessed musical systems long before our own was developed." But Engel wanted to go beyond this qualification to a more general reappraisal of music from what he called "a national point of view." By "national" he meant either folk music or music in a characteristic local style. Today the term sounds ominous: every claim to a "national" culture could, and in the nineteenth century often did, slide in the direction of demands for political autonomy and subordination of nonnationals who did not share the *Volksgeist*; national cultures were conceived of as timeless entities, metaphysical essences derived from some remote moment beyond the reaches of historical time. National culture could find expression in language, customs, character, or anything else setting neighbors apart. Music played a large part in the formation of this nationalist ideology and its transition from culture to politics. Yet this was not what Engel had in mind. Instead, he wrote in protest against the appropriation of music by the upper reaches of European society. "National" music extended to popular classes and had a dignity and vitality all its own. If there was a politics to his use of the term, it lay in his elevation of the lives and work of ordinary people.

Engel defended national music on both pragmatic and aesthetic grounds. For musicians to study music far and wide kept them from getting stuck in provincial preferences. Many national tunes, he added, were "delightfully beautiful" and improved the taste of the listener; Handel had borrowed from a song of Calabrian peasants, and Mendelssohn from a Scottish melody. Anticipating Bartók's research, he added that the music of the Hungarians and Wallachians might sound "strange and unsatisfactory" at first, but had "great charms for the initiated."[11] Exposure to foreign instruments, too, had practical value, suggesting ways of improving one's own.[12] Engel may have been steeped in German music, but from early on he had broadened his own taste (secretly playing Beethoven sonatas when they were forbidden by his first teacher). By the 1860s his taste had broadened to the point where he chided contemporaries who failed to grasp the utility of learning about foreign musical cultures. Later he completed the manuscript of a history of Chinese music which did not make it into print in his lifetime and has since disappeared, but was an unusual venture in the late nineteenth century.

Engel was not a cultural democrat. He shared his contemporaries' belief that there were more and less civilized nations, and that the same was true for their musical achievements. Yet the direction of his thought was a significant departure from the conventions of mid-nineteenth century Europe, a turn from qualitative evaluation and hierarchy to interest in all musical cultures as expressions of a common humanity. In contrast to the widely held belief in musical progress, he argued "that among the most ancient nations known to us—the Assyrians as well as the ancient Egyptians and Hebrews—music had already attained a degree of perfection considerably higher than we meet with in many nations of our own time." He also rejected the view that "savage" vocal compositions were imitations of the natural world; "expressive melody" was "an innate gift" of all peoples.[13] Never had the triumph of European civilization seemed more complete than at the mid-Victorian moment when Engel wrote. The critique of a hierarchical and evolutionary view of culture took place only slowly and irregularly in the last quarter of the nineteenth and first quarter of the twentieth century; Engel's plea for a universal ethnology was an untimely observation.[14]

Engel generalized his argument for an ethnology of music two years later in his *Introduction to the Study of National Music*. It was a plea for salvage anthropology, the enterprise for recording and preserving indigenous peoples' way of life before their inevitable destruction. Following a widely held belief of his time, he assumed that peoples like Polynesians and Native Americans were on their way to extinction, as was European folk music. Yet music cultures were a resource that his cultivated European contemporaries could not afford to ignore. On first impression, foreign music was apt to appear "unimpressive, strange, and perhaps even ridiculous, so that we find it difficult to understand how it can appeal to the heart at all." Engel combated this kind of musical provinciality with a Herderian belief that different musical traditions were varieties of the universal human expressive capacity: ". . . National music, be it ever so artless and simple, is in most cases, what music in the first place always ought to be—a faithful expression of feelings." Western music was just as unintelligible to others: intelligent Chinese, he tartly observed, could not make sense of the music of Rameau when the late eighteenth-century

Jesuit missionary Amiot performed it for them.[15] With all of his observations, Engel was an innovator poised between two more sympathetic epochs: the late Enlightenment as articulated by Herder, and the late nineteenth century with its comparative analysis of musical systems.

One argument that anticipated the course of musical cosmopolitanism to come was Engel's disagreement with the widespread belief in the naturalness of the Western diatonic scale. Europeans believed that it was natural, he wrote, because they were used to it. But the Greeks used other scales, and so did other countries in his own day, with everyone no doubt thinking that their own scale was the natural one. To counter European notions of naturalness, Engel pointed out the wide diffusion of microtones (a remarkable point to put forth, given that a half-century after he wrote, sophisticated Europeans still had trouble hearing them as anything more than off-key). Overall, he observed, the evidence showed that "the construction of the musical scales is not entirely dictated by physical laws, but that it rather has its source in taste. As in former centuries we have had scales different from those in use at the present day, so likewise there will undoubtedly be different ones in future ages."

Engel's conclusion in his work of 1866 overlapped with the assertion of the historicity of scales in Hermann von Helmholtz's work of 1863 on perceptions of tone, which documented in detail how the Western scale had undergone change over the centuries, with unacceptable intervals turning into an integral part of tonal systems. A connoisseur of classical music, Helmholtz, too, expected the Western musical system to continue to change in the future. The early 1860s marked an expansion of the definition of music and the human capacity to perceive it.[16] The definition of culture in general, not just of music, was undergoing change. National varieties of music, as Engel was beginning to understand them, were not the static types of the eighteenth-century imagination, but underwent surprising shifts, in which what had once been termed ugly or inharmonious turned into an acceptable or even pleasingly harmonious form of expression. Up to a point, Engel would seem to have put forth a concept of music as world culture—as a gallery of types, each one recognizable and separable from the others. But his thought was richer than this; he did not turn the varieties of national music into unchangeable essences, but emphasized their historicity. If his thought had its beginnings in inherited typologies, it also pointed the way to a more dynamic conception of cultures in an ongoing process of historical change.

Engel not only anticipated an ethnological approach in which the experience of music was embedded in specific times and places; he made one direct contribution to it, the section on music in the first edition of the *Notes and Queries on Anthropology*, the field guide for British anthropologists published in 1874. In it, he oriented the field worker right away to the difficulty of writing down extra-European music correctly, and the danger of rectifying "anything which may appear incorrect to the European ear. The more faithfully the apparent defects are preserved, the more valuable is the notation."[17] He expanded on the spare remarks of the guide in a far-reaching work published three years before his death, *The Literature of National Music* (1879). The classical pianist and connoisseur of harpsichords and clavichords was more insistent than ever on the value of folk music: he praised the originality of its melodies, its freshness and spontaneity compared to market-driven productions, the stimulating effect of listening to its unfamiliar scales, and its documentary importance. His scholarly contemporaries rarely did justice to it, however. Abrasive critique was Engel's reaction to most of the existing folk music collections. The valuable works were those that faithfully noted the melodies with their words, as opposed to the many books that added a piano accompaniment, "which is foreign to the original music and which obscures its characteristics." Harmonization, too, obscured the original nature of the music: most popular songs, he noted, were "sung by a single voice, or by a number of voices in unison," whereas harmony made them sound "ludicrous." If the tyranny of the Victorian household, which pressed everything into its preferred drawing-room mold, was one enemy of authentic folk music, another, wrote Engel, was the fantasy of travel writers. Natives were said to sing in harmony when they sang in unison; sad music was recorded as music in a minor key; if there was something peculiar about a performance, the traveler called it a "wild cadence." But Engel could also point to a handful of works that pointed the way to a reliable recovery of folk music. The liberal nationalist Hoffmann von Fallersleben's edition of Silesian folk songs showed how to do it right: the tunes were based on fieldwork, transcribed directly from the singers; the place of the fieldwork was recorded; footnotes indicated variations in the tunes; the accompanying verses were carefully treated; and Fallersleben and his coeditor worked comparatively, referring to other collections as they characterized the nationality of their songs. Engel could be a sympathetic listener as well as a scornful critic. He was intrigued by the antiquity of Jewish synagogue music, moved by a collection of slave songs from the United States, and charmed by the melodies of Mexican songs. His compassion as well as his erudition made him a founder of the modern approach to extra-European music, which, as he pointed out, depended on a feel for its beauty as well as exact knowledge—a rare combination, he wrote, among scientists.[18]

English Cosmopolitans

Engel wrote with the authority of a widely trusted expert. Walter Broadwood, the owner of the John Broadwood and Sons piano firm, the leading English piano maker, asked him to give a harpsichord in need of restoration to the craftsman who worked on his own instruments. Engel took care of the request by repairing the harpsichord himself—for he was the craftsman in question. August Manns, like Engel a German immigrant and for decades the conductor at the Crystal Palace of what today would be called a classical pops orchestra, called on Engel when he needed to have ready for the Prince of Wales so-called Indian music including "A Nautch Dance," "A snake-Charmer [sic] with his peculiar musical noise," "A Chant of the Children wherewith they greeted the Prince," "An Elephant-Procession," and "Music in Connection with Brahmin and Buddhistic religious ceremonies." In 1879 Luther Whiting Mason, a New England minister and modernizer of Japanese music, took Engel's book on national music with him on his trip to Japan. The erudite Belgian dealer-curator Victor-Charles Mahillon, one of Europe's leading authorities on extra-European music and instruments, turned to him for advice.[19] When the Western musical establishment wished to look out on the wider world, its members could turn to Engel as their guide.

Most important for his legacy, in 1870 Engel began a collaboration with A. J. Hipkins, who became his successor as the leading British expert on keyboard instruments. (After George Grove was turned down by Engel, he turned to Hipkins to write the entries on keyboard and string instruments for the first edition of his famous dictionary.) Their surviving correspondence circulates largely around their shared love of harpsichords and clavichords, but also points to a personal friendship.[20] Hipkins's later biographical entry on Engel in the Grove dictionary testifies to his admiration for the elder who in some measure must have been his mentor, guiding him into the lore of the instruments and music of early modern Europe, making him aware of the paucity of research on English folk music, and providing instruments and erudition to aid Hipkins's and Alexander Ellis's revolutionary research on the worldwide diversity of musical scales. Hipkins and Engel's friendship is a reminder of the larger pattern of German-English musical collaboration for a broad stretch of the nineteenth century.

Another enduring contribution to English public life was Engel's role in creating the musical instrument collection of today's Victoria and Albert Museum. He enriched it through donations, advice, and commentary. The capital the museum would inherit began to accumulate after Engel's arrival in London, when he began buying books on music and started his collection of musical instruments. By the mid-1860s, his library and instruments were a symbolic realization of Julius Klesmer's dream of a unified humanity, for they added up to an assemblage of musical cultures from around the world. The collections were at once the foundation of his own scholarship, a tangible realization of the idea of world music, and an inspiration to like-minded explorers of musical cultures. Engel's collecting activities converged with the ambitions of the world's greatest collection, past or present, of arts and crafts from around the world. The Victoria and Albert Museum became the eventual home for most of his musical instruments, and the site from which the next generation of scholars continued his project of a worldwide comparison of forms of musical expression.

German-British collaboration was part of the museum's story from the start, for it grew from the collaboration of Prince Albert, German in his upbringing and education (which included several semesters at the University of Bonn), and Henry Cole, a self-made manufacturer and reformer.[21] One of the experts who advised them was Gustav Waagen, director of the Altes Museum in Berlin. In answer to a question about how to elevate popular taste, Waagen "suggested that the Renaissance connection between workman and artist could be restored by organized educational efforts within such collections. . . ."[22] Following on this, Cole hoped that the new museum would provide samples of good workmanship for an audience including "artisans, designers and manufacturers."[23] Continuing the reliance on German vision and museum know-how, Cole was impressed by the writings of Gottfried Semper, who in 1848 had fled from Germany to London as a political refugee. Semper argued for an alliance of the fine and applied arts, as well as an understanding of art as the expression of its historical moment.[24] Arts and crafts implied a synthesis of good taste and practical skill. The South Kensington Museum was guided by this principle when it was founded in 1857, and remained true to it after its renaming in 1899 as the Victoria and Albert Museum.

From the beginning, Cole and the museum embraced a balance of local and worldwide acquisitions. He and Albert were the organizers of the Great Exhibition of 1851, which combined proud display of British industrial products with objects from abroad, including eighty-eight catalogue pages of Indian crafts, which were widely admired for their fine workmanship. The South Kensington Museum, too, embraced this balance of the local and the global. It displayed Western arts and crafts since the Middle Ages, with a special concern for the nuances of English culture; it also acquired foreign collections for the sake of comparison, and thereby became a repository for worldwide humanity's artifacts. The museum's aim was comparison of the best craftsmanship from different traditions.[25] Its simultaneous look backward in time to premodern Europe and across space to extra-European objects anticipated late-nineteenth-century scholarship's push beyond known temporal and geographic horizons.

By 1869, Engel had established a long collaboration with the South Kensington Museum, which stood not far from where he lived on Addison Road. In June of that year the art division (Art Museum, as it was called at the time) received a loan from him of fifty-four musical instruments. Eighteen came from Guiana, Morocco, Tunis, Senegambia, Egypt, China, Burma, Hindustan, and Siam, while the rest were early modern instruments from England, Italy, Spain, Portugal, and France. Among the extra-European prizes were a gunibry ("a sort of square guitar," according to the *Oxford English Dictionary*) made of "wood, and tortoiseshell covered with painted skin," from Morocco; a sancho or small stringed instrument, "mahogany the top covered with snake skin," from Senegambia; a qin, "kin or 'scholars lute' Wood, black lacquered in case of the same material," from China; and a sitar, "wood and pumpkin, with bridge & mount of ivory."[26] This was just the beginning of a series of fussy addenda and further contributions over the years to come. On July 8, 1870, Engel wrote that he would like "to assist as much as is in my power, in rendering the collection of musical instruments in the South Kensington Museum more comprehensive than it is at present"; and he offered on loan "a selection of eighteen instruments from my little Museum at home. . . . Some of them are tastefully ornamented, others are merely interesting in an archaeological or ethnological point of view." Among the European additions were an English bass flute from around 1600, a German lute from around 1700, a French "lyre-guitare" that was "said to have belonged to Marie Antoinette," and a border bagpipe from Northumberland. From elsewhere he listed a sarinda or Indian violin, a marouvané or string and bamboo instrument from Madagascar, and an ingomba or drum from Guinea, which was "made of the stem of a palm about 7 feet in length. Covered at both ends with the skin of an elephant's ear."[27] On November 11, 1870, Engel added two instruments from Egypt and Japan; on January 10, 1872, it was another twelve instruments, this time all but one of them extra-European, from Abyssinia, Congo, Persia, Hindustan, Vancouver, Burma, St. Lucia, and Brazil. He also mentioned some "twenty antiquated English and German musical instruments, most of them of the seventeenth century," which he could send for an exhibition planned for the following June. On July 26, 1875, the museum registered loans of many more instruments, including ones from Fiji and Tonga. Finally, on March 24, 1882, close to the end of his life, Engel wrote to Sir Philip Cunliffe-Owen, then the museum director, asking him to examine a list for sale, with the hope that it would help to realize what he called "my heart's desire to accomplish something last-ingly useful in the Art of Music." On June 17, 1882, the museum registered its purchase from Engel of 201 instruments for 555 pounds (then consid-ered a modest price), clearly offered in the spirit of a philanthropic gift.[28] Engel helped out the museum in other ways, too. He served as an advisor both for individual purchases and for the organization of the museum's contribution of musical instruments to exhibitions, including an 1872 exhibition (mostly of early modern European instruments) at the South Kensington Museum that was sponsored by Prince Albert. From the early 1860s until his death in 1882, Engel served as the museum's chief musical authority, presiding with expertise over the description of musical instru-ments from France, Italy, Africa, India, and China. He was the founding figure who gave shape to the museum's instrument collection. He insisted on understanding music in its local specificity and material particularity, but also as part of a unified whole through time and space.

One of Engel's most significant achievements was his catalogue of the South Kensington Museum's instrument collection, for it became the starting point for further attempts at classification of musical instru-ments. His erudition and ambition were staggering. In something over a hundred pages, a historical essay surveyed the instruments of the ancient Egyptians, Assyrians, Hebrews, Greeks, Etruscans, Romans, Chinese, Hindus, Persians, Arabs, and Native Americans, as well as medieval and postmedieval European instruments. This was followed by a catalogue of more than 150 pages listing the museum's holdings from Africa, Asia, the Caucasus, Turkey, Romania, Mexico, and Europe. The donor names in Engel's catalogue entries amount to a flowchart showing the path of objects to South Kensington. Offerings came from the Khedive of Egypt, the Paris Exhibition of 1867, the Annual International Exhibitions held in London in the early 1870s, the directors of the Alexandra Palace Company (the Alexandra Palace was a popular London entertainment center), private donations, and Engel's personal collection, which was partly derived from the collection of Mahillon.[29]

As remarkable as the abundance was Engel's mode of presentation. The instruments had little internal order beyond their grouping by nationality. One could perhaps regard Engel as the vestige of an earlier era, the creator of a cabinet of curiosities for the age of the public museum. Yet Engel mobilized his instruments with a sensitivity to comparative historical method. First, he argued that the current classification of instruments into the categories of string, wind, and percussion was "not tenable if we extend our researches over the whole globe"; to these one had to add "peculiar Instruments of Friction, which can hardly be classed with our Instruments of Percussion," and "contrivances in which a number of strings are caused to vibrate by a current of air, much as is the case with the Aeolian harp; which might with equal propriety be considered either as stringed instruments, or as wind instruments." Musicians could benefit from exposure to the music played on foreign instruments, which "mostly spring from the heart. Hence the natural and true expression, the delightful health and vigour by which they are generally distinguished." He continued with an important stricture on the value of Western music: ". . . The predominance of expressive melody and effective rhythm over harmonious combinations, so usual in the popular compositions of foreign nations, would alone suffice to recommend them to the careful attention of our modern musicians." Engel wrote these lines at a time when it was learned doctrine to praise the superiority of Western music for its elaboration of harmony; he pointed out the losses as well as the gains. His observations were prescient and especially noteworthy if one considers how little opportunity there was to hear performances of foreign music— not to speak of the unavailability of recordings, which were still several decades away.[30]

The Nationalist Challenge

What turned Engel into the advocate of expanded musical horizons? He had grown up immersed in the great tradition of the baroque and classical styles. To the end of his life he turned to the harpsichord works of

Johann Sebastian Bach as his joy and consolation. Yet from childhood he also imbibed a spirit removed from the confines of any one time or place. His early experience of German folk music prepared him for a comparative appreciation of popular musical expressions that transcended the vanity of any one nation; it may also have prepared the way for his later ability to cross class boundaries. More jarring, and a greater incentive to looking beyond established cultural limits, may have been his personal experience of border crossing. By moving to Manchester and London and marrying into the Paget and Bowman families, he came to know English society from the inside. At the same time he never considered himself anything but German. His double perspective was an education in seeing and thinking beyond local habits.

The broad stream of arts and crafts movements in nineteenth-century England also carried Engel into foreign territories.[31] The craft object and the craft of performance were the ends of his devotion. He spurned the cheapened values of the marketplace, and trained his eyes and ears on things of superior workmanship. With this dedication to the intrinsic value of things no matter what their origins, his attention wandered backward to the European old masters, both instrument makers and composers. But in globalized Europe, in which goods from around the world filled exhibitions and exotic instruments circulated into the metropolis, it was possible to make the leap from clavichord and viola da gamba to finely crafted sitars and kotos, and thence to curiosity about their music. Craft objects united the local and the global; the individual artifacts, embodiments of patient and creative workmanship, belonged to a constellation of times, places, workshops, cities, courts, and salons. The Victoria and Albert Museum provided a prominent showplace for Engel's cosmopolitan assemblage of instruments. In the next generation, early music proponents and the founding ethnomusicologists would join his embrace of forgotten and unfamiliar music.

Toward the end of his life, Engel fell into a deep depression. After his wife died in 1880, he suffered from intense loneliness. To be sure, his writing and work continued. Shortly before his death he wrote to a publisher with a promise of three book manuscripts, and his letters to Hipkins were still preoccupied with the search for more harpsichords and clavichords in church attics and country barns. Near the end, he made a trip to Thiedenwiese and Hanover, telling his English friends that he might just spend his last days in Germany. Instead, he got engaged to a young woman who had been his wife's servant. Decades of stability gave way to frenzied activity and struggle with inner demons. But in the end the demons overcame him; at his London home, the night before he was to be married in the fall of 1882, he ended his life.[32]

Engel had made one other attempt to restore his inner balance. In December 1880 Carl Peters, the son of one of his sisters, accepted his invitation to come and stay with him in London. For Peters, who had already completed his first years of university study, to join his uncle in Kensington was to leave behind provincial Germany and semipoverty—his mother was a pastor's widow—for a glamorous life in the metropolis. In Peters's eyes, his uncle lived and behaved like a prosperous gentleman. Through Engel's English family, he entered the salons of the privileged. Peters stayed in London for sixteen months with Engel, who urged him to settle and enjoy its pleasures as he had done. After wavering, Peters finally decided by April 1882 to return to Germany. His uncle's suicide a half year later transformed his and his mother's circumstances. She received thirty thousand marks, and he was heir to Carl Engel's "literary assets" (it is unclear whether this included manuscripts or books) as well as 3,672 marks, which was enough to finance his university studies.[33]

Peters also inherited his uncle's ambition to make his reputation by expanding beyond European borders. But he turned from romantic cosmopolitanism to criminal misdeeds, becoming one of the early German boosters of colonial empire and making his career as an explorer and administrator in German East Africa. There, he was a kind of Mr. Kurtz, whose sexual excesses and murderous treatment of Africans led to a trial in Germany, disgrace, and notoriety. Rehabilitation came from the Nazi regime, which celebrated him as a forerunner of its own methods and imperial designs. This bizarre turn—from humane early-nineteenth-century liberalism to the worst arrogance of the Wilhelmine colonizer gone bad—was also part of the history of cosmopolitanism. A desire to break out of German provinciality and explore the wider world could produce either compassion for all peoples or a limitless ambition for conquest.

Within the world of English music, an ironic appropriation of Engel's intellectual legacy took place in the next generation. Meirion Hughes and Robert Stradling, in their history of the English Musical Renaissance, credit Engel's *Literature of National Music* with initiating the English folk music revival. In it, Engel asked why the English were so far behind other nations—the Germans who had led the way, followed by the Russians and French—in documenting their folk music traditions. "The putative Renaissance,", "was galvanised by this German prompt," write Hughes

and Stradling.[34] But the young men who took up the call were English nationalists who squirmed away from acknowledging the German who had
led them to their appointed task. Cecil Sharp, the driving force behind the
movement, could only "reject and marginalize" Engel's work. Vaughan
Williams, who became Sharp's disciple and spent ten years gathering folk
songs, claimed to discover his vocation when a traditional English song
wafted to his ears as he sat in a vicar's garden. He and Sharp presented
folk song and Tudor song to the English public as a product of pure En-
glishness. They eradicated the inflection of a German immigrant who
belonged to the mass migration of Germans to Manchester and London
and turned away from intellectual and artistic exchanges between German and English music makers. This elision was, in turn, part of a greater
generational shift from admiration of German composers and criticism
to the assertion, at the turn of the twentieth century, of a homegrown English school of music.[35]

At this point, one might be tempted to imagine a growing cultural
chasm leading to World War I as the end of the story. Yet creative human
beings are too inquisitive, too insistent on following wisdom and aesthetic pleasure wherever they find it, to be corralled into such convenient
narratives. Gustav Holst is a counterexample from the same milieu as
Cecil Sharp and Vaughan Williams. From a Baltic family that came to England in the early nineteenth century after wandering from Rostock to
Riga and St. Petersburg, Holst had a deeply English sensibility, yet never
lost his Continental connections. During the mid-1890s, he fell under the
influence of Richard Wagner while joining the circle around William Morris, the guiding figure in the revival and preservation of English crafts. After the turn of the century, Holst became involved in the discovery of older
English music when he helped Vaughan Williams with editorial work
on *The English Hymnal*, a revised songbook that plumbed old sources for
riches from the musical past. Holst also composed three hymns for the
collection. He never turned against German music; instead, he continued the fruitful exchanges of previous generations. In the spring of 1903,
he and his wife vacationed in Germany and visited Berlin, Dresden, and
Munich, "sampling the musical life, art galleries, and museums wherever
they went. . . ." Even though his Wagner enthusiasm subsided, he kept
up his admiration for nineteenth-century German music.[36] Moreover, he
turned not just backward to an earlier England, and across the Channel
to a larger Europe, but abroad to the arts of India. Nalini Ghuman has described how, as early as 1894, Holst was able to attend a lecture by Charles

Day (an army captain befriended by A. J. Hipkins) with musical accompaniment, and had other opportunities to hear or learn about Indian music, especially after an intensification of interest in Indian arts and letters beginning in 1910.[37] In the late 1890s he developed a curiosity about Sanskrit that led him to take lessons in the language. He did not get beyond the alphabet, but that was enough to help him put original texts side by side with translations and work out his own libretti for works like the opera *Sita*, published in 1906. Indian literature and philosophy fired his imagination, as in 1913 did a related influence, astrology. Around the same time, he began sketching the work that became a popular favorite in the orchestral repertory after its first performance in 1920, *The Planets*.[38] Despite the incompleteness of his familiarity with India, Holst's work culminating in this piece continued the pattern of English receptivity to German musical culture, as well as his effort over many years to embrace extra-European arts and thought as an element in his own compositions.

The fate of Engel's instrument collection at the Victoria and Albert is another reminder that no single turn inward or outward is definitive. By 1910, the leaders of the museum decided that they had to rein in the eclecticism inherited from the exuberant but undisciplined Henry Cole, and instrument collecting was discontinued.[39] It was a decision that had repercussions for a century and more in which the foreign instruments given by Engel and other early donors were removed to the cavernous back rooms of the museum archive. That decision has at last given way to a renewed appreciation of the instrument collection. London, long a meeting place for peoples from around the world, has become a multicultural metropolis that wishes to show off its cultural diversity. Performances of Indian musical instruments have taken place, a small sample is on view, and more can be admired at the Victoria and Albert's online website.[40] Today's Victoria and Albert Museum is the inheritor of the ideals as well as the instruments cherished by Engel and like-minded cosmopolitans. It once again advances the admiration for musical craft objects from around the world, expressions of local culture and cross-cultural collaboration which Engel rescued for our own age of globalization.

2

An English Craftsman Discovers World Music

Where does musical imagination begin? We know that language takes shape with those around us, with family and caretakers who initiate us into *one* language (or two, or three) among the many that humanity has invented; they leave us with the stamp of a particular culture and personality through their use of language. This act is so fundamental for completing our humanity that it leads to more general reflection about the influences that inform our earliest years. If language is acquired, then what about musical language? Which is the language that we learn, and how and where do we learn it? The answer to these questions is more or less hidden from the biographer. It leads to questions of psychology that lie beyond the historian's scope. But it is at least worthwhile to pose the question.

A biographical appreciation of Alfred James Hipkins, written in his lifetime and with a degree of intimate detail that bespeaks interviews with him, provides a clue to his musical formation. He was born at Westminster in 1826. Westminster with its abbey, nearly a thousand years old in that year, the place of coronation of monarchs and burial of great men and women, an ancient contrast to the blur and buzz of the great city all around; a monument to stimulate the imagination of a child. And a musical place. As the biographer notes: "His earliest years were spent within sound of the Abbey bells."[1]

The cultural historian Johan Huizinga, trying to evoke for the twentieth-century reader the atmosphere of the Middle Ages, turned to the sounding of the bells as a regulating rhythm of its towns and villages. They broke up the mundane occupations of everyday life and announced common events, large and small; they were familiar but never lost their power to make townspeople listen. One of the odd things about this story is that we still hear bells today. Huizinga's example immediately registers with readers because they are with us: different, of course, from what they were and meant half a millennium ago, but strange enough to still modern chatter and transport our imagination. According to the abbey's official website, the chronicler Matthew Paris already noted in 1255 that five bells were in use, and a bell cast for the abbey around 1310 with the inscription "Christe audi nos" ("Hear us, O Christ") is still in the abbey's museum today. By the late fifteenth century, the time of Huizinga's famous portrayal of the late Middle Ages, six bells were in use; and it remained so, the website tells us, "until the twentieth century."[2] The young Hipkins could not have turned to the official website, and may have known more or less about the history of the bells than we can readily find out today. But he would have heard them and, with his exceptional musical gifts, been alive to them.

They had a specific musical feature that anticipated the objects of his later career: their wobbly tone. Bells emit the opposite of a pure pitch of the kind Hipkins would later know from tuning forks, and that we know today from the even greater consistency of electronically produced tones. Bells send out air waves in a broad span around their fundamental pitch. Sounding together, they do not harmonize with the mechanical snap of a modern instrument ensemble, but clang in something closer to a joyful anarchy of sound, a deviation from the expectations of modern European ears that is nonetheless welcome. The tension between harmonization and deviation can actually produce a pleasurable degree of dissonance. Bells offer moderns a respite from the regularities of industrial bureaucratic life, and a return to the freer expressiveness of distant times and places.

The Craft of Tuning

The discernment of irregularities of pitch became Hipkins's vocation. He wanted to become a painter, but his father asked him first to acquire a solid trade and apprenticed him at age fourteen to Broadwood, where he was to learn piano tuning. The agreement was that he could consider the fine arts again when he was seventeen, but Hipkins never looked back (though the visual impulse recurred in his son and daughter, both of them talented visual artists). Piano tuning was a skilled craft that depended on an ear capable of registering delicate differences in tone—but it also bordered on factory work, for Broadwood employed a sizable staff of tuners. Hipkins speedily educated himself beyond it. He learned to play the piano from an instruction book. His autodidactic efforts were supplemented by just three months of lessons from a kind Mr. Fentum "who kept a music shop in the Strand," played the flute for the opera house in the Haymarket, and made it possible for Hipkins to visit the opera. During his years of apprenticeship, the abbey did not lose its hold on him. It was where "he regularly attended the two Sunday services" and became familiar with the music of Handel and his lifelong favorite, Johann Sebastian Bach.[3]

Hipkins transformed the art of tuning within the Broadwood factory. Pitch systems at the time of his apprenticeship were in a state of uncertainty. Broadwood tuners continued to follow mean temperament. This had the advantage of being easy to use: the system was built on a perfect interval between the first and fifth notes of each scale, a discernible distance, and developed the other notes from there. Mean tone had the disadvantage, however, of creating some jarringly out-of-tune intervals which the tuners patched up but could not entirely overcome. While there was a long-standing European discussion of equal temperament, it was considered beyond the reach of most tuners to regulate the gradations of twelve notes placed at equal intervals from one another. Hipkins picked up a book on harmony that included a discussion of equal temperament, and taught himself the art of tuning with it. In 1846 Walter Broadwood took note of the innovation and gave Hipkins the job of teaching all the other tuners to use equal temperament, so that Hipkins, by then twenty, "had to instruct or re-teach those who had in the first instance taught him!" Change came slowly; five years later, at the Great Exhibition of 1851, the organs were still unequally tuned.[4] Hipkins lived, then, at a watershed moment of experimentation, with several kinds of tuning on one historical side and the introduction of equal temperament on the other. Over the course of his lifetime he embodied the age's tensions. Within the Broadwood factory he was an agent of mechanical progress who rationalized its tuning system; yet he remained sensitive to the virtues of older forms of musical scale and performance. This kind of intellectual and artistic breadth only widened over the course of Hipkins's lifetime as he explored novel arrangements of tone in every direction, temporal and geographic, listening for their distinctive qualities rather than validating any one.

The Craft of Listening: Chopin and Early Music

By the year of the Great Exhibition, Hipkins was no longer tuning pianos, though he remained a Broadwood employee for the rest of his life; his interests had grown to encompass central artistic issues of his time.

Musicians and musicologists turned to Hipkins for expert help. Chopin got in touch with him after arriving in England following the Revolutions of 1848. The composer had played a Broadwood piano in Paris and admired its sensitive touch; on returning to London (he had previously visited in 1837), he promptly went to the Broadwood warehouse in Great Pulteney Street. That was when Hipkins met him for the first time. On subsequent visits—Hipkins became his tuner and later owned a piano originally built to Chopin's specifications—he was able to hear the composer play. These private performances were a musical revelation. "It was the first near experience I had of genius: I had seen Mendelssohn conduct *Elijah*; I had heard Thalberg in his remarkable and original displays of piano-playing; but they were as prose to Chopin's poetry."[5] Hipkins was an unassuming, quiet man with a speech defect, but this did not keep him from campaigning for Chopin's music. At mid-century Mendelssohn was the favorite composer of *The Times* music critic J. W. Davison, who was reluctant to let Chopin share concertgoers' affections.[6] Hipkins publicized Chopin's music in 1851 by playing more than forty concerts to dense crowds on Thursday and Friday evenings at the Crystal Palace in the Great Exhibition.[7]

There was an irony to this mass education in Chopin's music, for what Hipkins admired in Chopin's own playing was the composer's quest for a subtle beauty best realized on small pianos, which Hipkins preferred to concert grands, as his daughter later recalled:

> Hipkins was well aware of the exhaustive demands made upon musicians in quest of technical perfection, but he greatly feared that this very perfection, tending more and more towards mechanical finish, would ultimately destroy the sensitiveness of the player's touch; his sympathies were altogether on the melodic side of music; he considered melody as essential to the enjoyment of music as an art, knowing that the cultivation of delicately graded tone with its wealth of values was an impera-

tive requirement towards the interpretation of Bach's expressiveness (*Vortrag*), and for the ultimate realization of Chopin's poetry.[8]

There was, then, a programmatic force to Hipkins's admiration of Chopin; the composer embodied sensitivity to note, tone and touch. As Hipkins interpreted Chopin's playing, he contrasted it to the mechanical athleticism of the merely brilliant virtuoso, whose outward showiness might be a crowd-pleaser, but at the cost of dynamic expression.

Hipkins did not limit this protest against the mechanization of music to his private notebooks. Later, he was able to promulgate his views to a broad musical public by writing for the Ninth Edition of the *Encyclopaedia Britannica* and the first edition of Grove's *Dictionary of Music and Musicians*. In these and other writings he advocated expressive versus mechanical performance. His concern naturally encompassed the construction of keyboard instruments as well as their use. At one distinguished occasion, his Cantor Lectures at the Royal Society of Arts, he made a masterful survey of strings and winds that included a discussion of keyboard instruments and their decisive role in the creation of modern music. Without them, he wrote, the orchestra might have remained a loose assemblage, the organ would not have accompanied church music, and the composer would not have had the piano as creative aid. By facilitating the playing of several notes at once, modern keyboard instruments had furthered the development of counterpoint and harmony.[9] European music could not have evolved into its present form without them—a conclusion with far-ranging implications for the larger place of music in modern cultural history.

Most European and American readers of this and Hipkins's other writings on keyboard instruments would have applauded the development of the modern piano as part of a story of progress. It was a given for music experts that the triumph of harmony in Western music signified a superior rationality and complexity. Even the handful of connoisseurs with a taste for extra-European musical traditions would only have said that they were more or less advanced, but not the peer of Western music any more than those cultures' other achievements had evolved as far as those of the West. More typical for the time were the sentiments of George Grove, editor of the dictionary and first director of the Royal College of Music, whose preface declared that "unless they ha[d] some direct bearing on European music," the dictionary had no space for the art of "barbaric nations."[10]

Hipkins's own article for Grove took a dissenting view of Western progress that planted a paradox into the heart of its history. He recounted the advances in the making of the pianoforte as a history of technological advance; his own research contributed to the clarification of the early history of the pianoforte by establishing the originality of the Florentine instrument builder Bartolomeo Cristofori in creating the hammer action between key and string that is the instrument's defining feature. Hipkins pointed to England, and to his own firm, Broadwood, for the invention of the grand piano with an improved "English action" in the 1770s—a mechanism that, according to Hipkins, was still used by Chopin as well as other pianists down to his own day. A limited use of iron to strengthen the frame and bear the tension of the strings permitted virtuoso playing technique to attain "its highest perfection between 1820 and 1850." Thereafter, the story took a dismaying turn: in 1859 Steinway patented a piano with two revolutionary changes, "a grand piano with fan-shaped overstrung scale in one casting." The cast-iron frame permitted the Steinway to bear more string tension and to string the bass over the long treble strings, which added to the bass's volume. The Grove article was not the place for polemic; Hipkins simply pointed out in his conclusion that the piano was not just a mechanical product but was also shaped by the manufacturer's personality and "a national taste in choice of tone."[11] The Cantor lectures were more critical: "For me, the tone of an over-strung bass is unduly powerful . . . soft, pure basses are not attainable. . . . What we want is a pianoforte tone that gives us all the power and all the charm of varying *nuance* we can desire, with a tone-quality as specialized in character as the harpsichord tone was, that shall have the brightness and energy of vibration of the trumpet, without the blare."[12] A similar objection applied to improvements in the action. The English action remained "wider and more various," and therefore "more open to the characteristic individual feeling for tone," while the newer action invented by the French piano firm Erard, generally adopted outside of Britain, "is considered more facile for the pianist's *technique*."[13] In the end, the advances in piano technology resulted in a monochrome kind of progress. The thunder of the Steinway virtuoso was drowning out the subtlety of Chopin playing on a Broadwood.[14]

In search of crafted expression—of instrument, of performance—Hipkins turned backward in time. He had an interest in old English music and became a mentor to Lucy Broadwood, a member of his employer's family, encouraging her in her life's work as collector, founding member of the Folk-Song Society in 1899, and editor of its journal. In Sunday concerts at his house, she and others enjoyed his performances on the clavichord and harpsichord. These intimate events were a world apart from some of her experiences in London's public musical life, where "the glamorous Liszt pupil Sophie Menter enthralled critic George Bernard Shaw and others as she pounded her way through the 1883 season, much to Lucy's disgust."[15] Through his writings, public concerts, and private performances, Hipkins became one of the leading late nineteenth-century advocates of historic instruments. His particular favorite was the clavichord. Its sound was produced when a blade struck from below and then (unlike the piano hammer) remained on a string until the performer released it. A delicate instrument, it was capable of dynamic gradations, and with pressure on the key the performer could slightly elevate the pitch of the note. Even though it was weaker in volume than the harpsichord, it permitted a greater range of expression. J. S. Bach preferred it to the pianofortes of his time, maintained Hipkins; Mozart composed *The Magic Flute* on it; and Beethoven, claimed Hipkins, praised its superior control of tone and "expressive interpretation."[16] Thus he took his campaign for this delicate early modern instrument right into the core of the classical tradition.

Historic instruments and performance had found advocates since the late eighteenth century. The first English concerts on instruments no longer in use dated from the 1830s, with the clavichord the first success for a revival. In the 1850s the critic-performer Charles Kensington Salaman enjoyed acclaim for his historical concerts of early English composers—Byrd, Bull, and Gibbons—on virginals, spinets, and clavichords, eventually performing for the royal family. In 1861 Ernest Pauer gave an acclaimed series of six recitals tracing the history of keyboard music from 1600 to 1850. Hipkins built on the work of these predecessors and, perhaps most important of all, on the instrument collection and writings of Carl Engel. His interest in historical performance having been initially awakened by Pauer, Hipkins gave a series of lecture-concerts on the history of keyboard instruments at the Musical Association of London that lasted from 1886 to 1896.[17]

Hipkins asked others to deliver his papers at these pedagogic events. His personal reserve seems only to have heightened the reverence that surrounded him. J. A. Fuller-Maitland, music critic for *The Guardian* and later for *The Times*, called him "a benefactor to all the young pianists who were trained in England or who flocked over from abroad. . . . It was a revelation to hear Hipkins play the 'Chromatic Fantasia' of Bach on his clavichord, for in the comparatively deliberate pace adopted one could realise the depth of Bach's poetry, which is generally hidden in the performances of those who will make it sound like a display of fireworks."[18] Hipkins' concerts, then, were a rebuke to the virtuosos who awed their audience through technical mastery; those who responded to music's hidden depths could find their way to it through his clavichord performances.

Arts and Crafts

Hipkins' mastery of the crafts of music won him admirers in the aesthetic milieu of the Arts and Crafts movement.[19] One of these was George Henschel, who was among the most celebrated singers of the late nineteenth and early twentieth century. German-born, a friend of Brahms, he visited England in 1877, fell in love with the country, and settled there as a leading tenor and orchestra conductor. He also pursued an influential musical career in the United States, where he became the first conductor of the Boston Symphony Orchestra in 1881 and taught in New York at the Institute of Musical Art, later renamed the Julliard Conservatory. His recollection of Hipkins in his memoirs is not just a touching evocation of a friendship, but underlines the place of the Hipkins style in fin de siècle musical life. With an introduction from Walter Broadwood, Henschel visited the firm shortly after his arrival in London. To do so was to enter a world of music hidden in the heart of the metropolis. The firm inhabited "three adjoining old houses situated in Great Pulteney Street, a thoroughfare in the midst of that labyrinth of little back alleys east of Regent Street between Piccadilly Circus and Oxford Street." These houses were filled with pianos unlike any Henschel had seen before, "built of oak, coated, like old violins, with a fine golden varnish which retained the colour and the grain of the wood." After showing him around, Broadwood handed him over to Hipkins. A great friendship followed:

> I shall always bless him for this introduction, for it marked the beginning of a friendship than which I have valued none more highly. I honestly believe a gentler, kinder, sweeter man than Alfred James Hipkins never lived. Nor a more modest one. For who, seeing him in his office at the Broadwoods . . . could have suspected in the simple, silent man the learned author of several standard books on various branches of the science and history of music, and an unrivalled authority on old keyboard instruments, on which he himself was a most accomplished and graceful performer, and of which he possessed several fine specimens?

To leave the giddy world and repair to the delightful home of the Hipkinses in Warwick Gardens, there, in the genial company of mutual friends upon a Sunday afternoon to partake of the spirit of simplicity, love, and harmony prevailing in the little household, consisting of father and mother and daughter and son, to listen to and join in the lively conversation from which anything even approaching gossip was ever absent, to see the look of supreme content and happiness in our dear host's face as, after a week's toil, he would sit down before his beloved harpsichord or clavichord and play us a Bach or Scarlatti in masterly fashion, has been among the purest joys of my life.[20]

To visit Hipkins's household was to enter something like the world of the Old Masters. Harpsichord and clavichord, Bach and Scarlatti, were the means and muses of the authentic spirit of art.

Is it the giddy world or genial devotion that is on display in a portrait of Henschel from 1879, painted by the artist Lawrence Alma-Tadema? Something of both, perhaps, as with George Eliot's Klesmer performing in a gentry salon. The painting shows the young baritone, not yet thirty, seated at a keyboard instrument with the little finger of his right hand visibly depressing a key, about to accompany his own singing as he often did in real life. He is turned toward us, his audience, with his mouth slightly open, head thrown back, as if a musical phrase had just begun or ended; he draws us into his art with his direct gaze, dark hair, and youthful good looks, his controlled but heartfelt exuberance. The props that frame the dark-suited artist convey color and antiquity. Behind him hangs a curtain suggesting a tapestry in an Old Masters painting from the painter's native Netherlands. Its bright, broad strokes add to the picture's cheerfulness, as does the light streaming in through fancy lattice windows. The picture transforms the Golden Room in Alma Tadema's home, the setting for Henschel's performance, into the successor to the patrician gathering places and masterly art of previous centuries.[21]

Henschel and Alma-Tadema had a warm personal friendship dating from two years before the painting.[22] They were also united in their admiration for Hipkins. The Broadwood employee did not belong to the high society of Alma-Tadema's mansion in St. John's Wood. Yet this did not preclude sociability between the modest master of the keyboard and the celebrated, wealthy artist. After Hipkins's death it was Alma-Tadema who designed a brass plaque in his memory for St. Margaret's Church, Westminster. His design memorialized the harmony of music and art with sinuous lines and other ornamental touches that might have come straight from an Arts and Crafts–inspired book illustration.[23]

Their admiration was mutual. Hipkins had turned to Alma-Tadema as an exemplary crafter of musical instruments. His praise for the artist grew from carefully weighed views on the relation between arts and crafts. Against the degradation of the instrument to a use-object, he wrote:

> Beauty of form and fitness of decoration demand more than the commonplace homage paid to simple use, and while we should never lose sight of the purpose of a musical instrument, its capacity to produce agreeable and various sounds, we can take advantage of its form and material, and making it lovely to look upon, give pleasure to the eye as well as the ear. It is hardly necessary to say that the love of adornment or ornament is an attribute of the human race. It is to be found everywhere and in every epoch when life is, for the time being, safe and the means of existence secure. . . . And so it was, until the marvelous mechanical advance in the present century has not only caused us to forget, by its overwhelming power, what our predecessors so steadfastly continued, but has induced us to regard the ugly as sufficient if the mere practical end is served. By thus chilling the appreciation and pursuit of decorative invention, that faculty has been numbed for the time being, and there is danger of its being lost altogether. . . . If there is any hope of an awakening of the love for musical instruments that finds expression in their adornment, its promise lies in the beautiful designs that have been, of late years, so meritoriously carried out for pianos. . . ."[24]

One of his examples of beautiful piano design came from Alma-Tadema. While he went on to observe that "good decoration need not be a privilege of the rich," the ensemble that exemplified fine ornament was certainly reserved for a paragon of wealth and privilege. He had in mind a work that was part of a set including a piano, two stools, two settees, and two armchairs. They were made for Henry Gurdon Marquand, a wealthy New York entrepreneur and patron of the arts who later became director of the Metropolitan Museum. Made in London between 1884 and 1886, with a Steinway as the piano, they were displayed in a shop in New Bond Street before being shipped to New York, where they furnished the music room in Marquand's house on Madison Avenue.[25]

How did the former piano tuner get mixed up in this exalted coterie? Whereas Hipkins stood by his craft and gradually expanded outward from it, many of the Pre-Raphaelite artists veered from one medium to another; whereas Hipkins's home was praised as an island of domestic tranquility, the love lives of painters such as Dante Gabriel Rossetti and Edward Burne-Jones were a tangle of liaisons; whereas Hipkins never left behind his petit bourgeois class status—often subtly registered in the affectionate testimonies to him—William Morris was born to wealth and Rossetti to status, while Burne-Jones and Alma-Tadema were both knighted. Yet the match made sense; the camaraderie of craftsman and aesthete fit the ethos of the Arts and Crafts movement. It aimed to rescue traditional crafts and work them up into models for contemporary design. Hipkins embodied just the qualities its makers were looking for. His mastery of the craft of piano building, scholarly expertise in its history, performances on historic instruments, and discriminating taste all made him a natural ally.

Hipkins's entry into highbrow artistic circles probably began in a milieu that may at first sight look unexpected: the Wagner cult in England. Hipkins was a follower of the first hour. An appreciation of Hipkins, written during his lifetime, mentioned that he "became attached to the cult in 1866, not from admiration—that came later and is now a passion—but from the feeling that Wagner was being condemned in England unheard."[26] The statement underlines Hipkins's independence: a craftsman he may have been, but he did not hesitate to question established prejudice. The connoisseur of historic instruments had open ears for new music and made a point of defying conventional taste in the case of Wagner, as he had already done with Chopin. In 1867 he joined a group of six called the Working Men's Society, whose members played forward-looking classical music at one another's homes: late Beethoven works, Schumann, Liszt, Berlioz, and Wagner.[27] Wagner's music stood apart from the others and became a collective cause.

The Wagner reception was part of the willingness of the English public in this period to let its taste be shaped by an Anglo-German musical alliance. Several members of the Working Men's Society were émigrés from Germany who came with a higher education (hence hardly "working men") and attachment to German philosophy that gave their dedication to Wagner its now-familiar ideological flavor. One of the most prominent of these was Edward Dannreuther, who grew up in the German community in Cincinnati, where his father owned a piano factory, and who entered the Leipzig Conservatory in 1860. Two years later he heard Wagner "conduct the first performance of the overture to *Die Meistersinger*." In 1863 Dannreuther made a sensation with his performance of Chopin's

F minor Piano Concerto in the Crystal Palace, and stayed in England to make his career there as a pianist and music scholar. He founded the Wagner Society in 1873; when Wagner visited London in 1877, he "lodged with the Dannreuthers at 12 Orme Square."[28] A detail from this visit, related by Anne Dzamba Sessa, illustrates the overlap of the Wagner cult with the Arts and Crafts movement. The interiors of the Dannreuther house were covered with William Morris wallpapers ("the design lemons and pomegranates") and paintings by Burne-Jones and his disciples.[29] Another émigré promoter of Wagner's music was Francis Hueffer. Born in Münster in 1844, he moved in 1869 to London, where he quickly rose to prominence and took over as music critic for *The Times* from 1878 to 1889. Hueffer made friends among the Pre-Raphaelites soon after his arrival in London; later he married the daughter of the artist Ford Madox Brown.[30] Hipkins too became a visitor at the Madox Brown household. With him came his son John, best remembered for his wood engravings but also a skilled caricaturist who made sketches of the artists he met at the homes of Alma-Tadema and Madox Brown. Dating from the 1870s to 1886, they belong to a time of creative work and public recognition for his father.[31]

The artists in this circle lend themselves today to a patronizing look backward. In our own time of frank acceptance of sexuality, their confused gropings after models and one another's wives, often leading to shame and unhappiness, may be a painful reminder of an age of repression. The showy display of female flesh and sentimental medievalism in their paintings looks self-indulgent, especially compared to the critical relationship to sexuality in the art of their French contemporary, Manet. Their work can be scorned as Victorian kitsch, as happened recently in a *New York Times* polemic against the art on display in a show dedicated to their work. And yet there was more to it than just that. In a direction congruent with Hipkins, their dedication to the techniques and ethos of craftsmanship merged with the Arts and Crafts movement, which in turn continued in the Bauhaus in Germany and with Frank Lloyd Wright in the United States. The English craft revival's rescue of traditional materials, methods, and designs and its concern for the relationship between artifact and environment remained timely for those twentieth-century successors.[32]

The prophet of their movement was John Ruskin. Little read today, Ruskin was a giant of Victorian public life. His writings expanded from their starting point in art and architecture to a critique of industrial capitalism and the meretricious taste of the middle classes who profited from it. Aesthetes, social reformers, socialists, and readers interested in a spiritual regeneration of modern society took heart from his lectures and books, which taught an appreciation of medieval civilization while condemning the moral poverty of modern Europe since the Renaissance. Morris and Burne-Jones were at Oxford while Ruskin was professor of art history; his writings, in particular *The Stones of Venice* and its famous section "The Nature of the Gothic," gave direction to their work. If they engaged in a kind of salvage anthropology, rescuing the remnants of traditional crafts from English towns and villages, thanks to Ruskin their mission had a clear and explicit program that criticized British manufactures and offered an alternative to them. Ruskin flung what he deemed the nature of the Gothic in the face of the Enlightenment belittlement of its productions as savage and imperfect. He turned the evaluation on its head, proclaiming that those were precisely the qualities meriting admiration. "It is true," wrote Ruskin under the heading "Savageness" as he defined the Gothic, "greatly and deeply true, that the architecture of the North is rude and wild; but it is not true, that, for this reason, we are to condemn it, or despise. Far otherwise: I believe it is in this very character that it deserves our profoundest reverence." What a challenge Ruskin made to his age of progress: "savage" and "wild," terms that his fellow countrymen applied to many of the peoples of the earth as offhand expressions of contempt, not only applied to their own past—that was nothing new—but could imply spiritual and artistic superiority. Gothic architecture, taught Ruskin, was the product of free labor, the freedom of the medieval craftsman who, however humble and subordinate, enjoyed the dignity of the individual espoused by Christianity. The ancient Greeks produced perfect buildings because their workmen were slaves, and as slaves they followed the formulas of their masters and reproduced them in stone. The ever-changing ornaments, irregularities, and roughness of the Gothic were the manifestations of a civilization that filled the craftsman's work with spiritual life.[33]

Ruskin imbued his followers with a similar love of craft and craftsmanship, a determination to rescue the remnants of it that they could still discover by combing through manuscripts or carrying out fieldwork in the pockets of craft tradition not yet swept away by industrialization. Ruskin's social program, too, deeply affected them. A Christian social reformer, he wished to bring the best in art and taste to working people; he practiced charity by giving away a fortune to support working men's education. Like his teacher, Morris dreamed of creating objects of good taste and workmanship that would be available to ordinary people. In the end, as is often noted, the wallpapers, weavings, and other furnishings from his workshops were too expensive for all but the well-to-do. Haunted by his own sense of social mission, later in life he joined the burgeoning socialist movement.[34]

When a figure like Hipkins came along, gifted and with something to teach them, Morris and his companions did not hesitate to admit him into their salons. They had done the same among themselves: even within the group there was a significant difference between Burne-Jones, who came from modest circumstances in Birmingham, and Morris, the prosperous Londoner. To be sure, they had met at Oxford; the social gap between them and the onetime piano tuner was far greater. But it was not too far for Burne-Jones to campaign with Broadwood to make pianos available to ordinary people, "the man with £20 as well as the duke with £1000 to spend." Burne-Jones's biographer, Fiona MacCarthy, writes that "in the early 1880s . . . Broadwood's produced several oak pianos specially commissioned to Burne-Jones's designs. . . ." The Pre-Raphaelites' gift for collaboration and creation of cultural movements extended to this cross-class alliance.[35]

Hipkins provided deeper evidence of the affinities between his musicological researches and Pre-Raphaelite art in a review of the musical instruments in Dante Gabriel Rossetti's pictures that he published in two parts at the beginning of 1883. Elizabeth Helsinger has pointed out that while Rossetti was not a concertgoer, he was interested in music for its affinities to poetry and its analogous power to transport its audience into a realm of the imagination. While Rossetti may not have been personally responsive to music, he inhabited a Pre-Raphaelite milieu that was. Morris and Burne-Jones "belonged to early music choral groups at Oxford," according to Helsinger. Burne-Jones's wife-to-be, Georgiana, was a gifted musician who played the piano and sang for friends in 1857 and 1858. Helsinger provides a poignant image of the innocent pleasures of musicmaking for three young married couples at the home built to embody Morris's design principles: "There was collective music-making, too, at Morris's Red House, where three newly married couples—Georgie and Ned, Morris and Jane Burden, Rossetti and Elizabeth Siddall—gathered in the summer of 1860." Turning away from the sentimental songs popular among the middle class of their time, they preferred old English songs and Scottish ballads.[36] Rossetti's use of musical instruments in his paintings did not require a personal dedication to music; rather it belonged to the broad current of *l'art pour l'art* and Symbolism that transported the listener-observer beyond the everyday world by synthesizing the arts.[37] Wagner, too, fascinated musicians and visual artists across Europe with his use of synesthesia: audiences were transported by operas that melded music, poetry, movement, and staging.[38]

Hipkins would have been fully cognizant of the mystique surrounding Wagner and his theories of synesthesia. At the same time, he did not succumb to its excesses and cloudiness. Rather, he set down his thoughts in an essay that was—like so much else about him—well-considered and far-reaching in its conclusions about Rossetti's visual version of synesthetic art. The occasion for his article was a posthumous winter exhibition of the artist's paintings at the Royal Academy of Arts. Hipkins took it upon himself to comment on the paintings with musical instruments, sixteen in all, and on seventeen more paintings in "a supplementary exhibition at the Burlington Club in Savile Row." He began by noting his impression that "Rossetti was endowed with no decided musical ear. He felt, however, intensely the harmony of line and proportion that many painters have noticed in musical instruments, inherent in their essential configuration, and had the deep instinct of their fitness as decorative objects, like flowers and other beautiful accessories." Hipkins went through the paintings one by one, identifying the actual kinds of instrument represented in them—or their fictionality. The task was an especially enticing one because the Pre-Raphaelites were supposed to be "ultra-realists, declining to represent any object not actually seen." The relationship between representation and instrument in the paintings was, however, more complicated. Hipkins's point was not to belittle Rossetti's accuracy: on the contrary, he recognized that Rossetti was "using musical instruments as symbols" and might give them a whimsical touch that transported them out of the realm of the prosaically real.[39] The introduction of the koto into the painting of a siren called *A Sea-Spell*, at first sight to innocent eyes a hyperaccurate painting, depicted neither a familiar instrument nor performance on a koto.[40] With his comments on this painting, Hipkins absorbed the teaching of the burgeoning modernism of his time. Art properly understood was not "useful"; the history of art was more than just an antiquarian activity. Rather, art permitted a kind of experience different from the consumption of commodities. The girl with the golden koto belonged to a realm of enchantment removed from the reproduction of use objects.

The Adventure of World Music

Hipkins was an adventurer. He had shown his pluckiness from early on when he revised the tuning system in the Broadwood factory and become the teacher of his elders. He confidently continued on his way, befriending artists and scholars who respected his expertise. He pushed beyond the musical boundaries of mid-Victorian Britain by championing Chopin, Wagner, and early music. He mixed with the avant-garde and contributed to it.

The explorations did not stop at the borders of Europe; instead, Hipkins became conversant with music from around the world. His methodological suggestions and cosmopolitan vision of world music led one postwar ethnomusicologist, Mantle Hood, to nominate Hipkins for the status of "the Father of Modern Ethnomusicology." What was the achievement, what were the words, that led to this admiring honorific?[41] Hipkins's handsome volume on rare historical instruments leads toward an answer. It is a picture-book, with forty-eight plates of illustrations and commentary on each one. The opportunity for putting it together came from two exhibitions. The first was the Loan Collection of Musical Instruments, exhibited at Royal Albert Hall in 1885. To draw and include instruments from this occasion, Hipkins received "the gracious permission of the respective owners of the instruments, including H. M. the Queen, H. R. H. the Prince of Wales, H. R. H. the Siamese Minister, and the Japanese Commission."[42] The second was a national event that has received widespread attention down to the present: the Colonial and Indian Exhibition of 1886. Millions of visitors came to see the displays devoted to India and other colonies. If it denoted imperial triumph, its mood was nonetheless of a nervous sort at a moment when Britain felt increasingly crowded by the growing industrial power of the United States and Germany. It was also a countergesture to the trauma of the Indian Rebellion of 1857, which tore away the illusion of grateful Indian subjects and left Britain's rulers grasping for means to legitimate their rule. The exhibition was a place for them to demonstrate how the colony was flourishing under their tutelage. In addition, it became a site for the admiration of Indian crafts: as Aviva Briefel has written, it carried the anti-industrial ethos of arts and crafts currents in a new direction, to an overseas society which, more than Britain, had preserved its craft traditions.[43]

First in Hipkins's volume came the European instruments: burgmote horns, bagpipes, a spinet, Queen Elizabeth's virginal, a lute, a portable organ, a dulcimer, a Welsh crwth, a Russian balalaika, violins, a bell harp, a hurdy-gurdy, a trumpet, a kettledrum, a dolciano, an oboe, a bassoon, an oboe da caccia, and a basset horn. Hipkins might have stopped with his European collection. It would then have been a folkloric celebration of European antiquities, the kind of thing that aided what Eric Hobsbawm and Terence Ranger called the invention of tradition, rummaging through historical attics for the materials of a modern national culture—or, in this case, a European musical inheritance to set against the resources of non-European musical traditions.[44]

This, however, he refused to do. His introduction turned with his typical curiosity to the subject of the Jewish shofar and its proper sounding:

> The Jewish Shophar, a simple ram's horn . . . is the oldest wind instrument in present use in the world. . . . . There seems to be little doubt that it has been continuously used in the Mosaic Service from the time it was established until now. It is sounded in the synagogues at the New Year and on the Fast of the Day of Atonement. . . . Through the mediation of a friend, whose assistance has enabled me to gather this information, I have heard the shophar flourishes played by a competent performer, and am enabled to give an authoritative notation of these strangely interesting historical phrases, for the final correction of which I have to thank the Rev. Francis Cohen.[45]

At a time when traditional Jewish religious practices were a source of embarrassment to assimilated Western European Jews and disdain by their Christian compatriots, Hipkins sallied forth to admire and explain. Somehow this infinitely active man, amid his duties at Broadwood and correspondence and advisory role for exhibitions, found time to get accurate information about the use of the shofar, report on the difficulty of playing it, consult with a rabbi, and listen to a performance. No substituting other writers' judgment for his own; he found an informant and listened.[46]

Hipkins's curiosity wandered further: out of the forty-eight plates, nine showed non-European instruments from India, Thailand, China, Japan, and South Africa. A koto made its appearance, and with his usual precision Hipkins described the instrument's relation to its Chinese predecessor as well as its construction and scale, the position of the player and method of playing, and the use of pressure on the strings to produce microtones. Thai instruments were singled out for their craftsmanship: "Siamese ingenuity, which has found a rich field for employment in the decoration of musical instruments, the Siamese, in this respect, bearing the palm in the East, as the Italians have done in the West." And he let his readers know that their ignorance of Indian music left them bereft of a high art: ". . . Throughout India, and more intensely in the south, music is felt as a poetic art and has a development in its own way, that still remains unrecognized in Europe, although we now have scholars from whose researches and zeal this ignorance may be in time, at least partially, dispelled."[47] Hipkins did not impose a word of hierarchy. Instead he added: "The persistence of noble traditions is shown in the exquisite ornament of the Siamese instruments . . . and of the Japanese Kote [sic]. . . . It would be grievous if this Eastern inheritance were lost through the engrafting of Western ideas and reception of our material civilization."[48] Amid the self-congratulatory European fanfares of his time, it was a remarkable statement. He admired the crafting of musical instruments wherever it flourished. The contrast between Hipkins's cosmopolitanism and others' narrowness encapsulates the contradictory mood of the 1880s. It was dominated by European presumption of superiority, but it was also a moment of revaluation of non-European cultures.

Hipkins's book was a gallery of distinctive types within the family of world music. It reinforced the image of separate traditions expressing the inner life of different peoples. Yet he was also aware of the patterns of transmission that went into the making of instruments like the violin or piano. To single out the distinctive elements of Thai or Japanese instruments was also a way of recognizing distinct histories and honoring their noteworthy creations. His readiness to entertain whatever fresh samples of artistic expression came his way made his writings a model of undogmatic reception.

India for Cosmopolitans

As Hipkins's comments hinted, an opportunity had come his way for a deeper engagement with South Indian music. A British army captain, Charles Day, asked him and Alexander Ellis for help with turning his researches into a book.[49] Day belonged to the long line of British soldiers and administrators who were charmed by Indian culture and tried to convey their knowledge of it to their countrymen. William Dalrymple has written eloquently about the "white Mughals" of the late eighteenth century who assimilated into Indian culture, taking on local wives, dress, and religion. That was no longer possible a hundred years later, for beginning

in the early 1800s British administrators adopted policies of racial separation; but debate raged back and forth between policy makers attempting
to repress Indian cultures and those who had developed a sympathetic
interest in them.[50] Day belonged to a different variety of admirer, more
detached than the "white Mughals" of the previous century, but nonetheless keenly interested.

The only son of a church rector, Day was educated at Eton and in 1880
joined the Third Lancashire Royal Militia. He served with his unit in India
from 1882 to 1887. During this time Day came under the spell of Indian
music, still seldom heard and little appreciated by Europeans. His goal,
according to Hipkins's obituary, was to become commandant of the military training school for marching bands, but he was killed on February 8,
1900, while helping a wounded man during an attack near Paardeberg in
South Africa. Day's book thanked Hipkins as his "friend . . . both for his
great help and sympathy, without which this work would never have been
published. . . ." It survived him as a successful synthesis of his immersion
in the music and resources of India and of the wider theoretical and musicological perspectives that Hipkins and Ellis could bring to bear on the
subject.[51]

Day's publication of a book on South Indian music marked an advance
in understanding the basic types of music from the subcontinent. The
music of India began to split after the sixteenth century into two great
styles, today called Hindustani and Carnatic. The Mughal emperors were
Muslims, and Persian was the language of their court and administration
in Delhi; from there, Persian culture flowed into their domains. Non-
Mughal courts went their own way and remained aloof from the Muslim
courts' Persian and Arabic admixtures. The division between Hindustani
and Carnatic music corresponded to the line between the northern and
southern linguistic areas of India. Contrasts arose in musical theory, the
music played, traditions of performance, and the masters who created
musical canons and dynasties of musical descendants, recital forms, and
instruments.[52] At an early date in the understanding of Indian music, Day
had embarked on a specialist project, asking his readers to have a regional
comprehension of Indian music at a time when the entire subject was
alien to all but a few erudite Western listeners. But he wrote with unusual
ethnographic zeal, countering the expectations of his readers and confronting them with the outlines of a specific musical culture.

As he tried to convey his musical knowledge, Day felt himself to be
fighting a difficult battle against European prejudice. He let the reader

imagine the frustration of the army officer on the spot, trying to pursue his passion amid the contempt of his compatriots for music that sounded like "mere noise and nasal drawling of the most repulsive kind, often accompanied by contortions and gestures of the most ludicrous description."[53] Day urged a different kind of attitude on his readers. To appreciate Indian music, "one must first put away all thought of European music, and then judge of it by Indian standards, and impartially upon its own merits."[54] The passage is a striking one. At a time when anthropology was often an exponent of racial theories, and when European observers generally took up a rigid post outside foreign cultures, Day made the plea for understanding a culture on its own terms. Exposure to it, he continued, was the first step:

> We shall perhaps begin to feel that music of this kind can be as welcome and tasteful to ears accustomed to it as the music of the West, with its exaggerated sonorousness, is to us; and so our contempt will gradually give way to wonder, and, upon acquaintance, possibly to love. For this music, let us remember, daily gives pleasure to as many thousands as its more cultivated European sister gives to hundreds.[55]

How had the idea of cultural appreciation reached Day? Spontaneously, after he was smitten by Indian music? Through conversations with Hipkins and Ellis? Or was it a symptom of a greater change taking place in British culture, of a piece with the appreciation for Indian crafts in the Colonial and Indian Exhibition of 1886? Day was not entirely sure of himself, and contrasted Indian music in this passage to "its more cultivated European sister." Yet he indicated the path for other listeners to follow. No one, he added later, could understand the principles of this music "without the aid of learned natives, a *practical acquaintance* with the capabilities of their instruments, and without consulting the best living performers—things that few persons have opportunity or leisure to attempt."[56] It would take decades for European musicology to catch up with Day and insist on what he called a "practical acquaintance" with a non-European music, which ultimately implied apprenticing oneself and learning to perform it.[57]

Day could not teach that "practical acquaintance" through his book. But he did give a wide-ranging overview of Carnatic music in discussions of the accompanying religious myths, the social standing of musicians, Sanskrit theoretical treatises, modern theory, the raga, European versus Indian performing arts, and instruments. Along the way, he clung to ideas about the inferiority of Indian music as stuck in a deep rut of melody "with the almost entire absence of harmony," which "prevented Indian music from reaching any higher pitch of development," a limitation that was "the chief cause of the monotony which causes Indian music to be little appreciated by, if not repellent to, European ears."[58] This kind of apologetic gesture alternated with observations about the conditions for apprehending a foreign musical culture. Western visitors, he noted, were not usually treated to very good samples of Indian music. His description of Westerners' impressions recalled grim evenings or tales from others: "Very little of the good or classical music of India is heard by Europeans. What is usually played to them consists . . . of modern ditties sung by ill-instructed, screaming, dancing women, at crowded native durbars, marriages, and other ceremonials. And when this is the case, it does not cause much surprise to hear native music often described as abominable, and devoid of all melody. But music of great intrinsic beauty nevertheless exists, and only requires to be heard by an unprejudiced ear to be appreciated."[59] There was a social contrast in Carnatic music between vulgar performances with dancing girls, and the low-status musicians who played at these events, and performances by musicians from high-status families.[60]

To explain the absence of harmony, Day turned to political history. He argued that the great age of Hindu music was pre-Mughal; he supposed that, with a puritanical attitude toward the arts, Muslim rulers had led Hindustani music into a decline. Despite the overthrow of the Mughal dynasty after the Great Rebellion, the prejudice against musicians lingered on: ". . . The old idea that music as a profession is a degraded employment, fit only for the stroller or the dancing girl, to some extent lingers on, so strong is the influence caused by the long ordeal of Mahomedan conquest."[61] Things were better in the south, where many musicians were "men of education and poets in their way," and music had flourished continuously since remote antiquity. At places like the courts of Mysore, Tanjore, and Travancore, Sanskrit was studied, and music was not left to "ignorant dancing girls and their attendants."[62] Day thus outlined an invidious contrast between the pure unbroken Indian culture of the south and the corrupted culture of the north, a description fitting into the late-nineteenth-century British obsession with racial and cultural purity, two terms casually intermingled. However, he reversed the usual British prejudice and favored the south—in this way challenging his readers to gain a specific understanding of the great divisions of Indian culture.

Day was devoted to Carnatic music, but also a little impatient with it.

"The voices of Indian singers," he complained, "are almost always weak and deficient in volume—one result doubtless of their system of training, by which a full clear tone is made to give way to incessant small inflections." Elsewhere he noted "a marked change for the better" because singers now had to perform in theaters or large halls and had to project their voice in a way that ruled out, he thought, the "continued small inflections of tone and unnatural falsetto notes so much practiced by native singers of the ordinary class."[63] Day's remarks offer a glimpse of how incipient modernization worked through the appearance of a new kind of theater, and with it a challenge to the existing singing style. His larger picture of modernization revealed how Western music insinuated itself into private as well as public performance:

> Throughout Southern India the native drama is exceedingly popular; the actors are generally well educated and of a high caste, and a good company always attracts full houses. Music is largely employed upon the stage, and there is a kind of orchestra attached to every native theatre. The songs sung at performances of the kind do not, as a rule, differ much from the ordinary music of the country, and of late years there has been a tendency to imitate foreign music, such as Arabian or Persian, and the English, Scotch, or other airs played by military bands at all large stations. These naturally find their way from the theatre into private houses—boys learn them and sing them in the street—and so their influence gradually extends and makes itself felt upon Indian music in general. The old melody types, or râgas, are being less jealously adhered to, and the better educated classes of Hindus are beginning to see that music is not necessarily confined to one or two particular systems, but that, like nearly everything else, it is capable of improvement and further development.[64]

Close observer that he was, Day takes us through the streets and into homes; and he notices the effect of his own professional ensemble, the military band, which in the late nineteenth century was one of the chief agents for the spread of Western music around the world.[65] An uneasy mixture of nostalgia and advocacy for improvement pervades his account.

Hipkins had no such doubts about the autonomous value of a non-European musical tradition. He introduced Day's book on a radical note, sweeping away evolutionary speculation about whether music was as old as speech, thereby making himself agnostic on just the kind of issue that exercised nineteenth-century thinkers who wanted to line up human achievements since remote antiquity in a neat progression. Instead he asserted that music was part of general culture: "From whatever point of view we overlook the human race, its history and development, we can nearly always trace music as having some connection, however slender, with the particular form of culture, or it may even be the absence of culture, under notice."[66] It was remarkable that Hipkins used the word "culture" when it had barely begun to establish itself as a general term for patterns of human expression. Boas was still in the early stages of developing his conception of it for anthropology. Yet Hipkins used it in precisely the significant context for modern thought of breaking away from evolutionary speculation and grasping human artistic expressions in their own time and place.[67]

After this repudiation of contemporary prejudice, Hipkins turned away from the European preoccupation with harmony, "indispensable" for modern European musicians, and asked his readers to contemplate the place of melody in other places, in particular India: "The object of this introduction will be gained if we, for a little while, allow ourselves to forget the glory and splendour of our modern harmony, in favour of those melodic systems which once satisfied the great nations of classical antiquity, and still content those hoary civilizations of the East which preserve so much that is really ancient in their present daily life."[68] He was urging on his readers the discipline of interpretation: instead of arguing which music was superior, he made it the listener's task to understand them. If the object of the introduction was to teach readers the habit of temporarily "forgetting" in order to further insight into a foreign musical system, then Hipkins had pitched his expectations very high indeed: he was not just pleading a special case for Indian music as Day did, but making a more general assertion about how to approach *any* culture, with initial like or dislike beside the point. His call for the suspension of judgment anticipated the modern practice of ethnomusicology, history, or any other hermeneutic discipline.

Hipkins went on to introduce a second general point for his reader's consideration, the Indian musical system's superior melodic resources:

> The greater freedom in musical intervals melodic systems allow must be reckoned as compensating in some measure for the want of those harmonic combinations of which our European music has such inexhaustible wealth. What we lose in the possession of this rich estate is that we

are effectually barred from the use and enjoyment of a more pliant melody, free from the fetters imposed by consonant chords, a melody which has a great privilege in easily touching the emotions.[69]

Hipkins knew "a more pliant melody" intimately well: the clavichord was able to deliver those stretches upward or downward in tone that added an extra emotional tug. Arabic and Persian musicians along with Indian musicians, he added, had developed the "powerful melodic freedom" that was also "widespread in antiquity"—an additional flourish undercutting the notion that there had been a permanent divide between the systems of Eastern and Western music. When it came to melodic expression, Hipkins had lived through debates over equal temperament versus mean tone going all the way back to his early days at Broadwood. In widening circles of argument, Hipkins's introduction disputed the special claims of Western music: its scale was supposed to be founded in nature, but this theoretical belief could not account for additional tones in "Eastern" music. And indeed, he added, after decades of work with different Western scale systems, it could not even account for the Western diatonic scale. A long history of modifications, in which he had played a part, was codified in the tuning of the modern piano.

The conclusion of Hipkins's opening remarks was the passage that since his time has won the admiration of Mantle Hood and other ethnomusicologists. Rightly so, for it was nothing less than a repudiation of provincial thinking and a demand for widening horizons. After praising Day for making his readers aware of a refined music outside Western experience, he wrote:

> What we learn from such inquiries is that the debated opinions of musical theorists, the cherished beliefs of those who devote themselves to the practice of the art, the deductions we evolve from historical studies—all have to be submitted to larger conceptions, based upon a recognition of humanity as evolved from the teachings of ethnology. We must forget what is merely European, national, or conventional, and submit the whole of the phenomena to a philosophical as well as a sympathetic consideration, such as, in this century, is conceded to language, but has not yet found its way to music.[70]

The theorists, the practitioners, the historians—all too many of these contemporaries were learned provincials: the theorists who confused the Western system with a natural system, the practitioners whose ears were not attuned to finer tonal distinctions, the historians who deduced one sole path toward musical superiority. One wonders which ethnology Hipkins was singling out for praise, since by the 1890s its practitioners had lost the cosmopolitan breadth of the Enlightenment and only inched beyond the mid-century's racial evolutionary theory. Might he have been thinking of his mentor Carl Engel's *Notes and Queries on Anthropology*? In any case, Hipkins himself set an example for his contemporaries of seeing beyond Europe, nationalism, and convention in order to conceive of different musical systems as the expressions of a single humanity.

PART II

SCIENCE

3

Sound in Historical Time

In the autumn of 1876, Alfred Hipkins received an invitation to a rendezvous that would widen his musical horizons: "I am very pleased to have your quotations of pitches of various tuning forks. I shall be at the South End of Room Q of the Soan Exhibition of Scientific Instruments, to-morrow (Wednesday) & also on Thursday from 11 to 3 for the purposes of trying forks. . . . I should say that I have none but a scientific relation to the instruments. If you come you will know me at once by bald head, white beard and stout figure."[1] So wrote Alexander J. Ellis, mathematician, phonetician, philologist, social reformer, humanitarian, and investigator of musical pitch. His letter was like a scholarly variation on the meeting of John Watson and Sherlock Holmes.[2] With a Holmesian indifference to social patter, Ellis's letter plunged right into the measurement of pitch and the qualities of tuning forks, as if that were the most natural subject of discussion in the world; and it invited Hipkins to join him in his place of experimentation, just as Watson and Holmes first met in the laboratory where the detective was carrying out his chemical experiments.

Ellis and Hipkins's collaboration lasted thirteen years. At the time they first met, Ellis was interested in the scientific determination of pitch: how the frequency of notes had changed throughout human history, and how the pitch of individual notes continued in the nineteenth century to vary across Europe. Later, his attention turned to musical scales, the sequential relationship of individual notes structuring a musical system. For his work on both pitch and scales, Ellis depended on his collaboration with Hipkins. The tasks required Ellis's skill in the use of tuning forks in scientifically controlled experimentation and mathematical calculation; but these had to be complemented by Hipkins's discriminating ear, contacts with Broadwood, and musical expertise.[3]

Hipkins was not at loose ends like the down-and-out Watson on his return from Afghanistan; he was a well known man in his own right, his musical expertise respected across Europe. As for the portly Ellis, he was certainly a physical contrast to the lean, athletic Holmes. Still, if one compares the two male friendships—two buddy stories from the recurring theme of male friendship in the scholarly and musical discourses of the imperial era—there was a social analogy worth contemplating: the collaboration across social classes. Watson had gone into colonial service and come out with barely the means to scrape by, whereas Holmes was an Oxford or Cambridge man (we are never told which) with a self-assured indifference to money. The contrast between the two musical authorities was at least as striking. Hipkins, as we have seen, was an artisan by origin, and to the end of his working days held a job at Broadwood. Ellis inherited a fortune, and though hardworking enough for any two normal human beings, he pursued his scientific passions as a private scientist-scholar.

Ellis was born in 1814 as John Alexander Sharpe. A wealthy relative of his mother offered to provide financial support for his education and a lifetime of learned endeavor if he would adopt the last name of his mother's family, a change which was made in 1823.[4] With his future secure, Ellis was able to receive a superb education. He went to Shrewsbury School, Eton College, and Trinity College at Cambridge University, from which he was graduated in 1837. His birthdate and years of education mark him out as a member of the Victorian intellectual world; John Stuart Mill was born in 1806, Charles Darwin (another Shrewsbury alumnus) in 1809, and John Ruskin in 1819. Like these eminent Victorians, he grew to intellectual maturity in the post-Napoleonic era of British self-confidence and rising prosperity. Ellis entirely fulfilled his relative's hopes. For his achievements in the study of language, music, and mathematics he achieved high honors over the course of his lifetime. In 1864 he was made a fellow of the Royal Society, the next year a fellow of the London Mathematical Society, and in 1870 a fellow of the Society of Antiquaries. From

1872 to 1874 and from 1880 to 1882 he served as president of the Philological Society; in 1890, months before his death in the same year, he was
awarded an honorary doctorate from Cambridge University. As a member
of the gentlemanly elite of Victorian science and letters, Ellis could count
on a respectful hearing for his views.

Trained in mathematics and philology, he usually turned his knowledge in practical directions, asking how one kind of reform or another
could improve human society. His first major enterprise beginning in the
early 1840s involved phonetics: he was convinced that simplifying English spelling would lead to a great advance in the education of ordinary
people. Later George Bernard Shaw, another phonetic reform enthusiast,
called Ellis "a man impossible to dislike," and recalled meeting him in his
old age when he "was still a living patriarch, with an impressive head always covered by a velvet skull cap, for which he would apologize to public
meetings in a very courtly manner."[5] Along with his disarming kindness,
Ellis embodied the passionate determination of the philanthropic wealthy
gentleman, most famously represented by Ruskin, to uplift the less fortunate in industrial society. For his moral ideals, Ellis turned to a favorite
of nineteenth-century believers in progress, Auguste Comte. The French
thinker preached a science of society that was one part sociology and one
part ethical movement, turning the intellectual methods hitherto applied
to natural resources to relations among human beings. Comte offered his
contemporaries a religion of humanity that combined fervent moralism
with a belief in the all-healing power of science. Ellis delivered sermons
on Comte's *Religion of Humanity* at South Chapel, a prominent gathering
place for devotees of ethical religion.[6] By all accounts he embodied the
Comtean ethos, turning his wealth and social privilege to the good with
his dedication to schemes for simplifying written communication.

Ellis almost comically fulfilled the received notion of a Victorian ec-
centric in the account of his "engaging personality" left by Hipkins's
daughter, Edith. If he was plump, it was not for lack of self-discipline: he
weighed himself every day with and without clothes, and lived mainly
on water with a little milk added to it, supplemented by a roll and but-
ter and a small portion of meat at midday dinner. His clothes contained
twenty-eight pockets filled with nail scissors, knife sharpeners, a cork-
screw (though, Edith Hipkins noted, "he never touched alcohol"), and
string "so that he could help others in need of such things," while the
outside pockets of his coats were filled with manuscripts. Her most telling observation was that Ellis "was methodical and almost painfully exact

in all his undertakings, he did everything for himself—posted his own letters—balanced his tradesmens [sic] books (to a farthing)—paid every account himself and gave the household orders." The eccentricities may have been partly an outgrowth of completely assured social rank, but they also matched the methodical drive of his research. In addition to being a scholar-scientist, Ellis was a family man, and the day-to-day life with his wife and three children—for whom he wrote and published a book of verse—may have tempered his scientific discipline and added to the patience that aided his ethnographic exercises.[7]

Hipkins and Ellis developed a heartfelt friendship. It grew partly out of the excitement of the chase for accurate readings of pitch and intervals; Ellis shared his enthusiasm as he worked his way through questions about bagpipe scales, tunings on the vina, correspondence with a Dutch professor on Javanese music, consultations with an Indian rajah about the sitar, and inquiries into Burmese and Chinese music as well as the tones and scale of the koto.[8] Throughout his letters, Ellis addressed Hipkins (always "Mr. Hipkins") with spontaneity and warmth as the partner to the endeavor, a role that Ellis also acknowledged in his published writings.

Since Hipkins was a working man, it was on Sunday afternoons (after mornings devoted to Comte) that Ellis would seek him out at home. Once their experiments and calculations were over, he would join the Hipkins family for tea, "never however sharing in the meal—as his milk-and-water supper was timed for 8 p.m. But he would join in the talk and beam on all—like the beneficent sun." When the experiments had to be conducted away from home, according to Edith Hipkins, "Dr Ellis would await my father, in a cab—at the foot of the Argyll Road—with a cake or scone—in case of an attack of hunger on his guest's part! It was never touched, but bears record of his solicitude and kindness of heart."[9] The friendship facilitated the collaboration of the craftsman-connoisseur and the university-trained scientist. Within the compass of uneaten scones and beneficent smiles, their differences were part of a powerful mix of ingredients that broke through the crust of European convention and reached an unprecedented understanding of the variability of non-European music.[10]

The Relativity of Sound: From Helmholtz to Ellis

By the time Ellis met Hipkins, he had already spent more than a dozen years investigating musical pitch. The work that inspired his interest was *On the Sensations of Tone* by Hermann Helmholtz, which he read in the year of its publication, 1863.[11] For decades to come, this work would serve as a foundation for the understanding of music, appealing to both scholars and artists for uncovering the hidden order beneath the surface of notes and scales. Henry Cowell took for granted Helmholtz's analysis of the formation of pitch as the basis for *New Musical Resources*, his 1930 manifesto for the avant-garde. The intellectual direction of the composer Harry Partch was set by his discovery of Helmholtz's book in a Sacramento, California, public library, and in 1949 he was still preaching a musicology according to Helmholtz in his *Genesis of a Music*.[12] As specialists in acoustics continue to debate how the perception of sound is formed in human beings, Helmholtz's theory remains part of their discussion.[13] It seemed to provide an irrefutable scientific foundation for understanding how certain combinations of sound appealed to human beings.

Helmholtz's model of musical analysis accounted for both the physical regularities underlying pitch and the particularity of different cultures' organization of pitches into musical systems; it was simultaneously a set of scientific generalizations and an acknowledgement of diverse aesthetic preferences. His schema contained three parts that linked physics, physiology, and psychology as methods for analyzing the sensations of tone. As a physical phenomenon, the human perception of sound originated in the vibrations of an object causing atmospheric vibrations that reached the human ear. When these vibrations were irregular, they were noise; when they were regular, as in the sounds generated by an instrument, they were intelligible as music. Musical pitch, the notes perceived as ascending or descending by human beings, depended on the number of vibrations per second in an instrument; the more rapid the frequency of vibration, the higher the pitch. A practical familiarity with pitch and with how to produce higher and lower sounds on a string instrument went back to the ancient world. The Greeks figured out the correct length of strings for a scale, and the use of bridges to control intervals. To do so, they invented "the *monochord*, consisting of a sounding board and box on which a single string was stretched with a scale below, so as to set the bridge correctly."[14] The knowledge that music was linked to physical relationships such as the different extensions of a string, which in turn could be described in mathematical terms, went back thousands of years.

Modern scientists since Galileo, observed Helmholtz, had advanced from this ancient knowledge of the length of strings and their effects to an analysis of the underlying cause, the frequency of vibrations per second; the shorter the string, the greater the number of vibrations and the higher the sound. The rise in pitch followed easily chartable mathematical ratios beginning with the octave in a ratio of 2:1, the higher pitch having double the number of vibrations per second. Following Helmholtz, if one imagines notes as on a piano keyboard and compares the relationship of lower to higher in the scale of C, the ratios continue: fifth 2:3 (the fifth note in the scale, G, vibrates three times for every two vibrations by C), fourth 3:4, major third 4:5, minor third 5:6. According to Helmholtz, the range of musical tones with a clearly distinguishable pitch extended from forty to four thousand vibrations over seven octaves. This physical basis of musical sound was well known when Helmholtz wrote, and was not controversial then or now.[15]

These physical regularities were just the first aspect of Helmholtz's analysis. He impressed on his readers a point that remains valid apart from the more detailed assertions of the rest of his argument: that the perception of tone is a *mediated* phenomenon, synthesizing several steps from instrument to mental perception of sound. We perceive a note as instant, and imagine it to be a single, unified event; but the sound obviously originates in the instrument, affects the auditory receiving capacity that we call the ear, and gets mentally processed in order to become an intelligible note. The subject of Helmholtz's book was the second stage in the sequence: the part in which the human ear analyzed the units of vibrations reaching it through the atmosphere. He prepared the reader to understand this by recapitulating what was already known about the physical production of pitch through regular vibrations. But that was only the prelude to the original part of his work, his theory of how the ear broke down and organized sounds into logical interrelationships.[16]

The seemingly insignificant feature of sound that captured Helmholtz's imagination and led to an original physiological theory was the presence of overtones. A musical note is normally not just a unit of one set of vibrations at a certain rate per second. Rather, the note is a compound: in addition to the predominant set of vibrations, it includes higher sets, or "harmonic upper partial tones." As Helmholtz explained to his readers, they were harmonic because they ascended in the ratios already described for strings for the fifth, the fourth, the third, and an ongoing sequence of notes. Helmholtz's triumphant assertion was that he had taken these so-called partials, long observed but bypassed as an insignificant phenomenon, and discovered that they were central to the human perception of musical order. The ear recognized them, and used them to compare notes.

When a chord corresponded to the main partials, the ear heard harmony; when it was further removed, the ear heard dissonance.[17]

Beginning in Helmholtz's own time, his theory of the auditory reception of overtones was controversial. To support it, he had to make tortuous arguments about the inner ear's reception of sound, and develop a theory of unconscious perception of overtones that were often inaudible to ordinary ears (Helmholtz and other experts made far-reaching claims about their own ability to hear a wide range of overtones). The evaluation of his theory, then or now, does not exhaust its historical significance. Even though Helmholtz's theory of the physiological reception of sound was criticized, it initiated a wide-ranging psychological and historical discussion of harmony.

After Helmholtz, musical notes and the systems they made could not be regarded as a fact of nature. Instead, the perception of certain sounds as fitting together into a meaningful whole could be analyzed on many levels. Helmholtz relied on the mathematical relationships between sounds that had long been established by modern science and premodern experience, but he went on to add a new dimension of uncertainty about how they were processed. Overtones created conditions for the possibility of establishing orderly relationships among sounds, but how human beings apprehended those relationships varied from culture to culture. The third part of his book emphasized this point as it passed from natural phenomena—the physical production and physiological reception of pitch—to the psychological and aesthetic principles of musical systems and how they had changed over time. He surveyed the historical evidence for recognition of the tonic, the note that is the reference point for all the other notes in the modern Western musical system (hence, in the scale of C sharp, the note C sharp is the tonic and organizes all the other notes in the scale); the Greeks, medieval authors, and Indian theorists paid attention to it, but none of them established the tonic with the logical consistency of modern Western music. The use of the fifth (the first harmonic interval after the octave) was universal, according to Helmholtz; even "the uncultivated ear" recognized it as a natural successor to a note played before or (in a chord) below it. But the same was not true for the third, even though this completed the triad, the basic chord of modern Western music, and was a natural-sounding note to modern Western ears; its functional role was not a historical given. Modern Western instruments using even tempering tuned the third a little higher than its natural ratio, a sharpening that Helmholtz disliked; he would have preferred a musical system in which the third was restored to its natural place (determined by its sound ratio to the tonic) and could fit fully harmoniously between the tonic and the fifth. The modern European scale was an artificial construction built out of a set of aesthetic preferences that had only recently, within the preceding two centuries, taken shape. Helmholtz ended his book with a far-reaching insight into the artificiality of notes themselves: they could never capture the tone production of the human voice, which did not hop from one fixed point to another but slid across pitches as it rose and fell. The Western diatonic scale selected only a limited range of possibilities out of a larger musical cosmos.[18]

Helmholtz's book had a breathtaking reach: starting out with the physical production of sound and the systematic relations among continuously vibrating tones, it ended with the cultural specificity of music as societies heard it. He made a critical break with the naive assumption that there was an immediate relationship between physical cause and the end result known as music; rather, the creation of music took place through a series of intermediate processes. While the end result was structured by the analyzable relationships between sounds and the constitution of human beings' physiological capacity for hearing, it underwent a further transformation in the perception of human subjects. Following the evolutionary historical thinking of the mid-nineteenth century, Helmholtz tried to chart the history of music as a progression from the simplest melody to polyphony and finally the development of modern harmony built out of chord progressions, the achievement of modern Western music. As long as this doctrine held sway in which the history of music, like the history of civilization in general, followed an evolutionary ascent, it would be impossible to understand non-Western musical systems as anything more than stages on the way to the Western diatonic system. Helmholtz himself, as recent scholarship has noted, had a strong personal preference for the classical style of the eighteenth century and was diffident toward Romantic music. In his own passionate musicianship, he was most at home squarely within Western music's most fully self-contained, logically ordered moment. Yet, with the self-detachment of a great thinker, he could see beyond his personal preference and recognize that other civilizations had developed highly sophisticated musical systems; the choice between them rested on motives of personally and culturally formed taste. If Henry Cowell's *New Musical Resources* was "the open sesame for new music in

America," as John Cage declared, its treasures came from the chest first stocked by Helmholtz.[19]

Helmholtz's book struck Ellis with the force of a revelation. Once he had read *On the Sensations of Tone*, his musical research took off on a clear course that led to more than two decades of demonstrating alternatives to the harmonic system of modern Europe.

Ellis's initial ambition was to make Helmholtz's book accessible to English-speaking readers. Arranging for the initial contact with Helmholtz was the easy part. Max Müller, the famous Oxford professor of language who was an important mediator between the scientific worlds of Britain and his native Germany, was lecturing at the Royal Institution in London when Ellis approached him and asked whether he would get in touch with Helmholtz about the possibility of a translation. Müller, who shared Ellis's interest in the physiology of speech, promptly wrote a letter to Helmholtz recommending the man and his work.[20] "I hardly think that you could find a better translator in England. He is entirely at home in German, he has been concerned his entire life with mathematics and acoustics." Ellis was a Cambridge man and a member of the Royal Institution, he added, whom Helmholtz could count on to be entirely reliable.[21] Ellis received Helmholtz's approval and set about finding a publisher for the translation during the spring and summer of 1863. The proposal met with rejection after rejection. English publishers thought it was too difficult and theoretical a work to have a chance of making a profit. "In Germany the musical Profession appears to study such works; in this country *few* do so," wrote one publisher. This frank statement was a marker of the preprofessional state of English musical culture in the 1860s, before the impact was sufficiently felt of the Germans who migrated across the English Channel. Nonetheless, when Helmholtz came to London the following spring, he visited Ellis at his home in the suburb of Colney Hatch Park. They would have to wait nine more years, however, until Longman, which was bringing out a translation of Helmholtz's lectures, suddenly accepted Ellis's terms for publication.

Despite the disappointing responses from publishers, Ellis set to work on the translation, which cost him long hours—137 days in eleven months, as he wrote with characteristic precision to Helmholtz, at a time of failing health. But he added that he never regretted the thorough study of the book that he labored to bring to his public in idiomatic English. The result was more than a translation. It turned Helmholtz's text into a dialogue partner for his own research into music topics, which he continued apace throughout the translation period and inserted into footnotes and appendixes. What he delivered to the English public was a double work: the translation of Helmholtz's text, which came to 371 pages—plus twenty appendixes coming to another 200 pages, which summarized his own investigations into everything from the experimental apparatus for measuring sound waves to recommendations for intonation in singing. Painstakingly scrupulous and eager to make the translation one that would satisfy Helmholtz, Ellis kept him up to date about his appendixes, which he added in part to reply to the views of others. In the end, then, the volume turned into something between a translation and a synthesis: faithful to the original text, but also significantly expanded by the translator's commentary.[22]

The Cultural Interpretation of Pitch

Helmholtz's book ended on a note of irresolution. Its observation about the inability of European common practice to capture the musical expressions of the human voice dissented from a narrative of European triumph over other musical systems. But its general historical narrative followed a path across the centuries from simple melody to modern harmony, a recapitulation of the conventional European understanding of musical progress culminating in the superiority of the system based on tonic and triad. Despite his admiration for Helmholtz, Ellis in his own work on the history of pitch in the 1860s and 1870s reexamined the historical narrative and ended up challenging it: instead of progress, he uncovered a power struggle between conflicting musical interests. His relentless drive for accurate measurement and research into the variability of pitch led him to undermine the evolutionary paradigm for the history of music.

Two public-spirited institutions of Victorian England provided the setting for Ellis's repudiation of the progressive narrative. He read his most important papers, on musical pitch and musical scales, before the Society of Arts. The society fit Ellis's character and ambitions very well, made up as it was of gentlemen who shared his dedication to public improvement through applied science. And the South Kensington Museum provided him with the tools for his scientific trade. Thanks to Carl Engel and other benefactors, Ellis could go there and conduct practical experiments in tone and scale on a sitar, vina, qin, or pipa. Helmholtz did not have comparable opportunities, and had to rely on travelers' reports for his views on Indian and Chinese music. Just a few years before his researches began, Ellis too would have been hard pressed to find these instruments, but with the new museum's resources at his disposal, he could carry out his empirical measurements. His attention to the acoustic qualities of instruments flourished within the Victorian encouragement of applied arts, collecting, and museum building.

One of the reform activities of the Society for Arts provided Ellis with a practical outlet for his interest in musical acoustics: the settlement of pitch in contemporary Europe. He addressed the society on his researches twice, first in a paper of 1877 and then in an expanded, definitive paper of 1880.[23] The 1877 report began by setting out the contemporary uncertainties over musical pitch. In France, an official decree of February 1859 had adopted the recommendation of a government commission to prescribe a lowering of the pitch used in orchestras and the construction of musical instruments. In June of the same year, the Society of Arts called together its own "committee of musicians, instruments makers, men of science, and amateurs" to adjudicate and ended up calling for a slightly higher pitch than the French commission. Almost a decade later, in January 1869, the Society of Arts "applied to the Secretary of State for Foreign Affairs to obtain information respecting the musical pitch used on the Continent." In reply it received reports from Copenhagen, Leipzig, Munich, Dresden, Stuttgart, Vienna, Baden, Berlin, Cologne, Florence, Bologna, Milan, Venice, Stockholm, and Brussels, which it printed in October 1869. As he reported three years later, Ellis was disturbed by the amateurish conclusions of the Society of Arts's previous inquiry, which were supposed to correspond roughly to the French conclusions but unwittingly recommended a higher pitch that never went into use. Motivated by the new survey, he decided to take up the whole subject of the history, measurement, and settlement of musical pitch.[24] It was to be a scientific intervention in a controversy that had roiled musical life for decades without reaching a satisfactory conclusion.

Ellis's first treatment of the subject in 1877 won the silver medal of the Society of Arts. Nonetheless, the accuracy of its numbers was questioned. He decided to make a more thorough investigation, and laid his results before the Society of Arts three years later. The first footnote of his printed report acknowledged 107 helpers. They included professors, private ladies and gentlemen, organ builders, piano makers, horn makers, tuning fork makers, bell founders, musicians, violin makers, and organists, as well as choir conductors and 542 members of their choirs. Craftsmen around

England as well as professors and musical practitioners were plied with questions. Foreign correspondents came to Ellis's aid too, from Germany, Italy, and the United States. An indefatigable researcher, Ellis did extensive fieldwork in England in addition to looking abroad for historical and scientific knowledge. If he was in the process of teaching his contemporaries to hear in a new way, he did so through a vast synthesis of craft experience with his scientific training, drawing on an army of hundreds to assemble his conclusions.

The pitch of a musical note, as Ellis defined it and as it is still defined today, referred to "the number of double or complete vibrations, backwards and forwards, made in each second by a particle of air, while the note is heard."[25] Ellis made a leisurely tour of the systems of tuning used to facilitate harmony since the European Middle Ages, since these had affected the pitch levels of individual notes. (For example, in the equal temperament system of modern Europe, the fifths are made slightly flat and the major thirds are made slightly sharp in order to produce a scale of equidistant tones.) He then used an ingenious mixture of sources to reconstruct pitch levels over the centuries. Organ pipes (often reused when organ builders dismantled old organs and put up new ones) and the recollections of organ builders formed a rich body of evidence, as did historical tuning forks and instruments, supplemented by written treatises. Ellis sketched the changes over time as the consequence of changing instruments and social configurations. The oldest basis for determining pitch was the requirements of the human voice, which dominated medieval music. According to Ellis, music makers at European courts slightly elevated pitch levels without altering the primacy of the voice as the determinant of pitch. However much pitch ranged up and down, it remained suited to singing until the early nineteenth century.

Then came the revolution. Ellis's 1877 essay turned for evidence to Handel's tuning fork of 1751 for C, "which was fully a semitone flatter than the present concert pitch. Hence vocal music of Handel's time should be transposed a semitone lower than it is written when played at concert pitch. The same remark applies to the music of Mozart, and, probably, Haydn, and Beethoven."[26] A few singers, to be sure, could master the new demands of heightened notes. "But the voices of others ought not to be fatigued by the exceptional acrobatism of the one." Most of the singers of choral works—here one thinks back to Ellis's interviews with chorus members—would strain to meet demands on their voices never intended by the composer.[27] He came back to the same point three years later, this time in possession of Handel's tuning fork for the A above middle C (especially interesting because this note was played then, as it is today, to set the pitch of orchestra instruments), lent to him by the Reverend G. T. Driffield, the rector of Bow (a district of East End, London). Handel's A had a pitch of 422.5 vibrations per second. Ellis regarded this as "the mean pitch of Europe during the 17th, 18th, and the early part of the 19th centuries, so important for musical art." He allowed for some variation, citing pianos used by Mozart in 1780 that had a pitch of A 421.6.[28] Again, the contrast with his own time was striking, amounting to a difference of slightly over half an interval.[29] "That is to say," he concluded, "the heroes of music, the founders and perfecters of modern musical art, all used this mean pitch, all thought out their music, and arranged their voice-parts to be played and sung in this pitch. This is, therefore, emphatically the classical pitch of music."[30] This story was anything but a history of progress; rather, it traced the emergence of an inflation damaging to singers and at odds with the composers' intentions.

What had caused the transformation? Ellis argued that the orchestra had displaced the voice as the measure of pitch. "Both church and chamber pitch were founded on the capabilities of the human voice alone, and the instruments were accessory. But the formation of large orchestras, for which especial music was written, gave an excessive power to the instruments, which could develop their powers independently of the voice, and then, when joined with the voice in operas, could often exercise—have certainly, often cruelly exercised—a tyrannical power over the voice."[31] According to the report of the French commission of 1859, the change began at the Congress of Vienna. Military bands set the new pace, just as in other respects they accelerated the rationalization of musical performance around the world. Emperor Alexander of Russia presented an Austrian regiment with a new set of musical instruments, and "this band became very noted for the brilliancy of its tones."[32] The band of another regiment received even sharper instruments, setting in motion a general fashion for the new brilliance, quickly diffused since these military bands were called in for large theater productions. Yet even for the orchestras, the added sheen came with an overall loss of quality: "Once set the ball in motion and instrument-makers keep it well up. Yet, heightening the pitch of wind instruments does not generally improve their quality of tone; they lose richness and roundness, and incline to scream; but it is continually the wind instruments which force the pitch up."[33] He traced the spread of the Vienna sharpening: to Dresden (where it remained comparatively modest), Italy (where Viennese influence was strong), Leipzig (quick to adopt it), and Berlin.[34] Finally there came the French reform of 1859, which brought the standardized pitch back to what Ellis thought was a tolerable A 435.4. Since the new setting was fixed by government decree, orchestras had made the adjustment and no longer complained that replacing their instruments would be too expensive.

As for England, its pitch settings had become chaotic. There was no standardized organ or orchestral pitch; piano makers used a sharp pitch for concerts and pianos with lower pitch settings for private performers. "Such is the very undignified and unscientific position occupied by our own country with regard to musical pitch—a position into which we have drifted without due consideration and which is the occasion of much practical inconvenience," Ellis observed. "It is entirely an orchestral or instrumental pitch, due to the makers, especially, of wind instruments, and maintains its ground on account of the expense of changing the instruments—£1000 is mentioned in [sic] the probable cost of the contemplated reduction of pitch at Covent-garden—as if the price of whole orchestras of instruments bore an appreciable ratio to the loss caused by the premature ruin of one great singer's voice!"[35] Ellis concluded that Britain would be required "to choose a pitch which, like the French, stands exactly halfway between" eighteenth- and nineteenth-century settings.[36] With the help of science, Ellis could recommend a reform that was humane as well as musically viable.

By the end of his second essay on pitch, with his diagnosis and prescriptions behind him, Ellis reached a point of expansive critical reflection. His opposition of voice and orchestra was in a larger sense an opposition of human expression on a human scale to the inhuman demands of the modern machine. As the sociologist Max Weber and others have since observed, the modern orchestra *is* a machine, the musical equivalent of the synchronized parts of a mechanical totality; in the grimmest versions of its effect on musical expression, its individual players have lost their independence and instead play their role within a larger division of labor in the assemblage of musical sound. On this view, its modern tempered scale does not embody an aesthetically superior sound, but facilitates the factorylike synchronization of the orchestra's parts. Against this collective dehumanization of sound, Ellis, following Helmholtz's lead, introduced the singer as the measure of musical expression. Choruses could not order new voices as orchestras could order new instruments; they were defined by natural limits. Ellis's compassion for singers under nineteenth-century conditions of production took its place alongside his contemporaries' widespread unease as they faced a mechanized society that chose productive efficiency over human needs. To make his criticisms, Ellis used a strategy of historical comparison. The sharpened pitch levels of his own time, he showed, were a historical anomaly. He was not a radical reformer proposing a return to the eighteenth century; historical authenticity was probably irretrievable. But his contrasts of past and present issued in a scientific refutation of the superiority of musical production in his own time.

The way was open for further relativization of modern Western music. Ellis's essays on pitch were diachronic, comparing European societies over time. But one could also look outward across space and compare Europe's tonal system with its counterparts around the world. More continuously than in his work on pitch, he joined forces with Hipkins to carry out his program of worldwide comparisons. Theirs was to be a joint venture in understanding music across continents.

4

Scales around the World

Ellis's studies of pitch sounded differences of musical perception through historical time; they revealed how individual notes in European music-making had changed their frequency, and how those changes were part of a larger, evolving context of technology and culture. This was a plumbing of temporal depths with large implications for the study of music, for it implied that pitch was not fixed and natural, but an outcome of changing preferences. Ellis's essay "On the Musical Scales of Various Nations" shifted his investigations from time to space. It roamed from Europe to East Asia, with stops in the Middle East and in South and Southeast Asia to analyze the variety of tonal systems. Apart from its value as a model of musical comparison, Ellis's essay documents the formation in nineteenth-century London of a global culture: how texts, instruments, and people were streaming into the metropolis and providing the materials for his comparative study. Technology, empire, and public curiosity made it possible to learn about different kinds of music that had come from a large portion of the earth and gathered as never before in one place.

Ellis is best remembered in the lore of ethnomusicology for his essay's division of tonal intervals. Instead of just the twelve different semitones of the piano, with its seven different white keys and five black keys, Ellis proposed a so-called cent system, fixing a hundred points from one semitone to the next (the distance from one key to the next on the piano). By charting tones on this finely graded spectrum, researchers could capture the distinctive sounds of musical systems from around the world. Instead of assigning a strange-sounding pitch to one of the twelve equidistant levels of European equal temperament, as travelers and scholars regularly did when transcribing foreign music, one could capture notes as quarter tones, eighth tones, or smaller fractions not recognized in Western music. The cent system was both a precise means of denoting other pitches and an acknowledgment that the world of musical sound was larger than could be recorded in Western notation.

To reduce Ellis's essay to this technical improvement, however, is to overlook the revolutionary nature of its approach. His essay is better remembered as a general confrontation of the difficulties of apprehending a foreign musical system—and by extension, a foreign culture. Ellis unraveled one methodological and practical issue after another that stood in the way of registering difference; he pointed out where errors crept in, and reflected on the misperceptions that filtered unfamiliar sounds into European categories. The result was a model of scientific inquiry, superior to other ethnologies of its time. When Erich von Hornbostel, a central figure in the history of comparative musicology, looked back from the 1920s, he pointed to Ellis as the true starting point for the field. Ellis did not leave behind a school of disciples to perpetuate his name, as Hornbostel did for the field that became ethnomusicology or as Franz Boas did for anthropology, and in part for this reason his essay has been remembered as a disciplinary forerunner rather than as part of a founder legend. But if one rereads Ellis's essay today, it belongs among the handful of writings before 1914 that radically challenged Europeans' hierarchical cultural assumptions. Ellis did not entirely discard contemporary prejudice; from time to time he casually took for granted the inferiority of non-European cultures. But the logic of his essay, repeated each time he addressed a different musical tradition, was detached from ranking their aesthetic value.[1]

Science and Craft

Ellis began his essay by thanking Hipkins for serving as his collaborator in the enterprise. The conception and the mathematics of the essay were his own; the fine ear for hearing differences of pitch and the general knowledge of music belonged to Hipkins. Ellis thus announced the union of science and craft that was indispensable to hearing differences and analyzing them as part of a foreign musical system.

Ellis brought home this alliance of science and craft by presenting his paper before the Society of Arts as a lecture performance with one part academic talk by Ellis and one part performance on musical instruments, some of them played by Hipkins. For the written version the performances fell away, and Ellis lengthened the written part. But his audience would have seen and heard, in addition to a piano, seven different kinds of unusual demonstration instruments from England, Java, India, Singapore, Japan, and China—an assemblage of a kind that had rarely if ever been brought together. The stage show plunged his readers into his work of listening to the music as well as analyzing it.

Local craft skill and globalization made it possible for these instruments to travel to London of the mid-1880s from different parts of the world, and take their place alongside one another. The first instrument was a so-called dichord, consisting of two strings "with a beautiful sounding board," constructed for Ellis by Broadwood. With the help of markings made beforehand, tuning forks, and Hipkins's tuning skills, Ellis could, he said, "render any scale distinctly audible. This must have been entirely new to almost every one [sic] of the audience." The second was an English concertina, made to order for Ellis by a Mr. Saunders of Lachenal and Company of London. Ellis was familiar with the concertina from childhood, and could tune it to demonstrate different kinds of scales. A sitar had been presented to Ellis by one Rajah Ram Pal Singh. This Indian prince worked with Ellis and Hipkins to make an accurate transcription of some Indian scales—a task that would otherwise have been completely beyond them, as Ellis's correspondence makes clear. Two vinas had been lent to Ellis by Victor-Charles Mahillon.[2] A gambang ("that is, a wood harmonicon, played by a hammer") had been sent from Singapore to Hipkins, who also provided Ellis with a koto. Hermann Smith, who later published books on world music, lent "a small Chime of Chinese Bells, and a set of Japanese Pitch-pipes. . . ." As in his work on pitch, Ellis showed himself in his study of scales to be an able organizer who corresponded and collaborated, borrowed and bought, until he had the collection of instruments that could provide a real-life demonstration of the diversity of scales.[3]

When foreign musicians came to London, Ellis went to great lengths to meet with them in order to understand their scale systems. To be sure, he had many instruments available for his use at the South Kensington Museum; but he realized that he could not reconstruct the scales of a vina, gambang, or koto without user expertise. Without going abroad, he took advantage of the opportunities at his doorstep for detailed investigations into performance practices.

The point of departure for Ellis's comparison of musical scales was Helmholtz's analysis of the physical and physiological basis of tone. Helmholtz himself emphasized that this *basis* was something different from music. To be sure, the basis created a material foundation for the consonance of sounds. But he emphasized that there was nothing natural about a music system based on harmony and its ever more thoroughgoing integration of parts into a logical whole. With *Sensations of Tone* about to appear in English in the same year as his talk, Ellis had powerful scientific support for discarding the prejudice that foreign scales were deviations from a Western norm. Instead, he and his readers now inhabited an open musical universe in which one could examine different scales as equally valid systems.

Ellis explored numerous different scales, scrutinizing scraps of evidence from around the world to establish different ways of arranging notes. A few stand out for the richness of their evidence at a time when European prejudices were firmly entrenched, and it required ingenuity to probe into their autonomous structures. The scale systems of the Middle East, Japan, China, and India were the ones Ellis could best document. They illustrate the great diversity of ways in which foreign music reached Europe, and the challenges it presented even to Ellis's and Hipkins's sympathetic ears.

These scales were not mathematical or musical abstractions. They reached Ellis and Hipkins through a welter of personal ambitions, nationalist political programs, and conflicting claims about what constituted the musical traditions.

Middle Eastern Microtones

Ellis was never able to hear a performance of Arab music. Instead, he relied on a theoretical tract by Mīkhā'īl Mishāqa, a well-known merchant, physician, historian, and mathematician born in Lebanon in 1800. Mishāqa's family had emigrated from Corfu to Tripoli in the early eighteenth century as part of a larger wave of Greek immigrants attracted by changing patterns of commerce. As the power of the central government in Istanbul waned, southwest Syrian merchants profited from connections to the pilgrimage route to Mecca, and developed ties to British and French merchants. Most of the Syrian Greeks remained rather conservative in their way of life and outlook on the world, but Mīkhā'īl Mishāqa responded to the community's new circumstances by developing novel perspectives on religion, politics, and ideas. He seems to have been disturbed by the religious quarreling of small communities in Syria, and he took the unusual step of converting to Protestantism, much to the consternation of his family; yet it was a move that opened up new educational opportunities and contacts with Europeans and Americans. In politics he contributed to a nascent nationalist ideology that would transcend community differences and create a common Syrian identity. In intellectual life he was influenced by readings in the European Enlightenment. Altogether his family and personal history made him well placed to act as a mediator between Arab and European cultures, for he was both a local patriot with a deep knowledge of Arabic learning and an eager conversation partner with Westerners.[4]

With his lifelong self-confidence, Mishāqa taught himself to play Arab musical instruments and familiarized himself with the tradition's theoretical writings. He still attracts the interest of musicologists today, who view his work as an important advance in the theorization of modern Arab music.[5] His analysis of Arab music was translated into English as the result of a practical challenge faced by the Presbyterian minister Eli Smith. Smith wanted his missionary associates to be able to teach music, but found it impossible for Arabs and Westerners to communicate musically back and forth:

> The obstacles arising from the peculiarities of Arab music are such, that, not only do we find the singing of the Arabs no music to us, but our musicians have found it very difficult, often impossible, to detect the nature of their intervals, or imitate their tunes. The first intimation I had of the nature of the difficulty, was derived from observing, that a native singer, in attempting to repeat the octave in company with one of our musical instruments, did not observe the same intervals, and of course the two were not at every note in unison.[6]

That peculiarity left the would-be music teachers baffled. One of Smith's colleagues tried to write Arab songs on the Western stave "and found that he was unable to do it, owing to some peculiarity in the intervals." Not until he read his "friend" Mishāqa's work could he make sense of Arab music.[7] Smith assumed that the diatonic scale, with its division into seven different notes, was "according to nature." But Arab music did not conform to his expectations of the natural scale. Instead, he learned from Mishāqa, Arabs divided notes into two classes, greater and less. The greater intervals contain four quarters, and the less three. The entire octave contained twenty-four intervals divided into these two groups of unequal length. Having understood this principle, Smith could grasp more: the notes of the Arab scale did not include a third (part of the basic chord of Western music); Arab music dealt only with melody, not harmony; if a musician changed the tonic, the melody was rearranged over the long and short notes and came out sounding different.[8] As the record of a Western/ Arab musical encounter, Smith's description is a striking demonstration of the obstinacy of Western norms: even after he grasped Mishāqa's explanation, he could not see it as a valid system in its own right, but continued to insist on the naturalness of the diatonic scale.

For the intervals of the Arab scale system, Ellis turned to the transcription of ninety-five Arab melodies given in Smith's translation of Mishāqa. Generalizing from Arab to "Oriental" music—that is, music from today's Middle East to East Asia—Ellis introduced two bold points. One was that these musical systems contained "neutral" notes, that is to say, notes that could not be assimilated to a harmonic system built out of chords. These notes were meaningless to Western listeners; "the European ear does not know how to appreciate them." This in turn had led Europeans to mistranslate Arab and other musical scales, distorting them in order to fit them into familiar patterns. With this statement Ellis recognized the systemic musical character of microtones—tones at smaller than Western intervals—as meaningful in its own terms, but only properly discernible by a European educated to listen for it. Ellis went on from this to a second important point: "A solo player on a stringed instrument without frets, who is absolutely unchecked by harmony, is able to amuse himself by taking all manner of strange intervals, or occasional variations of established intervals." The performer had greater latitude to rely on improvisation, taking his audience where he chose to lead it.[9] This insight built on the conclusion of Helmholtz's book: just as the human voice eluded the boxlike divisions of diatonic notes as it rose and fell, so the Arab or Asian musician had an unfamiliar freedom of musical expression. Ellis's description amounted to an expansion of the horizon of musical sound beyond anything that modern Europeans had imagined, encased as they were in their neatly fitted harmonies.

As a mediator between Middle Eastern and European music, Smith was part of the long line of missionaries who, with varying degrees of sympathy and hostility, attempted to enter into non-Christian cultures. Through the centuries, his predecessors and contemporaries could combine appalling insensitivity with genuine interest and respect; it is not easy to unravel their complex relationships to the peoples they encountered, and impossible to do so without examining their encounters one by one. The difficulties were augmented in the case of Americans from Smith's organization, the American Board of Commissioners of Foreign Missions, whose outlook was defined by early nineteenth-century New England puritanism. As with its counterpart, the London Missionary Society, its point of departure was a Protestant culture that defined religion primarily around doctrine to the detriment of ritual, myth, and vision.[10] Mishāqa was an unusual interlocutor, however: self-assured, literate, and cultivated, politically or socially independent of the missionaries and able to impress his own musical analysis on them. Smith's translation of Mishāqa's tract was a fortunate find for Ellis: a written document which, even in the absence of teachers and performers, could serve as a starting point for his analysis.

The gift was an ambiguous blessing, however. Mishāqa's theory and Smith's translation furthered the notion of music as a logical, intellectualized form of communication. This had the advantage of giving Arab music a dignity it otherwise would not have had for European readers: it could be admitted to the club of rational musical systems. It was a status comparable to the possession of a classical literature or "canon" comparable to nineteenth-century European nation-states' creation of a classical literature for themselves. Where European scholars did not find such a fixed body of core texts in other parts of the world, they could always select and proclaim the special status of a central tradition. This understanding of music as part of a self-enclosed history was at odds, however, with the practice of Arab music then and now. As A. J. Racy has commented, European observers were struck in the nineteenth century by the emotional impact of Arab music on its audiences, which could rise to the level of mystical ecstasy. Its effect had as much to do with many-sided conditions of religious tradition and the bond between performer and audience as with the music's purely formal qualities. A missionary source relying on a critical intellectual and convert as its informant was not a place to discover this cultural context; in any event, Ellis was interested in a formal analysis that tended to exclude religious and performative contexts of cultural meaning. There was a paradox embedded in Ellis's methodology:

it had the valuable function of confronting European readers with the autonomy of a foreign system of music, but it did so only by narrowing it to the point where some of its essential qualities vanished. The reduction of the music to a formalized system was facilitated by the fact that Ellis, an inveterate researcher in Britain but not an overseas traveler, knew only the tract, and never experienced the music.[11]

Musical Japonisme

For their excursions into foreign music, Ellis and Hipkins were not always limited to written theories. A spectacle offering a different kind of introduction, the Japanese Village, opened in London in 1885 just four months before Ellis's lecture on scales at the Society of Arts. It was a remarkable year for *Japonisme*. On March 14, just eleven days before Ellis's presentation, Gilbert and Sullivan's operetta *The Mikado* opened at the Savoy Theater in London, the beginning of a run of 672 performances; by the end of the year the opera was performed in more than 150 theaters. It mocked the fashion for Japanese arts and crafts that had taken hold in England since the mid-nineteenth century and was in full bloom thirty years later.[12] Ellis's research led into a far richer history of reformers from Japan and Western countries collaborating to represent Japan's traditional music. His search for the Japanese scale system drew him into ideological arguments about Japan's modernization.

In 1885, Londoners might have pointed not to an operetta (or a scholarly talk) but to the Japanese Village as the place to immerse oneself in the country's arts and crafts. Like many of the late nineteenth-century exhibitions featuring foreign peoples, it operated at the borders of commerce, craft, and cultural exchange. An entrepreneur named Tannaker Buhicrosan recruited between ninety and a hundred Japanese, among them dozens of craftsmen who laid out the village, built it, and filled it with craft exhibitions. Buhicrosan charged one shilling for admission. The import and export firm Rottmann, Strome & Co., admired in Europe for its high-quality leather wallpaper from Japan, helped him recruit craftsmen; it was stimulating visitors' appetite for its fine crafted goods by playing a role in establishing the village. To add to the village's classy tone, it was opened by Sir Rutherford Alcock, former British consul-general to Japan, on January 10, 1885. The venture was a great success: in its 112 days to May 1, some 250,000 visitors came. Once inside, they could not buy Japanese crafts, for the organizers wished to avoid the atmosphere of a "bazaar." Instead, one entered a broad street of shops and houses, "well-built apartments of varied appearance, each with its own characteristic ornamentation of parti-coloured bamboo, on solid panels, with shingled or thatched roof," according to an anonymous journalist for *The Times*. Landscapes painted by artists at work in the village decorated sides of the hall. Craftsmen demonstrated the lacquering of wood, pottery making, cloisonné, ivory and wood carving, and the making of sandals, pipes, lanterns, fans, and umbrellas, as well as the weaving and embroidery of silk, satin, and crepe. A music teacher was in residence, his house a favorite gathering place for the Japanese themselves. Musicians played at the tea house, reported *The Times* journalist, where visitors sat cross-legged on mats "to be served with tiny cups of tea by a smiling and most polite little maiden whose chevelure of jetty black could only be matched by one of her sisters of the East." While this was polite entertainment open to all, the dominant audience, as these lines from *The Times* suggest, was imagined as male, part of the implicit gentlemen's fraternity that controlled almost all of the reception of foreign music in the late nineteenth century. In the Japanese Village, Ellis had his chance to interview performers on the scale of the koto, in face-to-face encounters facilitated by a global concatenation of commerce, entrepreneurship, and taste.[13] But it was not in the Japanese Village that Ellis and Hipkins ultimately unraveled what they imagined to be the secrets of Japanese music. Communications were hobbled by the embarrassing circumstance that the performers knew no English and the Dutch interpreter knew nothing about music. Proximity was no guarantee of comprehension; one needed capable mediators.

Ellis found such mediators elsewhere. A rapidly modernizing Japan already had its own Western-educated experts who could guide his analysis, as could Westerners with experience living in Japan. With their aid, Ellis could make good use of his face-to-face time and come to his own conclusions about Japanese music's place in the diversity of musical scales.

Random scraps of evidence came his and Hipkins's way: a set of Japanese tuning forks lent to them by Hermann Smith, and previous measurements of the koto taken by the Reverend P. V. Veeder, a Western professor at a college in Tokyo. The forks and measurements contradicted one another and "were in all probability much out of order," wrote Ellis.[14] He and Hipkins made their own first imperfect attempt to measure Japanese music at the International Health Exhibition of 1884. This little-remembered gathering was an ambitious and high-minded demonstration of upper-class Victorian concern for the public weal. The Queen served as patron, while the Prince of Wales (the future Edward VII) was president and chairman of its general committee, which was made up of a dozen members of Britain's social, political, and scientific elite. The exhibition's aim of illustrating "in as vivid and practical a manner as possible" the "food, dress, the dwelling, the school, and the workshop, as affecting the conditions of healthful life," was capacious enough to include almost any elevating subject. Even though the event was built on the site of a previous exhibition, two acres of new buildings were constructed for it, and the exhibitions spilled over into buildings in central London. The catalog filled several hundred pages and listed large exhibitions sent by the French and Belgian governments. Attendance averaged about 140,000 visitors per week, who received heavy doses of pedagogy on the conditions for a healthful life.[15] It is rather stunning to observe in retrospect that a lesser-known exhibition like this one—which has not survived in collective memory as have the Great Exhibition of 1851 or the Paris Exposition of 1889—could attract large masses of visitors by the standards of any age. Middle-class and working-class people who would never travel to Japan and rarely saw Japanese visitors at home would have their impressions formed by their visit to an exhibition such as this one.

Attached to the International Hygiene Exhibition in the Japanese Section of its Educational Division was "a considerable display of Japanese musical instruments, but unfortunately no one who could play them, or who knew anything of music."[16] This was imperfect evidence, but Ellis and Hipkins did what they could with it. Tightening the four strings on a handsome biwa, a traditional Japanese instrument similar to the lute, they came up with a pentatonic scale. There was a sho in the exhibition, a mouth organ similar to the Chinese sheng, and they tried to blow through it but without getting any satisfactory results. Once again, as with Indian music, they found that it was not enough to have the instruments; they needed performances and expert guides.

They found a written guide at the Health Exhibition: an English summary of a report on Japanese music written for the Japanese Department of Education by Shūji Isawa, the director of the Institute of Music in Tokyo. With his usual care, Ellis recounted how Isawa came to his results about the tones of Japanese music. His American advisor, Luther Whiting Mason, "after attentively hearing Japanese popular and classical pieces of music for the purpose, said there was no difference as to tonality (meaning evidently *intonation*), but only a little difference in the mode of the tonal combinations." Mason was declaring that Japanese music closely resembled European music: the intervals between notes were the same, and the scales were virtually the same too. Replying to a letter from Ellis, Mason, drawing on a pamphlet published by Isawa as well as his own researches, wrote that traditional Japanese musicians tempered the intervals between tones to produce scales comparable to modern European systems of tempered scales.[17] This would have been a remarkable statement if it had been correct. In that case Japan alone, in contrast to every other musical system in the world, would have had scales comparable to those of the Western musical system. The comparison would have been a flattering one, suggesting that the Japanese were the equals of Europeans when it came to music, just as they were rapidly catching up with them in their general level of technological and military prowess.

Isawa and Mason insisted on the identity of European and Japanese tonal intervals as part of their radical program to modernize Japanese music. From 1875 to 1878, Isawa rounded out his education for a career as an administrator by studying in the United States, attending the Bridgewater Normal School in Massachusetts for two years, followed by studies at Harvard in 1887 and 1888. While at Bridgewater, he found vocal music a difficult subject and ended up going to Mason, forty miles away in Boston, for musical instruction. Mason was then thriving as an organizer of music instruction for Boston primary schools, and he took advantage of the opportunity to extend his influence by accommodating Isawa, who was being groomed to rise in Japan's bureaucracy. Every Saturday afternoon, Isawa went to Mason's home, stayed for dinner, visited music schools and libraries, and returned the next day to Bridgewater. During these sessions Isawa and Mason worked out a program for teaching Western music in Japan, creating charts for instruction and discussing how to add Japanese texts to Western melodies.[18] Their collaboration was a friendly meeting of two worlds. Isawa, trained as a scientist, viewed the Western musical system, like Western science and technology, as superior; Mason was interested in understanding a culture different from his own. When Isawa arranged for Mason's 1880 visit to Japan in order to advise him on reforming Japanese music, Mason, according to his biographer, "collected pentatonic folk songs of Ireland, Scotland, and Wales because he thought they would be similar to Japanese melodies."[19] He also took along a copy of Carl Engel's *National Music*, which he had bought on an 1872 trip to London.[20] The outcome of Isawa and Mason's collaboration was profound: they established the music curriculum for Japanese schools and universities that lasted into the post-1945 era. One of the first fruits of their efforts was a

volume of thirty-three elementary school songs published in 1881; it included "Go Tell Aunt Rhody," "Auld Lang Syne," and "Schlaf, Kindchen,
Schlaf" ("Sleep, Little One, Sleep") as well as "Our Land of the Rising Sun"
and "The Imperial Reign."[21] One of Isawa's principles was to combine the
best of both worlds, as represented by such melodies as these. Another
was the melding of Western scales and harmony to Japanese words and
sentiments. With the help of Mason's reforms, Japanese music would absorb the superior system of Western music but—with Engel's definition
of national music enlisted into the enterprise—maintain the spirit of the
Japanese nation.[22]

Ellis was skeptical about the claim that Japanese intervals already
matched those of Western scales. Other observers cautioned him against
Mason and Isawa's facile equation of European and Japanese music. One
of them was William Edward Ayrton, a British electrical engineer who
served as a professor at the newly created Imperial College of Engineering
in Tokyo from 1873 to 1879. After Ellis read a paper on nonharmonic scales
to the Royal Society in November 1884, Ayrton commented "that the Japanese intervals were often very different from the European." The head
of the Japanese section at the 1884 Health Exhibition put Ellis in touch
with an "anonymous Japanese gentleman" studying physics in Europe
who answered "a long string of questions that I sent him on the subject."
He wrote that the intervals deviated mathematically from their Western
counterparts, and that the Japanese had no harmony. The Japanese correspondent had also compared two sets of tuning forks, one from the
Japanese court and the other European, and found pitch discrepancies.
Isawa refused to send him a set of tuning forks because he thought such a
comparison would be "misleading," which led Ellis to dismiss his claims
of similarity and conclude that Japanese notes were not in fact comparably tempered. Ellis had a second suspicion about the comparability of
Japanese and European music: individual musicians, he guessed, made
their own idiosyncratic tunings. The scale of the koto, he thought, was not
fixed across Japan. He did not go very far, however, toward reflecting on
how the music of the koto and other instruments had changed over time.
From his study of pitch he was aware that Western music had undergone
fundamental changes, but he tended to treat non-Western scales as part
of static systems. Yet the definition and construction of the koto had indeed fluctuated. According to William P. Malm, in the nineteenth century
it came to be seen as a suitable accomplishment for well-bred girls, its appeal heightened by its court origins and gentle tone, qualities that also

made it attractive to Victorian taste.[23] The very use of the koto to represent Japanese music was a cultural choice conditioned by a morally infused aesthetic in both Britain and Japan.

At the Japanese Village, Ellis and Hipkins could work, despite the linguistic barrier, with two koto players "from country districts, and hence certainly unprejudiced by scientific research"—and, more broadly, by the prestige of European music. The two musicians effectively refuted Isawa's claims for the Western qualities of Japanese music. They did perform ensemble pieces, and there were moments when the musicians briefly played different tones together, but those did not add up to the systematic stacking of different intervals known as harmony.[24] Isawa's misleading assertions led Ellis to reflect more broadly on the uses of theory: did Greek musicians really conform to the symmetries stated by their mathematicians? Observing in passing a similarity between a Japanese and a Greek scale, he added: "Perhaps Olympos himself tuned no better, and it is only theorists who have rendered his intervals exact, precisely as Mr. Isawa, in his praiseworthy efforts to raise Japanese music, has defined the intervals with a mathematical precision, which the ordinary musician, whether Japanese or European, fails to appreciate."[25] Ellis, the experienced phonetician, was used to comparing sound patterns from textual evidence and contemporary speech. Familiar with the class and national vanities that went into claims about dialects, he punctured Isawa's claims to a traditional Japanese music that lived up to Western ideas of sophistication.

Isawa's reforms have been criticized for obliterating traditional Japanese music in the schools and replacing it with a hybrid that gave a Japanese inflection to trivial Western songs. Yet, in the context of the late nineteenth century, Isawa had altogether different choices to make from those of the post-1945 world in its preoccupation with preserving premodern tradition. In music as in other areas of culture, reformers around the world were without guides or historical precedent as they tried to preserve their cultural autonomy but incorporate the allure of Western modernity. Isawa's resources were a court culture that was far too difficult and refined to serve as a basis for mass education, and a popular musical culture that he considered vulgar and immoral. Discarding these unsatisfactory choices, he tried to create a synthesis of Western and Japanese genres that would embody social principles of order, participation in collective life, and patriotic loyalty.[26] Other societies made different choices, including a reassertion of folk music in England and, as we shall see, the argument in India that the music of princely courts was a national music. All of these reworkings were gambles with uncertain outcomes in response to the rapid changes confronting political and cultural elites.

Chinese "Noise"

At the International Health Exhibition of 1884, Ellis also had the opportunity to hear and interview Chinese musicians. The exhibition included a band of six Chinese musicians in the so-called Chinese court of its Education Division. How it got there is a story of global trade and diplomacy that depended on the incursion of British interests into late-nineteenth-century China.

The mediator was an organization called the Chinese Maritime Customs Service. Its well-documented history permits us to retrace the worldwide connections that led from Peking to a representation of Chinese music in London and Ellis's comparative analysis. The Customs Service was an amphibian organization, the outcome of shared Chinese and Western interests in seaborne trade. Administrators of China's Qing dynasty were unable to assess duties on foreign trade goods in Shanghai, which were controlled by secret societies. They agreed to the formation of an international organization that was staffed by Europeans but under the authority of Qing officials. Robert Hart, who was appointed acting inspector general of the Chinese Maritime Customs Service in 1861 and full inspector general two years later, turned the agency into a powerful engine of economic and social improvement, celebrated ever since in British imperial lore. Under Hart's administration, which lasted to 1910, it became "a model of an empire-wide organization, centralized in Peking, administered efficiently and honestly"; it was already fulsomely praised by *The Times* in 1899. Hart turned an office for tax collection into an agent for improving harbors, gathering statistics, and creating a national Chinese postal service. By 1907 it was operating in fifty-seven cities and had a staff of close to twelve thousand persons. In his position of responsibility to two governments, Hart worked well with Qing authorities, who awarded him high honors and in his last years of service were reluctant to let him go.[27]

Hart also turned it into a conduit for Chinese-Western cultural exchange. He devoted himself to learning Chinese soon after his arrival by studying with a tutor in Ningbo while still in the consular service. He also had a long-standing liason with a Chinese woman by whom he had three children. It was a testimony to the deep involvement of Hart and his employees that on short notice they could put together the International Health Exhibition's Chinese court with a many-sided presentation of elite and popular life. The request came from the exhibition commissioners in February, and Hart and his colleagues set to work gathering exhibition materials in "Peking [Beijing], Tientsin [Tianjin], Hankow [Hankou], Kiukiang [Jiujiang], Shanghai, Ningpo [Ningbo], Foochow [Fuzhou], Amoy [Xiamen] and Canton [Guangzhou]." Despite Hart's worries about timing and money, the materials for the exhibition arrived in England in the first week of June, a feat of organization that impressed contemporary observers.[28] The Chinese court contained exhibitions of dress in general, official costume, court dress, the wedding chair, silks and satins, boots and shoes, funeral ceremony, crematory ovens, the sedan chair, the Peking cart, the mule litter, the wheelbarrow, bows and arrows, stoves, books, furniture in the reception room and bedroom, soapstoneware, grain and pulse, decorations, shops—and a restaurant and teahouse where the Chinese musicians played, as well as an exhibition of Chinese musical instruments. One wall of the restaurant was painted by a Chinese artist with a "laburnum tree in full bloom," while other walls were decorated with "wreaths and bouquets of artificial flowers from Amoy." Nine Chinese cooks and waiters took care of food in the restaurant, while the teahouse served "tea of the very best quality." (One newspaper reported that one of the Chinese chefs was already working in West End clubs, and that "the Health Exhibition of 1884 will be memorable for the introduction of dinners à la Chinoise.") The Chinese band performed "daily in the tea-house" from four to six and evenings, and in the restaurant from half past seven to nine. Beyond any connection to health or education, the Chinese band was part of the exhibition's robust entertainment program.[29]

There are no recordings of these performances, which came too early for wax cylinders to capture them. But the exhibition catalog gives a full program of the music they played. The ten instrumental selections ranged from the grand "Hoa Tchou Ko—Chinese National Anthem" to the piously everyday "Mama Hao Ming-Pai—Mother Understands Me Well." The thirty-five vocal selections were more theatrical, with tales of separated lovers, selfish and self-sacrificing husbands and wives, cruelty and kindness of the gods, the song of a fan-painting girl, and the silliness of a donkey driver.[30] As did the Japanese Village, the Chinese court offered both popular entertainment and a chance to learn about the performance of instruments that until then, if they sat on museum shelves, had been enigmas.

When Ellis turned to Chinese music he had no guides to prepare him, as he did for the Japanese performances. Initially he was at a complete loss: "Wild horses can't drag the secret of Chinese music from their instruments," he wrote to Hipkins toward the end of their work with the band in the Chinese court. "But it *is* music all the same, & does not sound amiss though strangely unlike ours."[31] A buoyant statement, hopeful and enterprising despite the initial puzzlement! He and Hipkins were given complete access to the Chinese musicians and interviewed them "on four mornings in July and August 1884, for two hours at a time, with the help of an interpreter, in the large dining-room of the Chinese contingent of thirty-one natives. . . ." The two music researchers asked the musicians to play their scales and measured them with tuning forks; the musicians good-naturedly obliged them. But taking the pitch was not so easy, perhaps because the unusualness of the intervals threw off even Hipkins's fine ear. In a sense, what was most intriguing was the musical incomprehension Ellis and Hipkins were able to observe:

> There was present on two occasions an English violinist, who was engaged to teach the musicians English tunes, and he said that he had the utmost difficulty with passages involving semitones. We also heard one of the Chinese on his fiddle attempting to play a Scotch air, and the difficulty he had in hitting the intervals—although, of course, on the violin, however made, there is not much immaterial impediment to taking any intervals, was a sufficiently convincing proof that the modern Chinese intervals are not the same as ours.[32]

Here was an on-the-spot demonstration of musical diversity: with the best will, neither the English violinist nor the Chinese violinist could hear one another's intervals well enough to reproduce them. If ever one wanted an example of the difficulty of "hearing" another culture, this was it.

Ellis and Hipkins initially experienced Chinese music as noise. This was a frequent reaction to it in the late nineteenth and early twentieth centuries. Within Western music, not all notes fit into a harmonic pattern; on the contrary, part of the art of the harmonic system was pushing against its limits, producing dissonances which served as moments of tension before their resolution. But Chinese music—at least the samples of it that baffled Ellis—was something else, a breakdown of meaningful order, or noise. This could be a term of contempt, as when it was used to describe Jewish music. The case of Ellis is a reminder of something else:

the genuine barriers in the way of comprehension. His initial reaction was a telling moment not of deep prejudice, but of deep culture, the differences in patterns of meaning-making that limit understanding. What the Chinese example also demonstrated was Ellis's rare determination to work beyond differences and make sense out it.[33]

In the face of difficulties, Ellis and Hipkins made their utmost effort to take down intervals—and not just with the musicians at the Chinese court. At the South Kensington Museum and in the private collection of Hermann Smith as well as the Chinese court, they worked with unnamed wind instruments, a sheng (reed mouth organ), two sets of gongs, a dulcimer, two types of guitars, several pipas, and a chime of bells. Having the instruments was no guarantee of knowing what to do with them: it was hard to know how to play the wind instruments, it took guesswork to arrange the gongs, and string instruments had to be tuned. All in all, concluded Ellis, his and Hipkins's observations were not enough material to form the basis for a theory. But they sufficed to show that all the missionary and travel texts at their disposal, which recorded Chinese music as if it were composed in the Western diatonic scale, were "utterly misleading" and had to give way to further experiments testing the sounds of Chinese instruments.[34]

None of Ellis's criticisms was more scathing or, in retrospect, more misguided than those he flung at J. A. van Aalst, who had written the first modern monograph on Chinese music, a serious introduction to a previously unknown subject. Van Aalst was an official working for the Chinese Maritime Customs Service. Like several members of the organization, beginning with Robert Hart himself, he was interested in exploring Chinese culture and wished to interpret it for a European audience. Hart liked but worried about him. "He is well educated and brilliant, but somewhat impatient of control and very unwilling to let anybody 'sit on' him," he wrote to Campbell, his secretary in London, after Aalst got into trouble for mistreating Chinese at the Chinese court of the International Health Exhibition.[35] Hart and Aalst shared a passion for music, and Aalst played in an ensemble at his superior's house on Saturdays. When the time came to prepare the Chinese court, Hart asked Aalst to prepare a section of the exhibition catalog on music and to lecture at the Health Exhibition. In response, Aalst published in 1884 a small treatise on music which (as Ellis noted) he condensed for the catalog. The result was, if not perfect, at least a point of departure for a difficult subject.[36]

Van Aalst began his monograph by combating the reigning prejudices toward Chinese music. If foreign writers mentioned it at all in their books, he commented, "it is simply to remark that 'it is detestable, noisy, monotonous; that it hopelessly outrages our Western notions of music,' etc." As a first step toward understanding it, he introduced a principle that scholars continue today to emphasize. In Confucian teaching, music was viewed as pragmatic and political: it could change people's souls, and correct music contributed to the order of the state. Nonetheless, wrote Aalst, "serious music," once considered an essential part of a gentleman's education, was now "totally abandoned." Hence, it was a challenge for any outsider with an interest in understanding classical Chinese music to do so. One would have to gain the trust of literati who, despite the general decline of musical training, cultivated the playing of a classical instrument; gain entrance to a house for intimate social gatherings; or be a witness to Confucian ritual—all unlikely situations.[37] While the decline of the classical music tradition is usually associated with the overthrow of the monarchy and founding of the Chinese Republic in 1912, Aalst's comment is a noteworthy documentation of the turn away from it decades earlier as epitome of the supposedly stuffy, outdated culture of the mandarins. There was also popular music that filled the streets. One got glimpses it now and then: Aalst gave a charming description of passing by shops at twilight when the shopkeeper's selling of "candles or sugar loaves" gave way to the sounds of a fiddle. But he looked down on it, and left the reader with these tantalizing hints of Chinese cities' vital street life.

Aalst's catalog offered the first modern overview in English (aside from his own monograph) of Chinese music, as preparation for visitors' walk through the musical instruments on display. Here they would have learned about features of Chinese musical notation that affected its European reception, and which continue today to stimulate commentary. As recent scholarship has emphasized, the notation system guarantees that the music passes from generation to generation as an *oral* tradition handed from master to disciple. The notation has no indication of time units for individual notes or pauses. As Aalst wrote, the *principle* of musical production differed from that of its Western counterpart:

> The best Chinese musician could only conjecture the general form of a written piece shown to him for the first time; to be able to decipher it he must first *hear it played*. Therefore all the tunes are learned by tradition, and are continually modified by the individual taste of the performer, so that after a lapse of time the tunes become quite different from what

they were originally, and scarcely two musicians will be found to play exactly the same notes when performing the same piece of music. But Chinese musicians do not exhibit any peculiar anxiety about exact justness of pitch or intonation. They content themselves with an "*à peu près*," an approximation, and within the compass of ten or twelve unchanging notes they find an infinite number of airs, which amply satisfies the requirements of their simple tastes.[38]

Aalst was ambivalent toward Chinese music. On the one hand, he paired the limited repertoire of its classical musicians with "simple tastes." He went on to the more sophisticated comment that Chinese music puzzled Europeans because it did not have the major or minor scales, the modulation from key to key, or the dramatic dynamics of European music. On the side of complexity, he pointed out that the Chinese "understand and appreciate the beauties of their own tunes," an admonition that cautioned the reader against turning away from it before adjusting to the appeal of a foreign art. Like Charles Day writing about the music of South Asia, he seems to have been inwardly divided, by turns apologetic for and an advocate of the strange beauty of a music outside Western experience. That even these enthusiasts coupled their sympathy with self-doubt is a marker of how difficult it was for nineteenth-century listeners to hear beyond inherited expectations.

Even a mildly curious visitor would have been intrigued by the Chinese instruments in the exhibition and Aalst's comments on them. His descriptions of a profusion of music-making devices did not just present them as aesthetic objects, or instruments for sound production; they transported the reader into court, religious, and everyday life. Especially intriguing were the objects that Aalst introduced in their social contexts. Under percussion instruments there were the t'ang-ku, large drums for imperial and religious ceremonies: "They are richly ornamented with dragons, flowers, and other designs." The pa-chiō-ku was a tambourine, "used sometimes by ballad-singers to accompany their songs." The y'ao-ku, or peddler's drum, was "used mostly by hawkers in millinery goods to announce their approach. It is a peculiar feature of Chinese hawking," wrote Aalst, "that each corporation has a signal of its own by which it can be readily recognized." The chu was a square book painted with "the five Chinese colours, and is used only at the Imperial Religious Ceremonies to give the signal to begin the music—a rather cumbrous mode of producing a simple result." The wu, another wooden device, had "the form of a creeping tiger," and was used only in imperial ceremonies together with the chu. Buddhist priests used mu-yü, wooden fish, "to mark time in the recitation of their prayers." Tê-ch'ing, sonorous stones, were cut to yield musical tones. Once made sometimes of jade, they were now made of "a black calcareous stone" and were considered sacred instruments to be used only at imperial ceremonies. Bells came in many different sizes and shapes, including the chung, sets of five bells cast with dragon statues on top. Hai-lo, stone conches, were "used by soldiers and watchmen to convey signals." La-pa, trumpets, were "used by soldiers to convey signals, but principally by knife-grinders to announce their approach." There were la-pa trumpets on display that lamas used in their religious ceremonies and kang-t'ung or dragon trumpets also used by the lamas. And, as a pièce de résistance thrown in after the catalog's listing of forty-two other instruments, there were pigeon whistles:

> PIGEON WHISTLES.—A collection of whistles to be tied to pigeons' tails. One of these whistles is bound, so as to stand erect, round the tail of one pigeon in every flock in order to keep the flock together. As he circles round, the wind whistling through the organ-like tubes gives forth a weird, plaintive sound, which after a while becomes anything but unpleasing to the ear.

By the time one reached the pigeon whistle, musical instruments themselves had undergone a redefinition from a means of creating a solely aesthetic experience to artifices linking buyer and seller, emperor and court, monk and the supernatural in unexpected social, political, and ceremonial communities.[39]

There is no record that Ellis tried out the pigeon whistle. Nor was his imagination teased by the panorama of knife grinders, milliners, soldiers, priests, court attendants, and pigeon-tormenting idlers who made life in Chinese cities a bewildering sound cosmos to Western visitors. Nor did he appreciate the work it took to bring together social observations and the fantastic variety of instruments on view at the exhibition.

What instead grabbed his attention was what always drew him: the accurate measurement of pitch and scale, and in this case Aalst's failure to register anything like the difference between Western and Chinese tonal systems. Going through instrument after instrument, Ellis discovered intervals different from those of the diatonic scale. As for Aalst's scales, he judged them to be erroneous for instruments like the sheng and the gongs; even worse, the samples of Chinese music at the end of Aalst's book were completely Westernized for use on the piano, transcribed to correspond to Western notes and harmonized in a Western key. "We may, therefore, pass it by as not Chinese music at all," sniffed Ellis after describing the harmonization of Aalst's first example, "though it is called the National Anthem."[40] (The selection begins with a grand procession of seven-note chords, enough to make a reader cringe more than a century later.) Ellis's analysis demonstrated the superiority of his scientific method to centuries of travelers' tales—including those of a serious, well-intended traveler such as Aalst—when it came to grasping the formal dimensions of a foreign music. Ellis also pounced on notation as a point at which the attempt to record a foreign musical systems revealed irreducible cultural differences. Even a sympathetic listener immersed in a culture would not necessarily comprehend what he was hearing—and Aalst, like centuries of Western observers before him, reduced Chinese music to a Western schema.

Yet Aalst's text remains a significant historical document in its own right, with contributions beyond the reach of Ellis's mathematical mind. His inclusion of whimsical oddities like the pigeon whistle and his alertness to the social and political uses of sound called into question the very category of "music." From his tour of the city street and the Confucian temple, one could begin to perceive the category of music itself as a historical construction, and not a universal cultural form, as Ellis assumed. Avant-garde musicians down to our own time, with their exploration of a wide range of sounds long ignored or treated as noise, are the successors to Aalst and his description of the varieties of Chinese music.[41]

Indian Melodies

To Ellis, Indian music was more approachable than its East Asian counterparts. It readily enriched his case for the widespread use of microtones that had no equivalent in modern Western music. In this instance more than any of the others, he had insider exponents of the musical system, educated and anglophone, who were prepared to explain it. His and Hipkins's tutor for Indian music, Rajah Ram Pal Singh, played for them on his sitar. In addition, he had a theoretical guide: the writings of Sourindro Mohun Tagore, including one book in particular, *The Musical Scales of the Hindus*, which Ellis called "the only English modern native authoritative work on Indian music extant." With the help of Singh and Tagore, he could do what was impossible for Arab or East Asian music: compare musical theory and performance practice.[42]

The results matched fairly well. The Hindustani scale, according to Tagore, contained seven fixed notes that roughly corresponded to the European scale. In addition, there were tones that musicians produced by making the fixed notes flat or very flat, sharp or very sharp. Ellis could turn to a vina in the South Kensington collection that confirmed this result: it had twelve frets corresponding to the twelve European semitones, with additional tones to be produced by increasing the pressure on the strings. When Europeans transcribed Hindu music, however, they assimilated the additional tones to the fixed notes. "These confusions necessarily injure the original character of the music, and give it a harmonisable appearance which is entirely foreign to Indian music." While Indian music did not have harmony, it constructed an enormous number of scales with the aid of these additional tones. Tagore's writings were a satisfying demonstration of a musical system that was distinct from Western music, yet equally ordered and articulated.

There was another implication to using this source: by accepting Tagore's explanations of Indian music as authoritative, Ellis was also embracing a newly created program of what Indian music *ought* to be. For Tagore was the maker of a modern agenda that looked to and at the same time transformed the written tradition while making drastic selections within performance practice about what counted as authentic Indian music. A conservative Hindu, he repudiated the music making of most contemporary musicians in North India. These were usually either court musicians or popular entertainers, groups that in his eyes had contributed to the corruption of the ancient foundations of Indian music. Mainly Muslim and uneducated, the court musicians were regarded by Tagore as incapable of understanding or transmitting a highly intellectualized musical tradition. As for popular entertainers, they were associated with erotic dance by nautch girls. The puritanical Tagore campaigned to elevate the reputation of music and musical performance and turn it into an art that could take its place as an adornment of middle-class families and guests at the high table of world cultures. This was music reworked to be part of a program of Hindu national revival.

In 1871 Tagore founded the Bengal Music School, which in 1874 had about five hundred pupils. Newspapers reported on the annual awards ceremony of that year, which included a distribution of prizes to the best students and "a series of *tableaux vivants*, accompanied by verbal explanations, and illustrated by the students of the school on their respective instruments." After tableaux representing the six principal ragas (beginning with "a nymph, gathering fresh blossoms in the bosom of a grove" and ending with "a mighty warrior on horse-back in the battle-field, besmeared with blood"), Tagore stepped forward and spoke to the assembly. He "expressed his joy at seeing the thriving condition of the Bengal Music School," but also his belief that "Hindu Music was on the whole in a deplorable state," which had to be remedied by schools across the country.[43] The Calcutta school seems to have quickly achieved the respectability he sought, to judge from a laudatory account of one of its music festivals two years later in The Hindoo Patriot.[44]

To advertise Indian music to the rest of the world, Tagore sent collections of musical instruments and books to learned institutions across Europe, Australia, and the United States. Thanks and honors reached him from the Royal Swedish Musical Academy, the Hague (one Count H. Du Moncean thanked him on behalf of the king), the Academy of Music of St. Cecilia in Florence, the Hungarian Academy of Sciences, the Lisbon National Library, the University of Parma, the Académie des inscriptions et belles lettres in Paris, the Academy of Sciences and Letters in Palermo, the Royal Academy of Urbino, and the Philharmonic Society in Melbourne, Australia. He also sent collections to the Metropolitan Museum in New York and the South Kensington Museum (Victoria and Albert); the Victoria and Albert collections still contain a box of twenty-two tuning forks which, according to Tagore, illustrated the intervals of the Indian scale.[45] Professors praised his writings. G. B. Vecchiotti of Urbino wrote a discriminating review of his account of microtones and harmony in Indian music, adding his "voice to that of the civilized world" in praise of Tagore, and welcoming his expansion of Europeans' musical horizons.[46] Albrecht Weber, professor at the University of Berlin and one of the leading Indologists of the day, testified in 1875 that up to this moment, little direct contact with Indian music had been possible; Tagore deserved recognition for changing this with his instruments and books.[47] Tagore's campaign played a large part in creating admiration for Indian music in late nineteenth-century Europe. While it would be decades until Indian music began to influence Western composers or reach a general public, expert readers were already intrigued by his introduction to treasures awaiting further exploration.

Tagore's skills as educator were on full display when he hosted the distinguished legal scholar Julius Jolly, who was giving the Tagore legal lectures at the University of Calcutta. Jolly asked S. M. Tagore's elder brother, Jotindro Mohun Tagore, to arrange a meeting. He soon received an invitation to come to the family palace (where both brothers lived with their families) for an evening concert. Together with some of his musically inclined German friends, Jolly made the long trip from the European part of town to the Tagore house. The performers were an orchestra made up of teachers from Tagore's Music Academy. They started out with a "cantata" composed by Tagore himself in honor of the Prince of Wales, a Westernized piece of music that was easy to enjoy. Next, they went on to classical Indian music. Jolly and his companions had trouble comprehending it, but appreciated the precise execution and ability to play from memory (he did not recognize improvisation as a dimension of the performance), as well as the Indians' ability to discriminate microtones that could sound like out-of-key notes to uninitiated Western ears. The secretary of the academy later showed Jolly an Indian "harp" and answered questions about the theory and practice of Indian music with a satisfying eagerness and thoroughness. Jolly left Calcutta an admirer of Tagore and his works, which he publicized in his travel account, published in a prominent German journal.[48] The visit and Jolly's account demonstrated Tagore's ability to win friends for Indian music; it was also a reminder that, even for discriminating and sympathetic Western ears, it was difficult in the late nineteenth century to understand a foreign musical idiom.

Tagore campaigned successfully to preserve the integrity of Indian music from the attempts of one British administrator, C. B. Clarke, to Westernize it. Clarke belittled the Hindu system of notation that Tagore had publicized a few years before, arguing that it was a novelty and that Indian music would be better served with Western notation. Music was not Clarke's usual beat; he was by training a botanist, and after his retirement moved to Kew.[49] Tagore was guided in his ambitions for reviving Indian music by the writings of Carl Engel, and through Engel he would have been familiar with European arguments for respecting the idiosyncrasies of national music from around the world. He may also have read Engel's complaints about the distorting effect of using Western notation. In similar fashion he criticized what he called Clarke's mathematical approach:

> At first sight it would seem as if Mr. Clarke's chief object in writing the essay was to mystify the subject by enveloping it in a cloud of mathematicism. But no one is better aware than himself that mathematics is no

more indispensable for one to be a musician than it is indispensable for him to be a painter or statuary. In learning music the student requires, above all things, an educated ear capable of detecting and feeling the sense of all tonal combinations. The susceptibility of an art being examined by mathematical tests is something different from mathematics being indispensable to its comprehension or acquisition. Principles of music, embodied into scientific theories, may be based on mathematics, but it does not necessarily follow that one must know mathematics in order to understand those principles. We may say without fear of contradiction that those principles which go to form the science of Acoustics enter fully into Hindu Music. But that science in its improved form is still incomplete and imperfect. . . . There is nothing to make us regret that the principles of Acoustics, as they exhibit themselves in our music, differ in form from the European system.[50]

Tagore was putting forth a view of rationalization that looked beyond the identification of music with the Western diatonic system and pointed instead in the direction of understanding the distinctive logic of Indian music. He was closer than his English critic to Helmholtz (not yet available in English translation) when he noted that a different system could still be compatible with the "principles of Acoustics," which historically had taken different musical forms. Tagore challenged Clarke's notion of science at a deeper level, however, by rejecting the entire notion that one could impose a foreign schema. An understanding of music grew from the experience of the music, or what Tagore called the educated ear that was responsive to its tonal combinations. This was a fundamental point for expanding the musical cosmos: the ability to listen was the starting point for theorizing any particular kind of music.

After criticizing Clarke's many misunderstandings of the basic features of Indian music—the raga, the sruti, the presence of harmony, the notes on the sitar—Tagore turned to their disagreement over musical notation:

We now come to the discussion of our critic's remarks on our musical notation, which he condemns by saying "that the nationalist Bengali musical notation is valueless and ought to be superseded at once by the stave." To say the truth we do not very clearly understand the gist of his objection. We may, however, tell him that the Indian notation as far as it goes is all that we require. It is simple, convenient, and sufficient

for all practical purposes. We beg Mr. Clarke to bear in mind that the
notation he condemns is based on the original Sanscrit [sic] notation,
of which he will find a full exposition by Sir William Jones in the Asiatic
Researches . . . .[51]

Tagore himself appears at this point in the role of reformer in the original
sense of the word, taking ancient texts and restoring them to their full
meaning for his contemporaries. There was an original Sanskrit notation,
but, he added, ". . . many of the signs and symbols of that notation have
now become obsolete or have been entirely lost. What we have done is
simply this, we have endeavoured to introduce such improvements in the
system as are necessary to adapt it to modern requirements."[52] He generalized that every nation with its own music had its own system of notation
which could not be improved by borrowing notation from another nation.
"Anglicized as we have become in many respects, we confess we prefer
our national system of notation for our national music."[53] This was, then,
a playing back to Clarke of the critique of universalist conceptions of culture that went back to Carl Engel.

The debate had special relevance to India. Since the late-eighteenth-
century conquest of Bengal, British administrators had quarreled over
cultural policy. William Jones set the tone for those who insisted on
understanding Indian cultures for the sake of effective rule; James Mill,
writing in the early nineteenth century, delivered an Enlightenment critique of Hindu culture as corrupted by the rule of the priests (the Brah-
mins), and insisted on the need for sweeping Westernization. The question of musical notation was but one field where combatants, for the rest
of the nineteenth century, continued to battle over their missions of nurturing local culture versus imposing a universal civilization.[54] Tagore's
arguments were telling blows against Clarke's naive insistence on West-
ernizing Indian notation. At the same time, they exemplified the nationalist imagination at work. Following the example of Western nationalists,
Tagore sought a primeval origin and found it in texts that were never unified in the past and could only be reconstructed retrospectively into an
intelligible whole. Jones, whom he cited, wrote with cosmopolitan intent.
He sought to open up Indian culture to his contemporaries in Britain, define it in what he imagined to be its purest form, and elevate it to a bur-
nished seat in the order of world cultures. By contrast, Tagore wrote to
exclude Muslim contributions to the music of South Asia. This kind of
cultural fundamentalism was especially ironic as a strategy for reviving

musical tradition in Bengal, with its Persian influences and Muslim musicians. Tagore's invention of an ancient musical tradition belonged to the larger emergence of nineteenth-century nationalist histories that located a mythically pure culture in a remote past.[55]

Although Tagore refused to travel to Europe (in keeping with the conservative Hindu belief that one lost caste by traveling overseas), he lived between two worlds. The Tagore family had risen to greatness since the early nineteenth century through their loyalty and usefulness to their British rulers. The Great Rebellion of 1857 did not weaken the alliance. He and his elder brother were extremely wealthy aristocrats (by one count they had 600,000 peasants on their lands) and gained the new titles respectively of rajah and maharajah. The Prince of Wales (the future Edward VII) attended a special pageant in his honor at the Bengal School of Music, and Tagore dedicated his book *Six Ragas* to him. As a British subject and host to foreign guests, he was an accomplished diplomat.

At the same time, a spirit of national resistance and cultural renaissance was stirring; only a decade separated the tour of India by the Prince of Wales from the founding of the Indian National Congress in 1885. Tagore's campaign for musical independence was part of a larger movement away from acceptance of British authority. Tagore belonged to a worldwide generation of privileged colonial elites that were finding their way into a space between loyalty and independence. Teresa Segura-Garcia has illustrated this for India in her study of Sayaji Rao III, Maharaja of Baroda, who was handpicked by the British to become ruler of this formally independent princely state and received his education from an English tutor-regent, but took up contact with nationalists even as he continued to profess his imperial loyalties.[56] Rulers and intellectuals elsewhere, too, navigated the narrow channel between dependence and independence. Isawa chose to use Western musical structures as a vehicle for patriotic melodies in Japanese schools. The Hawaiian monarch, David Kalākaua, and his sister and successor, Queen Lili'uokalani, faced yet another set of choices and constraints. Aware that their rule was threatened by the white American planter elite, they gathered folklore and artifacts in a concerted effort at cultural revival, with significant success for the future of national cultural identity despite the overthrow of the monarchy in 1893. Both of them highly musical, they created a corpus of Hawaiian song and dance that drew on missionary as well as native sources, which had become intertwined since the 1820s.[57] Tagore, Isawa, and the Hawaiian monarchs were complicated, mediating figures. There was no single or inevitable choice for them between non-Western and Western cultures, nor was there an inevitable movement in a single political direction. Their syntheses informed and shaped their national cultures: whatever tradition had been, it underwent change as soon as they appropriated it in global context.

This was the pattern for the the sources used by Ellis and subsequent researchers. What they found was not pure, but the outcome of an encounter. Overall, it is a fundamental misconception to imagine the late nineteenth century as a time when Western colonizers imposed and the colonized reacted by simply deferring or rebelling. Rather, in an age of globalization a *circulation* of ideas and sensibilities took place. Carl Engel developed his conception of national music with the help of sitars and vinas; Tagore developed his conception of an independent Indian musical culture by reading Carl Engel; Alexander Ellis defined Indian music by relying on Tagore texts shaped by Western ideas of authenticity. Vecchiotti welcomed exchanges of this kind in his review of Tagore's writings:

> Now, when in music no less than in other arts, an ardent desire to try new paths and to take wider views, is apparent, it is more than ever necessary that we should expand our knowledge to appreciate the beautiful under whatever form it may appear, as also to repudiate what may be opposed to its fundamental principles. In this manner, without giving up our precious traditions, we may draw profit from the artistic treasures of all times and of all peoples. Neither intelligence is raised, nor is the heart developed by isolation. It is only from social contact, from comparisons, and from wide syntheses that the true incarnation of the beautiful can be formed, and the true progress of art—rising higher developing in proportion as it becomes eclectic and universal, can be found.[58]

As Vecchiotti imagined the partners in this exchange, they were not defending primeval cultures. Rather, they were joining the logic of human dialogue, in which a shared widening of horizons took place.

Ellis's entrance into the Indian harmonic system was facilitated by literate, English-speaking interpreters. He had Rajah Ram Pal Singh to guide him in London. From afar, Tagore was not only fluent in English but wrote with expert authority, analyzing Indian music from within and comparing it with its Western counterpart. Guided by an interlocutor and authoritative texts, Ellis could learn about Indian music with relative ease and accuracy. His respectful interpretation belonged to a tradition that looked back a hundred years to William Jones, and forward to the twentieth-century reception of Indian music.[59]

An Egalitarian Diversity of Scales

The diversity of musical scales in Ellis's survey surpassed the expectations of the ear and the simplifications of theory. He was a rigorous experimenter and mathematician, but qualified logical symmetries with the phonetician's ear for idiosyncrasy and the philologist's sensitivity to context. The only "naturally recognized" interval he could find was the octave, but even that was not always comparably tuned. Other intervals occurred frequently; none was universal. Within societies, radical changes took place and individual pitches rose and fell. The Greeks changed their scales over time; medieval Arab and Persian music went their own ways with tuning systems, and in modern times Arab music worked from a system of twenty-four equal semitones; India had "a remarkably complex system" that allowed individual musicians to shift frets and press strings; Japan and China used quarter tones; and Javanese scales worked without a fourth or fifth, which elsewhere seemed essential. The more Ellis cut through prejudice, ignorance, and pretension, the closer he came to universal anarchy. Across time and place, different societies constructed musical scales. Beyond that he could discern patterns, but not universals.

Aware of the limitations of his own undertaking, Ellis looked back across all that he had surveyed: "The final conclusion is that the Musical Scale is not one, not 'natural,' nor even founded necessarily on the laws of the constitution of musical sound, so beautifully worked out by Helmholtz, but very diverse, very artificial, and very capricious."[60] At just the moment when Ellis could anticipate the publication of his translation of Helmholtz—more than a decade after he first proposed it, and after exhausting labor to render the work into English—he left the master behind. Helmholtz continued to have a belief in music founded in nature—certainly Western music with its foundations in the natural set of overtones—and, equally important, a music *history* that followed a natural evolutionary form as it rose from melody to polyphony and harmony. The logic of Ellis's essay was different: it did not trace a historical movement from simplicity to complexity in an ascending hierarchy, but instead placed musical systems side by side for comparative analysis. As Ellis most readily admitted for Indian music, a non-European system could have a sophistication fully equal to that of European music.

The divide separating Ellis from Helmholtz carried over into the politics of culture. As recent commentators on Helmholtz have observed, he embodied the outlook of northern Germany's Protestant educated elite. The son of the Potsdam Gymnasium director, Helmholtz as a mature scientist remained close to the humanistic education exemplified by his father. Music played a large part in this: Helmholtz was a devoted pianist, attended several concerts a week, and took sides in the stylistic debates of the nineteenth century. He identified German culture with the superiority of Western music in *The Sensations of Tone* and its history of harmony. According to Helmholtz, the decisive moment of breakthrough to the organized succession of harmonic chords came about through the Lutheran Reformation. In unprecedented fashion, the Lutheran church chorus embodied the vox populi, the people's collective voice, which became a whole unifying equally valued parts. Helmholtz took the further step of identifying the chorus with the modern age's drive toward the freedom of all citizens in the modern nation. This would not have sounded strange to his educated peers at mid-nineteenth century. Even anticlerical northern European thinkers—for example, John Stuart Mill—looked back to Luther as the liberator of modern man from the chains of medieval Christianity. Helmholtz took this ideology and gave it a peculiarly German form.[61]

Ellis cast away this kind of ideological claptrap. His outward eccentricities and Comtean nonconformity were manifestations of an inner independence that extended to his taste and judgment. Unlike German Protestants, locked in a heated battle with Catholics for political domination of Central Europe as a German nation-state took shape, he was a self-confident member of a United Kingdom and an expanding empire. German Protestants tended to remain *cultural* Protestants even if they were religious skeptics; Helmholtz is a good example of the claim to a culturally superior *Innerlichkeit* or spiritual depth that persisted as a point of pride even among those who cast off formal religious belief. Ellis abandoned Christianity altogether for Comte's Religion of Man, a self-proclaimed universal creed in contrast to the ethnic and cultural specificity of Helmholtz's Lutheranism. A cheerful do-gooder, Ellis certainly belonged to a specific stream of humanitarianism within Victorian Britain, but he was not the bearer of a cultural ideology projected back through the ages. He rarely expressed any kind of musical preference at all. Scientific curiosity, and a certain reform impulse when it came to questions like singers' voices or popular access to music, formed part of his motivation. But he was an impartial arbiter when he compared musical scales, and did not build an evolutionary ideology into his comparisons. Scales were just various.

It was a rare intellectual honesty that underlay his enquiry—which for decades to come impressed readers and aided the formation of a musicology worldwide in its breadth.

5

Is It Noise, or Is It Music?

London occupied a central place in the story of Europe's expanding musical horizons. Britain's empire brought it into direct contact with foreign musical cultures. London as imperial capital attracted musicians, foreign guests, instruments, museums, and spectacles. By the late nineteenth century, metropolitan musical life itself was enjoying a general expansion that was broad enough to embrace the early instrument revival and nascent interest in extra-European scales. A taste for traditional crafts ran through the elite culture of the time, and extended to vinas and kotos. Contributors came from social ranks as far apart as A. J. Hipkins and Prince Albert, makers in their different ways of the South Kensington Museum.

This growing awareness of non-European musical traditions could hardly have happened without the contributions of German music lovers. Carl Engel was a product of north German family life, musical training, and concerts. Thousands of other German émigrés raised the general level of musical connoisseurship in England by serving as performers, critics, and audiences. The global cultures of empire converged with the émigrés' taste and learning to create a cosmopolitan musical milieu.

Slightly later than their English counterparts, Germans in Germany developed a growing interest in music from around the world. Their starting point had different features: a proud musical tradition which, in combination with rising nationalism and the formation of a nation-state, led them to think of German music as *the* great music; and a network of modern research universities that fostered disciplinary musical scholarship alongside other branches of higher learning. Late in the nineteenth century, Germans began to assemble the scraps and pieces of an empire. Theirs was a new creation and a puny one compared to Britain's overseas realms. But it sufficed to initiate a new era of intellectual curiosity that turned faraway places into objects of careful examination.

Germany Enters the Global Age

Sometime during the late nineteenth century a change of atmosphere took place: Germans looked out to the world, almost as if a sea breeze had stirred them to venture forth with a new, reckless urge for adventure. The quickening animated the Berlin Congress, which opened in 1884: Otto von Bismarck, the German chancellor, summoned statesmen from the imperial nation-states of Europe and—as is often noted, without a single African present—deliberated with them over how to divide the African continent into spheres of influence. Students used to learn about this conference as an event that signaled Germany's new prominence within the European order of things, which it certainly was. But the Congress also demonstrated Bismarck's interest in serving as Europe's arbiter within a *global* order. This new role was all the more remarkable because Bismarck was such an unlikely instigator of it. He started out as a Prussian patriot, a member of a stolid landowning class that did not have much use for members of other German states, much less the larger world. Part of Bismarck's greatness was his steady ability to outgrow the provinciality of his peers and push for the creation of a nation-state; he once again demonstrated his ability to size up the political necessities of his time when he presided over a European division of colonies. Romance for the world beyond Europe was alien to this arch-European, who did not share the French or British association of overseas empire with grandeur for the nation at home. But he recognized the importance of the colonies for Germany's status among the European great powers. And by summoning the conference he registered something more: the impatience of his compatriots to play a role around the world. If even a skeptical conservative felt the need to cross horizons, something had changed in German politics.

The change comes into fuller view if we recall the historical conscious-ness of middle-class Germans. They regarded themselves as latecomers without the secure historical rise of their Western neighbors; they looked back to their own past as a tragic one in which the religious wars following the Reformation divided and impoverished the German-speaking lands while Britain by the end of the seventeenth century was setting out on its path to commercial fortune at home and conquest overseas. It deepened the Germans' sense of grievance to recall that France under Louis XIV be-came the invader of German territories and the model for court life and cultivation throughout Europe. Late nineteenth-century German profes-sors and politicians still felt that theirs was the *verspätete Nation* or late-comer nation compared to the Atlantic powers.

German anxieties only deepened during the first half of the nineteenth century, when the devastation of the Napoleonic wars was succeeded by economic crisis. The decades from 1815 to 1848 were a time of hunger on the land, modest means for most people of property and education, and decline in traditional crafts and trades, which were overpopulated and outmoded by burgeoning industrialization. Even before the outbreak in 1848 of revolutions from Berlin to Vienna, the mood of the 1840s was one of foreboding, filled with worries about revolution and a descent into chaos.[1] Before and after that crisis year, Germans were engaged in a fierce debate over how to unite their independent principalities into a modern nation-state, a question that was only resolved by Prussia's victories over Austria in 1866 and France in 1870–71. The wars of unification had the effect of shaking people out of their provincial identities and—despite on-going local patriotism, as well as class and religious divisions—creating larger national perspectives. Only after resolution of the national ques-tion did Germany's educated elite turn its collective attention overseas. As Sebastian Conrad has pointed out, we should not think of Germany's newfound worldliness as just finding an outlet in its own empire.[2] Since the eighteenth century, individual Germans had done business and set-tled and traveled in the empires of other countries, emigrating in large numbers to the United States and South America; wheeling and dealing in China, India, and remote Pacific islands; and serving on scientific expe-ditions to the far reaches of the earth.[3] This heightened attention turned into a national intoxication with worldwide expansion after Wilhelm II came to the throne in 1890 and set his "new course" for German foreign policy. Fanfare over colonies, indignation over French and British refusals to grant Germany its place in the sun, opportunities to escape the tightly organized class society at home and seek a better life abroad—all of these were elements of Germany's leap into imperial adventures.

An imperial fever gripped Germany's educated elite. By the late nineteenth century, German scholars and scientists were confident in the superiority of their universities, which included the three great research institutions of Berlin, Leipzig, and Munich as well as a network of smaller institutions and neighboring universities, which functioned as part of the same system, in Switzerland and Austria (above all the University of Vienna, another great research university). They had not been planned as gathering places for cosmopolitan information; their main historical purpose was to train civil servants for largely landlocked state governments. Suddenly in the late nineteenth century, academics could turn outward as never before and occupy global fields of knowledge.[4] The famous German social scientist Max Weber illustrates the transition. He grew up receiving a gymnasium education in Berlin with a heavy emphasis on the Greek and Roman classics; his first major work was a study of the economy of ancient Rome. As a young scholar on the make, trained in economics and law, he made a splash with a study of Germany's rural laboring class, a critical topic at a time of transition from an agrarian to an industrial economy. But in later years he turned his attention outward and produced comparative studies of Chinese, Hindu, Islamic, and ancient Jewish society. The world was now his social science laboratory. He could only conduct his comparisons because a generation of German scholars had gone beyond the bounds of Europe and become serious scholars of societies from the Mediterranean to East Asia. By 1914, German university scholarship was global scholarship. Or rather, global scholarship—which existed in many European countries—took on a German university cast of objective scientific knowledge, with a special emphasis on massive accumulation of facts, critical attention to sources and methodology, and the formation of specialized disciplines.[5]

With the research university as its chief setting, the German reception of music from around the world took on a distinctly academic character. Germans did not have the advantages of a global metropolis and long-established colonies; they could not examine instruments pouring in from imperial outposts in India as could Ellis and Hipkins, nor could they talk to a comparable stream of officers and administrators returning from colonial service. But they had a critical community and habits of institution-building that furthered the systematic accumulation of knowledge in newly founded departments and institutes. It was no accident that Franz

Boas became an institution builder for modern anthropology—including the study of music—in the United States after receiving his university education in Germany and working in the Berlin Ethnological Museum; he arrived fully confident in the superiority of his scholarship and was self-assured in assembling a discipline, founding departments, training students, and directing research expeditions. The study of world music grew in Germany with the same yen for high standards and lasting institutions that Boas brought to his new home across the Atlantic.[6]

Professor Stumpf Meets Nuskilusta

On November 18, 1885, Professor Carl Stumpf went to a concert by nine Bella Coola Indians at the Geographic Society of Halle, Germany.[7] The meeting took place in the same year as Ellis's lecture on the diversity of scales. The following year, Stumpf published an account of his experience with the Bella Coolas—or Nuxalks, as they call themselves—that became one of the founding documents of comparative musical studies.[8] Like Ellis, Stumpf wrote with methodological self-consciousness, scrupulously recording his own process of discovery, so that we can look back today and situate his enquiry in its contemporary cultural context.

At the time of the encounter, Stumpf was a thirty-seven-year-old professor of philosophy on his way to a brilliant career; the novelist Robert Musil and the philosopher Edmund Husserl would be among his students, and he would become one of the founders of experimental psychology.[9] Like many educated Germans of his generation, Stumpf was devoted to classical music. To his ears—attuned to works like the Bach B minor mass, which he heard shortly after attending a Bella Coola performance—the Native Americans' singing that evening was cacophony. The music making was part of a dance show, and the racket was enormous: the performers stamped with both feet at once to an ongoing drumbeat, and there were other distractions too, like a rattle and enormous animal masks, with the music growing louder and the notes harder to tell apart, as the performers danced and sang.[10] The performance first impinged on Stumpf's ears as noise.

Most Germans would have been happy to forget the experience and go back to their Bach. But Stumpf was a curious, patient man who wanted to bring his love of music into his work. So he went to Captain Adrian Jacobsen and his brother Fillip, who had brought the Bella Coolas from British Columbia to Europe, and asked them for help: could they provide him with an Indian who would sing the music again for him? The show-men were willing to let the professor spend time with Nuskilusta, who often lulled himself to sleep in the evening by thinking up new songs.[11]

Stumpf's request to the Jacobsen brothers is a reminder that his en-counter with the Nuxalks was an incident in the worldwide business of producing ethnographic shows. The entrepreneur-impresario behind the Jacobsens was the celebrated Carl Hagenbeck (1844–1913), who cre-ated, in the memorable phrase of the historian Eric Ames, an "empire of entertainments."[12] Hagenbeck took over his father's already flourishing animal trade in 1866. The moment for expanding the Hamburg business could hardly have been more fortunate. Germany was in the midst of the tremendous growth that was turning it into one of the world's three eco-nomic great powers along with Britain and the United States. The mood was particularly ebullient after Prussia's 1866 victory over Austria. Glob-alization and imperialism were the novel conditions for building this kind of global commercial empire. Hagenbeck's publicist and biographer, Heinrich Leutemann, wrote that this entertainment empire was made possible by the new technological means of globalization: "'Only in the now highly developed system of railways and shipping lines, in connec-tion with the telegraph and everything else that makes commerce flow today—only in this system was Hagenbeck in a position to plan and carry out these activities.'"[13] But technology would not have carried him across mountains and deserts without the personnel and military force of colonizers. Hagenbeck searched through numerous colonial empires–American, British, Danish, and Dutch, according to Ames—from Africa to India, from the German-controlled market of Sudan to the steppes of Siberia and Mongolia—for animals to supply the rapidly growing number of German zoos. European and indigenous hunters, colonial administra-tions, paid local agents, and travelers all participated in bringing the ani-mals back to Europe. Even though Germany had not yet begun to acquire its own colonial possessions, Hagenbeck was one of those Germans who worked fluently through foreign empires to give his business its bound-less scope.[14]

From the dozens of actors in the Hagenbeck empire, Adrian Jacobsen rose to become a legend in his own right as an importer of exotic people and ethnographic objects. A sailor from the remote, impoverished north of Norway who came to Hamburg in search of work in 1874, Jacobsen was hired by Hagenbeck in 1877 to "import a group of Inuits from Greenland." Business conditions turned from ebullient to frustrating in Germany after the stock market crash of 1873; Hagenbeck responded by adding shows of "natives" to his business. As Ames emphasizes, he rivaled the scientists of the time in his search for authenticity: he wanted his people collectors to gather ethnographic objects and whatever else could duplicate their original setting. Jacobsen turned out to be a skillful businessman who negotiated with reluctant Danish authorities as well as missionaries, and with the Inuits themselves, to bring six Inuits back to Europe in 1877. They went on a successful tour of German cities and Paris, Brussels, and Copenhagen before returning safely to Greenland in mid-July 1878 with large earnings and gifts. Ames reports that in Hamburg alone, "more than 44,000 people attended the shows on Easter weekend." In 1880 Jacobsen recruited a new group of Greenland Inuits, but this time the tour ended in disaster. After performing in Hamburg, Berlin, Prague, Frankfurt am Main, Darmstadt, Krefeld, and Paris, they fell ill and died of smallpox in January 1881. This tragedy shook up Jacobsen but hardly slowed down the circulation of people and objects—and their crossover into the burgeoning empire of ethnographic museums in Germany. Adolf Bastian, the first director of the Ethnological Museum in Berlin, "had already commissioned the Inuit performers to create objects for the museum during their visit. Now he expressed interest in acquiring the show's collection of artifacts"; and he hired Jacobsen to bring back more artifacts.[15]

Jacobsen's expeditions reveal how different actors pulled together to make a global network. Jacobsen himself came from the fringes of Europe. He was one of those knowledge brokers who through birth or upbringing knew how to profit from working both sides of colonial frontiers. Many different parties could make life difficult: missionaries and administrators might be brutal toward their charges, but they were jealous and paternalistic when he came as a recruiter on his first foray, only releasing a small number of Inuits after negotiating the conditions for their wages, working conditions, and return. The Inuits themselves were skeptical recruits who bargained hard on their own behalf. After the success of the first ensemble, others were eager to follow; they made their own decision to go abroad despite the loneliness and health risks. Jacobsen could not bully the Moravian missionaries or Danish officials; working in the Arctic, he was dependent on them for his physical survival. It would be a historical fantasy to imagine that an entrepreneur like Jacobsen could magically whisk away performers and hope to find further recruits on a second visit.[16]

When the Nuxalks came to Halle, Stumpf met with Nuskilusta for four days, an hour or two each time. A patient teacher, Nuskilusta sang slowly, without emotion, in a soft and light voice. Stumpf's first step, he recounted in his article, was to listen to the melody without writing it down in order to get a feel for the melodic and rhythmic structure. Regardless of the pitch, he then transposed it into C major or A minor, keys without sharps or flats, so that he could work more quickly and get down the sequence of notes without worrying about rhythm markings. Even though Stumpf was a keen listener who could usually write up music as soon as he heard it, he needed for Nuskilusta to sing the beginning of a song repeatedly—ten times or more—in order to be able to reproduce the notes with the correct rhythmic markings. As an additional check, Stumpf would have him sing it again on another day. According to European prejudice, Nuxalk music was supposed to be simple; by transcribing it, Stumpf got a feel for its complexity.[17]

The experience made Stumpf suspicious. Plenty of travelers to exotic places had transcribed local music, but they made no mention of the difficulties of writing it down. How carefully had they listened?

Just three years earlier, in 1882, an American named Theodore Baker had published a book containing thirty-two transcriptions of Native American songs. It was admirable, conscientious work, thought Stumpf, that did not indulge in speculation. Instead, Baker stuck to the important thing: he just wrote it down. (Stumpf was not yet worried about the problems of notation that had led S. M. Tagore into controversy and which later created unease among ethnomusicologists.)[18] Baker was an inspired outsider who had worked as an organist, attended MIT for a year, worked in a Boston business, and moved to a farm in Olympia, Washington, before traveling to Europe and enrolling at the University of Leipzig in 1878. He took his research a step further than Stumpf would do, traveling in the summer of 1880 to the Senecas in Upstate New York and sitting in on their harvest celebrations. Then he took aside one of the more accomplished singers, who performed fifty or sixty songs for him. Nor did Baker stop there: his next field trip took him to the Training School for Indian Youth in Carlisle, Pennsylvania, where he gathered more songs.[19] He was a dedicated researcher, and writing down the songs raised an important question. Did Indians recognize a scale like the Western scale? After careful consideration, he was sure that they did. He checked the notes by singing the melodies himself after listening to his informants. Their singing, he emphasized twice, was clean on the mark with Western intervals.[20]

But that was exactly what Stumpf did *not* find.

Instead, Nuskilusta sang notes that by Western standards were impure, for they fell between the notes of the Western scale. He sang the same unusual notes again and again at the same spots, and when another singer substituted for Nuskilusta, he too sang the in-between notes. These microtones were what Baker had failed to discern. Stumpf used an *x* and an *o* to indicate notes placed a fraction higher or lower than Western notes, a makeshift solution that pointed to the difficulties of hearing and transcribing non-Western music.

After his four days with Nuskilusta, Stumpf went back for another public Bella Coola performance. This time he was a more competent listener. When the troupe performed songs he had worked on with Nuskilusta, he could begin to appreciate what he was listening to. The noise of the first night had turned into melody.

Collaborators, Technologies, Methods

At first sight it looks easy to cross into Nuskilusta's world. One just had to take the time, as Stumpf did, to listen. But why, then, did Stumpf succeed where Baker and previous generations had failed? Part of the answer is that Stumpf's breakthrough required collaborators. He did not just work alone with Nuskilusta; a network of like-minded people informed his account of the experience.

From the far side of North America, in Metlakatla, British Columbia, an Anglican bishop named William Ridley offered on-location impressions of Pacific Northwest Indians and their music. He had a difficult and, in the end, tragic assignment. Another missionary, William Duncan, had turned into a utopian sect leader. The church sent Ridley out from England to lead the Tsimshian mission in Metlakatla back to religious law and order. He tried. Most of the locals left with Duncan for a place in Alaska they once again named Metlakatla; Ridley hung on with the remaining Tsimshians, learning their language and translating the Gospels into it. In 1904 his wooden church burned down—some suspected arson by Duncan supporters—and he returned to England.[21]

Somehow Stumpf learned about Ridley's work and wrote to ask him about native music. Ridley wrote back with the fervor of a man who loved his charges and knew their music intimately. He spoke confidently about the different peoples of the region. Every tribe had its war and funeral songs, he wrote, with music that superbly fit the occasion. The performer at funerals was usually a poet who modified his song to fit the character of the deceased. Every chief had his own song, which was passed down to the next chief and was the sign of his rank to any approaching stranger. (Ridley noted that it was almost impossible to persuade Indians to perform their funeral songs outside an actual burial; as a result, Stumpf could appreciate that it was unusually forthcoming of Nuskilusta to sing one for him, something that he might have been more reluctant to do at home.) Overall, concluded Ridley, Indians had a highly developed capacity for music, and not just their own: they were quick to learn Western music, which they preferred for church services. He made it clear to Stumpf that Nuskilusta belonged to a whole culture of able musicians among the Nuxalks and their neighbors.[22]

To ease his entry into Nuskilusta's world, Stumpf could turn to Boas, just twenty-eight when his article was published. Working at the Berlin Ethnological Museum at the time, Boas was responsible for organizing Northwest Indian artifacts brought by Jacobsen. The artwork of peoples like the Kwakiutls and the Haidas fascinated him; he developed a lifelong interest in these peoples and their neighbors, including the Nuxalks. In 1886 Boas was in Berlin at the right moment to attend a show by Nuskilusta and his fellow performers; he transcribed two songs, one used to accompany a game with sticks and the other to accompany ceremonial gift exchanges. He had already begun learning Chinook Wawa, the widespread trade language of the area, getting far enough to read a paper on it to the Berlin anthropological association. With this knowledge he translated the texts of some of Nuskilusta's songs for Stumpf.[23]

While Boas helped with the words, a fortunate coincidence opened Stumpf's path toward microtones: Alexander Ellis mailed Stumpf an offprint of his talk "On the Musical Scales of Various Nations," which he had delivered to the Society of Arts eight months before Stumpf heard the Nuxalks in Halle. Stumpf published a lengthy review of Ellis's essay; it appeared in the same journal issue as his article on the Bella Coolas. His review praised the "rich, original contents" of Ellis's lecture and its value for historical and psychological studies. Until Ellis, wrote Stumpf, researchers had relied mainly on the comments of theorists, which did not necessarily correspond to musical practice. As for travelers, even if they had above-average knowledge of European music, they could only capture the rough outline of foreign musical systems. Ellis, by contrast, delivered exact measurements of intonation. Stumpf called the results "a priceless foundation for reliable knowledge of the actually used scales and therewith also for the psychological-historical study of their origins."[24] He himself could rely on the vocabulary and empirical findings of Ellis's essay as context for his own account of the Nuxalk concert.

There was one more group that Stumpf depended on: the Nuxalks themselves. Stumpf tells one story about a lesson learned from the entire ensemble: When he asked Nuskilusta and the other performers to sing a song from their games, they looked at each other and laughed until at last one of them explained that they had thousands of songs.[25] Perhaps an answer with its own patronizing touch toward the earnest German philosopher? At least Stumpf was honest enough to record this along with many other details of his encounter. What it hinted at was a culture that he could hardly grasp through his interest in scales and pitch.

The subsequent research trips of Boas and, in the 1920s, of the Cambridge-trained Canadian anthropologist T. F. McIlwraith began to reveal the interweaving of natural setting, religion, and social order in Nuxalk music. Boas made this clear in his later account of the astonishing beauty of the Nuxalks' territory in British Columbia. To reach it, he had first to cross a wild plateau and walk to a mountain summit; after hiking past a few small snowfields, he could see Bella Coola River almost five thousand feet below. On the opposite side of the valley rose the high peak Nuskulst, "which plays a most important part in the mythology of the Bella Coola," flanked by glaciers and other beautiful mountains. It took another day for Boas's party to descend and enter a Bella Coola village.[26] McIlwraith and subsequent researchers learned that this landscape was "dense with sacred meaning." According to the editors of McIlwraith's field letters, Nuxalk "ancestors' names, their associated cloaked forms, and their places of landing and settlement form an eternal and inalienable unity. Throughout their lives people inherit ancestral names and associated prerogatives, place names, and histories. These names must be validated before witnesses at potlatches and then released to succeeding generations upon the deaths of their temporal custodians."[27] While Nuxalk society was greatly diminished by the 1880s—the number of tribe members had shrunk from perhaps 2,910 before first contact in 1797 to 402 by 1868—it was still possible in the early twentieth century to reconstruct something of the internal complexity of its music. Nuxalks used it in ceremonial events where they competed for status and wealth; two secret societies made use of the music at their gatherings. In addition to reinforcing social status, it served as a medium between Nuxalks and their animal and other guardian spirits. Tribe members also sang love songs, gambling songs, and animal songs to attract game during hunting and fishing and communicate with it. Their professional class of musicians rehearsed carefully for ritual events (at which errors could lead to severe sanctions) and performed with a division of labor between leader, chorus, announcer, and a prompter who whispered words to the announcer. Stumpf could not yet begin to imagine the meaning of music that was not an isolated form of artistic expression but was deeply embedded in its makers' total way of life.[28]

Despite its limitations, Stumpf's work was a breakthrough in understanding as a result of both its discovery of microtones and its auto-ethnography of the path from prejudice to widened perception. It benefited from an eclectic assortment of collaborators: a recent PhD, a missionary, a sea captain, a young academic, and the musicians themselves. Collaborators do not just appear, however; somehow you have to get in touch with them. This was not unthinkable in earlier times. Europeans had for centuries been used to exchanging letters, and during the Enlightenment, intellectuals in Paris and London had correspondents scattered around the world. But the improvements of the industrial era accelerated communications. Jacobsen and the nine Nuxalks traveled by train across North America, by steamship across the Atlantic, and by train again to Halle. A hundred years earlier, the trip from the Pacific Coast around Cape Horn would have taken them through tropical heat and antipodean cold, the kind of adventure that aged travelers if they survived it at all; modern transportation turned it into a tourist's vacation. After arriving in Europe, the musicians would once have had to travel on mottled roads to reach a provincial town like Halle; the train turned it into an easy stop. When an eighteenth-century traveler like Captain Cook brought a Tahitian to London, it was a sensational event that turned the heads of royalty and high society; a century later, non-Europeans were regular visitors. Stumpf mentioned Zulu performers who visited Halle in 1885 (alas, their handler was not as forthcoming as Jacobsen), Nubians in Halle, and a Sudanese group that performed at the Dresden Zoo. With his own ears, supplemented by reports from other scientific observers including Ellis, Stumpf could compare live singers from different parts of the world in a way that would have been unlikely at any earlier moment in human history. Living encounters once reserved for a handful of world travelers were now part of the fare of popular entertainment for small-town Germans.

Cultivation, Cosmopolitanism, Science

Stumpf's essay combined scientific method with humanist learning and cosmopolitan openness. It took an unusual personality to bring these qualities to bear on indigenous music. Perhaps it helped that Stumpf started out at a distance from metropolitan society. He was born in the hamlet of Wiesentheid in 1848, and grew up after 1863 in the small town of Aschaffenburg. Both were in Franconia, which was politically incorporated into Bavaria but maintained a regional identity looking back to its prosperous era in the Reformation and turbulent decades as one of the theaters of the Thirty Years' War. By the nineteenth century the region was, like Carl Engel's north German home, a sleepy place where an older tradition of learning hung on at a remove from the full blast of industrialization and political unification.

Stumpf grew up with the natural authority of a member of the local educated elite. Looking back in an autobiographical sketch of 1924, he recalled that on the paternal side his father was a physician and his grandfather was a historian of Bavaria, while his father's "two brothers were also active as academics, publishing work on statistics, biography, and forestry." His mother's family "included a remarkable number of doctors," among them his great-grandfather Adelmann, "a forensic physician" who "had studied eighteenth-century French literature as well as Kant and Schelling."[29] Both parents were musical; he took full advantage of the offerings at home and the "excellent opportunities" for musical education in Franconia. Starting violin when he was seven, he learned five other instruments, and began composing when he was ten. He arrived at university, he commented, "with more love for music than scholarship."[30] That is hard to imagine, for he plunged himself into a challenging course of studies in physics and philosophy, receiving his doctorate in 1868. After a detour into theology and a brief stint in a Catholic seminary in 1869 and 1870, he returned to philosophy and wrote his second qualifying work, the habilitation, at the University of Göttingen. In 1873, at the unusually young age of twenty-five, he was appointed professor of philosophy at the University of Würzburg in his native Franconia.[31]

By the time Stumpf entered university in the 1860s, the age of German Idealism had come to an end. The great philosophers of the late eighteenth and early nineteenth century—Kant and his successors Fichte, Schelling, and Hegel—were well informed about the natural science of their day and developed their own philosophical systems in response to it. But they rejected any confusion of philosophy and natural science and instead emphasized the autonomy of human mind for the production of valid knowledge, ethics, and taste. In particular, they repudiated the notion of any psychological conditions on philosophical conceptions of truth, whether in the transmission of impressions from the external world to the human mind or in the receptive faculties of the human mind itself.[32] But by mid-century the conditions of higher learning had changed. German industry began its takeoff after the failure of the Revolutions of 1848, a process that accelerated throughout the 1850s and 1860s and provided the muscle for political unification culminating in the formation of the German Empire in 1871.[33] In intellectual life there was a new boldness about investigating the human psyche as an empirical phenomenon, a path of inquiry that was no longer marginalized as illegitimate or vulgar compared to philosophy, but moved to the center of academic inquiry with claims on laboratories, personnel, and academic appointments. The novel attention to empirical psychology became one of the prominent features of fin de siècle culture. Wilhelm Wundt's establishment of the first psychology laboratory at the University of Leipzig made a great impression on his contemporaries at home and abroad, stimulating them to develop rival laboratories. The fiction writing of the era, too, began an exploration of human stream of consciousness, turning characters from embodiments of fixed traits into bearers of a fluid surface of impressions.[34]

Stumpf combined an ongoing dedication to philosophy with an early interest in empirical psychology. He approached psychological phenomena in two ways. One was introspection, the examination of the data of experience given in one's own consciousness. This was a procedure analogous to the novelist's rendering of stream of consciousness based on personal experience, though Stumpf worked with a commitment to scientific principles of empirical veracity, public debate, and conceptualization of data. His first major work, The Psychology of Tone (published in 1893 as the start of a projected five-volume series, though he got no further than a second volume), was precisely such a work of introspection. Although it operated completely within the bounds of self-examination, it did so with a novel scrutiny of objects of subjective experience. Stumpf was staking out his distinctive territory between empirical analysis and reflection on its larger philosophical implications.[35]

Stumpf continued this navigation between the empirical and the philosophical with a series of experiments that required laboratory conditions and research assistants. The very title of his book, Tonpsychologie, partially echoed but also suggested a challenge to Helmholtz's *Lehre von der Tonempfindung*, signaling a shift in focus away from physiological sensation (*Empfindung*). As we have seen, Helmholtz proposed a three-part model for understanding it: physical, physiological, and psychological. Tone originated in the sound waves produced by a vibrating object; it impinged on the inner ear and set off an analogous process of oscillation; this physiological reception had in turn to be processed as an object of personal experience. With his firm sense of disciplinary limits, Helmholtz restricted his analysis primarily to the physical and physiological moments in the creation of tone. He was mainly interested in proving that the mental comparison of primary tone and overtones created a rational foundation for perceptions of harmony and the organization of tones into scales. While his book also made ingenious observations on the historicity of scales, it did not systematically investigate how the perception of consonance and dissonance formed in individuals. The examination of subjective perceptions was Stumpf's point of entry into tone, and his approach was the opposite of Helmholtz's. Instead of following out a causal sequence originating in the physical production of sound, Stumpf began at the other end, with the fact of tone perception. What did individuals hear? Stumpf began with his personal experience as a pianist: he heard a chord not as a series of separate notes, but as a single sound. He called this perception fusion, the melding of the different notes into one in individual consciousness. From this starting point, he went on to develop a series of experiments designed to refute Helmholtz's notion of a fitting together of primary tones and overtones. He tested listeners' perceptions with tuning forks that were poor in overtones, and found that this reduction did not affect listeners' impression of dissonance. Stumpf separated the sounds of notes going into the two ears with the help of tubes, so that no layering of sound waves took place in the air or the ear—yet, in the absence of physical proximity, impressions of dissonance or consonance continued to arise. A physical explanation did not suffice; an independent level of psychological activity had to account for perceptions of dissonance and consonance.[36]

As Mitchell Ash has shown, Stumpf was developing a program for the investigation of structured wholes in psychological perception. This line of inquiry simultaneously demanded measurement of the objects of perception and conceptualization of patterns of meaning. Stumpf's balanced strategy, with its quantification of empirical evidence and imaginative grasp of totalities, made his teaching an important starting point for the cluster of his students who founded Gestalt psychology.[37] Stumpf himself found one early application of his approach in his study of the Nuxalks. Here was sound that he as well as his contemporaries first heard as noise, the category we have already encountered in Ellis's struggle to comprehend Chinese music. It took not just speculation, but an active questioning of the Nuxalks as human subjects, to discern the patterns of their music, which were cohesive and complex in ways not apparent to European ears. *Both* parts of Stumpf's program had to be observed in order for it to be successful. Well-meaning sympathy toward the Nuxalks would not have gotten him far; it took several hours of sessions with Nuskilusta and his fellow singers for him to recognize their singing as moving through the unfamiliar intervals of scales using microtones. The fieldwork was a crude start; its interviews were brief, and probably took place with the aid of an inadequate translator. But this first step was large enough to yield a gain in comprehension.

Stumpf's subsequent science of non-Western musical systems, and that of his disciples, built on the methodological foundation laid by Ellis's essay on the diversity of musical scales. As Stumpf took it up, Ellis's distinctive achievements involved a turn to musical *practice*. Ellis was not the first, he noted, to analyze foreign musics by using their instruments. In the early nineteenth century, François-Joseph Fétis had pioneered original instrument performance and experimentation with non-European instruments. But his description of the scales after studying the construction of the instruments did not always match Ellis's results. Stumpf also called attention to the critical role of Hipkins in determining the pitch of instruments, again a nod in the direction of attention to musical practice.[38] Stumpf did not construe Ellis's mathematical reconstruction of scales narrowly, but made his readers aware that it was part of a broad-based effort to capture the texture of music in lived human experience. His ability to comment and build on Ellis is a testimony to the cosmopolitanism of late-nineteenth-century science: the unraveling of the workings of non-European musical systems was not a national achievement, but contained contributions shared between Germany and England. Ellis himself developed his musical research out of the program laid down by Helmholtz; Stumpf, in turn, recognized the advances that brought Ellis's work closer to his own psychological approach. Stumpf's students would expand on this continuous line of research in collecting and analysis that led to the history, sociology, and present-day practices of music around the world.

Despite their similarities, Stumpf was a philosopher with a universalizing bent that was alien to Ellis. He struck out on a separate path of philosophical speculation when he argued that psychological-historical studies might serve an inquiry into musical *origins*. At this point he and his English contemporary parted ways. Ellis was stolidly matter-of-fact. He had no interest in grand philosophical statements. As Stumpf noted, with his concluding observation that scales were not uniform or natural but very different, artificial, and arbitrary, Ellis refused "to go beyond the bounds of exact physics." Stumpf did not stop there; his philosophical ambition drove him to pursue the origins of music in the human psyche and to search for the singularity of Western compared to non-Western musical systems. Like most of his contemporaries, he derived historical significance by placing his subject in an evolutionary framework in which non-Western forms of music had more value and interest than had previously been thought, but ultimately ceded the place of honor to the modern Western harmonic system. The other musical systems, he argued, all remained attached to their mechanical origins, starting with the folding in half of strings in order to construct a scale of notes. Only Europeans had freed themselves from this dependence on the physical construction of instruments, and had created a purely intellectual system based on the inner ear, and ultimately on the discovery of the natural relationships of tones.[39]

Stumpf concluded his review essay with a return from evolutionary history to exact research, calling for more study of the growing number of exotic visitors, exact experimentation in scientific settings, and interdisciplinary cooperation. This empirical approach would lead away from speculative comparison and back in the direction of musical cultures appreciated as self-contained wholes.[40] At the beginning of the disciplinary study of music, then, Stumpf left his readers with a tension between two choices: they could pursue either the particularity of individual cultures or their enclosure in a universal evolutionary paradigm, either Ellis's detachment from cultural hierarchy or a reassertion of it closer to the norms of the late nineteenth century. He and his students would struggle for decades to come to terms with this uncertain legacy.

The Thai Performers, 1900

Fifteen years after his encounter with Nuskilusta and the Nuxalks, Stumpf had another encounter with extra-European musicians that led to an important essay. This time it was an ensemble of Thai dancers and orchestra on a world tour that stirred his scientific imagination. The best-remembered outcome of this moment was recordings of the Thai musicians, for they inaugurated the great repository of world music, the Phonogram Archive. Yet to limit Stumpf's work with the Thai performers to this product is to miss his larger purpose when he founded the archive. Stumpf set down his response to the performers in an article containing a program for the scholarly study of music. Part of the article's ingenuity is that it is not limited to the analysis of sound, but embraces music as what Marcel Mauss called a total social fact, broadly meaningful for understanding human psychology and culture as well as the nature of music in its own right.

The Nuxalk listening sessions of 1885 were a kind of first encounter for Stumpf, a moment when he strove to understand an alien form of aural expression as music. With the Thai musicians, Stumpf was no novice; he had had fifteen years to absorb Ellis and advance his own research into the psychology of listening. The quantitative measurement of scales and pitch served as the foundation for a more elaborate interpretation of the meaning of music.

Once again there was a global framework for this immediate encounter in Berlin. A Thai orchestra: how did it end up in the German capital at the beginning of the new century? In a sense, the answer is no surprise: we have already encountered the worldwide circus business of Hagenbeck, and one can easily imagine that performers of many kinds were traveling by steamer and train to distant destinations. But the Thai musicians belong to a different circuit: not the vulgar entertainment world of Hagenbeck, but a crossover zone of artistic entrepreneurship. Historians of theater and music have begun to tease out the means by which artists from the vaudeville stratum to the highbrow could try their luck on international circuits. Nic Leonhardt has pointed to the period from 1850 to 1920 for its novel networks of "agents, impresarios, managers and entrepreneurs" across the arts on a global scale. Theatrical brokers, she notes, "had a truly transnational dimension: an agent in Vienna, for example, would book acts for a circus in India, an American impresario would organize a tour of performers in South Africa, a German agent could become the representative for German playwrights in France. . . ." She reminds us of the many modern means of shortening the passage from place to place: "newspapers, professional photography," and the telegraph and telephone, as well as mechanized transportation. The theater broker, as she calls this kind of entrepreneur, emerges as an agent not just of entertainment, but of the artists who represented exotic high cultures in the metropolises of Europe.[41]

The transnational network was not just a one-way street from the colonies to the metropolis; artists moved in multiple directions. Christopher Balme has reconstructed the routes of business empire for two entrepreneurs whose ventures overlapped in India, but whose origins and destinations point to the many possibilities of building business empires. Since the early modern era, according to Balme, theater management was small-scale: theaters were often family-run, with actors doubling as entrepreneurs. By 1900 these casual arrangements had given way to the dominant role of full-time, capitalized businessmen dedicated to the formation of multinational circuits for touring artists. One of these was Maurice E. Bandmann, the Anglo-American son of a famous German-Jewish actor, Daniel Bandmann. In 1905 he set himself up in Calcutta and built an entertainment circuit that filled theaters across the British Empire, from the Mediterranean to India and East Asia. An Indian example was J. F. Madan from Bombay, a Parsi impresario who started out as an actor, made money provisioning the British army, operated playhouses and cinemas in Calcutta beginning in 1902, from there bought up theaters across India, represented the French phonograph company Pathé, and began producing films.[42] Although Calcutta was the hub of business empire for Bandmann and Madan, it was not the only starting point for the diffusion of artistic performances. MeLê yamomo has called attention to the migrant musicians from Manila who filled the entertainment halls of Asian metropolises from the late nineteenth to the mid-twentieth century. At least some of these Manilan ensembles played Western music: yamomo mentions a Manilan band that at the end of the 1890s was playing Strauss, Verdi, and Bizet in the city of Medan, Sumatra. There was movement and mixture that defied the shorthand of national identities. One Cosme Buenaventura, who had played in a Spanish military band, joined a group of Filipinos in Phnom Penh in 1869 to form the core of the military court band of King Norodom I of Cambodia. In May 1886, Giuseppe Chiarini's Circus arrived in Manila for a two-month stint; local musicians joined them for a tour of Macau and China.[43] Whether they were proffering popular or highbrow entertainment, musicians in search of work could overcome linguistic and cultural differences to team up and cross political borders. By 1900, global tours were a well-established big business.

The Thai theater company was following these emerging opportunities for global profits when it arrived in Europe. Like many musical ventures across borders, it originated in older precapitalist traditions of performance that were giving way to a global, market-based musical economy. In the late nineteenth century there was a fundamental divide in the Thai kingdom between popular and elite entertainment. Wealthy and princely households had their own performers for the private plea- sure of the household masters and their guests. At the same time, Bang- kok was filled with popular entertainment houses; Europeans could visit them and were assigned to special boxes. The performances were many- sided spectacles. Female dancers had tight-fitting, gold-embroidered jackets, epaulettes on their shoulders, long artificial fingernails, and powdered faces; they surprised Western observers with their emphasis on finger, hand, and arm movement as they narrated tales of heroes and gods. The performances were strange, but not unappealing, to two late- nineteenth-century Western travelers in Thailand, the sober Swedish naturalist Carl Bock and the sensationalizing German traveler Ernst von Hesse-Wartegg.[44]

One Thai prince, Phya Mahin, blurred the line between aristocratic spectacle and popular entertainment by opening a theater starring his own performers in commercial concerts. Hesse-Wartegg called the mu- sic of the twenty to thirty orchestra members a *Heldenlärm*, an outsized noise that practically drowned out the singing.[45] Once again, a European observer turned to a colorful expression for noise in response to an alien genre of musical expression. This kind of European reaction did not slow down Phya's son, Boosra Mahin, who took his father's company on a world tour. According to Nic Leonhardt, the journey originated in a princely invitation. In 1890 the future Tsar Nicholas II went on a voy- age around the world that included destinations in South Asia and East Asia. On his visit to Thailand in the same year, he was so impressed by the Boosra Mahin Theater that he invited the princely entrepreneur to St. Petersburg. If the ensuing tour was partly a commercial venture, it was also an act of cultural exchange: the Thai king, Chulalongkorn, who had gone on his own trip to Europe in 1897, gave his official permission for the ensemble to make its way there. Taking up the invitation, it made stops en route in Singapore, Alexandria, Vienna, Paris, and Berlin. Its impresario was one Victor Bamberger in Paris. At the beginning of August the troupe performed in the large Venice pavilion of the Viennese park, the Prater, where it mixed absurdities and serious artistic performance. A Thai resident diplomat and a prince receiving officer's training were invited to the premiere (but did not attend), as were Thai students in the metropolis. The show itself featured traditional Thai "dance, music and theatrical scenes, all referring to Siamese traditional stories and costumes." For its next stop after Vienna, Bamberger arranged for performances in the Zoological Garden, the large park and entertainment site in the center of Berlin. From Berlin the company finally traveled to St. Petersburg. Its performers impressed the Russian dance world and were an inspiration for Nijinsky's *La danse siamoise*, which was performed at the Paris Opera in 1910.[46] The tour was, then, an amalgam of aristocratic display, officially sanctioned cultural mission, and public amusement.

Stumpf does not relate whether as a German professor—now one of the eminences of the University of Berlin—he felt comfortable amid the holiday atmosphere of the city's Zoological Garden. But he seems to have enjoyed what was, as he emphasized, above all a dance performance. Women danced while men made up the orchestra. The splendor, harmony, and subtlety of the women's clothes won his praise, as did their strange but astonishingly varied, daring, original, and expressive hand movements, which he called without peer on the Western stage. His article on the Thai performance, published the year after the visit, focused on its musical dimension.[47] His point of departure was a critical examination of Ellis. At the simplest level, he wished to check Ellis's measurements of the Thai scale; and he concluded that they were accurate. This straightforward initial aim also opened up wide-ranging questions about how to attain valid knowledge of another culture and, in turn, about that knowledge's philosophical and social-scientific significance.

Stumpf's essay is a reminder that he was venturing out at an early moment of scientific inquiry into extra-European music. He made little steps and sober conclusions, alert as he proceeded to methodological sources of error. Ellis had reported that the Thai scale consisted of seven equal steps; Stumpf was not convinced. The evidence did not seem to sustain a conclusion that he found important but paradoxical. Ellis had relied on his examination of two Thai instruments and the statement of a Thai diplomatic envoy. But the envoy could only repeat a theory that did not necessarily correspond to practice. Stumpf had to hear the music for himself.[48]

To test Ellis's conclusions, Stumpf described the instruments, measured their scale, speculated about the scale's origins, interviewed Thai musicians, and worked with his own aides. He walked his readers through his methods of testing intervals and pitch. To begin with, he described the orchestra's xylophones (ranats), gongs (khongs), flutes, drums, and cymbal, recommending to readers an illustration showing the xylophones and gong chimes in Hipkins's *Musical Instruments*.[49] Next, he went into measurements of the tones of each instrument, which he took with the help of an Appunn tonometer. This was a tuning fork set of 120 pieces, encompassing the octave from 400 to 800 oscillations: forks measured two oscillations apart between 400 and 480, three between 480 and 600, and five apart from 600 to 800. Recognizing that the pitch of the forks was never completely exact, he had two assistants independently test them against other forks and compare each tuning fork with its neighbors. He also combed European accounts going back to the late seventeenth century for impressions of Thai music.[50] Within the limits of what could be done with mechanical tools and written description, he checked and cross-checked his results.

An important source of error had already been discovered by Ellis but continued to creep into the results of later researchers. Ellis had been puzzled by the tuning of two Thai instruments in the Kensington Museum. As soon as he could get his hands on the instruments used by a visiting ensemble, he found that the museum pieces were out of tune. Nonetheless, contemporaries continued to rely on museum instruments uncritically. With his indefatigable pursuit of accuracy, Stumpf related one case of scientific neglect that he could refute by going back to the evidence. Richard Wallaschek, who was teaching musicology in Berlin, had taken measurements of Thai ranats in Berlin without noticing that they were supposed to have lumps of wax on the undersides, some of which had fallen off. Examining khongs used by Wallaschek in his monograph *Primitive Music* (checking the inventory numbers to be sure they were the same ones), Stumpf went back to the Berlin originals and found the account of their pitch to be impossibly erroneous. "I regret this all the more," added Stumpf, "since Herr Wallaschek undertook the entire investigation at my suggestion. Because I was pressed for time, I had to limit my participation to lending him the acoustic measuring tools (Tonmesser), but I remember explicitly warning him about possible defects in the instruments."[51] The right procedure, Stumpf concluded, was to go to instruments in use. It was an anecdote with a wide reach: in general, nineteenth-century European scholars and scientists had little hesitation about relying on secondhand materials removed from immediate experience. Texts drawn from high literary traditions were readily taken to be accurate distillations of cultures from abroad or from the distant European past. In this case, instruments were treated to scientific measurement without regard for the vagaries of material decay and incorrect performance practice.

Taking accurate measurements sounded straightforward, but in practice it took a methodological self-consciousness that culminated in the principle of relying on musical practice, not theory or instruments at one remove from the hands and ears of concert musicians. The result of Stumpf's investigations was a confirmation of Ellis: the Thai instruments did indeed form octaves in even steps, and corresponded to other instruments in the Thai repertoire. The scale tested by Stumpf was an even-toned octave with seven steps. To his European ear, the result was clear and bewildering: the distinction between whole and half-steps disappeared; what replaced it was steps that came between European intervals. As Stumpf described it in Western terms, major and minor thirds as well as major and minor sixths and sevenths gave way to neutral thirds, sixths, and sevenths. The fourth was higher, the fifth lower. "Not one of our intervals is present," he added, "neither purely in itself nor tempered within our acceptable range."[52] This was, of course, a translation of the Thai scale into a foreign language in which it made no sense; it was as if an English-language speaker had reported astonishment over the German placement of verbs at the end of sentences. But by doing so, he made a point for his readers: the Thai scale was the architecture of a foreign musical cosmos.

Stumpf forcefully met a potential objection: Could the Thai musicians really construct a scale with such precise divisions? His reply to such skepticism was to register his admiration for the exactness of the Thai musicians' ear, and his doubt that European musicians could match their tuning precision. Ellis had actually tested different instruments—pianos, an organ, and a harmonium—that had been tuned in the Broadwood factory, and he had discovered significant variations. By contrast, the Thai musicians reached their high level of accuracy without any kind of instrument to guide them, working solely from their impression of the successive tones. Of course, there were better and worse Thai musicians. Ellis used two xylophones that belonged to good artists, but their deviations were great enough to make Stumpf doubt the principle of the evenly spaced scale and presume that the Thais were simply using the steps of the European scale carelessly. But his own measurements proved otherwise. They led to an unexpected conclusion: the foreign scale was not a degenerate form of the familiar, but something unimpeachably different.[53]

Stumpf concluded his essay with a call for the study of music as a window onto the history of mankind. "Whoever considers the dominant place of music in primitive cultural conditions, the variety of its forms, the astonishing similarities and differences, whoever considers its connections with the most general questions of the origins and forms of human civilization, with the development and spread of the human race, needs no proof of the importance of researching extra-European music for the general ethnology and history of the human species."[54] This was an evolutionary plea in the long trail of the nineteenth century: history for Stumpf meant a universal ascent from primitive origins to modern civilization. As in his study of the Nuxalks, Stumpf remained poised between sympathetic insight into non-European cultures and a hierarchical vision that placed them on a scale leading up to modern Europe. He could appreciate the skill of Thai musicians, he could hear the originality of their musical forms and challenge the provinciality of his readers, but he then dropped his methodological strictures and hinted at a speculative evolutionary history. The rest of the passage continued to waver back and forth.[55]

With greater prudence he observed that the science of exotic music, as he called it, was still in its infancy. Above all, he added, it required reliable materials. Countless travel accounts recorded uselessly superficial impressions; notations were of doubtful quality. Ellis had laid the foundation for the scientific study of foreign scales. But now one ought to equip scientific travelers, missionaries, and other Europeans abroad with tuning forks and the rudimentary know-how for accurate recordings. Travelers should make recordings, although, he added, one should not underestimate the difficulties of using the phonograph, starting with the need to ensure constant turning speed. They would face the challenge of developing a transcription system that would accurately convey the qualities of the original. In addition, scholar-scientists would have to go to all the concerts of exotic music that were now available to them in Europe.[56]

This was the rudimentary sketch of a program for a new science. Ellis had had no such thing in mind: he was a mathematician and a humane observer who had spotted a specific problem, the measurement of scales, and considered his work done once he presented his conclusions. Stumpf took Ellis's work as his starting point, and with his usual methodological rigor he reviewed its integrity before trying to build on it. But the greater edifice he had in mind was a cultural science of music. That was the task he embraced, first in feeling his way in his essay on the Nuxalks, and then with a mature sense of purpose in his study of the Thai musicians.

Heterophonies

With his curiosity about European harmony, Stumpf wondered how a Thai musician might perceive it. To test this, he invited one of the orchestra members to his home and asked him to judge various chords on the piano. An attaché to the Thai mission, named Nai Chorn Nond Buri, served as translator. Minor chords were consistently called unpleasant, major chords pleasant. But beyond this, when Stumpf played two strings on the violin simultaneously, the musician remarked that he preferred hearing them in succession, which he was more used to. Hearing thirds did not give him pleasure, even though he was familiar with them as part of European music, which he had heard aplenty in Vienna and at home. When Stumpf played some Thai themes with a simple harmonization, the musician responded: "Not bad, but too many tones."[57] From a Thai perspective, Western consonance was discernible but not an aesthetic revelation.

From a European perspective, Thai music had a stylistic feature that was confusing, irritating or maddening: its ensemble members played different melodies or variations on the same melody that seemed simply to go off in different directions without the recognizable harmonic connections of Western music. For this jarring (to Western ears) contention of parts, Stumpf proposed the name heterophony.[58]

Perhaps it was this feature of Thai music that made the Swedish naturalist Carl Bock hear only noise. The Dutch musical scholar respected by Ellis and Stumpf, J. P. N. Land, thought it resulted in "a sort of barbarous harmony, which has, however, its lucid moments, when the beautiful tone of the instruments yields a wonderful effect." As for Ellis, on listening to the Thai orchestra he was baffled: "Although many instruments were played together, there was no harmony in our sense of the word. Either all the instruments played in unison, or one, generally with the highest and most evanescent tone, flourished away between the notes, regardless apparently of what the other instruments were doing, but falling into unison sufficiently to show that it was playing a part in the same music." In a rare aesthetic judgment, he called the voice accompaniment "so dreadfully, and apparently intentionally, unmusical, that it could not enter into our examination."[59] Even Ellis's tolerance had its limits. The Thai orchestra lay somewhere on the other side, in a zone of unintelligibility.

Stumpf mentioned Land's remark about the "barbarous harmony" of the Thai orchestra as his point of departure for an extended meditation on this baffling musical form. As with the Nuxalks, he did not content himself with an immediate aesthetic response, but tried to understand it—and in this case a parallel within Western civilization readily came to his broadly educated mind: "Should we think of the music of the ancient Greeks as in some respects similar to this music from Asia? Enthusiasts will perhaps reject the suggestion with horror. But to be frank, as far as the melodies are concerned, the difference is only that the Siamese are more attractive to us than the preserved remains of the ancient Greek. What I am suggesting, however, concerns not the melody, but the interplay of the instruments with the song and one another."[60] An enigmatic passage in Plato's *Laws* pointed to an analogous juxtaposition of disparate elements: "In fact," commented Stumpf, "one could hardly describe better the Siamese accompaniment to the melody. Taking note of this, we have already preferred above to speak of heterophony rather than polyphony."[61] With this observation, Stumpf opened the door to an intelligent conceptualization: instead of just assimilating it to the ready-made categories of his time, Stumpf adopted a fresh term. Heterophony took its place as a category in its own right; he did not speculate on whether the playing of unharmonized sounds led to aesthetic civilization or barbarism, the pleasure of euphony or the pain of cacophony. Instead, he asked how this combination of sounds, discordant to European ears, belonged to a distinctive pattern of culture.

Stumpf's reflections on the Thai orchestra's musical techniques belonged to a larger European discussion of heterophony, not always by that name, in the decades before and after he wrote his essay.

Critics recoiled from simultaneous performance of disparate melodies in Chinese music, as in Javanese, before they even knew what to call it. The heterophonic overlay was perhaps what the musicologist August Wilhelm Ambros had in mind when he wrote in the 1880s that Chinese music was "meaningless noise." Ambros was repeating the impression of European travelers to China, relying on the eighteenth-century French missionary Joseph-Marie Amiot and the nineteenth-century British diplomat and naval official John Barrow. From their reports Ambros learned that heterophony cropped up in popular bands, which he contrasted to the Confucian theoretical tradition and its analysis of music in the service of a calming, orderly production of notes.[62] J. A. van Aalst, in the context of writing about the Health Exhibition, reacted with ambivalence to the riotous tableau of Chinese street life: "The populace, as every foreigner in China has experienced, delights in the deafening noise of the gong, accompanied by the shrieking tones of the clarinet; and such music requires no scientific study." But he added a note of cultural caution: Foreigners' first impression of a band might be that the individual musicians played in a noisy anarchy, but with patience one could discover "that the performers play in time and well together." Bands of musicians paraded through the streets, every festival was celebrated, and there was constant singing by "children, domestics, hawkers, and passers-by." Aalst continued: "What matter that we foreigners find the popular music detestable if the Chinese themselves are contented with it?"[63] Aalst put his finger on a quality of Chinese music that had nothing to do with the London and Berlin preoccupation with scales: it seemed to be bursting with life, an effect partly generated by its unfamiliar use of heterophonic melodies, jostling one another like hawkers and passersby on a crowded intersection. Aalst also alluded to another feature: its social stratification. He bemoaned the passing of China's classical music; clashing tones came from the ordinary people of the villages and cities.

Seven years after Stumpf wrote his essay, heterophony became a well-established topic in musicological discussions. Guido Adler, a professor of musicology at the University of Vienna, who edited the scholarly journal in which Stumpf's essay on the Bella Coolas had appeared, published an essay on heterophony that drew on sources including Stumpf's article on the Thai orchestra and an essay by two members of Stumpf's circle, Erich von Hornbostel and Otto Abraham, comparing heterophony in Japanese and medieval European music. Adler agreed with Stumpf that heterophony was a distinctive musical style that should be held apart from polyphony; like Stumpf, he put it in an evolutionary scheme and regarded it as a more primitive style preceding polyphony and harmony. Unlike Stumpf, Adler also related heterophony to the contemporary cultural scene in art and music. He viewed it as part of modern primitivism: "We have something analogous in modern music, as in the plastic arts, in which there is even frequent recourse to primitive forms and means of expression. After the Pre-Raphaelites there was a tendency in the so-called period of Secession to borrow from exotic original forms, especially Asian ones, for aesthetic purposes."[64] With fine sensitivity to the cultural currents of his time, Adler identified the artistic milieu around Hipkins, led by artists like William Morris and Dante Gabriel Rossetti, as a vector for the entrance of "exotic" forms into European culture.[65] Adler's essay bore witness to the general change in mood since the 1880s, when Ambros's book deplored and Ellis struggled to make any sense of Chinese music. Instead, during the first decade of the twentieth century, discussions of heterophony took shape in a general atmosphere of experimentation with Asian cultural resources; Adler's essay suggested that the receptive mood stretched from London to Vienna. Whether from the scholarly side of Stumpf and Adler or from the artistic side of the Pre-Raphaelites and the Secession, Europeans were engaged in a journey of discovery that mingled their own artistic language with the expressive capacity of a form as remote yet strangely appealing as heterophony.

6

Music's Global Archive

In 1900, Carl Stumpf created the first archive of world music. Recordings of the Thai orchestra were the initial item in the collection called the Phonogram Archive (Phonogramm Archiv). From the Archive's home in Stumpf's Psychology Institute, his collaborators carried out the day-to-day work of gathering and analyzing thousands of cylinders etched with strange rhythms and microtones. By the outbreak of World War I they had more than 6,300 cylinders from Asia, Oceania, Europe, Africa, and the Americas.[1] To create a music archive of this kind was a historic achievement. For the first time, recordings of music from around the world could be heard in one place.

The Phonogram Archive sponsored a new kind of network of knowledge. We may distinguish it from its predecessors, the traditional and the high imperial networks, by its path of transmission and the kinds of objects that were in motion.

The traditional network transmitted knowledge through texts: it consisted of the occasional reports that scientists, missionaries, and other travelers sent home in their written accounts. These had the well-known dangers of translating aural into verbal forms of expression, and music into literary description. The inadequacy of moving from one medium to the other was heightened by the use of Western notation, which created a pseudo-accuracy of transcription that covered over the distinctive features of non-Western musical art. Not all extra-European music was domesticated to the point of harmless similarity or dismissed as noise; the example of William Jones's essay on Hindustani music is a reminder that witnesses on the spot could become appreciative and analytical listeners. Yet it was impossible even for sympathetic readers to make very much out of texts and transcriptions without the music itself. The philological revolution that Jones set in motion with his pronouncement that Sanskrit and Western classical languages were linguistic cousins fed into the stream of nineteenth-century historical linguistics, which, even in the absence of direct contact, could use texts as articulated documents for analysis. Comparable materials for music simply did not exist.[2]

The global circuits of modern empire created a second, revolutionary network of knowledge. Steamships and railroads permitted human beings and material objects to travel across continents with unprecedented speed. Foreign musicians like the Nuxalks and the Thai orchestra visited Europe; foreign instruments arrived in Western markets and found permanent public homes in newly created museums. Connoisseurship on a new level flowed in too, from sources as diverse as colonial officers, missionaries, and non-European intellectuals. The accelerating speed and volume of this influx facilitated a new level of expertise. From about 1850, the home of this second kind of network was exhibition at world's fairs, entrepreneurial shows, and museum exhibitions.

Neither the first nor the second kind of network disappeared. Travelers and reviewers continue to the present day to write accounts of concertizing in reviews, magazines, and books; the Rough Guides to world music are testimony to their enduring popularity. Authentic musical experience continued to go on display in the twentieth century and beyond, though today the music festival has replaced the world's fair and the museum as the chief site of spectacle. Musical instruments and musicians continue to pour into Western metropolises. But the advent of the phonograph set in motion a third kind of network, one characterized by aural documents or "records" in the dual sense of the word (documents as well as recordings) rather than by texts or live performance, and also by their circulation with novel speed and volume. Recordings were an entirely new medium that permitted a direct musical experience, yet one profoundly shaped by its own constraints, beginning with the reduction of all musical genres to a few minutes' playing time. Those responsible for making the recordings went out from Europe or North America, made their recordings abroad, and returned to their place of origin. This system remained asymmetrical; most of the knowledge sponsored by scientific-scholarly sites like the Phonogram Archive stayed in Western metropolises, and it was pulled together by the large numbers of Europeans who for reasons of business, state, diplomacy, or curiosity were traveling through exotic places and returning with scientific documents for learned enquiry.

The phonographic network of knowledge took shape in less than a decade. In 1900 its makers produced their first recordings; eight years later they could write an overview of their global music collection. We can best retrace their work by starting from their innermost core and working out in widening circles. It originated with Carl Stumpf and encompassed correspondents across continents. What this circulation of researchers and cylinders reveals is the transition from the world galleries of the late Enlightenment to the *global archive*. This global archive was more differentiated than its predecessors. Suddenly as never before, researchers confronted fine shades of local musical tradition; suddenly they could assemble sound records in one place to compare and contrast across continents. As a result, one could no longer be satisfied with a small number of national types. Instead, a far more complex picture of music in motion began to take shape.

The Berlin Archive

The recording network grew out of the imperial network of artists and travelers touring in Europe. In the familiar mode of Ellis and Hipkins, Stumpf started out by making use of the resources coming to his door, hearing the Nuxalks and interviewing Nuskilusta in Halle. He was once again taking advantage of a traveling ensemble when he worked with the Thai orchestra in Berlin. These experiences marked the end of the exclusive reliance on text and performance, and the beginning of the new network of phonographic musical knowledge. Together with Dr. Otto Abraham, a physician in Berlin, Stumpf made three recordings of the Thai orchestra. By doing so, they made an instant leap beyond their English predecessors, using the new technology not commercially available a decade and a half before. The Thai orchestra recordings initiated a new kind of collection.

The achievement was a historic one. The notion that all music productions from around the world deserved comparison and study was anything but self-evident. A century before, German intellectuals had imagined a world literature and set about discovering its classics. J. G. Herder went far toward creating a textual archive of music that went beyond the conventional categories of European art forms and turned to popular as well as high art, Slavic alongside Western European song. But of course he did not yet have the machines for sound recording that would create the materials for a sound archive comparable to the literary texts that could be assembled in a library. A century later, Stumpf and a handful of like-minded cosmopolitans quickly grasped the possibility of collecting and comparing the different sound productions of all of humanity. Like Herder, they looked beyond the intellectualized productions of cultural elites. Later generations may reflect critically on their reluctance to give up cultural hierarchies, their complicity with colonialism, and their reliance on the term "music" itself as a Western imposition. But the alternative would have been to dispute the notion of a common humanity and to fall into a lack of curiosity about alternatives to one's own culture. Such were the more typical attitudes of their contemporaries. Imperfect though their efforts were, when Stumpf and other comparative musicologists around 1900 founded a cosmopolitan archive of sound, they created the possibility of opening one's ears to diversity.

The Phonogram Archive took shape in a setting of institutionalized science, embedded in the German university and museum systems of the late nineteenth century. This scientific setting distinguished their work from that of their London counterparts. Even though the sources of the recordings might resemble Ellis and Hipkins's Japanese villagers or visiting Rajah, the context had shifted. The Phonogram recordings were no longer the notes of a private gentleman like Ellis, but documents in a state archive. To be sure, Abraham too was working as a private scholar; a gynecologist by profession, he aided the Phonogram Archive and wrote scholarly articles in years to come without title or remuneration. Yet the example of his involvement makes the power of the institutional setting all the more striking: it could corral resources wherever it found them— whether from private scholars, native informants, colonial bureaucrats, missionaries, or adventurers—and turn them into the building blocks of its house of learning. The public status of the Phonogram Archive guaranteed its lasting place in scientific discourse.

Then as today, comparative study of music was a marginal enterprise, one that attracted academic outsiders and adventurers; and yet, flush with its young empire and awakened to a global consciousness, the Prussian political and cultural establishment made space for it. The archive was able to garner enough resources to survive and even flourish within German institutions of higher learning. Several of its early researchers, in addition to Abraham, were Jewish and therefore faced almost insurmountable barriers to an academic career. Erich von Hornbostel, the central figure among them, grew up in a refined Viennese household, his father from a noble family, his mother Jewish; this was enough to make life difficult for him in Central European universities. In 1905 Stumpf asked Hornbostel to become the director of the Phonogram Archive, a position that he assumed in 1906.[3] It came without salary; he devoted himself to building up the global music undertaking while living on his private means. Another young Jewish would-be academic was Max Wertheimer, later one of the founders of Gestalt psychology, who was friendly with Hornbostel and used the archive's recordings occasionally for his research. Jewish, too, was Erich Fischer, who wrote his dissertation on Chinese music and likewise relied on the archive's recordings. Stumpf himself seems to have been completely free of the casual anti-Semitism that was widespread in polite society and the university. Instead, he mobilized his circle's academic skills and curiosity about foreign cultures to create a novel kind of center for cross-cultural studies.

Even though resources and recognition were meager, they began to filter in rather quickly once the Phonogram Archive could point to concrete achievements. First and foremost was the collection of recordings. These arrived from around the world in the form of Edison wax cylinders. With a doctorate in chemistry, Hornbostel decided to preserve the music through a galvanization process that created a copper negative of the original. The procedure destroyed the wax cylinder, but from the etched copper mold an unlimited number of copies could be made; a master was created in metal form, and copies could be disseminated to other institutions. Creating the copper negatives was a farsighted decision. According to Hornbostel, the copies made from the metal master were, with rare exceptions, satisfactory reproductions of the originals. The wax originals could in any case be played only a limited number of times. Beyond that, they could be irreparably destroyed by mold (this was already a problem in the field for the many recordings made in warm and damp climates) and damaged by rough handling—a danger for a collection that was later transported by the Soviets to Leningrad and then moved to the East Berlin State Library. Copper masters guaranteed the survival of the recordings to the present day, when the entire collection is being digitized.[4]

In 1908 Stumpf could report that the archive had almost a thousand recordings from around the world. Three years later, an article in the trade journal *Phonographische Zeitschrift*, summarizing an essay by Erich Fischer, reported that the number of recordings had risen to more than three thousand, a figure that would more than double by the outbreak of war. The archive clearly tapped into a movement by largely self-proclaimed ethnographers from around the world who had the curiosity to preserve local forms of music and sought an institution that would serve as its enduring repository.[5] Susanne Ziegler has assembled tables that give the number of recordings by continent and region from 1900 to 1914: 2,066 from Africa, 896 from the Americas, 1,166 from Asia, 1,415 from Australia and Oceania, and 725 from Europe. A large number of recordings came from German colonies in East Africa, with 863 recordings, and the South Pacific, with 810. But overall it was a widely diffused collection, with musical samples from a total of twenty-five regions of the earth. For example, 408 recordings came from North America and 464 from Southeast Asia, where there were no German colonial sites, and the collection included smaller but significant collections from North and Central Asia (106 recordings) and North Africa (104 recordings).[6] There was a danger that the musical snapshots in such a collection could freeze into immutable types, functioning in a fashion analogous to that of stereotypical images of exotic peoples in eighteenth-century travel accounts. But the very size and specificity of the collection was a leap beyond anything the eighteenth century had known, and even for this reason it provided a glimpse of a far greater human diversity. It provided a rich source base for cultural *comparison* —and, with it, investigation into migration and musical influences. The recordings' diverse geographic origins encouraged measuring the *global* culture of music in motion.

The Inner Circle

Hornbostel, Stumpf, and their collaborators did not just collect the cylinders; they wrote about them assiduously in articles demonstrating that the Phonogram Archive was a serious scientific enterprise. Hornbostel brought musical connoisseurship and performance skills to his work alongside his scientific education. His personality had a bohemian side at odds with the stiffly correct protocol of prewar Germany. According to the ethnomusicologist Jaap Kunst, who first met him in the 1920s, he stayed up late playing the piano and woke at midday to make his way over to the Archive; in later years he belonged to a gentleman jugglers' club.[7] None of this was visible in the prewar memoranda he sent to his correspondents near and far. As for his scholarship, it bordered on hard science, much of it a continuation of Ellis's exact measurement of pitch and scales, which he and his colleagues reported on in article after article.[8] If Ellis's work was the foundation for an expansion from music to a science of culture, Hornbostel added a painstaking comparison of musical instruments from around the world, culminating in the creation of a system of classification created with the musicologist Curt Sachs and famous ever since.

Following the model of historical linguistics, Hornbostel believed that by combining attention to scale and pitch with comparison of musical instruments, one could trace the diffusion of culture around the world. A similarity of scales might be accidental, and did not in itself point to contact between two cultures. But absolute pitch, he argued in 1911 in a paper to the Berlin Society for Anthropology, Ethnology, and Prehistory, was purely arbitrary; precisely for this reason, identical absolute pitch along with identical instrument construction signified cultural borrowing. Mobilizing musical scales, pitches, and instruments, he made confident judgments about the diffusion of music. Was the African xylophone native, or was it imported from Southeast Asia? Despite some negative indicators, he noted that the African instruments used seven intervals very similar to those used in Asia, but this evidence alone would not suffice. He compared four instruments—one used by Ellis in London, and others that he had used in Washington, Hamburg, and Berlin—and found that their absolute pitches were close enough for him to attribute them to a Burmese origin. He made a similar case for diffusion of the pan flute. It was widespread around the world, but only two regions had a double row: the Solomon Islands and western Polynesia, and Peru and Bolivia. To this he added their similarities in absolute pitch. The comparison did not quite hold, for the Brazilian pan flute did not have double rows; but he made allowances for this by pointing to similar forms of construction. With this much evidence in hand, he argued for mutual influence. The method was by today's historical standards a speculative one. But he deployed it with great erudition in order to map the movement of music and instruments across vast spaces and reaches of time. Whatever his personal quirks may have been, his objective scholarly achievements and formal propriety in writing represented the Phonogram Archive to the world with all the dignity required for a young scholarly enterprise that had to establish its legitimacy.[9]

An especially revealing publication was the instructions for musical ethnography that Hornbostel wrote in a general guide to ethnography published by the Berlin Ethnological Museum. It began with a proclamation that every traveler in little-studied areas should be equipped with a phonograph in order to record as many musical performances as possible. The would-be ethnographers were warned not to be Eurocentric about their selection: "When selecting pieces, do not prefer those that appeal to European ears," he wrote, urging researchers instead to include the greatest possible range of useful scientific examples.[10] Other injunctions to be good listeners followed, but so did a procedure that seemed guaranteed to stifle musical spontaneity. The ethnographer had to be sure to prepare his phonograph for accuracy, fully winding it up and setting it at the right speed. He was then responsible for an entire protocol of procedures: setting it firmly and not disturbing it during the recording; starting the recording with a tuning pipe and then stating the journal number and title of the recording; bringing the apparatus as close as possible to the musicians; having a performer mark the time with hand claps or drumbeat; alternating nearness of the musicians to the recording device in pieces not sung in unison; capturing singers' highest and lowest notes after the recording; asking instrument makers to play the complete scale of their instruments; separately recording the words of a sung performance; playing back the recording right away; noting journal number and title on the cylinder box; writing the journal entry; and making another recording of the piece on a different day.[11] If one followed these prescriptions, bureaucratic procedure would invade the ethnographic moment with shattering thoroughness.

The instructions capture the underlying paradox of Hornbostel's approach. On the one hand, it asked travelers to abandon their prejudices and enter into an alien culture. "Take care to avoid judging extra-European music from a European standpoint: general descriptions like 'musical,' 'beautiful,' 'ugly,' 'peculiar,' are worthless. By contrast one should collect native aesthetic judgments of their own and of European music (sing or use phonograph to demonstrate)."[12] This was music appreciation class, global-style; the "native" was supposed not just to make music, but to speak about it. On the other hand the advice was so heavy-handed that it was bound to transform the music. Furthermore, the assumption that the scale was the natural unit for music simply took a Western notion of musical structure and projected it onto other musical cultures that might have different ways of organizing sound. One wonders how the roving colonial administrator or expedition member could issue Hornbostel's directives without a great deal of confusion and bellowing at informants. The manual's simultaneous insistence on sensitivity and protocol was part of the larger struggle of well-meaning early-twentieth-century researchers to create order out of the oceanic abundance of new evidence about non-European cultures. Hornbostel and the museum authorities were determined to get beyond the impressionism of earlier generations of travelers, and they tried to do so by using the well-sharpened tools of modern field science. Since the eighteenth century, generations of naturalists had made the transition from unlabeled, misrecorded flora and fauna samples to exact record keeping; musical ethnography, too, would have to insist on orderly collecting.

Stumpf and Hornbostel worked wonders to turn the idea of an ethnological music archive into a reality. They were only able to do so by forming an alliance with Felix von Luschan, a virtuoso at promoting his own interests and those of the Berlin Ethnological Museum. Like Hornbostel, Luschan came from a comfortably placed Austrian household. Trained as a physician, he showed an early interest in ethnology and archaeology, taking part in expeditions to Eastern Europe, Asia Minor, southeast Anatolia, and Syria. After arriving in Berlin in 1885 for an initial three-year stint as assistant in the Ethnological Museum, he rose to the position of director of the Africa/Oceania section in 1904. Racial and cultural anthropology overlapped in his work. He developed skull-measuring and color schemes as aids to racial classification; he also had a connoisseur's appreciation for the arts of Africa and Oceania, and worked with entrepreneurial brio to gather an outstanding collection for the museum.[13]

A decisive organizer, Luschan recognized early on the importance of the phonograph for field researchers. Even before his collaboration with Stumpf, he began outfitting the researchers with machines and cylinders. By 1903, he and Stumpf were going back and forth about how to get funding for the Phonogram Archive and how to set up a cooperative relationship with the Ethnological Museum. Luschan wrote to Stumpf with gossip and advice, telling him that he could expect a favorable reception from the Ministry of Culture and urging him to write up something that could go to the Academy of Sciences and the Berlin museums for evaluation. They agreed that about 1,500 marks was needed for start-up costs—mainly the purchase of phonographs and cylinders—and an annual income thereafter of 1,000 marks, again mainly for equipment. There was not even mention of a salary for Hornbostel. By a year and a half later, Stumpf had filed a formal request for funding with the ministry, and the five section heads of the Ethnological Museum had weighed the pluses and minuses of funding the archive. The museum director's evaluation came down in its favor "so that material missing until now for the study of the languages, stories and songs of analphabetic peoples could be gathered at a central location, therewith permitting a systematic processing and evaluation of the materials." In the end, an initial 1,500 marks came through from the Rudolf Virchow Foundation—not an odd choice, since Virchow was one of the founders of German anthropology. At the beginning of 1906, Hornbostel could thank Luschan for his help and announce that he and his colleagues could at last establish the archive and would have the space they needed to do so. By 1908, Stumpf could report on receiving further support from the Academy of Sciences and two private sources. Luschan had campaigned successfully for an archive that added a dimension to the scientific expeditions supported by his museum but also maintained its connections to the Institute for Psychology, where it continued to be housed. As he made his case to the Ministry of Culture, the Academy of Sciences, and the Colonial Office, he sized up how they would respond to aesthetic, scientific, and pragmatic arguments; all three seem to have entered into his own thinking about the preservation of indigenous cultures.[14]

State support for the Phonogram Archive created a distinctive blend of aims with a long history behind them. Since the eighteenth century, the pursuit of science had gone hand in hand with ambitions of overseas expansion. On a modest scale—after all, the sums involved were tiny compared to the expenses of outfitting an entire expedition—the Phonogram Archive fit into this larger pattern of archiving the resources of the earth to satisfy the multiple motives of metropolitan European elites. Colonial intelligence gathering and scientific idealism continued to merge in this example of the German pursuit of higher learning.

Boas and Dorsey in America

The Phonogram Archive's network of knowledge extended from its inner circle to the university and the state's cultural bureaucracy. It also reached overseas in Stumpf's cooperation with Franz Boas. Their youthful exchange of knowledge about the Nuxalks did not end when Boas emigrated to the United States. The standards of American scholarship left Boas impatient and at times scornful; he was glad to keep up his good relations with his contacts in Germany. In 1893 he sent Kwakiutl (Kwakwaka'wakw) recordings to the Phonogram Archive. In 1897 he followed up with what he described as dancing, lyric, religious, women's, potlatch, gambling, and medicine songs, as well as a "grizzly bear song for the birth of twins." They were collected with the aid of "James Teit, a Scotsman married to a Thompson River Indian woman." Hornbostel and Abraham used these recordings to write an essay for the Festschrift in honor of Boas; it appeared in 1907. The collaboration continued after World War I: during the 1920s, Hornbostel's student George Herzog went to New York and wrote his dissertation under the guidance of Boas, going on to become a founder of ethnomusicology in the United States. The comparative musicology of Berlin around 1900 enjoyed a new life across the Atlantic, thanks in part to Boas's and Hornbostel's combined efforts.[15] While Boas was not a major contributor to the Phonogram Archive or deeply involved in the collection of music, the link is a revealing one. Boas's work stood for the highest standard of ethnography; beginning with his early work on the Inuits of Baffin Island, and continuing in his studies of the Native peoples of the Pacific Northwest, he documented indigenous ways of life in extraordinary detail. His dedication to rigorous empiricism and self-critical methodology matched the aims of Hornbostel and his disciples; they provide a larger context for the Phonogram Archive in the intellectual history of its time.[16]

The number of contributors of recordings grew year by year. From North America, George Dorsey rattled his competitors with his speedy gathering of artifacts for the Field Museum in Chicago; he seemed to show up everywhere. His name surfaced in the correspondence of the Berlin Ethnological Museum when Karl von den Steinen, director of its American section, alternately joked about his frenetic collecting activities and negotiated with him in 1903 over North American collections, including a seventy-five-page catalog of Arapahoe art for which Dorsey demanded a stiff $1,900. In September of the same year, Dorsey bragged from Victoria, British Columbia, that he had just returned from "an extremely interesting and profitable trip to Alaska, where I secured about fifty very rare and interesting Tlinkit specimens." (The Tlingits were famous for their attractive masks and other artifacts.)[17] In 1909 a member of a German expedition in New Guinea wrote to Luschan in a panic over the sight of a steamship with Dorsey on board. (Luschan wrote back that there was plenty of material for everyone).[18] For the Phonogram Archive, Dorsey became a valuable ally. In October 1906, Hornbostel wrote from Chicago to Stumpf in Berlin that "Dr. Dorsey is a very lovable man who arranges everything for me as comfortably and advantageously as possible."[19] By

November, thanks to Dorsey's assistance, Hornbostel was working with Pawnees in Oklahoma, learning that adults objected to seeing themselves written into note cards, trying to work with children while discovering that they had learned white men's songs in school—and, despite the difficulties, making some recordings. It was a valuable personal experience in building connections between Germany and the United States, and it confronted Hornbostel with the difficulties of fieldwork. Ethnography could be subjected to lengthy checklists at home, but even in relatively comfortable and safe North America, it was a hit-and-miss business.

Austrian Correspondents

The career of Rudolf Pöch is a reminder that "German" ethnography at the beginning of the twentieth century should not be conceived apart from its Austrian counterpart; together they belonged to a Central European discourse about non-European peoples and their music. From a wealthy Viennese family, Pöch studied medicine in Vienna and then spent 1900 and 1901 in Berlin, where he heard Luschan's university lectures on anthropology and ethnology. With the museum director's encouragement, he did his first ethnographic work on carved figures from German New Guinea. From 1904 to 1906 he took a self-financed trip to New Guinea, the Bismarck Archipelago, and Australia, making anthropological measurements and gathering skulls and skeletons. His financial investment was rewarded at the University of Vienna when he became adjunct professor of anthropology in 1913, and its first professor of anthropology and ethnology in 1919.[20]

Pöch was an avid user of new technologies, but also a thoughtful one who reflected on their advantages and disadvantages. The old-style anthropologist had pencil and paper in hand as the zoologist and botanist loaded up their boxes. But the modern anthropologist, Pöch wrote in 1907 about his work in New Guinea, had a whole series of new methods and technical inventions at his disposal. Having taken a phonograph from the Imperial Academy of Sciences in Vienna, and having turned to Hornbostel for advice, Pöch was acutely aware of the technical requirements of recording, including the need to keep track of the machine's speed and eliminate background noise. Altogether, to get "a really natural recording" took a lot of "practice and skill." The scientific traveler determined to load up with still photography camera, motion picture camera, and phonograph might have too much of a good thing and be less well off than his predecessor with pencil and notebook. The amount of mechanical labor it took to run all those machines was overwhelming, beginning with just unpacking them and setting them up. "Natives" would not be able to offer much help, and Pöch advised against traveling with another European, which would double the cost and make it harder to get to know the people one was studying. At the same time, he valued the new technologies as aids in salvaging native cultures before they were destroyed by contact with Westerners. Such cultures had to be documented as thoroughly as possible before they disappeared forever. In his experience the phonograph had a special magic: photographs held no special attraction, but fifty or sixty Monumbos, the people he worked among in New Guinea, might gather to hear a recording. In retrospect, however, Pöch's doubts about the new style of ethnography continue to resonate. Like Hornbostel's questionnaires, the mechanization of fieldwork rationalized and distorted the very society and culture one was attempting to preserve. Hornbostel never called his own methods into question, but Pöch approached his research with a seasoned skepticism. Changing methods and new technologies did not belong to a uniform history of progress. The old techniques had their own strengths; abandoning them brought about losses as well as gains in cultural insight.[21]

A thoroughgoing dedication to the phonograph as the foundation for fieldwork came from Béla Bartók, who after the turn of the century made an intensive drive to collect folk songs in Magyar villages. There he briefly had to endure the discomforts of cold weather and simple food while working to tease songs out of villagers, including old ladies who were suspicious of an educated stranger and fearful of being ridiculed by their neighbors if they sang for him. Together with his collaborator, Zoltán Kodály, he collected and classified hundreds of Magyar folk songs; he soon extended his collecting to Romanian, Slovak, and other music from the rich variety of nationalities settled in the geographic Hungarian portion of the Habsburg Empire.[22]

In 1913 Bartók mailed to Hornbostel a collection of wax cylinders containing Romanian folk songs. That was the material testimony to an enduring relationship between the composer-ethnographer and the scientist at the Phonogram Archive. Bartók's library contained more than a dozen of Hornbostel's publications from this period; his own methodological reflections on fieldwork show the influence of Hornbostel's writings.[23] Their approaches were different: whereas Hornbostel was interested primarily in the analysis of scale and pitch, Bartók focused on the stylistic analysis of melody. Hornbostel thought of himself as a scientist carrying out exact empirical research to be shared with his fellow scientists, whereas Bartók was a composer turning to folk sources for artistic inspiration. Yet they shared a determination to professionalize fieldwork. For Bartók, the insistence on scientific exactness was manifest in his ambition of collecting as many melodies as possible; by 1912 he had gathered more than three thousand and was planning to turn his attention to unexplored Romanian areas.[24] He was convinced that the phonograph had revolutionized the musical ethnographer's task or even made it possible for the first time. "Every transcription," he wrote in 1919, "even those of European melodies, is inadequate from the folklore viewpoint, because not only our notation but even the newly invented, supplementary diacritic signs are by no means suited for truly representing the mode of performance (tonal glide, rhythmic transition, rubato performance)."[25] Bartók thereby put his finger on one aspect of the transformation wrought by the phonograph. European representation of non-European cultures was heavily dominated by the authority of the word; writing down their performative arts gave the authority of the document to living encounters. Music, however, was an art that dramatically revealed the limitations of this exclusion of nonwritten sources. Descriptions and notation of music led to systematic omissions and distortions. The phonograph captured cultural peculiarities that had eluded transcription.

Germans in the Field

Most of the Phonogram Archive's prewar collection came not from foreign correspondents, like Boas and Dorsey in the United States or Pöch and Bartók in the Habsburg Empire, but from Germans abroad.[26] Luschan was one of the driving forces behind the first flurry of business for the archive, outfitting military and colonial visitors with phonographs and showing them how they worked. In March 1906, Luschan wrote to Hornbostel about cylinders of music from the Masai people (seminomadic cattle owners in East Africa); an unnamed officer owned them but might permit Hornbostel to make copies. In June, Luschan wrote to Stumpf that Augustin Krämer—a navy physician on his way to a career in anthropology—had left his phonograph with a German naval officer in South Africa; could Stumpf get another one into the hands of Frau Professor Krämer, who would be leaving in a few weeks to join her husband in the Bismarck Archipelago? Within the past few days, Luschan added in the same message, First Lieutenant Julius Smend, "one of our most energetic collectors in Togo," had sent in very interesting cylinders, some of them damaged by moisture but apparently still usable. A month later, Luschan copied out a letter from Max Girschner, a colonial doctor in Pohnpei, an atoll in the eastern Caroline Islands. "It would be a pleasure for me to make phonographic recordings," Girschner had written. "This will actually be the fulfillment of a long-cherished wish. The melodies (namely those of the Ruk inhabitants) cannot be reproduced with our notation system but are, it seems to me, musically not without interest." Girschner had discovered microtones. Hornbostel must have welcomed this naive confirmation of their existence from a Micronesian atoll. In October, Stumpf learned from Luschan (who apologized for writing to him while Hornbostel was in America) that Georg August Zenker, "an old benefactor of our museum," was passing through Berlin. Luschan wrote that he had instructed Zenker in the use of the phonograph; Zenker would use it to capture dance and songs in Cameroon.[27] These contacts with potential contributors all resulted from colonial connections linking Berlin and its outposts in Africa and Oceania. Without the navy ships that regularly plied back and forth between Germany and its colonies, without the colonial doctors who were curious about local cultures and ambitious to make a name for themselves, the Phonogram Archive would never have received recordings from places so difficult for Europeans to reach.

These contributors were among the many Germans roving the earth via the paths of empire. Their biographies offer a small sample of the diversity of backgrounds and fates that contributed to the archive of world music. Like Luschan, Krämer was an intriguer and a go-getter: stationed in Samoa, he meddled in island politics while gathering a rich ethnography of island society and culture, bullying islanders for information like the family genealogies that reached back for centuries. Later he had a successful career as the founding director of the Linden Museum, the ethnological museum in Stuttgart. As for Smend, he had a successful career as colonial officer, gathered a large collection of ethnographic materials in Togo, and—in 1916, after being badly wounded on the French front—became a major in the War Ministry. Max Girschner was a physician who arrived in Pohnpei in 1899 and spent nearly sixteen years there. Warmly interested in the islanders, he worked assiduously to document their world and published several articles on his research. After his return to Germany, he tried without luck to get a doctorate on the basis of his work and to publish his manuscript monograph. Georg August Zenker was a gardener and adventurer who served in the German colony of Cameroon from 1889 to 1895; notorious for having a large polygynous family, he left the colonial service after arguing with his superiors, and became a plantation owner in Cameroon, all the while pursuing his scientific interests.[28] The careerists, the curious, the kindly, and the wild: a mixed assortment of characters and motives fed into the labors of the Phonogram Archive in an imperial era. Just this little cast of characters from 1906 suggests the varied, but on the whole high, level of education to be found in Germany's colonial service. The university system, churning out educated doctors and administrators, supported the care and accuracy required to make recordings, document them, and ship them back to Berlin. Once again the resources of the state worked together with the prestige of cultural achievement to further the worldwide collection of music.

The Phonogram Archive profited from scientific expeditions. As part of the long trail of scientific travel going back to the eighteenth century, early twentieth-century travelers were commissioned by learned bodies at home and were expected to gather collections and documentation about the societies and places they visited. The transition from eighteenth-century expeditions to the modern disciplinary field work of anthropology was a gradual one. In the case of Franz Boas, for example, his first foray beyond Europe was a trip to Baffin Island with stated aims of mapping and surveying, very much in the tradition of eighteenth-century voyagers like Captain Cook, who had begun his career in Newfoundland a century earlier with similar tasks. Mapping of coastlines, geographic surveys of interiors, collection of botanical specimens, comments on the soil and natural resources—all these were duties of such expeditions, along with investigation into the society, culture, and political organization of local peoples. New technologies were heaped onto the old research methods; cameras and phonographs joined pencil, paper, and surveying tools as travelers' equipment. Expeditions in this updated naturalist tradition made recordings that ended up in the Phonogram Archive.

The travelers were bold adventurers who took risks with their health and their careers. Karl von den Steinen sponsored one of them, Theodor Koch, to gather materials for the Ethnological Museum in the border area of Peru, Brazil, and Bolivia—remote terrain in the South American interior. The local tribes ought to be visited right away, von den Steinen wrote in his proposal to his colleagues in the museum's assistance committee, since their extremely interesting languages and cultures were endangered by the incursions of the rubber trade. As the trade grew, it was enormously disrupting the Amerindians' lives, driving them from one waterway to another. Von den Steinen recommended Koch, a young museum assistant who had already completed his doctorate and taken part in a South American expedition, for research among the Pano speakers. The committee approved von den Steinen's request for six thousand marks (a large sum, as von den Steinen noted) for a one-year journey. Koch was hard to manage—he got distracted by other indigenous groups, and with the museum's reluctant approval and some scolding, he ended up staying two years, from 1903 to 1905—but his patron and the other museum directors did not lose their patience. In the end, Koch must have satisfied them, for he went on to an academic career, further field trips, and eventually directorship of the Linden Museum. He had photographic equipment, but not yet a phonograph, on the first expedition. The phonograph was added on a later expedition of 1911 to 1913 to northern Brazil and southern Venezuela, where he made cylinder recordings for the Phonogram Archive. His ardor for fieldwork finally killed him; in 1924 he contracted fatal malaria at the start of a further expedition to Brazil. His beginnings in the expedition of 1903 are a reminder of how globalization and fieldwork could be intertwined in the most remote places. As his sponsor noted, the exploitation of the rubber trees in South America, a scandalous story of human and natural destruction, also created the commercial contacts that permitted Koch to make his journey.[29]

Even the toughest correspondents endured physical and psychological duress. From the German colony of New Britain (then part of the Bismarck Archipelago, off the coast of Papua New Guinea), Richard Thurnwald, a man who sneered at tropical disease, sent Hornbostel a stream of complaints about his phonographic equipment.[30] His phonograph had fallen into the water, he wrote in March 1908—an accident that would probably be the death blow to the long-suffering instrument.[31] The last shipment of blank wax cylinders to New Britain was so badly packed that it had arrived with many of them broken or damaged. "I wish to ask you to knock the responsible mischief-maker upside-down," Thurnwald added. "Next time, i.e., as soon as possible, please send me well-packed cylinders."[32] In May he wrote that his supplies were used up—at precisely the moment when the locals enjoyed working with him and were urging him to make more recordings. As for the new phonograph: "Its little transmission belt tore. I repaired it with my all-purpose helper: book glue." But this caused new trouble, "a buzzing noise."[33] Despite all the problems, after his return home Thurnwald could brag about his haul for the Phonogram Archive, which included 145 texts of songs and 340 phonograph recordings on wax cylinders.[34]

Just a few years later, Thurnwald found himself back in the Solomon Islands as part of the Empress Augusta River Expedition, sponsored by the Berlin Ethnological Museum.[35] In a letter of March 1913 he growled once again to Hornbostel about his struggles with the phonograph: "I have to tell you right away: the phonograph is my problem child." When he had arrived to join the expedition, it would not work at all. His machinist had had to take everything apart and clean it, but it still made noise as well as starts and stops. The cause? "The needle seems to be rusty, in the opinion of the machinist." Thurnwald asked for a new one, the strongest there was, well oiled, to capture the islanders' charming ("recht hübsch") songs.[36] At the beginning of September, Thurnwald wrote that the expedition's two machinists had gotten the phonograph to work. Its spring had been matted by too much oil, the axles had too little, and the drive belt was out of place. Half a year later, in March 1914, he had a cheerier report: The phonograph was working better, and he was hoping at the next opportunity to send a box of cylinder recordings. The letter ended on a poignant note as Thurnwald recalled a shared study group in Berlin and hectored Hornbostel to find "new blood" to keep it lively. He yearned to get back to the intellectual work that was his and Hornbostel's shared passion.[37]

Thurnwald's reports from the field document the third phase in the formation of a global network of musical knowledge. Helmholtz had relied on travel accounts, as generations of Europeans had done before him; these were the impressions of isolated individuals who were often not musically trained and who, even if they were, did not belong to a scholarly community. Ellis and Hipkins expanded their pool of information by taking advantage of the new mobility of musicians, scholars, and instruments arriving by modern means of transit in London. Thurnwald belonged to a different kind of enterprise: the materialization of sound in wax cylinders and its circulation to a research center in Berlin.

Music and Meaning in History

By 1908 Stumpf could write that the Phonogram Archive had contributed to a transformation of its source materials for extra-European music. Just as in travel accounts illustrations of "savages" had once been made to look like Europeans—a state of affairs decisively altered by photography—so the phonograph had decisively challenged the assimilation of foreign music to European expectations, and could instead reproduce its rhythmic and tonal features exactly and unchangeably.[38]

Recordings, Stumpf predicted, would have a transforming effect on Europeans' conception of music. "One's first impression of exotic music is that of the curious and incomprehensible. One's amazement only grows with exposure to different kinds. Our scales, our rhythms, our melodies are such givens to us that everything else seems abnormal, unnatural, and therefore unpleasant, even repulsive."[39] The incomprehensibility was far stronger than for literature or fine art, in which concrete representations could guide foreign audiences. However, science could come to the rescue of curious listeners. Understanding foreign music diminished its strangeness; listeners could make works of musical art from the entire world their own. These could be aesthetically satisfying and a gain for scientific, cultural, and ethnological knowledge.[40] Who knew, he speculated, if the future of European music did not lie in the direction of more complex rhythms after the possibilities of harmonization had been exhausted? In any case, even if Europeans could not get beyond their own aesthetic preferences, it would be foolish to dispute the scholarly value of listening to ethnographic recordings.[41]

By the end of the decade, Stumpf took advantage of the global comparisons now at his disposal in a series of lectures published in 1911 as *The Origins of Music*. They were delivered to the Urania Society in Berlin, a forum that gave experts the chance to reach a broad public audience. The lecture format had the fortunate effect of leading Stumpf to write with clear, nontechnical and openly stated conclusions. Even to this audience Stumpf adopted a scholarly approach to the question of music's origins, reviewing his subject's history, surveying the list of nineteenth-century contributors, emphasizing the revolutionary centrality of the phonograph, and giving a full account of his sources from the Phonogram Archive.[42]

One of his most important tasks was to criticize the assumption that music around the world was fundamentally identical to Western music, with the different varieties representing more or less sophisticated approximations of it. For an example of this homogenization, he turned to Wilhelm Wundt's sampling of "primitive" music in his textbook treatment of popular or folk psychology. Stumpf intensely disliked Wundt, his rival in the field of empirical psychology, and Stumpf's impatience comes through in his attack on his Leipzig colleague's use of ethnographic evidence. "A psychologist as famous as Wilhelm Wundt gives four specimens of primitive songs, of which the third and fourth, as they stand, could not possibly be real." One of these, an "Australian melody," came from *Among Cannibals* by Carl Lumholtz; the second was from *In the Heart of Africa* by G. Schweinfurth.[43] The first had "Tempo di Valse. Allegro" written underneath the notes in Lumholtz's book. As a piece, it sounded in fact like the main waltz from Oscar Straus's operetta *Walzertraum* (1907). Any expert, added Stumpf, would say that it had "about as much chance of originating with the primeval inhabitants of Australia as a silver soup spoon or a typewriter." Stumpf then tracked it down: it was probably a European song first sung by Aborigines in Rockhampton who had migrated to the faraway Herbert River Mountains. "The European ear may have done much more in addition, it may have 'assimilated' the things heard. . . ."[44] As to the second example, Stumpf went to the source: "Since the example from Schweinfurth's book struck me as no less astonishing, I asked the great explorer of Africa by letter for information about the way in which he transcribed this song, and whether it might not have migrated to that region." Schweinfurth's reply: He had overheard the melody, then hummed it while marching, and had it transcribed by his brother Alexander, a musician. Stumpf commented: "What transformations must a melody undergo if one hums it to oneself on long marches, and what a complete transformation if, after this first unintentional arrangement, it is transcribed by a dyed-in-the-wool European musician who has perhaps never heard exotic melodies in the original! . . . what he sees as a guarantee for loyal transmission is in fact the opposite." All of this was a demonstration "of how indispensable phonographic recordings are on location. . . ."[45] Colorful, silly anecdotes had no place in scientific work; they withered away under Stumpf's critique. The annexation of Australians and Africans to a caricature of Victorian popular culture had to give way to a serious inquiry into foreign musical systems and what they might reveal about musical cultures in general.[46]

Stumpf's conclusion returned to Western music as the norm that others imperfectly approximated. It ended with an arrangement of the major types of music in order of their integration of voices into a complex whole. The typology ranged from single voices to polyphony and other forms of internally differentiated melody, and to modern Western harmony. Other systems, wrote Stumpf in a footnote, had "multiple simultaneous sounds," but not "our chordal system, as it gradually developed with its main triads in major and minor on the tonic, dominant, and subdominant; with scales derived from triads, in which each note is first obtained from the triads out of feeling and effect, and also first attains its exact tuning; with dissonant chords (discords) that turn into the main triads and finally into the tonic triad according to particular rational rules—that is something thoroughly new for which we find no equivalents before the last millennium or in present-day exotic music."[47] For Stumpf this was a dialectical process in which Western harmony assimilated earlier forms of voice differentiation like the drone (the sustained note best known to European ears from the bagpipe, and also a feature of South Asian music) and polyphony into its all-encompassing totality.[48] By this point, Stumpf's argument had retreated to an affirmation of Western music as a universal language. While at other moments he could qualify his preference for it as a question of taste, and point out the superior rhythmic or melodic possibilities of African or Indian music, at the end his line of thinking tipped toward an identification of Western music with music making in general at its most complex.

A commentary on Stumpf's conclusions—and more broadly, on the development of comparative music studies—came from the sociologist Max Weber, who approached music from an entirely different disciplinary background. Weber was not by training a natural scientist like Helmholtz or Hornbostel, a mathematician like Ellis, or a philosopher with strong scientific training and inclinations like Stumpf. Rather, he was an economist and jurist, a student of societies past and present, who grappled from his earliest work with the interaction between objective economic conditions and psychological structures of motivation. Guenther Roth has explored the cosmopolitan dimension of Weber's family and upbringing: on his mother's side, the wealthy Souchay family had strong business connections to England and America, and in particular to Manchester, whose German colony had welcomed Carl Engel. There was a strong musical legacy in the Souchay family, with Felix Mendelssohn marrying one of the daughters.[49]

A late romance turned Weber's attention in the direction of music as a subject for cultural comparison. In 1909 he befriended the Swiss pianist Minna Tobler, then living in Heidelberg. It was a relationship that turned into an affair. Intellectual companionship did not lag behind; their conversations at the piano spilled over into Weber's study of comparative musicology as stuff for his comparisons of world civilizations. Between approximately 1909 and 1913, Weber wrote the rough draft of a sociology of music. His progress on it was interrupted by World War I; despite revisions and the writing of a second fragment, he had put it aside by the time of his death in 1920. His widow, Marianne Weber, published it from his papers, and a critical version has appeared in the complete German edition of his works. Even after his concentration on it gave way to other projects, the subject remained a favorite of Weber's, one he turned to with guests at home and students in the classroom.[50]

For his research, Weber read in the scholarship on indigenous music. Carl Engel, Ellis, Stumpf, and Hornbostel taught him that the music of "primitive" peoples was far more complex than he had previously imagined; he recognized that the phonograph swept away inherited stereotypes and created an entirely new, rigorous, and quantifiable documentation of extra-European music.[51] Before then, Weber had never paid much attention to anthropological writings; his comments on popular classes tended to be superficial and dismissive. Yet in this case he registered an important lesson: that there was no "natural" basis for the music of "primitive" peoples. In evolutionary schemas since the eighteenth century, there had been a recurring search for a natural foundation that was part of mankind's original state. Weber discarded this and sketched his own evolutionary schema: Music was originally subordinate to magic, cultic, and medical ends; next it became the property of status groups and priesthoods, the moment of incipient aestheticization and rationalization; and after that came the need to tune instruments, which heightened the rationalization of music in its Greek and Arabic forms, but still contained no tonic as an organizing principle. Finally came the emergence of a "melodic center of gravity" in Western music, with its logical structure firmly moored to the tonic, around which all the other notes assumed their functions.[52]

After exposure to the work of Hornbostel and his colleagues, Weber arrived at a sophisticated interpretive approach to the production of music around the world: No matter how crude or simple, music was a localized form of human expression, the product of a specific culture.

He directed this insight against the argument of Helmholtz—whom he otherwise praised as a model scientist, and whose analysis he recapitulated at length—that acoustic relationships could account for the specific choices of intervals and scales adopted by a given society. This was a scientistic view of behavior, which assumed that sound frequencies caused aesthetic pleasure or displeasure and led to the adoption of certain systems of scales and tonal intervals. Underlying it was a neoclassical conception of human behavior as grounded in a timeless natural order. Weber was profoundly opposed to this perspective. In his own thinking, an infinitely complex world contained no intrinsic meaning for human beings.

Instead, they had to shape the world into a particular historical order; that was the work of culture. Weber's observations on music balanced different causal factors: class interest, status loyalties, political power, technical developments, and the state could all enter into the choices. According to Weber, it was the antipathy of elites far and wide to emotional extremes—he was especially thinking of East Asia—that led to the adoption of pentatonic musical scales viewed as orderly and calm.[53] Religion played a role too: the antisensuous disposition of the ancient Christian churches, he maintained (according to one of his student's recollections), led them to separate music from dance, and guided the monks of the Middle Ages, especially the Cistercians, toward constructing an orderly musical system that eventuated in harmony.[54] Apart from these considerations, Weber pointed to the Western system of notation as a technical aid that was an indispensable support for the complexity of modern Western music.

From his own time, Weber took up the peculiar impact of the piano: an international commodity, the bourgeois musical instrument par excellence, which gave an unprecedented rationality to the tonal order. The same instrument that accompanied his ardor for Minna Tobler created a musical iron cage: it was capable of refinement and range, pianissimos and power, concentration and scope; but at the same time it excluded other worlds of musical possibility. Like his predecessors going back to Helmholtz, Weber believed that the piano had led to a loss of ability to discriminate fine shades of intonation. It was a well known fact of his time, he wrote, that North European singers who grew up with greater exposure to the piano had less sensitive voices than Southern Europeans, who were more attuned to tonality in its microtonal gradations.

Weber offered a tragic perspective on the development of modern global culture. What it brought about was not an exchange between local communities of art and knowledge, but an expansion of Western rationality around the world, a cultural counterpart to the overwhelming force of Western imperialism. Weber was both an aggressive proponent of the expansion of Western expansion and its reflective critic. He could treat other cultures with sarcasm and contempt, but he realized that a universalization of Western rationality was also tantamount to an impoverishing uniformity. This was a point that he had argued as early as his essay on the Protestant ethic, whose conclusion famously stated that the early Puritans had wanted to create a world dominated by ascetic discipline, while subsequent generations, inheriting this cosmos of modern capitalism, were forced to live in it. Music illustrated an analogous argument for the arts: the diatonic scale, the triad, and all the other building blocks of Western music excluded rhythmic and melodic alternatives. Weber left his contemporaries and later generations with a question: Were they in fact doomed to inhabit this world and no other?

The question took on unexpected urgency after 1914, when Europe's prewar civilization gave way to mass carnage, demoralization, and revaluation of the relationship between Europe and the rest of the world. But already in the prewar years another causal factor entered into the formation of global musical culture and disrupted previous assumptions about the relationship between West and non-West: the phonograph industry. As with many other aspects of globalization, its effects were paradoxical. It could both advance the Westernization of music around the world and add to the durability of local forms; it could provide vulgar entertainment or refined concerts; it could reinforce or erase the lines separating national and class identities. How the phonograph resulted in a globalization of music and challenged its established categories of reception is a story that looks back to the late nineteenth century, and forward to the interwar years and their newly arranged world order.

PART III

COMMERCE

7

Phonographs around the World

After the Flood, as the visionary poet Arthur Rimbaud imagines it, heaven and earth are briefly at peace. Nature is awake and all but speaks: a rabbit says its prayer to the rainbow, and the flowers look all around. But then mankind starts up its slaughters and false pieties. In a caricature of nineteenth-century Europe, Rimbaud evokes the work of butchers, shop stalls, and boats setting out for distant ports. Along with all the other businesses there is the return of music: *Madame *** établit un piano dans les Alpes*— "Madame so-and-so sets up a piano in the Alps." Pristine nature gives way to commerce. Commerce sullies the sublime heights of nature and art. The piano spreads bourgeois pretension. By the end of the poem, Hotel Splendid has been built at one of the poles and nature's pantheistic intelligence has gone into hiding. The poet can only wish for a second flood.

Rimbaud began writing his *Illuminations*, the collection of prose poems including "After the Flood," in 1873. Aged nineteen, he was as precocious as Mozart, had visited England, and combined arresting imagery with attention to the global expansion of European commerce. There is something breathtaking about the accuracy of his inclusion of the piano, then the epitome of the mechanization of music and the worldwide spread of Western musical practices. By 1886, when *Illuminations* was published,

Rimbaud himself had abandoned his poetic fantasies for two of the dirtiest African trades, arms and ivory. His lines about the piano were prescient: on its ivory keys and mechanical tones, the Western octave made its way around the world.[1]

Between the time Rimbaud wrote his poem and its publication, a new form of musical mechanization had come into being: the phonograph. Thomas Edison invented the first talking machine in 1877. It took a decade longer to turn it from a novelty into a commodity and to recognize that its most attractive use was musical, but by the late 1880s there was already a fad for coin-slot-operated phonographs in the United States. In the decade and a half after the publication of Rimbaud's visionary collection, the phonograph turned into an industry. Emile Berliner, a German immigrant to America, applied in 1887 for a patent for the first talking machine with a flat disc record, called a gramophone to distinguish it from Edison's cylinder phonograph. It was the prototype of all the disc record machines to come and had the decisive advantages that it was easier to mass produce and to use. By the end of the 1890s, many of the major record companies had been formed that continued to dominate the industry until the outbreak of World War I and beyond: Edison's North American Phonograph Company; Berliner's early corporations, which survived crises and emerged after 1900 as Victor, under the leadership of Eldridge Johnson; Victor's sister companies, Gramophone in England and Deutsche Grammophon in Germany (the latter's factory managed by Berliner's brothers in their native town of Hanover); Victor's American rival, Columbia; and Pathé in France. The German industry rapidly expanded after the turn of the century, with the leading competitors consolidated by 1912 into Lindström, a giant to rival the Anglo-American and French firms.[2]

One of the remarkable things about the talking machines, as they were then sometimes called, is how quickly they spread to Europe and the rest of the world. In 1888 Edison's phonograph was exhibited in London. The following year it appeared at the Paris World's Fair and could probably be bought in Shanghai.[3] A decade later, when phonographs were still of poor quality, advertisements for them began to appear in Indian magazines.[4] Technical improvements—above all, Eldridge Johnson's creation of the first spring motor to operate at uniform speed, for Emile Berliner in the late 1890s—and the resolution of patent disputes by the early 1900s led to mass marketing of the phonograph and its expansion to the great urban centers and remote villages of the earth. In 1900 Gramophone's managers in London sent an agent to Australia, Victor and Gramophone made an agreement to divide world markets, and Gramophone's sound engineer Fred Gaisberg made a six-month tour of Russia.[5] In 1902 and 1903 Gaisberg followed up with a recording tour of India, China, Singapore, Penang, and Japan, with Columbia agents not far behind in East Asia.[6] By 1904 one could buy *corrido* ballads in Mexico, calypso in Trinidad, and rumba in Cuba, while classical and popular recordings of Arabic music spread from Cairo to the rest of the Middle East.[7] By mid-decade, German newcomers like Beka and Odeon (which within a few years became subsidiaries of Lindström) were startling Anglo-American managers by flooding foreign markets with cheap machines and taking over a large share of the low-end business. The rival companies recorded in multiple languages and dialects across Asia, the Middle East, and Latin America, while also appealing to immigrant groups in the United States.

By 1907, the peak business year before World War I, the giant phonograph firms had spun a network of phonographs across continents. *Talking Machine World*, the leading American trade journal, carried snippets of news from near and far. Often its accounts had the bright tones of pep talks for its audience of industry marketers. Columbia's Detroit branch "gave an extended demonstration of their new records for the benefit of the newsboys of the city." On the same page, readers could learn that the Russian government was afraid of talking machines. It was "seeing ghosts every day now" and "designs to look upon the talking machine as a revolutionary vehicle. . . ." Panicked, it had "forbidden the use of graphophones in Russian Poland when the discs or records reproduce Polish patriotic airs. All these found have been destroyed and even the machines seized by the police."[8] Scared or not, the Russian government could not hold back the flood of recordings in its own society; Russia became one of the biggest phonograph markets in the world.

To the Ends of the Earth

Like an unironic Rimbaud imagining the bourgeois lady who installs a piano in the Alps, *Talking Machine World* reported on the spread of the phonograph to the pristine places of the earth, hitherto without exposure to Western music. The same issue from 1907 reported that phonographs in Africa were "penetrating even into some of its dark and remote corners." The first traveler to take a machine into the interior initially was threatened by the "savage" locals, but they "fled in abject terror" on hearing a voice from it, and thenceforth regarded him as "a white god who had

at his command a terrible and amazing magic." The article itself embodied a mindless discourse: the racial stereotypes of the white explorer-god,
passed down from generation to generation and now part of the twentieth-
century press's repertoire. The moment of first contact was supposed to
be a prelude to opportunities for profit. An initial encounter in German
South West Africa had given way to scenes of natives sitting around in a
circle and listening to the magical sounds. Soon, predicted the journalist,
the whole of the "Dark Continent . . . from the Cape to Cairo" would be
buying phonographs. The roar of the lion and tiger and the trumpeting
of the elephant, he imagined, "will be mingled with the melody of 'Bill
Simmons' or 'Because You're You.'"[9] Month after month, stories piled up
about the worldwide triumph of the phonograph. In March and June of
the same year came reports of booming business in Mexico, with Walter
Stevens, manager of the foreign department of Edison's National Phonograph Company, making a visit to his Mexico City office.[10] In July came a
warning that the "Japanese will bear watching," for "they cheerfully steal
patented and copyrighted articles for their own profit." During the same
month came the helpful advice to American dealers to use foreign records
in their record recitals—such events were a publicity stunt of the early
recording years—to reach the "cosmopolitan element" in the cities (Wagner, Verdi, Donizetti, and Bizet operas from the Edison catalog were cited
as examples of cosmopolitan fare).[11] In October came news of a Yankee
"push" in the South Seas with the help of the phonograph: A New England
sea captain ferried recruits from the New Hebrides and the Solomon Islands to the sugar plantations of Queensland, Australia. Their misgivings
were calmed as soon as he showed them pictures and played recordings
of their friends who had already signed up. "The Yankee captain certainly
displayed the National traits of enterprise in this transaction," commented
the journalist.[12] In the same issue, royalty was called into the service of
a New York needle maker: "His royal self, the Rajah of Rajputana," announced the advertisement, used a brand of needles called Petmecky.[13] In
November the magazine reported on the outfitting of a US-government-
sponsored trip to the Philippines with phonographs "to secure dialects
of fast disappearing tribes." And a December story gave coverage to the
New Guinea expedition of Rudolf Pöch, and showed a picture of a group
lustily singing while one member of the native ensemble concentrated
on operating the machine.[14] Phonographs were everywhere: that was the
collective message of these bits of news and self-promotion in *Talking
Machine World*. Their agents were as ingenious as Yankee commerce and

as thorough as German science when they crossed the world under the sun of European imperialism. Or so it seemed in the news reports up to 1914, which mixed truth with propaganda to promote an industry that was marked by downturns and frustration as well as achievement.[15]

Beginning in 1905, *Talking Machine World* published weekly figures for global phonograph exports from the Port of New York. As a continuous file they add up to a valuable overview of the early phonograph industry. While confirming the general impression of rapid growth, they also raise questions about the fragmentary nature of the process, the limits of what we can know about it, and the need for qualitative context in order to make sense out of it. The figures are overwhelming as they appear in compact paragraphs on the printed page, with the destinations shifting week by week: for March 13, 1905, they report that packages went to Auckland, Berlin, Buenos Aires, Cardenas, Calcutta, Gibraltar, Hamburg, Havana, Havre, Liverpool, London, Manchester, Montevideo, Mauritius, Rio de Janeiro, Santiago, Sydney, Valparaiso, and "Wina" (Vilna?). Five days later the destinations were Alexandria, Berlin, Brussels, Bombay, Buenos Aires, Callao, Curacoa (Curaçao), Glascow, Hamburg, Havana, Havre, Hong Kong, Kobe, Liverpool, Manchester, Maracaibo, Melbourne, Para, Santos, Santiago, Sheffield, St. Petersburg, Valparaiso, Vienna, Warwick, and Warsaw.[16]

Just these two dates, with their dizzying array of destinations, are enough to suggest the wide variety of places receiving phonographs—but one should multiply their effect to imagine how wide, irregular, and dispersed was the outpouring of packages. Week after week, they landed on different shores, for a total of over four hundred destinations before World War I. They arrived in obscure and out-of-the-way places in addition to the great metropolises and port cities, which for their part bought phonographs but also served as conduits to smaller towns. Overall during the period from 1905 to 1914, the journal recorded 8,086 shipments containing 283,829 packages. These aggregate figures amount to an enormous wave—or, one should say, successive waves, from gentle lappings to floods—of articles shipped around the world.

With the help of optical recognition technology, one can now bring order into this mass of materials and create an overview of American exports. Among the first impressions to emerge is the export industry's breakneck ups and downs. In 1905 the total number of packages (excluding the disproportionately large London exports) was 24,431; it doubled by 1907 to its largest prewar figure, 55,268. Thereafter, it slid to some 30,000,

20,000, and a thuddingly low figure of 13,011 in 1913—less than a quarter of the figure from six years earlier.[17] The unpredictability of exports created a frenzied atmosphere among trade journalists and businessmen. They sensed grand opportunities for profits but came up against unpredictable shifts in the market, and struggled to keep up with their competitors (table 7.1).

A pie chart of the phonograph packages' distribution reveals that despite their great numbers, the destinations are peculiarly limited to certain regions (figure 7.1). About a third of all exports went to the Latin American market (including "North America," made up of shipments to Mexico and Central America). Another 29 percent went to London. This is not a surprising figure, if only because the giant Gramophone Company in London imported products from its American partner, Victor. At the same time it leaves open questions about what portion of the great number of packages shipped there was intended for the British market versus other places in Europe, the British Empire, and other parts of the world.[18] While 14 percent of the packages went to Europe, almost as much—another 13 percent—went to Oceania, primarily Australia. That left only

Table 7.1. Global shipments of phonograph packages from the port of New York, value by year, 1905–1914

Year	Value of shipments to world, excluding London*	Number of Packages to world, excluding London	Value of shipments to London*	Number of Packages to London
1905	$666,781	24,431	$359,859	22,850
1906	859,124	42,115	533,868	38,129
1907	1,237,048	55,268	445,464	29,725
1908	770,814	30,969	335,891	19,904
1909	857,271	33,195	424,074	20,856
1910	1,022,489	32,173	288,231	10,001
1911	999,747	28,998	311,328	10,148
1912	885,841	20,095	286,761	6,803
1913	652,294	13,011	252,323	6,719
1914	175,664	3,574	22,757	639
Total	$8,127,073	283,829	$3,260,556	165,774

*Values given in US dollars. Source: *Talking Machine World*.

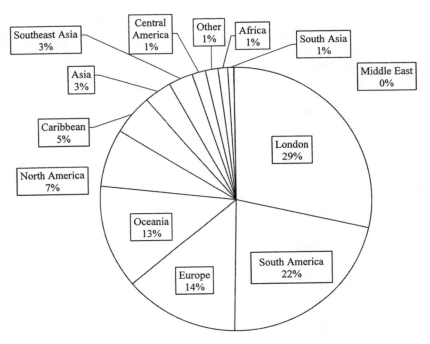

Figure 7.1. Phonograph package shipments from the Port of New York, value by region, 1905–1914. Source: *Talking Machine World.*

tiny smidgens for East and Southeast Asia. Yet a collection of reports by US consuls makes it clear that the story was more complicated. The US consul in Shanghai wrote that in 1909 the United States supplied around 27.5 percent of the imports. Other places certainly hungered for phonographs, even if the numbers and market share were unknown: in Manchuria around 1910 to 1912, reported the consul, "the phonograph has become very popular," and "there is now a moderate demand for machines and records in the larger towns of this district." Did these imports arrive via London, or from an Australian port? As for India, it did not have to import its records, according to the Bombay consul, because Gramophone had started its record factory in Calcutta, and "its output is the most popular in India." The consul estimated: "Probably 75 per cent of the records sold in India are manufactured in this country. The greatest demand is for records in the Hindustani, Gujerati, and Urdu languages, comprising songs, humorous sayings, speeches, etc., just as in the English language." Borders were porous; points of production and transport were various;

Table 7.2. Numbers of phonograph packages shipped from the Port of New York to select cities, 1905–1913

	1905	1906	1907	1908	1909	1910	1911	1912	1913	Total
Brussels	165	1,055	1,161	81	220	83			24	2,789
Buenos Aires	829	1,686	2,176	2,217	2,748	2,869	3,498	2,780	2,832	21,635
Cairo		3	5				13			21
Fremantle			3,725				19			3,744
London	22,850	38,129	29,725	19,904	20,856	10,001	10,148	6,803	6,719	165,135
Melbourne	2,837	1,067	3,756	9,525	4,293	6,406	1,934	772		30,590
Sydney	1,232	8,093	7,208	2,736	6,972	3,769	2,096	1,318	819	34,243
Yokohama	259	533	1,538	364	70	275	1,241	152	48	4,480

Source: *Talking Machine World*

and on the local scene, the success of a hard-driving salesman, the loss of a trusted middleman, or the breakdown of a homesick company employee could change business for better or worse.[19]

The instability of the global market emerges from the statistics for package destinations by city and year (table 7.2). Cities like Buenos Aires, Sydney, Veracruz, and Yokohama (serving as the port city for Tokyo) were regular customers throughout the decade. Even there, however, wide variations in demand qualify the aggregate picture of 1907 as the boom year for phonograph exports. London conforms neatly to the overall pattern, with its 29,725 packages in 1907 and a dropoff to 6,719 by 1913. But Buenos Aires remained strong to the end of the decade and beyond, rising from 2,176 in 1907 to a high of 3,498 in 1911. As a boom town, rapidly building a center to rival European metropolises and attracting large numbers of European immigrants, Buenos Aires followed its own rhythms and demands for entertainment. The table also shows odd gaps: why does Melbourne, in most years a strong market, show a blank for 1913? Why were American manufacturers completely absent from the Brussels market in 1911 and 1912, only to creep back with twenty-four packages the following year? The American consul in Cairo reported large phonograph sales, with most machines imported from the United States—yet the figures from the Port of New York are mostly blank.[20] How, then, were records reaching Cairo? Possibly via London, possibly by another export route; but in any case the Cairo figures are a reminder that, despite its vastness, the *Talking Machine World* information is incomplete.

Smaller places, too, have intriguing stories to tell about phonograph exports. Fremantle, Australia, made a strong showing for exactly one year, 1907. With 3,725 packages worth $63,648, it ranked among the top twenty sales destinations for the entire period from 1905 to 1914. But why Fremantle, not an obvious choice for such a strong showing? There was in fact good reason for it to indicate a strong demand for phonographs. Western Australia was a gold rush site in the 1890s, and it continued to prosper in the following decade with a pattern of ongoing immigration, building in the towns, and diversification of its economy. By 1900 Fremantle was a major port for the interior. It had become a place with money to spend on an entertainment luxury like phonographs. Why it showed up for just one year is a puzzle probably answered by decisions about distribution within the Australian market—but the yearly figures do not reveal anything about alternative routes.[21]

Another place, tiny Curaçao, then a Dutch plantation colony, provides a striking contrast to Fremantle's boom and bust, instead showing a steady run of healthy import figures from 1907 to 1913 (table 7.3). But why? The total population of the island was small (33,361 in 1916). In the early twentieth century it had a small merchant and official elite with a hunger for culture and novelties like the cinema, but the rest of the population was poor. and after a brief boom in phosphate exports in the 1880s it lived on the verge of a subsistence crisis. While Curaçao enjoyed a certain

Table 7.3. Phonograph packages shipped from the Port of New York to Curaçao, 1905–1913

Year	Shipments	Total number of packages	Total value*
1905	1	8	$158
1907	1	3	104
1908	3	11	523
1909	1	3	170
1910	2	139	515
1911	3	14	492
1912	3	7	360
1913	1	6	307
Total	15	191	$2,629

*Values given in US dollars.
Source: Talking Machine World

fashionable reputation and its Dutch masters enjoyed showing off its hats, dolls, cigars, rum, and other products at 1859 and 1883 exhibitions in Amsterdam and at the Brussels World's Fair in 1910, none of this advertising led to satisfactory profits for the island. The phonograph imports had to do not with Curaçao's domestic consumption but with its usefulness as a strategic location. What mattered was the island's good harbor and ample storage place, which made it a convenient point of transit for goods heading for nearby Venezuela and the rest of the northern coast of South America, as well as the Eastern Antilles.[22] Phonographs probably passed through Curaçao along well-defined trade routes. The export figures for this island, then, take us into a local network of distribution—and suggest how phonographs could diffuse through a web of arteries to reach places that do not make it into the statistics. To understand where globalization happened, one has to go from place to place and reconstruct local histories. Stories like the ones from Fremantle and Curaçao take us beyond even the hundreds of ports listed in the export figures and reveal how far and wide mechanized sound was spreading across the earth.

These examples can stimulate more general curiosity about the hundreds of places receiving phonographs: What mixture of factors—fashion, systems of distribution, local economies, legislation—accounts for the unstable numbers in each case? And how accurate were the figures? Only rarely and anecdotally does one get to glimpse the oddities that went into the reporting. According to the 1912 United States consular report, in 1910 Argentina claimed imports of 2,073 units of phonographs valued at $7,053. Compare this statement with the figure from *Talking Machine World* for exports from New York for 1910: 2,901 packages valued at $144,351! What could explain this enormous disparity in the export figures? Did it have to do with the method of counting, or exaggeration by the customs officials in New York? From Buenos Aires the consul, General R. M. Bartleman, suggested a different explanation: The valuations he reported were "those assigned for customs purposes, and not necessarily representing the true value of the phonograph. . . ."[23] In plain language, the local figures were falsifications, on the order of a twentyfold minimalization, to reduce import duties; there is no reason to doubt the accuracy of the *Talking Machine World* valuation.

Altogether, the figures from *Talking Machine World* teach us a great deal that we did not know before, if only the global breadth of names and places that got exposed to phonographs in the early years of the twentieth century. This is in itself an expansion of our retrospective view of globalization, which tends to shrink the movement of goods, commodity, and knowledge to a handful of metropolises, with only hazy guesses to guide us beyond them. Instead, the export destination names are windows into the specific histories of hundreds of less obvious places with their own booms, busts, and appetite for the new sonic world of recorded music. The tables also give the impression of a business with wild ups and downs in sales year by year, and of a new form of entertainment that may have come and gone from smaller places. The impact of phonographs was complex: both revolutionary—bringing a new technology and great changes in musical life—and fragile and uncertain in its duration. On this evidence, globalization was less a steady onward and upward than a staccato of sound that could give way to silence.

The quantitative evidence for the global spread of phonographs is valuable, then, but also a maze of uncertainty unless it is complemented by qualitative sources. A critical corrective requires description, commentary, and attention to human interests. The consular reports come to our aid by offering a display of anecdotes from a far-flung collection of American observers. By 1912, according to the consul on the spot, door-to-door canvassers sold machines and records in Chihuahua. "Everybody has a phonograph in Belize" was the saying in British Honduras. Brazilians cherished "small machines with large, decorated horns and showy cases and fittings." Record music blared at all hours in Bombay. Alexandria, Egypt, was filled with advertising "both in newspapers and on billboards, as well as by elaborate window displays," with opera music the most prominent. The settler states of South Africa, Australia, and New Zealand were all strong markets for American products, with the Australians singled out as "lavish buyers" who went for "phonographs of superior grade."[24] Phonographs were the first form of audio entertainment to be marketed to individual consumers around the world. They broke through the constraints of time and place to bring the pleasure of music by outstanding performers to metropolitan cities and faraway villages. With cars an expensive rarity and household machines a thing of the future, it was phonographs that first brought to rich and poor alike the excitement of consumer goods, whether in the form of tinny-sounding contraptions for bars and dance halls or heavy wooden cases for bourgeois living rooms. Yet music did not just go out from the centers of production to the peripheries of consumption. Markets were unpredictable and contested; the taste in phonographs and music varied from place to place; and American manufacturers struggled against British, German, and French competitors. Capitalists from all of these places did not dictate modern sounds to the world; if they wished to sell phonographs and recordings, they had to adapt to local taste. Like quantitative export figures, the consular reports' descriptions of different markets are a warning against viewing globalization as a process of cumulative growth. Their reporting was sometimes blurred by the expectation that they would serve as the agents of American business interests: consuls often wrote in an upbeat tone, a little like the reporters in the trade journal, as if doing their job meant pointing out opportunities for entrepreneurs. Still, their reports are a collective snapshot of testimonies from a single moment in time, the cumulative effort of observers spread out around the world. They were not always boosters; their reports commented on the shortcomings of American businesses (for example, their loss of markets to lower-priced German phonographs) as well as their prominence in many places. Despite their limitations, the consuls bore witness again and again to the creation of a novel form of global entertainment.

Brash and up-to-date, the phonograph industry did its part to capture one of the characteristic spectacles of the age: polar expeditions. These adventures looked back to the heroic age of exploration, when explorers from Martin Frobisher in the 1570s to Captain Cook two centuries later braved the icy north in search of a watery passage between Atlantic and Pacific. Mary Shelley made a journey to the North Pole the framing story for *Frankenstein*, announcing the glory and the madness of the modern quest for knowledge; over the course of the nineteenth century travelers kept up the romance, dreaming of the Northwest Passage and a flag at the North Pole. By the end of the nineteenth century, polar expeditions had turned into a vast theater for audiences around the world. Eager for attention from the beginning of his career, Franz Boas went to Baffin Island, vast and remote between Greenland and mainland Canada, for his first fieldwork; he was enticed by the German public's fascination with polar expeditions, and went with the sponsorship of a Berlin newspaper. At the turn of the twentieth century he reached out for attention from the American public with the Jesup North Pacific Expedition, an enterprise encompassing the Siberian and American sides of the Bering Strait. Arctic and Antarctic expeditions combined commerce, scientific enterprise, national competition, the will to claim uncharted lands, and the prospect of fame and money for the lucky few who reached their goals and made it back home.[25]

Explorers at the Bering Strait showed off their phonograph in a picture from the very first (January 1905) issue of *Talking Machine World*. It blared at a group of tired-looking Aleutian Islanders, a people enslaved and abused by Russians for more than a century, while an anonymous European traveler, towering over them in his black hat, stared at the machine's long slender megaphone. "It is possible [that] they are hearing for the first time modern music of the leading orchestras, as well as songs and witty sayings which are current in the large cities," wrote the reporter about the Aleuts. "Through the aid of the talking machine their lot has been made a happy one, and the world made smaller in a comparative sense." The incident was a telling example of the prewar idea of the civilizing mission, in which Europeans and Americans readily assumed that the trinkets and songs of the big city were a welcome replacement for a lost way of life.[26]

In another magazine story, Joseph Hutchinson, a politician and mining magnate prospecting in Port Barrow, Alaska, bumped into the phonograph and its works. According to a report in *Talking Machine World*'s second issue of 1905, ". . . He and his American companions were startled one day to hear an Indian coming slowly among the fir trees softly and musically humming 'The Holy City' song. He had its air, its keys, its intonations and its harmony chords well trained in his throat. Its rendition away up there made the white men stand on their feet." A few months earlier, they learned, a prospector had traded a phonograph and seven music cylinders worth forty dollars for three grizzly bear pelts worth a thousand dollars. Among the cylinders was the evangelical favorite from the 1890s (on its way to lasting fame through a bit part in James Joyce's *Ulysses* and, more recently, recordings by Mahalia Jackson, Jessye Norman, and the Mormon Tabernacle Choir). "'It goes to show,' said Mr. Hutchinson, 'that <music hath charms to soothe the savage breast> even so far north as Port Barrow, where it would seem the weather would freeze and hold and chill every poetic thought or sentiment that had song in it.'" Of all the music the "Indian" had gotten from the prospector, "'The Holy City' struck him the most forcefully. And it seemed strange and out of all reason that we should hear that sacred anthem hummed and rendered prettily away up there amid the snows and the ice crags of the Arctic."[27] The phonograph accompanied scientific explorers too: Vilhjalmur Stefansson took a talking machine with him on a 1906 trip to Coronation Gulf, Prince Albert Land, in Canada, and three Victor phonographs on an Arctic trip of 1913. In the meantime, he had made sensational (and absurd) claims to have discovered "Caucasian" Eskimos on Victoria Island in the Canadian Arctic Archipelago. He went on to become one of the founders of modern Arctic studies, and a professor at Dartmouth College.[28] Captain Robert Falcon Scott took two gramophones with him, gifts of the Gramophone Company, on his tragic expedition of 1912 to the South Pole. Scott and his men perished, but one gramophone was rescued and returned to the company.[29]

In the trade propaganda, the phonograph comforted brave men in the darkest and loneliest nights. It taught oppressed and isolated peoples at the edge of the inhabitable earth the cheerful sounds of the latest popular songs from the metropolises of Europe and America. It introduced them to the promise of eternal life, making the exchange for a few pelts a very good deal indeed. It was not just about profits; it was about a machine that was all-pervasive, traveling to the most remote regions as a bearer of European imperialism's civilizing mission, as grand and absurd as Rimbaud's satirical image of Mme. ***'s piano in the Alps. Through the phonograph, Western imperialism around the world declaimed like Caruso and enticed like a gospel tune.

The Labor of Globalization

To recount the numbers and names and places is to create the impression of an effortless spread of phonographs around the world. The trade magazines often imagined it thus as they cheered on the salesmen who carried their wares to customers in domestic and foreign markets. Beneath the surface of a smooth circulation, however, obstacles of many kinds—technical, legal, financial, organizational—beset the inventors, managers, and marketers who dreamed of making millions from the magical talking machines. The patent wars of the turn of the twentieth century almost destroyed the American industry from within. The flood of cheap machines from Germany overwhelmed Anglo-American manufacturers in South American and Asian markets. Market saturation led to declining sales and a consolidation of the German industry, with well-financed Lindström swallowing up the smaller producers. World War I leveled the German industry, which made an astonishing recovery in the 1920s; radio almost destroyed Victor, which barely survived as an acquisition of RCA.

Even to describe the industry's collective failures and successes is to make it sound too much like a roller coaster that careened its way forward through ups and downs with the force of a machine. It was not; that is again the fantasy from afar. Human beings created the industry and sometimes failed. For every Eldridge Johnson, who rose from semieducated mechanic to decades-long strategist behind Victor's triumphs, there were others like William Barry Owen, who brilliantly led Gramophone in its early years, only to end his days in poverty, supported by a pension from his former colleagues. Fred Gaisberg thrived on six months of wild travel through Russia, recording and signing up the "talent," as musicians were called; but other foreign agents fumbled their sales and lost their health.

The labor history of the industry—as opposed to the chronology of its profits and losses—has only begun to be written. We have glimpses of factory workers in Berlin and Hanover, Germany, but know nothing about workers in the factories of Camden and Orange, New Jersey; Hayes (in greater London); Riga; and Calcutta. What were their wages and hours? How skilled were they, and when did they protest, strike, and organize unions? Some were skilled craftsmen who would have been prime candidates for political and economic organizing in an age of unionization. Their stories of sweat, nerves, and ingenuity in assembling phonographs and getting them to markets are difficult to tease out of newspapers or archives. For now, we have only a scattering of archival records and published accounts to evoke the craft and class dimensions of early machine and record production.

The recording sessions have left deeper traces. One of the best professional recording engineers, Raymond Sooy, started out working for Victor in 1903 and developed a high level of skill for recording on the road. According to the autobiography he set down for the firm—later rescued from the streets of Camden outside the abandoned record factory—he and his three brothers left school early to support his widowed mother and keep the household together. After working for five years as a machinist, he got a job thanks to his brother in the recording department of the Victor laboratory, then located in Philadelphia. By 1905 he was recording William Jennings Bryan at home in Lincoln, Nebraska; in 1908 he recorded President Taft in Hot Springs, Virginia. From his beginnings on the shop room floor, Sooy rose to mastery of a newly invented form of craft labor.

In the same year as his Taft recording, Sooy took his first foreign trip, sailing from New York to Veracruz and taking a night train from there to Mexico City. His wife accompanied him, and they had "many amusing experiences due to our not being able to speak Spanish," which was, he added helpfully, "the language of Mexico." He must have done well despite the linguistic adventure. In 1909 he recorded in Havana; in 1910 he made a grand tour of Bahia, Rio de Janeiro, Santos, Montevideo, and Buenos Aires. The Argentine capital was "an up-to-date city in every respect." The one thing that seemed strange to him and his companions was that it was cold in summer and hot in winter. Sooy, who later recorded Vladimir Horowitz and Sergei Rachmaninoff, may have been a simple-minded chronicler of foreign places. But his were the kind of determination and skills that account for Victor's success in Latin American markets.

When it came to capturing sound, Sooy's naiveté gave way to thoughtful observations. "A good recorder must have at least five years of experience," he wrote. "He must be a very quick thinker and patient—must know how to meet and handle all kinds of temperamental people, and govern himself under some very trying conditions. He must get the confidence of the artist with whom he has to work, whether they be good, bad or indifferent—also must not show any signs of disappointment whether the voice he is recording be good or bad, but try under all circumstances to get the best record possible." The recorder had to have negotiating skills, for he dealt with everything from symphony orchestras to "Hillbilly songs," handled large amounts of money to pay artists, paid them in countries where he did not know the language, and was responsible for the name of the music and composer as well as the holder and date of copyright. Technical challenges abounded. On the road he had to judge the acoustics of unfamiliar rooms and make mechanical and electrical repairs on the spot. His ears had to be sensitive to the distinctive vibrations of each instrument and voice; his eyes followed the grooves in the wax masters after a recording was made and could pick out lines that experience had taught would not record correctly. ". . . I can safely say that nine times out of ten, a good recording man can walk out in the studio and put his hand on the man or instruments causing the trouble, move them a little farther away from the microphone, [and] make another record, which will prove to be perfect." In a sophisticated version of the home recorder's task, he had to place all the instruments of an orchestra so that they had the right balance; for example, the piccolo would record louder than any other wind instrument, and thus required special placement. "I have always contended that a good recording man must be the same as a good musician—he must feel his work in order to get the best results out of it, as this cannot be done mechanically and prove successful," he contended. There was a large area of overlap, then, between musicians and engineer. The engineer was not a passive recipient, but actually shaped the sound with his eyes and ears. He taught the musicians to rework their performances for the new medium; his judgment determined volume and pitch. He was technician, coach, conductor, and critic. Sooy was making an arresting statement of fact when he wrote that like a musician, he had to *feel* the music.[30]

While Sooy turned helpless when it came to comprehending the temperature and tongues of foreign places, management—at least, successful management—knew better. It took both technical ingenuity and cultural alertness to make records abroad. As Edward N. Burns, the export manager and mastermind behind Columbia's overseas empire, noted in an interview, challenges abounded: it took several years just to figure out how to package wax masters so that they would survive their outbound and return journeys unblemished. Like Sooy, he emphasized how much time and patience went into training local musicians to sing for the recording machine. For example, according to Burns, Western recording artists learned to take high notes slowly, whereas in Japan, China, and Thailand "the voices are explosive"; the Western companies developed a special diaphragm for the recording machine "to take up or absorb these sharp inequalities of sound." Outside the recording session, too, a process of accommodation had to take place. Western agents relied on local dealers for their choice of recordings, but the dealers were not good at gauging their customers' taste, and one simply had to use trial and error to figure out local markets. Chinese compradors, the wholesaler-mediators whom Western agents turned to throughout East and Southeast Asia, must have had high translating and negotiating skills, for Burns praised their honesty and reliability. He estimated that out of six hundred Chinese records, only about fifty were profitable. It was hard to get the color of the labels right for local preferences: no yellow, an imperial color, in China, but brilliant red would do; black and gold were best for Japan and also acceptable for Thai, Malay, and Arabic labels. The titles "cause[d] no end of trouble": the sound engineers sent them "transcribed in the native tongue, without a translation. . . . Then on their arrival in New York we are compelled to get a translation somewhere, somehow." More timid minds resented the risks and wrinkles of the foreign trade, but Burns forged ahead with conquering the audio world.[31]

As it reached out to the world, then, the recording industry did not fit the model of a soulless destroyer of culture. Many contemporary observers thought of it that way: Rimbaud's image of a world littered with Western sound machines (pianos, in his case) belonged to a larger wave of anxiety about musical mechanization. Yet the transformation of musical sound was far more paradoxical than the poet and his contemporaries

could comprehend. It was not an exaggeration to speak of a vast rationalization that gripped the modern orchestra, the piano, and the training, production, and circulation of music in the late nineteenth and early
twentieth century. Yet these changes did not undermine music's expressive potential as composers, performers, business agents, and entrepreneurs took up the mechanization and commercialization of sound with
many-sided creative responses. Capturing sound on recordings inspired
adventure and imagination; it carried an unforeseen potential for widening humanity's sonic horizons beyond Europe.

8

Americans Abroad: Innocents and Transnationals

By 1903, a quarter century after Edison's historic recording of "Mary Had a Little Lamb," the phonograph industry had reached an initial stage of technological and business maturity. Recordings and phonographs were ready for mass distribution, and the leading firms plotted competing strategies.[1] Before his rivals Columbia and Victor existed, Edison made a splash with national and international audiences. An article under his name on "The Phonograph and its Future" in the *North American Review* of May 1878 announced his invention to a highbrow readership just a few months after his patent for the new invention went through. Edison imagined numerous uses for the phonograph, from business dictation machine to toy; he only mentioned music in passing, without foreseeing its singular importance.[2] After his initial breakthrough, however, Edison put aside the phonograph in order to concentrate on improving the incandescent light. By the turn of the century, when the craze for recorded music was spreading, a swarm of newcomers in the United States and Europe were working on technical improvements, pouring capital into new firms, and strategizing to take over worldwide markets.

The nimbus of his name and prowess of his business and technical enterprise still made Edison a power to reckon with. At the turn of the century his attention had turned back to the neglected invention, and he did become a major maker of phonographs. But by 1914, competing American, German, and French manufacturers had outstripped the National Phonograph Company, especially in appealing to consumers overseas. In the United States it was an immigrant inventor, Emile Berliner, who had the transnational skills to achieve what eluded Edison and his business partners: the creation of a global phonograph empire.

The American Market

If Edison faltered, the reasons were partly technical—and partly personal. Berliner's alternative to the Edison cylinder was the flat disc with a needle and arm bearing down on it, the lasting design for the recording market until the late-twentieth-century advent of digital technologies. Within a few years of Berliner's release of his first commercial discs in 1895, Columbia followed his lead and made the leap from cylinder to disc technology. Edison, however, insisted on the superiority of his original invention: he stuck with the cylinder. Commentators—beginning with his employees at the time—have pointed to Edison's insistence on retaining the cylinder as the cause of his company's lag behind Victor and Columbia. Edison publicists confronted their customers' frustration with their finicky machines by giving them operating manuals. As late as 1912, one had to set up the little cylinder machine, and once it was set up, it had to be adjusted to stay at 160 revolutions per minute. Making home recordings was more demanding. "The first efforts are disappointing," warned a 1908 manual, comparing the effort to the "time, care and study" that went into photography, and giving detailed instructions for placing the musicians when recording solos, duets, quartets, bands, violins, string orchestras, banjos, and mandolins. For example, tenors were supposed to occupy the center of all-male quartets, and soloists were to step forward to the receiving horn for solos and then step back.[3]

Historians also point out Edison's competitors' superior skills at signing up star artists and appealing to consumer tastes. Edison sized up the phonograph's attractions differently from his competitors. He cared passionately about sound quality, and had decided ideas about what made for good or bad recordings; he was also convinced that consumers would recognize the superiority of his product and prefer it.[4] A memo in his handwriting of December 1911, which went to his London branch manager, lay down his methods and preferences. He was skeptical about the big opera stars: "Take [Titta] Ruffo—I heard his voice on Victor Record & I would not put his voice on our new disc even if he paid me—his voice is attuned to a large place like an opera house which transcribed on a phonograph & put in a Home gives poor results, Bonci [Alessandro Bonci], has not this effect." Edison declared in the same memorandum that he had "personally listened to all our records made in last 7 years 3600 all together to determine, what is wrong in recording—& the kind of voices wanted. . . ." New Jersey church choirs and glee clubs had plenty of talent suitable for the phonograph; he was "getting ready . . . to test all the Church Choir voices in Orange & Newark [New Jersey]" and had already found two tenors who he thought were only surpassed by Caruso.[5] Edison's judgment determined the fate of every candidate for recording at the Orange, New Jersey, plant. When an artist wrote from Newark that he had been in a state of nervous suspense ever since making a trial record several weeks before, an employee explained that often "several weeks will elapse before Mr. Edison finds time to hear trial records of singers."[6] The inventor-businessman kept a tight grip on the decision of which recordings would be associated with his name.

What Edison did *not* judge was the aesthetic qualities of a recording. While he might have casual personal preferences (he was partial to the harp, and his employees made many trial recordings with a Miss Maud Morgan before deciding not to use her harp recitals), he had no interest in qualities of personal style or artistic innovation that might have led him to admire a voice even if it recorded imperfectly.[7] In other words, Edison listened as an engineer. Recording quality was purely a technical issue for him. But audiences did not listen to records just for their sound quality. They cared about *what* was being played: whether it was in fashion, whether they liked the lyrics, whether they were moved by the voice. And they cared about *who* was performing; then as now, people sought out star performers, who before 1914 were likely to come from Italian opera. Edison preferred New Jersey talent and small-town taste, but that was not enough to satisfy audiences at home and around the world. In a fast-moving business, Victor (followed with less success by Columbia) snapped up most of the stars, and left Edison's hapless managers on the sidelines.[8]

As Edison's managers became aware of the problem, they made frantic efforts to sign up top talent. In 1906 they had the intriguing idea of recording opera in English as a way of expanding their list to reach classical music lovers.[9] But this would not have taken care of their basic deficit; three years later, William H. Miller, manager of the recording division,

was complaining that he could hardly find a single artist to sign up beyond the "middle class."[10] In 1912 the National Phonograph Company was
still trying to buy up Italian talent; it paid Adelina Agostinelli Quiroli the
round-trip costs of travel from Milan to London for a recording session
as part of her contract agreement to make two masters of ten different
selections, for which the company promised to pay her $2,500 in the
signed contract of March 23, 1912.[11] There was also talk of adding instrumental selections to bolster the classical offerings: in 1909 the National
Phonograph Company tried and failed to sign up the celebrated violinist
Fritz Kreisler.[12] Reaching the upscale market was not easy. The big stars
demanded big bucks, and they already had contracts with Victor and Columbia; Edison's company found itself outclassed.

Edison's taste and choice of market may have been provincial, but his
genius came through when he turned to phonograph quality and technological improvements. It is remarkable to see how much time Edison
sacrificed to ensure—in his own way—nothing but the best for his phonographs and recordings. Several of his laboratory notebooks are filled with
his comments—scribbled in pencil, often in broken sentences—on hundreds of recordings. They bear out the image of Edison the sound engineer, able to differentiate fine qualities in the reproduction of tone, but
unsophisticated or uninterested when it came to artistry. One comes away
from these judgments of hundreds of recordings impressed by his frank-
ness (the notebooks were for his personal use), preferences (he thought
tremolo was horrid), and folksy American language (an excellent record
was a "crackerjack"):

B 182 Should get this tune—the voices interfere very badly = the basso
has a fat frying voice—the combination seems to be very good—
769 = This man has a good voice in this tune, at least—has no
evidence of the Vaudeville Tone—Tune not enjoyable but might use the
man in something—
44 = Enjoyable—Lay yourself out to get this—Important to get it
perfect
Try other singers, for instance another woman—Want to make this a
Crackerjack, Everybody loves it possibly a grand opera woman
If you use a tenor the womans voice will not blast against the
Barytone [sic]—
35016 Rotten accompaniment
Blasts in womans voice part—

> This may not show on disc
> V o i c e R i c h
> Record is somewhat Enjoyable—*get it*
> This woman is a pretty good
> Singer, think you will have good luck with her, only trouble
> Is those wheezy blasts at several places[13]

And so it went, often in brief comments, in his evaluation of hundreds of recordings. As Sooy testified, it was a delicate craft to produce a satisfying sound: placement in relationship to the recording machine, the constellation of voices and instruments, and the timbre and other features of an individual voice all affected the final product. Edison analyzed these aspects of recording with a self-assured sense of what sounded right and what would sell. Meanwhile, his managers watched their competitors bound past them.

When it came to immigrant markets, American manufacturers had to come to terms with foreign cultures. How well prepared to do this were Edison and his managers? Their response was a tale of communication between cultures.

The advertisements and catalogs of record manufacturers document the contemporary belief that there was money to be made in foreign records. Indeed, they suggest an imperial imagination of ever greater markets at home and abroad. Inside their offices, the Edison managers worried about stumbling; but to the outside world they offered robust listings of foreign records. A handsome 1904 Christmas pamphlet in Christmas colors, with a dark fir green background, a gold Art Nouveau winding frame, and red balls or fruit hanging from the gold, advertised Edison Gold Moulded Records (hardened black cylinders introduced two years earlier) for 35 cents each or $4.20 per dozen. Customers could order cylinders by mail, many of them recorded abroad: British music, most of it from the British Military Band; Bohemian music; French songs, including numbers by Saint-Saëns, Verdi, Meyerbeer, Gluck, Halévy, and Bizet; Canadian selections, most of it folk and military music, including "Blue Bells of Scotland" and "La Marseillaise"; and German, Hebrew, Hungarian, Italian, Mexican, Polish, Russian, and Spanish selections, most of them vocal music. Chinese listeners could order "To Destroy the Four Gates" (song and orchestra), "A Widow's Lament" (song and orchestra), "Comic Recitation by Sher Doy Wong," and "Travelling by the West Lake." Their Japanese counterparts could enjoy "Song of Mount Fiji," "A Student's Thoughts of

Home" (sung to the tune of "Bonny Doon"), and "Nearer My God to Thee."[14] The languages and the recordings changed year after year. In 1908 the comprehensive brochure added music from Cuba, Denmark, Norway, and Sweden. In 1910 four catalogs covered twenty nationalities, including novel Belgian, Dutch, Argentine, Puerto Rican, and Philippine numbers.[15] Their offerings for immigrant consumers were hardly less capacious than the ones mentioned in the Victor trade journal for 1913, which announced twenty-six foreign languages in fourteen special catalogs.[16]

Edison's quest for foreign markets at home—that is, immigrant audiences—began with an impressive recording campaign. German titles were a recurring favorite. The first issue of the *Edison Phonograph Monthly*, in March 1903, announced a jumble of record entertainment including Germanica ("Heidelberg: Stein Song"); the May 1904 issue advertised the multicultural "Du Du Lichs mir im Herzen (or The Wearin' of the Green)," calling it "a comic and yet clever mixture of Irish and Dutch [German] dialect and singing. . . ."[17] Inane music for Jewish immigrants also abounded. A "Hebrew" vaudeville parody, "Rip Van Winkle Was a Lucky Man," spoken and sung by Julian Rose, was announced in March 1903.[18] The May issue followed up with Rose's new records for its "Hebrew" collection: "They open with the usual talk in Hebrew dialect, followed by singing. The song in 8417 is a parody on 'When the Boys Go Marching By,' and that in 8423 is a parody on 'Go 'Way Back and Sit Down.'"[19] The "Hebrew dialect" would have been Yiddish, bathed in a blend of American popular tunes, European opera, and brass sections. Not that Edison hesitated to reach for the sublime. The only foreign listing for June of the same year was the Kol Nidre, "the great Hebrew religious song" (more precisely the opening declaration of Yom Kippur, the Day of Atonement); the singer was Frank Seiden, best known as a recorder of humorous songs.[20]

Chinese music also attracted the National Phonograph Company's attention. A record engineer went from the Orange, New Jersey, compound to San Francisco in order to record some samples, resulting in forty-six records with nineteen subjects (nine songs took up more than one record—for example, "To Destroy the Four Gates," on twelve records).[21] By October, the magazine was also promoting Japanese titles as bizarre as its German and Jewish fare; it expected a good Anglophone trade for the Japanese songs, since "some of them are sung to well known English tunes."[22] A jumbling and jostling of cultures, a variety show that spanned Atlantic and Pacific danced across the Edison listings alongside hometown favorites like "I Wonder Why Bill Bailey Don't Come Home," and a medley of

"Southern Patriotic Airs" played by the Edison Military Band.[23] Catalog entries like these sometimes blared an almost defiantly racist humor, but also signaled an emerging American attempt, without European counterpart, to cross cultural borders.

The National Phonograph Company made the recordings, but lacked the imagination for successful marketing. A 1909 memorandum outlining its advertising plans reveals what a modest place foreign markets occupied in its strategic thinking. Edison was personally curious about how his company's advertising was keeping up with Victor's, and a report was prepared to give him overall figures for its own expenditures, plus some educated guesses about its competitor. About $125,000 of Edison money went to "general weeklies and monthly magazines." Many of the names still look familiar today: *The Saturday Evening Post, Cosmopolitan, Ladies' Home Journal, Redbook, Sunset, Scientific American, Harper's,* and *Good Housekeeping,* among others. These were publications for a white middle-class audience across the United States. Another $100,000 had been budgeted for newspapers, but after deciding at a meeting the previous October to give up newspaper advertising, the company had instead invested most of the money—more than $60,000—in farm papers and country weeklies. Edison was supposed to be investing roughly the same amount as Victor and Columbia in these general and farm serials. The company also experimented with advertisements in a small number of foreign-language newspapers. Nine of these were German-language papers in St. Louis; Chicago; New York; Lincoln, Nebraska; and Milwaukee; followed by smaller numbers of Norwegian, Swedish, Bohemian, Jewish, and Italian publications. The total budget for the foreign-language serials came to a little over $3,000, only a fraction of the English-language budget. Edison's company pursued the immigrant markets, then, but not strenuously. The impact of records on these communities may still have been considerable; star performers and popular tunes could cross class, racial, and national lines. But the Edison center of gravity was white, small-town, and rural America, to whose tastes and prejudices it gladly gave a voice.[24]

Global Edison

The National Phonograph Company shared its rivals' attraction to world markets. The *Edison Phonograph Monthly* announced in its second issue of April 1903: "The demand for Edison Phonographs and Records in Europe, South America and Australia is rapidly becoming one of the most important features of our business. During the past year the business of our Foreign Department was more than double what it was the year before. . . ."[25] If Victor was making its mark in part by using its London affiliate, Gramophone, as a springboard to the wider world, Edison's company had its own plans for opening up London and continental branches. In August 1903 its trade journal reported that it was making "extensive arrangements for the increase of its business abroad" and had already set up a plant for making master records that would be shipped to New Jersey for mass production until plants for this purpose could be opened abroad.[26] It was a hopeful and ambitious moment.

Compared to their rivals, however, the Edison managers were slowpokes. In response to the Edison company president's hesitant request to keep a complete stock of Russian records in Berlin, the foreign sales manager wrote that there would not be a lot of Russian business in the near future and that the list of Russian records was "practically obsolete." Yet by this time Fred Gaisberg, sent out by Gramophone, had already made a first tour of Russia and signed up a bevy of superb artists. It was rather lame of the Edison manager to write from London that they should "begin making a good class of Russian music" when Gaisberg had already found an excellent class of Russian music and cut the records.[27]

As for India, another foreign market eyed by competing companies, the Edison company's entry was hobbled by timid managers who hesitated to leap feet first into a new continent. Writing from New York in 1907, a year in which American record exports were booming, Walter Stevens, the manager of the foreign department, reported to W. E. Gilmore, the company president, that export sales had slipped from $45,145.95 in 1905 to $30,309.04 in 1906, a loss of almost a third. "Naturally," he wrote blandly about this disaster, "I set about to ascertain the cause." He put his finger on the company's deficiency: "For several years the only things we could offer the Indian trade were our Phonographs and Records of instrumental and vocal music made in the States. We were, however, on an equal footing with our competitors, in this respect." To make records in India, Edison's wholesalers and dealers there purchased Edison blanks and made their own records. "The finished product was very crude, indeed. . . ." Meanwhile, Stevens admitted, contradicting his own statement about "equal footing" with the competition, Gramophone of London and the Beka Company of Berlin had "sent their experts to India, and recorded a large number of selections." Other companies too, he added, were talking about sending sound engineers to India to record native records.

Hence it was "imperative that we send our people to India, unless we wish to surrender this very valuable territory to our competitors." The role of local businessmen, Stevens recognized, was critical: "It would be impossible for us to undertake this work without co-operating with our principal jobbers, who understand fully the situation, and are in close touch with the talent, as all have made native Records for their own trade." He proposed sending an "expert" accompanied by "a tactful man from our office" who had experience dealing with Indian merchants on a trip to Bombay (where Edison did most of its business) at a cost of $13,000 for an output of eight hundred to one thousand records. At its height, Edison's business in India had brought in $50,000; he thought it would not be difficult to double that figure if the company did not cede market control to its competitors.[28] Another letter to Gilmore, from a company employee in Newark, made a now-or-never plea for starting to make recordings in India: Gramophone had recently opened a factory there, and at least two other companies were recording "on the spot." Yet these pleas for action were disregarded. No Edison expedition to India took place. Instead, by the end of 1908 just nineteen Indian recordings were left in the catalog (in the category "miscellaneous, India") and record sales had sunk to almost nothing.[29]

Edison made a more serious effort in Mexico. The United States government report of 1912 stated, "Phonographs are purchased by all classes in all parts of the Republic of Mexico—in the large cities and towns, in mountain villages far removed, on haciendas, and in isolated mining camps."[30] This was a rich market, and five years earlier the Edison company had made a concerted effort to compete in it with Victor and Columbia. Walter Stevens himself took a trip to put the company's business there on a firm footing, at roughly the same time that he was unsuccessfully pleading for a similar trip to Bombay. Setting up a sales and distribution network in Mexico gave him a close-up view he could share with Gilmore, then president of the National Phonograph Company, and with Thomas Edison himself.

In his correspondence during the trip and in his final report, Stevens described problems that reached down to the everyday details of doing business. To be sure, Rafael Cabañas, Edison's office manager in Mexico City, was capable and widely respected: "Personally," Stevens wrote on May 2, 1907, "I have never met a more gentlemanly fellow and a more loyal Edison man. I do not think that if offered double the salary, he would leave our Company." Stevens haggled with him about salary, and at a time when competent Mexican executives were in demand, they finally settled on $550, which was below the going rate of $600 to $1,000.[31] It was short-sighted stinginess. A few years later, Cabañas would confound Stevens's confidence in his loyalty and jump over to Columbia, where he became the director first of Mexican and later of Canadian operations. Beyond the search for a manager, it was so difficult to find a competent clerk for Cabañas that Stevens decided to have someone sent from the New York office to help him. Cabañas had "a fairly good bookkeeper," but "his accounts needed systematizing," so he arranged with an auditor named Mr. Johnson to review the accounts with Cabañas and his bookkeeper. An overdue bill from the Columbia store had to be collected, and payment of accounts due after thirty days had to be made the rule. Stevens could feel satisfied that he had shown his managerial mettle and was leaving the Mexican business in good hands.

Despite the petty day-to-day annoyances of running a business, Stevens thought that Mexico City had excellent prospects as a phonograph market, estimating that in this city of almost half a million people, perhaps a fifth had "plenty of money, which they spend very freely" and were candidates for purchasing phonographs. Victor and Columbia were one step ahead, for each of them had "four stores in different parts of the city" at a time when Edison was trying to establish one. With the same urgency with which he had written about Bombay, Stevens insisted that Edison immediately open a retail store in Mexico City. He and Cabañas had already found a good building for rent on San Francisco Street, "the Broadway of Mexico City," in a fancy hotel neighborhood. They had bargained for a rent of seven hundred Mexican pesos a month, and he estimated that it would take another three thousand "for shelving, redecorating the walls, repainting the front, putting in booths, and arranging to have an exhibition room, to have Phonograph concerts, installed in the rear." This would be an expensive undertaking at a time when Edison's cylinder recordings sold for a dollar apiece and Columbia had just dropped its price to seventy-five cents. Edward N. Burns of Columbia and Mr. Lightner of Victor were already "giving this field their special attention, and there is no doubt we should do the same."[32] Edison sound engineers had already made recordings for the Mexican market, and Cabañas expected to issue a new list every month. They were up against formidable rivals—Burns was the master strategist of Columbia's worldwide prosperity—but Stevens could feel that Edison was solidly in the running for Mexican business.

On his return trip Stevens stopped in several provincial cities, where he got a glimpse of how excitement for the phonograph seeped into the daily life of remote places. In Torreón his wholesalers, who were partners in the Warner Drug Company, were "the most enthusiastic Phonograph people I have ever met."One of the partners said that the other, a Mr. Warner, "talks Phonographs if a man comes in to buy a box of pills." A young lady in their company worked full time to run a phonograph "from morning to night." Its printing press turned out fliers every day that a young man hawked on the streets. For mail order, the source of most of the company's business, they had "a standing semi-monthly order for 65 Machines and 5000 Records."[33] Back home in New York the following week, Stevens wrote that he had met with Edison and spent some time giving him a report on his work; Edison "seemed very much interested in the matter" and approved of the Mexican venture, in particular the plan to open a retail store.[34]

A year later, Stevens and Cabañas followed up with a second trip: Stevens reported that they left New York by train on March 16 and reached Mexico City on March 21. They made arrangements for a recording space (calling it a sound studio would be an anachronistic description for the time, since recordings were usually made in hotels or other improvised rooms), made contracts with local talent, and were joined by two sound engineers from Edison's recording department, George J. Werner and Frederick Burt, who made about a hundred selections. They also hired the assistant leader of the Orchestra of the Conservatory of Music in Mexico City to assess recordings and arrange orchestral and band selections. Cabañas and his business partner, a Mr. Parker, proposed to take over the retail store.[35] The details reveal a rather complex pattern of collaboration, with Edison's managers taking certain initiatives while depending on Mexican businessmen and musicians for their success. No magic wand waved from afar could bring about a Mexican phonograph trade, especially not when Columbia and Victor were swarming across Mexico City with their phonographs and records.

Despite their serious efforts to set up their business in Mexico, the Edison managers had trouble understanding what it took to operate abroad. A letter of 1907 from a music dealer in Quebec laid out their shortcomings. Joseph Beaudry, a music dealer and publisher, wrote in response to a questionnaire to explain the reason for Edison's weak sales:

The reason is that the supply and the choice of French records are not up to the demand. In fact, most of the French records in your catalogue are old songs (comic or ballads). The French records (ballads or operatic) are not as clear and as plain as could be desired, most of them make an awful vibration. The comic french songs (made in canada) [sic] reproduce better, but the songs are not to be heard by any lady or young people. I suppose you understand what I mean, they are too free. Besides, any one will tell you that they heard the songs five or six years ago. Having to compete with the French Phonograph "Pathé" whose catalogue of french song is simply beautiful and of course, up-to-date, there is the difficulty of securing the french trade for the Edison, although the Edison phonograph is far superior to the Pathé or any other machine.

The deficiencies went back to Edison's personal strategy of producing a superior sound and ignoring consumer tastes. By technology alone a market could not be won, so long as Edison recordings were vulgar and out of date. Pathé's machines may have been inferior, but the music matched the market. The comparison was especially telling because Pathé sold cylinders, so the contrast with disc technology did not enter into consumers' preference. McChesney, who forwarded the letter to Gilmore, commented: "It seems to thoroughly typify the situation in Canada with respect to French Records."[36] Yet the bosses did not change their listings; five years later, the French Canadian list was still a string of corny and comic titles which might have sold in American towns but did not appeal to French Canadians.

Two years later, a visit to the competition close by confirmed that Edison's phonograph company had fallen far behind its chief competitor. At the end of January 1909 an Edison employee named Joseph McCosh made the trip to Camden, where he was given a tour of the Victor factory and offices. (This visit may have been facilitated by friendly discussions between the presidents of Victor and Edison about a congressional copyright bill.) His report contained dismal news for Frank Dyer, the president of the National Phonograph Company. Even though it was the slowest time of year, the Victor factory could not keep up with the demand for high-end Victrolas, the two-hundred-dollar phonograph that came in a dignified wooden cabinet. Victor catered to "the educated people of the country, who are fond of music, and are willing to pay for the best," versus the Edison company, which was selling phonographs and records "in the small towns and country places." The hard economic times of the previous year had made no dent in Victor's sales, for while "they did not sell as many of their popular priced machines," the sales of Victrolas and Auxetophones (a luxury line of phonographs) remained brisk. How the Victor employees bragged to McCosh! In the past few years "business had increased to a marvelous extent, as they were doing more than 65% of the business now done in the cities." No other company could equal their lineup of "renowned musicians, and the greatest operatic stars." No one else would pay for talent what they did: $45,000 in commissions just to Caruso. Nearly a thousand people worked at the Camden plant, which was valued at six million dollars; and this miracle had happened in just the past eight years, when they had gone from a small company to a commanding position in the industry, "the largest and best Talking Machine Company in the world."[37] While Thomas Edison insisted on turning out records for small-town American taste, Victor understood the yearning of Americans of all classes for something more glamorous.

Thomas Edison's poor market instincts came at a high cost for his record company's exports. McCosh's January tour of the Victor factory coincided with a moment of review of export sales and debate over the profitability of foreign production and sales. Even though London showed a healthy profit, it did not bode well for exports that Edison's Berlin and Paris plants showed losses for 1909: these had been producing for export markets, but the foreign director, Thomas Graf, could only complain about cylinders losing out to discs.[38] In February 1909, Stevens sent Dyer the complete figures for orders received by the foreign department in November and December 1908 for Latin America and the Pacific. The total number of records sold was 346,756 for November and 141,669 for December. Australia was by far the largest buyer, with 339,080 records for November and 132,448 for December, leaving only smatterings for runners-up the West Indies (1,253) and the Philippine Islands (1,096), and even smaller amounts for other Caribbean countries, Latin America, India, and Korea. The report also included a list of December requests for catalogs. The total number of requests was just 139, but they came from a wide variety of places across Latin America and the Pacific as well as Europe, the Canary Islands, Japan, Java, and Syria—evidence of stirrings of interest. "Dyer I wonder if we got a 1st class reliable man as a general traveler around the world to establish a factor [retail agent] or wholesaler we could make it pay—It would all depend on getting the right man—we could give the factor a low price & require advertising & then establish a biz," mused Edison on the report, in his neat script. Despite his tardiness in exploiting export markets, he remained intrigued by the possibility of doing more with them.[39]

The numbers alone do not reveal what was happening to musical *cultures* around the world. Beyond the questions of profit, loss, and mass sales, the exposure to phonographs and records, even in small numbers, could kindle big changes in foreign listeners' taste. Records blaring from a bar or store exposed listeners to new kinds of music. Direct requests for catalogs could come from anywhere in the world: Hong Kong, Madras, Boston (for a West African missionary), Adana.[40] The phonograph business had gone through rapid ups and downs year in and year out; overall business was booming, and the hunger for phonographs seemed limitless. It was apparently worthwhile to make new proposals and continue to invest in foreign records. Edison's phonograph business started out with the advantages of having made the original invention; having the factory in Orange, New Jersey; linking scientific research and commerce; and possessing an initial flair for the dramatic gesture and the magic of the Edison name. Yet the company lost out on the global markets, and stumbled in the United States. One source of the disappointing outcome was clear: Edison's insistence on sound quality above all else, whether in his stinginess about advertising, his disdain for divas, or his indifference to consumer tastes. The failure of communication was most complete as he moved into global markets. Records were all about what foreign people wanted—but Edison and his team could not get beyond what *he* wanted: the music of small-town America, endlessly turning on etched cylinders.

Emile Berliner, Transatlantic Networker

Emile Berliner occupies a modest place in American history as one among its many inventors. His most memorable achievement, the flat disc, was efficient to make, convenient to ship, and easy to play. But that adds up to a footnote compared to Edison's embodiment of American ingenuity through his many contributions to the technology of everyday life. Edison is a household name in the United States for his homebred genius, transforming everyday life with inventions like the phonograph and the light bulb. It does not diminish Edison's deserved place in American collective memory to turn to the skill that made Berliner a force for globalization: his ability to weave together partners across the Atlantic. Berliner was a transatlantic networker. He knew how to move across classes and countries: fellow tinkerers, family on both sides of the Atlantic, Philadelphia financiers, and London executives cooperated in a business that brought together the triangle of America, England, and Germany in the businesses of Victor, Gramophone, and Deutsche Grammophon. The partners in the enterprise became the agents of a global empire of sound.

Berliner turned an ordinary trip into an organizing success when he and his family made a return visit from his adopted to his native country. On September 3, 1889, Cora Adler Berliner began a diary of their voyage from the United States to Germany. With her were her husband, Emile, and their four children, Oliver, Edgar, Hanna, and Herbert, aged two to seven. Emile was then thirty-eight, while Cora was eleven years younger. In 1870 Emile had started out in the United States as a haberdashery clerk who pursued his self-improvement program—learning to play the piano and violin, reading about physics and electricity—after hours. By the time they married, Emile had sold a telephone invention to the Bell Company and landed a job at the Bell laboratory. By the time they boarded ship together, Emile was a well-known inventor who could support his growing family—three children were yet to come—in middle-class style. It was both a business trip for Emile and as a chance to visit his family in Hanover, which he had left nineteen years earlier to make his way in America.[41]

Cora herself may have come from a German Jewish family, but if so, she had completely lost any feel for the country. Her first diary entry gave an account of her and Emile's arguments with the crew aboard the German ship—with each side, as she wrote, thinking their own country was the best in the world:

> Our captain Herr Schmölder is a most pleasant & amusing man. He has a fund of stories & anecdotes which he always assures us are facts—at his tongue's end. He has travelled a great deal on the Lloyd Steamer, to Australia, China and other countries, but he has lost his heart to Samoa. We have been shown a map of the island, of the beauty of the females, great size of the men, & the excellent qualities of both sexes, together with many facts concerning their ways, habits & customs. He is much incensed at the U.S. for their interference in Samoan affairs; considering that no Country has or should have a "voice in the land" but Germany.

Samoa had shaken up diplomatic relations between Germany and the United States just a few months earlier. American and British boosters of empire had their eyes on the island as a convenient Pacific stopping point for trade and refreshment. Nearby Fiji was already under British control. But the Pacific network of the German merchant firm J. C. Goddefroy and Son was centered in Samoa, and Germans had extensive plantation holdings on the island. In June 1889 the three colonial countries reached a power-sharing agreement, but the compromise was an uneasy one that gave way to conflict in 1897, leading to partition of the Samoan islands and the formation of a German colony in 1899. Aboard her ship, Cora Berliner had run into the rising German public mood of determination for that country to take its place as a great power with a world empire. Captain Schmölder's praise of Samoa's female beauties and handsome men fit into a propaganda campaign stylizing Samoa as the pearl of the Pacific. Cora was bemused by the exchange at the beginning of her overseas adventure. But her diary entry also reveals her unfamiliarity with the world beyond home.[42]

Things only got worse when Cora met her husband's family. An undated entry goes back to their arrival in Bremen: "On the dock were Moritz & Uncle Meyer. They both looked different from what I expected being both small men, when I had pictured them to myself as tall & of commanding stature. However, although I was disappointed in their appearance, I liked them in every other way. Each brought me a bouquet, Uncle Meyer brought chocolates for me & the children, & Moritz had Kuchen etc which Elsa had baked & (Marianna?) sent." They arrived at eleven o'clock that night in Hanover, where the whole family was waiting for them at the train station "& what kissing exclamations etc. Not one of them came up to my expectations excepting perhaps Manfred & Franziska." One wonders what the family thought of Emile's American wife, so fixated on appearances, impressed by the train station and the city of Hanover, but cool toward the family affection. Cora recovered from her initial distaste for the men of small stature and kissing cousins: "Later when I knew their habits & myself got into their routine of living, I could better understand why they were as they were."[43] A steamer could bring Cora across the Atlantic; the passage from East Coast to North German culture was a less certain journey. She was crossing continents of looks and customs, and not everyone could make it to the other side as she was beginning to do. Yet her family's prosperity depended on it: her husband was rising in the world not just because of his inventive genius, but also because of his skill at assimilating into American society while retaining close ties to Germany.

Berliner's Wanderjahr in America

The image that Emile Berliner's biographer, Frederic Wile, broadcast to the world in 1926 was a story of the immigrant as self-made man. The book's dedication ("to the youth of America") came with a fragmentary quote from Calvin Coolidge: "Whether their ancestors came over in the *Mayflower* three centuries ago, or in the steerage three years ago." The author's preface praised the story of "the German immigrant boy" and his "successful taking advantage of America's proverbial opportunity for any youth of brains and industry, from anywhere in the world, to rise to greatness." Herbert Hoover's foreword added to the same melting-pot narrative of how people from all sorts of nations had contributed inventions to American technology.[44]

Emile Berliner did in fact emigrate as a German Jew without money or status, and his story was a remarkable one of inventive genius and American opportunity. But he also grew up with educational resources garnered from German, Jewish, and family sources. [45] As Peter Schulze has written in his historical sketch of the Berliner family, the founder was Jacob Abraham Joseph Berliner, who settled in Hanover in the early 1770s. He had a protected legal status with guarantees of life, property, and religion, but was limited to small business occupations and was known for his deep piety. His son, Moses Berliner, displayed the business drive and public spirit that continued to characterize the Berliners of Hanover until the destruction of their community by the Nazis. Moses's fabric business flourished during a brief period of trade freedom under Napoleonic occupation. In 1812, at the age of twenty-seven, he was elected chair of the Jewish community's charitable association; for the next forty-two years, until shortly before his death, he remained its director—a record that his famous grandson still recalled with pride many decades later. Emile's father, Samuel, belonged to the first generation of Jews in Hanover to enjoy citizenship and full freedom of trade and manufacturing, rights granted in the 1840s. Samuel Berliner and his wife, neé Sally Friedmann, had thirteen children between 1848 and 1869—including Emile, born in 1851, and his two later business partners: Jacob, born in 1849, and Joseph, born in 1858. All seven Berliner sons received business or banking apprenticeships after their schooling ended (Emile, in a clothing store), and all surpassed the existing social bounds as they went on to remarkable careers.[46] Emile also received a special education, boarding at the famous Samson School in Wolfenbüttel for four years until he was fourteen, while his brothers went to trade school at home. Most of Emile's fellow pupils came from modest backgrounds like the Berliner home, which was almost inevitable in a Germany that placed heavy restrictions on Jewish occupations, which were largely limited to petty trades. Despite these limitations, about a quarter of the Samson School graduates from 1807 to 1847 seem to have gone on to educated professions.[47]

While Emile's formal schooling was brief, it was also thorough enough to prepare him for his later self-taught study of electricity and physics. He also came to the United States at age nineteen with business education and experience. And he could count on family solidarity: after their early years of hardship, the brothers developed the mutual warmth that still surprised Cora Berliner in 1889. Emile Berliner was never just self-made; schooling, business training, and family solidarity were the capital he drew on to create an international business enterprise.

Emigration and journeyman years did not take him away from this family network. Like many immigrants, Emile Berliner started out in America with help from family friends. Samuel Gotthelf returned from Washington to Hanover for a visit in 1869 and promised to give Emile work in his dry goods store on Seventh Street. Just shy of nineteen years old, Emile departed on the *Hammonia*, a Hapag (Hamburg America Line) ship, via Hamburg on April 27, 1870, and arrived two weeks later in Hoboken, where he was greeted by Jacob Davidson, a friend of Gotthelf's. After half a day of sightseeing, Emile took the train to Washington and began working for Gotthelf and B. J. Behrend.

Family had got him started; but then, by his own efforts, Emile plunged into the life of an unfamiliar continent. His first aim, by his biographer's dutiful account, was to turn himself into "a good American," which he did by anglicizing his first name with the final "e" and learning English from church sermons, the highbrow *Quarterly Review* in a YMCA reading room, and pages of the *Congressional Record* that were used as wrapping paper in the store. Three years later, he still did not know what he wanted to do and had no plan to become an inventor. By moving to America and leaving behind the constricting German system of apprenticeships, he had opened up a novel freedom of occupation that he first sought to explore. In New York, his first destination beyond Washington, he sold glue, painted portrait backgrounds, and gave German lessons. Then, in response to a newspaper advertisement he set out for Milwaukee, where he arrived in freezing winter weather and ended up traveling by river barge on the Mississippi and Missouri Rivers as far as Omaha. By late 1875 he was back in New York, working as "a general handy man and bottle-washer" in the laboratory of Constantine Fahlberg (who in 1878 discovered the substance he later named saccharine) before switching jobs to become a better-paid "bookkeeper in a feed store." Evenings were spent at the Cooper Institute, the famous technical school founded by the self-made industrialist and inventor Peter Cooper, where Emile could attend adult education classes or visit the reading room. His wanderings ended with a return to Washington at the end of 1876, where he worked once again in the dry goods store, now owned by Behrend.[48]

Berliner's years of wandering were not in vain; they were a period of getting to know his adopted country. He was improving his English along with his knowledge of production, sales, and marketing—aspects of business later critical for success in the phonograph industry. Near the end of his journeys, he finally discovered his vocation. A friendly drug store owner, August Engel, gave him a physics textbook by Johann Müller that captured the imagination of the insatiable self-improver. Müller, a professor of physics and technology, specialized during his years at the University of Freiburg from 1844 to 1875 in writing accessible illustrated textbooks. They included chapters on acoustics and electricity that would especially have gripped Emile's imagination. It is a testimony to his personal intelligence and determination that he was able to master what he read. But Emile was also the beneficiary of Germany's attention to instruction for all classes, and to workers' hunger for education and culture, which stimulated the production of popular editions like Müller's textbooks.[49]

A German-American Business

Berliner is sometimes portrayed as a fumbling businessman in the phonograph industry, but his early success in developing and marketing the telephone demonstrated boldness and grit. In 1877 he deposited his patent in Washington for an improved transformer and microphone that magnified the volume and improved the quality of voice transmissions, turning the telephone into a commercially viable means of communication. The next year, the Bell Company, impressed by the inventor as well as the invention, offered him a modest salary and a royalty on the transformer in return for control of his patent applications. In November 1878 he moved to Boston to begin working for Bell. The arrangement turned out to be a point of departure for his subsequent achievements. As a Bell employee he began the transition from struggling immigrant to part of a scientific elite that included both the company and, thanks to introductions from the Bell family, the upper-class network of Boston scientists. In addition, the Bell settlement provided him with enough capital to launch his own business ventures. With these resources he was on his way to a career as a creative entrepreneur, investor, and inventor.[50]

Berliner wasted little time in putting his old and new resources to work. In summer 1881 he took a leave of absence from Bell and returned to Hanover. By then he had arranged for his younger brother Joseph to come to the United States and work in a Bell telephone factory. He proposed that his older brother Jacob partner with Joseph, and found a telephone factory in Hanover. Jacob would serve as the financial and business manager while Joseph would take over the technical side of production. Two years later, Emile sent Jacob to the United States for firsthand experience with American technology and marketing. In the same year, 1883, the German state's telephone network reached Hanover. The fortunate timing facilitated the founding of Telephon-Fabrik J. Berliner, which started out with a capital of ten thousand marks. Business grew rapidly within and beyond Germany; the new company soon had branches in Paris and other French cities for making telephones that used the Berliner microphone. Meanwhile, the Prussian telegraph director, Louis Hackethal, was promoting the use of underground cables. The Berliner brothers invested in the invention, and by 1900 were partners with Hackethal in a company for the production of cable wire. Again they entered the market at just the right moment for their Hanover factory to meet a tremendous demand. Throughout these years Emile Berliner pushed himself to the limit, suffering two nervous breakdowns and pulling himself together to get on with his businesses. Despite the harsh demands he placed on himself, he had winning qualities toward those around him, avoiding resentment in an atmosphere of ongoing litigation over patents, setting an example of generosity rather than self-gain, and building relations of trust that were indispensable for a long-distance business held together by letters and occasional visits. Machinery spun the cable wire in the Berliner factory; family solidarity permitted the Berliners to spin nets of credit and create a transatlantic flow of know-how and capital. [51]

The telephone factory in Hanover later became the location of the Berliner brothers' record factory, Deutsche Grammophon. But a long path of inventions and transatlantic crossings led from Emile Berliner's first set of inventions to his launching of a global record industry. After setting up his brothers in business, he returned to the United States in fall 1881 and married Cora Adler. She was a former Washington neighbor whose mother had permitted him to string wires from house to house as part of his early telephone experiments. After two more years of work for the Bell Company in Boston, Berliner returned to Washington and concentrated on creating a commercially viable record player. At his newly built home in "suburban" Columbia Heights (today in the heart of the city), and in a few rooms rented closer to the Smithsonian and the Patent Office, he developed the flat disc record. In contrast to Edison's phonograph, in which the recording stylus followed an up-and-down ("hill and dale") motion, Berliner's gramophone used a lateral cut, a side-to-side transmission of vibrations. Berliner's work did not stop there. He collaborated with "Max Levy, of Philadelphia, a technician of great ability," until by spring 1888 he could manufacture discs from matrices; by 1892 he had perfected high-quality matrices for commercial production. It was Berliner, too, who looked for an improvement over rubber as the material for records and came up with a shellac-based substitute, which continued to be used for decades to come. By the early 1890s he had assembled most of the component parts for the mass production of record players and their discs.[52]

Berliner was quick to publicize his new invention. In his first presentation, of May 1888, he showed it off to a scientific gathering at the Franklin Institute in Philadelphia. To demonstrate his talking machine in Germany, he made the Atlantic crossing in the following year with Cora and their children. His initial presentation at the Hanover Institute of Technology was followed by a visit to the German Imperial Patent Office. He was asked to repeat his demonstration for a group of engineers and scientists that also included the famous conductor, Hans von Bülow. Fascinated by what he heard, von Bülow predicted a great future for the gramophone. In November, Berliner appeared at a meeting of the Electro-Technical Society in Berlin for a comparison of his lateral cut disc record with Edison's cylinder phonograph. It was an "ordeal" for Berliner to face the audience of five hundred, with officers in uniform present, including the society's president, Rüdiger von der Goltz. Werner von Siemens, the famous German inventor and industrialist, was in the audience; he praised Berliner's invention while also expressing his admiration for its competitor. This event attracted the attention of Hermann von Helmholtz. At the beginning of January 1890, Helmholtz wrote to Berliner, who was still in the German capital, and asked whether he might see the gramophone at work. On

Wednesday, January 8, in the Hotel Kaiserhof, where Berliner was stay-ing, Helmholtz and his research assistants—an audience of about thirty in all—showed up to listen to the new invention. They were "delighted," and urged Berliner to visit their physics institute to make some records, but he lacked the recording equipment to follow up on the offer. The hotel meeting with Helmholtz was an extraordinary event in its own right, as the culmination of a series of demonstrations giving scientific prestige to Berliner's achievement.[53]

Berliner had started out in the world of small business, turned him-self into a trial-and-error tinkerer, relied on the mechanical skills of Max Levy, and received legitimation from his demonstrations before the Ger-man and American scientific communities. Commerce, craft, and science all entered into his transformation of Edison's original invention into a marketable product. On November 6, 1898, Deutsche Grammophon was founded with a starting capital of twenty thousand marks and Emile and Joseph Berliner as its owners. Its initial core of skilled workers drew on the workforce of the existing telephone factory. The record business was highly profitable in its early years, yielding annual dividends of 25 per-cent until 1903 and 1904. At a cost of 250,000 marks, a new factory for record production was built on the edge of Hanover with a yearly capacity of ten million records. It opened in fall 1904 with forty-five employees. As Dieter Tasch points out in his account of the firm, this was an ambi-tious undertaking but, compared to other enterprises in Hanover, still a modest one. The tire factory of Continental Caoutchouc and Guttaper-cha Compagnie employed ten thousand men and women; other factories for building locomotives and textiles also operated on a large scale, as did the factory opened by Hermann Bahlsen, on the same street as the Berliners, to make the cookies that still bear his name. Deutsche Gram-mophon was a medium-sized enterprise that stood for high-quality craft production.[54]

High wages and esprit de corps complemented the craft skills of work-ers in the Berliner enterprise. Joseph's workers had twelve-hour shifts, but were paid well: the pressers (who pressed the blank records against the matrix) earned 44 marks per week—considerably more than typesetters, famously a craft elite among workers, who in Hanover earned 33.6 marks per week in 1913. Joseph played the role of master in an expanded work-shop, going in to work every day, arranging outings with his factory and white-collar workers twice a year, and asking workers to make personal household repairs for him in the slow summer season. At Christmastime the workers were summoned one by one to Joseph. He gave each of them a ten-mark gold coin.[55]

From Transatlantic Triad to Global Empire

Emile Berliner returned to the United States in 1891 and began the work of founding an American phonograph company. By 1893 he had assembled a small circle of investors who together put up twenty-five thousand dollars to found the United States Gramophone Company in Philadelphia. No less remarkable than his technical skills was Berliner's talent at attracting collaborators who would become the makers of a global record industry. The most important of these for the United States was a machinist named Eldridge R. Johnson. A defect of the talking machines of the early 1890s was their lack of a steady power source; hand cranks and batteries were in different ways clumsy and unreliable. Berliner and his team—among them Alfred Clark, a lawyer from a well-to-do New York family who was hired to manage the business's Philadelphia retail shop—searched for an inventor who could provide them with a spring motor that would turn a record evenly from beginning to end of the needle's spiral motion across the record surface. Johnson, the owner of a small machine shop in Camden, New Jersey, across the Delaware River from Philadelphia, delivered the spring and a sound box in 1896. With this addition, Berliner and his team had taken a large step toward turning the talking machine from a toy into a reliable technology.[56] It turned out that they had also taken on a large business talent. Johnson, who came from a family with social pretensions but unstable households, endured a traumatic period as an apprentice machinist who was determined to rise in the world and turn himself into a gentleman. Deprived of a higher education, he created his own *Bildungsjahr*, traveling across the United States and spending a year in Washington state. In the end, despite the high wages on the West Coast, he decided to return to the East Coast and its greater business opportunities, but he remembered his time away as an adventure that broadened his mental horizons. More than any of the other phonograph industry founders, he had a fine feel for middle-class American taste; it was he who in 1903 invented the Victrola, which hid the phonograph and tin horn inside a wooden cabinet, turning the phonograph from a machine in the living room into a genteel piece of furniture. Like Berliner, Johnson had a masterful ability to put aside personal differences, reward generosity, and build alliances at home.

A storm of litigation destroyed the Berliner phonograph company in its original form. Frank Seaman, a former advertising agent whom the Berliner company had contracted to market their talking machines, founded his own company, which put out phonograph products under the name Zonophone and contested the Berliner company's rights to its own patents. A battle ensued that drew Columbia, Berliner, Edison, and Seaman interests into a legal maelstrom. In 1898 a court injunction forbade Berliner's company "from using the word 'gramophone'" on any of its products in the United States. Berliner responded by founding a firm in Montreal that remained under family control.[57] But he had also prepared a greater rescue from this denoument by sending agents to London in the preceding year to found a partner firm.[58] There they had attracted a wealthy British lawyer, Trevor Williams, who traveled across the Atlantic in February 1898 to meet Berliner; he agreed to invest up to five thousand pounds in a new British enterprise, the Gramophone Company, in return for the British rights to Berliner's patents.[59] By 1901, Johnson had emerged in the United States as a skilled negotiator who could persuade most of the warring parties to put aside their differences and come together for their mutual profit. By the end of the year he was the president and dominant shareholder in the Victor Company, in which Berliner and his investors were large minority shareholders.[60] It was Johnson, too, who arranged for patent exchanges with Columbia and Edison, leading to an era in which the competing firms could do business unimpeded by legal conflict.

Agreements were woven around the three businesses in Philadelphia, London, and Hanover that balanced coordination and freedom. While Trevor Williams was chairman of the Gramophone Company, Berliner was one of its directors. Gramophone became the majority shareholder in Deutsche Grammophon and controlled the Berliner and Johnson patents in Europe.[61] Gramophone bought its talking machines from its American partner, and the two companies had the right to sell one another's recordings.[62] Friendships undergirded enlightened self-interest to hold together this transatlantic business. Alfred Clark initially helped to bring Johnson into the Berliner company, and the two men became close friends, rooming together for a while in Philadelphia. Clark migrated to London and soon became one of the founders of Gramophone, rising to be managing director in 1909.[63] Trevor Williams, too, took a personal liking to Johnson and invited him to his country home on Johnson's visits to London. Seaman, the maverick who turned on his bosses and created havoc in the young industry, definitively lost his court cases by 1901 and no longer counted as a serious competitor. By contrast, Williams, Clark, and Johnson were canny survivors: tough, hardworking, and—no less important—capable of building a culture of cooperation.

Perhaps their most remarkable move was a division of the earth that sounds like a modern Treaty of Tordesillas. By an agreement of 1901, Victor could sell in the Americas and East Asia while Gramophone took South Asia and Europe. By the end of the decade, Edison was faltering while the Victor-Gramophone empire extended across continents. The newer company's global reach called for cosmopolitan skills requiring new agents—not just the inventors and executives of its transatlantic partnership, but the roving dealmakers and recorders who in a handful of years captured music from around the world.

9

A Global Empire of Sound

At the beginning of 1900, when Victor's management was still trying to cut its way through a thicket of litigation between phonograph companies over patents, William Barry Owen, the founder and managing director of its sister company Gramophone, was already spinning his web of agents reaching all the way to the Pacific. Owen is a legendary figure in the early history of the phonograph business: the son of a Yankee whaling captain with an Amherst College degree, he brought the sea captain's boundless pursuit of his prey and the college man's disciplined intelligence to bear on the phonograph business.[1] New Englanders had once chased the whales down the coast of the Atlantic and around Cape Horn, swarming into the far side of the world and trading in Asia; now their descendant pursued profits from canned sound across oceans and continents.

Whaling ships often crossed the line from bold to foolhardy, staying out too long, exhausting their stock of prey, and ruining the health of captains and crew. Dangers awaited, too, for the global phonograph industry. Some ventures flourished; others ended in disaster. Brimming with brio, Owen sent an agent named Peter Bohanna to Australia in 1900. Everything seemed to go wrong. First, Bohanna could not even get off his ship because of an outbreak of the plague in Sydney. Once he landed, he had to contend with damaged parts and stiff competition from Columbia, which was under-selling Gramophone. He was dismayed to discover how vast a continent Australia was, and suffered the humiliation of having his traveling sales-man run off with a woman, to be last seen at a casino. His health broke down, and he died five years after his adventure began. Owen was right to detect gold in Australia, which in the end turned out to be a large market for recordings, but Bohanna's experience was a reminder of the hazards facing pioneers.[2]

Others had the nerves and canniness to make a go of overseas busi-ness. When Norbert Rodkinson, one of the toughest and most effective Gramophone executives, grappled with Gramophone's business in Rus-sia, he had to master wild business cycles of boom and bust, dubious credit conditions, and labor conflict. In October 1903 he visited the com-pany's factory in Riga and complained that Hanover was failing to deliver raw materials, causing a five-day work stoppage. (Two years later, factory production came to a halt for a different reason: a general strike in the city.) Studying conditions in Russia from Germany in October 1904, and visiting in December of the same year, he identified serious competition from Columbia and from the German firms Beka and Odeon. Rodkinson himself was an uncontrollable character who refused to follow orders from London; in June 1904 his bosses discussed transferring him to Ber-lin, but decided that the turbulent Russian conditions required his pres-ence.[3] If one simply looks at the prewar figures for the profitability of the Russian market, it looks like a place for easy success; but the correspon-dence between London and the peripatetic Rodkinson tells a different story. The recordings now stored by archives and collectors are the mate-rial outcome of years of human toil and cunning to survive an explosive, uncertain enterprise.

Gramophone's Indian Empire

In a letter of January 13, 1900, Owen opened the new century by describ-ing India as a land of limitless commercial opportunity to J. Watson Hawd, a manager who had proven himself in the firm's Deutsche Grammophon partner factory in Hanover. For example, wrote Owen, Calcutta was a city of one and a half million inhabitants and was known as the "city of pal-aces" for its large number of people with lavish means. Owen promised to have all the preparations for a trip ready within three or four weeks, and proposed that Hawd go out by steamship with five hundred phonographs and thirty thousand records to Calcutta and Bombay for the next three to five months. After setting up the business, he could turn it over to a local firm that would work on establishing a chain of record distributors. In December 1901 Hawd, writing from bustling Chowringhee Road in Calcutta, could already report that demand for records was strong; by the second half of 1906, the Calcutta branch had more than a dozen employees plus servants, and despite internal management troubles sold more than ninety thousand records. Gramophone's India catalog for 1906 contained records in Tamil, Telugu, Malayalam, and Sanskrit. They ranged from Vedic recitations to comic imitations of birds and the roar of a passing train. By December of the same year, the incoming manager was scouting out the best site for an Indian record factory. A stream of complaints about doing business in India runs through the letters, but they also document the managers' realism and their success at overcoming obstacles.[4] India fulfilled many of Western entrepreneurs' dreams for success in a foreign market. With its rich musical traditions and its rapid embrace of the phonograph, it also became the stage for one of the most self-conscious redefinitions of culture to accompany globalization.

Maddening obstacles threw off Gramophone's successes in India. Records were hard to store in the heat, Indian distributors broke their promise of an exclusive relationship and handled records of the upstart Beka firm from Berlin, and the Gramophone manager, Charles Gilpin, was demoralized by his wife's sickness and departure from India. The Londoners could not imagine the difficulties of "keeping things in Calcutta straight," he wrote in 1906. The Gramophone "catalogues were all rubbish"; the "southern Indian labels got all mixed up and our Tamil and Telugu catalogue is a mess of errors." In the Calcutta office the staff was sickly, and he could not get good work out of them; records came from the factory warped, they warped in Calcutta, and the water table was so high that one could not store them in cellars.[5] When Norbert Rodkinson arrived in Calcutta at the end of 1906 he found a shambles of employee incompetence, orders negligently filled, and customer complaints. He quickly restored order. After the Indian dealers told him that Gramophone records were too expensive, he slashed prices. He also praised the dealers as worthy members of the Calcutta merchant elite (Gilpin's relationship with them had degenerated into one of mutual recriminations), though their fondness for gossiping with him for hours on end, day after day, tried his patience. Rodkinson created forms for documenting transactions step by step, and recommended elevating the accountant to assistant manager and firing a brutal Mr. Duncan who mistreated both European and Indian employees. Among the in-house staff, the "Bengali Babus" were "expert office men," and three could be hired for the price of one European.[6] This was sensible administration; though tinged by prejudice, it recognized merit. One cost of this efficient regime was a readiness to leave the comforts of home and plunge into the daily life of a foreign society. Where the Edison managers were squeamish, their Gramophone counterparts jumped right in. Rodkinson's human resource management was not a high intellectual achievement like Ellis's analysis of foreign scales, but in its own way it built a bridge between cultures.

Calcutta was the point of entry for an Asian empire. In October 1902, Owen called the Indian agency "a small affair" and announced a profit for the preceding year of £3,271. But he reminded his fellow board members that he was "laying the foundation for a business in the East"; his plan called for overseeing 1,200 to 1,800 recordings over the next six months "in many dialects of China and Japan, and the surrounding nationalities."[7] A year later, a manager wrote from Calcutta with an anxious report on the competitors who had entered the market. Things were going all right in India, where he was pouring money into advertising and had "about twenty good and fairly good agents." But he heard from the company's representative in Kobe that "our friends the Victor Talking Machine Company continue to flood our territory with their goods at prices far below those I am allowed to quote, and the Columbia people are also now in the market at almost any prices to affect sales. . . ." China was worrisome, too; Gramophone's Chinese distributor, Moutrie & Company, had promised only to purchase Gramophone products, but Moutrie's correspondence made clear that it intended to purchase gramophones from Victor.[8] Others, too, thought they would strike gold in India, China, and Japan.

Despite the challenges from competitors, Gramophone's international pooling of business experience gave it a know-how that no other company could match. From Calcutta, Gilpin bragged to his London bosses in 1906 that Will Gaisberg (brother of the more famous Fred), who was on his way, would be able to record "the best singers":

> No common singers like in past. The people out here have their high
> class Artistes just as well as we in Europe. We cannot stick any old singer
> in front of a reproducer and imagine we are going to sell the Records well,
> because we cannot. Although at first all Records sounded alike to me, I
> am now beginning to see and know wherein lie the good and bad points.[9]

Gilpin was worn down by disease and everyday frustrations in Calcutta, but he also had company experience, an ongoing business, personal contacts, and the acumen of the Gaisberg brothers going for him. It was a register of widening horizons when the businessman declared that he had gone from ignorance to an awareness that the Indian market was discriminating, and that even he could begin to recognize artistic quality.

Gramophone's answer to competitors like Columbia and Beka was to build a factory in Calcutta that could supply all its Asian markets. After Johnson declined the invitation to make it a joint venture with Victor, the directors of Gramophone led by Trevor Williams decided at the beginning of 1906 to open their own pressing plant.[10] Again the pooling of talent came to its aid: Joseph Berliner was a member of the board who frequently came to the meetings in person. By March, his colleagues were awaiting his assessment of their plans.[11] At the board's June meeting, it was announced that Joseph Berliner recommended Siegfried Sanders, a Berliner family relative, as manager of the Indian factory, advice taken up by the board, which went ahead and hired him.[12] Michael Kinnear writes that most of the senior executives of Gramophone, including Fred Gaisberg, made the trip from London to Calcutta for the grand factory opening on December 18, 1908. It must have been both a chance for them to get a close-up look at their investment and a powerful message to Indian audiences of how seriously the European managers took their business. The factory immediately began pressing a thousand discs per day. It was part of Asian operations centralized in Calcutta and extending by 1910 to China and Southeast Asia; the company's factory, use of first-rate recording engineers, and aggressive advertising made it dominant in India and a major commercial power elsewhere.[13] In the space of five years, Gramophone built an Asian empire.

The Education of Fred Gaisberg

Some of the memorable early encounters were the recording sessions of Fred Gaisberg, recording engineer, with Gauhar Jaan. In the blaring commercial language of then and now, one might say that the era's greatest talent scout teamed up with India's greatest diva. A first encounter, a confrontation of cultures as alien as Mars and Venus? At first sight, perhaps. Gaisberg, the recorder of Caruso and later Vladimir Horowitz and Arturo Michelangeli, was still making the transition from small-town boy to worldly wise music maven; Gauhar Jaan was already the lover of princes and a master of India's classical music. He was a white businessman, and therefore by definition privileged in the Raj; she comported herself like a princess, bejeweled and trailed by dutiful attendants. He made his way in English; she knew English and many more languages. Yet we should be wary of staging this as a West-meets-East encounter. Other factors of gender difference, professional ambition, complex cultural identities, and personal idiosyncrasy entered into the successful collaboration.

The meeting of artist and entrepreneur was the outcome of a long preparation on both sides. Twenty-nine years old at the time he arrived in India, Gaisberg had already developed a sure sense of taste in Western music, had learned the technical side of making recordings, and had traveled widely. Through his education in widening spheres—from Washington to Philadelphia and New York, and then to London, Western Europe, and Russia, followed by trips to India and China—Gaisberg embodied the expanding horizons of the early phonograph industry.

Like A. J. Hipkins, Gaisberg came from an artisanal background; had he been less musical, he might have ended up as a machinist. His father Wilhelm's family arrived in New York from Germany in 1854. Following in the trade of Fred Gaisberg's grandfather, in 1869 Wilhelm went to work for the Government Printing Office in Washington as a bookbinder. Frederick William Gaisberg, the future talent scout and recording engineer, was born in 1873. His mother was musical; he became a serious pianist and sang in John Philip Sousa's choir. Then he was in the right time and place to get in on the phonograph business just as it was starting up. At age sixteen he began making recordings with wax cylinders for the Columbia Phonograph Company, which was founded in 1889. After graduating from high school two years later, he got an apprenticeship on the technical side of building and working with phonographs at Columbia while also accompanying performers. He worked for a year in the research department of the American Graphophone Company, the parent company of Columbia, in Bridgeport, Connecticut, and spent some time in the Volta Laboratory of Alexander Graham Bell in Washington. He also assisted the Bells' associate Charles Sumner Tainter, a gifted inventor whose innovations contributed to the founding of Columbia; Tainter sent him to the Chicago World's Fair of 1893 in order to find talented performers. There was nothing classy about phonographs at the time; they thrived as a "coin-in-slot business . . . in shops and saloons." That did not put off Gaisberg; his apprenticeships served him well in his career, for they had combined a performer's appreciation of classical music, an understanding of how to make the machinery work in recording sessions, and experience at sizing up and negotiating with musicians. Science, craft, and taste all entered into the business of making records.[14]

In 1894 Gaisberg was taken by a friend named Billy Golden to meet Emile Berliner, then established in Washington. "We found Emile Berliner in his small laboratory on New York Avenue," he recalled, "and received a warm welcome from the inventor." He gave a witty and enticing description of Berliner as "dressed in a monkish frock" and greeting them in his "guttural, broken English." Berliner immediately had Golden sing while Gaisberg played the piano and the inventor cranked his recording machine "like a barrel-organ." Berliner then took "a bright zinc disc" from the machine, plunged "it into an acid bath for a few minutes," took it out, washed it and cleaned it. Then he played the record. "To our astonished ears came the play-back of Billy Golden's voice." Gaisberg was enchanted: "Acquainted as I was with the tinny, unnatural reproduction of the old cylinder-playing phonographs, I was spell-bound by the beautiful round tone of the flat gramophone disc." In addition to the charm of the flat disc's sound, the cultural fit would have attracted Gaisberg to Berliner. Both men had acquired a thorough practical grounding in the sound technology of the phonograph despite their lack of higher education. Gaisberg wrote about another quality that bound them together: Berliner, he recalled, was for a long time the only person in the industry "who was genuinely musical and possessed a cultured taste."[15] This was the legacy of the love of classical music that extended deep into modest but socially ambitious German families.

It was not just spring motors and disc records that propelled Victor and Gramophone, the successors to Berliner's record company, to world dominance of the record industry. When it came to sound quality, Edison was generally thought to have the better product (although one notes with interest Gaisberg's suggestion to the contrary), and he staked the success of his record firm on its technical superiority. Berliner and Gaisberg set their empire on a different course. Along with an intense interest in improving the sound quality of their recordings, they moved the phonograph beyond its beginnings as a cheap amusement to a classy purveyor of musical culture. In 1897, the same year Eldridge Johnson delivered his reliable motor, Gaisberg went to Philadelphia, where he "installed and operated the first commercial studio for recording sound on discs." The offerings started out lowbrow, with "only popular and comic songs, valses, and marches in their simplest settings." On a trip to nearby Atlantic City,

however, he discovered "the handsome tenor Ferruccio Giannini in a provincial Italian opera company." The next day he and Giannini went to the
studio and made recordings of "La donna è mobile" and "Questa o quella"
("The Woman is Fickle" and "This Woman or That," from Verdi's opera
Rigoletto). They were the company's first opera songs and were highly successful. "They filled us with pride and for many months represented our
only concessions to highbrow taste." Sentimental and silly numbers still
filled the catalog, but Giannini, a serious artist who established himself
as a leader of operatic life in Philadelphia, quickly went on to make more
recordings for Berliner and then Victor and Columbia. His opera hits led
the way to a galaxy of classical stars and cultural prestige for the early record lists.[16]

The following year Berliner sent Gaisberg to London in order to work
with the firm's newly established partner company, Gramophone. He arrived on a Sunday, and the director of Gramophone gave the innocents
abroad a first taste of the good life in Europe by taking him and two fellow novices out to dinner: "We were all small town boys, and Owen was
in the seventh heaven of delight at our astonishment at the luxury of
the Trocadero Grill and the 'wickedness' all around us on that sabbath
night."[17] Gaisberg's way of recalling that initiation points to a feature of
the early phonograph business: its all-male cast. Singers, of course, might
be women, but on the management and production side it was all men
alternating between camaraderie and combat (in the form of litigation).
It was Owen who had the vision and energy to introduce American advertising methods to staid London, taking out "a whole page ad in the *Daily
Mail*" for the company; Owen who purchased the artist Francis Barraud's
painting of the dog known as Nipper listening to "His Master's Voice," after having Barraud paint a Berliner gramophone over its original Edison
phonograph; and Owen who moved with breakneck speed to occupy foreign markets.

He sent Gaisberg on a European recording tour; the former small-
town boy went to Leipzig, Vienna, Budapest, Milan, and Madrid, recording a few hundred titles on each stop. He recalled getting "vast experience
in recording under various conditions," and producing "a rich harvest of
musical records, both exciting and delightful to my provincial mind."[18]
Gaisberg had the endurance for the grueling travel schedule, as well as
the drive and satisfaction in his work that were indispensable for building
a global recording network.

His master coup came on his second continental tour. In March 1902 he and his brother Will left London and settled into Hotel Spatz in Milan, close to La Scala and the former home of Verdi, who had occupied a whole suite. Expecting a conventional round of recording "opera, ballads, comics, and bands," he was thrilled by a performance of the young Caruso singing in the role of an Italian patriot urging an uprising against the invader Napoleon. By the next day he had the makings of a deal: Caruso would sing ten songs for one hundred pounds. It was big money for the time. He wired his London bosses and made his case—only to receive a quick reply: "Fee exorbitant, forbid you to record." Gaisberg ignored orders. "One sunny afternoon Caruso, debonnaire [sic] and fresh, sauntered into our studio and in exactly two hours, sang ten arias." Gaisberg and his team "paid Caruso his £100 on the spot." The original recordings went to the Hanover factory for manufacturing. From there a record made its way to Alfred Clark, who was by then in Paris. Clark played "E lucevan le stelle" ("And the Stars Were Shining," from *Tosca*) for Heinrich Conried, the Silesian-born director of the Metropolitan Opera; Conried carried the record to New York and played it for his associates, who were so impressed that they cabled Caruso a contract immediately. Gaisberg had launched a career that would not only bring Caruso and the recording industry huge sums of money, but also, as Gaisberg observed, broke down "all the barriers of prejudice which the great artists held against recording." The Victor executives capitalized on their success by creating the Red Seal line of recordings as a prestige label that would appeal to artists jealous of their reputations and a public eager to share in the glamour of great performers and glitzy opera houses.[19] The success of the recordings was instant—and international because of the multinational agencies already opened by Gramophone and its affiliates. Philadelphia, New York, Hanover, London, Milan, and Paris: Victor and Gramophone agents in all these places worked to sell the first recording superstar. No wonder the Edison team was too late when it looked for opera talent. By the time it woke up, Gramophone was scouring Europe, and Gaisberg was leading historic expeditions to Russia, India, and East Asia.

From Europe to Russia, with Love

If Western Europe turned Gaisberg from a provincial to a sophisticate, the Russian Empire gave him a yen for wild, colorful world travel. At his bosses' behest, he stuffed the visit to Russia in between his first and second visit to Italy and its neighbors. On Gaisberg's 1900 expedition the

Russian businessmen were ruthless, sharp, and corrupt. Graft was "rampant"; Russia did not recognize international patent and copyright laws; Victor had to fight back against pirated copies of the company's recordings; Gaisberg helped organize a police raid on one illicit competitor's factory. He recalled the amiable swindlers who sounded like extras from a threepenny opera:

> Our agent was Max Rubinsky, the well-educated son of a Russian-American Rabbi. Max was handsome and ruthless in business and love, his two absorbing pursuits. . . . The combination of American and Russian business methods, introduced by him, showed a versatility that amazed even the hardened Polish and Russian-Jewish dealers of the old Russian Empire. . . . The dealers also were a comic crowd. One, Rappaport by name, would draw me apart and whisper in my ear: 'Don't trust Lebel, he'd cheat his own father.' Then Lebel would take me in a corner and advise me: 'Look out for Rappaport, he seduced a girl-pupil and was transported to Siberia. . . . These people, particularly Lebel and Rappaport, tried to win me over from my Company and make me join them in forming a rival gramophone syndicate; naturally, I did not succumb.[20]

Gaisberg was as canny as his Russian counterparts. His main business, however, was not wheeling and dealing, but recording. In Petersburg he met Panina, "a Tolstoyan type of gypsy with a deep-throated alto voice," and Tamara, also a great chanteuse, but "easygoing and not too fond of work: she frequently broke off a tour in a particular town if she found agreeable company and was well entertained; it took a bottle or two of champagne to put her in her best mood for a Russian gypsy song and then she could melt a heart of stone." In Moscow he recorded "church choirs, Cossack soldier songs, military band marches and Little Russian choruses of the Don River." On a stop in Warsaw he discovered the Jewish cantor Zavel Kwartin, later a world celebrity who would sing at the Metropolitan Opera in New York after emigrating to the United States.[21] Gaisberg struck gold in Russia: he discovered great singers, recorded them first, and turned a handsome profit for his firm.

His successes only stimulated his appetite for more adventure. On Easter holiday 1901 he traveled down the Volga to Kazan in search of Tartar music. The boat ride plunged him and his companions into a riot of song that rose up from the rhythms of everyday life: "Interesting, if for no other reason, was the fish dinner on the open deck of the steamer, during which the ragged, half-naked stevedores sang while loading sacks of meal and cement. Shall I ever forget the rhythmical swing as the green water-melons were passed from deck to barge? On every hand one heard music. Cossacks mounted on their sturdy, shaggy ponies rode through the streets singing soldier songs; their leader in a high-pitched tenor sang four lines and the chorus of a hundred masculine voices shouted to the refrain. It was grand. The haulers moved in rhythm to their song; the loafers on the docks or the passengers on the decks below, with a small concertina, mouth-organ or balalaika, joined in groups. Through all these sounds threaded the clang of Russian church bells, with their distinctive changes of five tones."[22] On reaching their destination, he didn't find much among the educated Tartars, who preferred Western music: "So to the working-man's cafés and to the low-class brothels we went, since they were the only avenues for the Tartar songs we wished to record." Altogether the Russian expedition was one more foray into new worlds, this one "begin-ning in a zero winter of deep snow, fur coats, and troikas, and finishing in a blazing summer of buzzing bees and flies, with scarcely a lull interven-ing." Over the course of his trip he had seen "unbelievably lavish" opera paid for by the Romanovs; he had negotiated with "a bevy of the greatest and perhaps most spoiled artists of that epoch"; he had gathered "first im-pressions of Russian music, ballet, and decorative art, then at the height of their freshness and vigor." He left determined to go back to Russia as often as he could. But his adventures had also turned him into an explorer eager for "newer and stranger fields of travel," and he began to plan a trip to East Asia.[23] Just a year later he was on his journey to Calcutta, compar-ing himself to Marco Polo as his steamer approached the city.[24]

Gauhar Jaan

Gaisberg first heard Gauhar Jaan on November 6, 1902, at the end of a long day of searching for musical talent. It began in the office of the superin-tendent of the Calcutta police, who provided Gaisberg and his business companions with an officer to accompany them to the clubs and theaters along Harrison Road—today Mahatma Gandhi Road, a main Calcutta thoroughfare. Their first stop was the Classic Theater for a performance of Romeo and Juliet, where they were startled by a chorus of nautch girls, bleached with rice powder and dressed in transparent gauze, who sang "And Her Golden Hair Was Hanging Down Her Back." "Nautch girls" was the term Westerners used broadly for women in dance; like the ballet

dancing girls who performed between acts in the Paris opera, they could
offer high art in their performances but were also prey for their gentleman audience. Nautch girls lost caste, just as Violetta in *La traviata* had
lost her social standing; but in India as well as Europe, skilled artists could
sing their way to wealth and social triumph. Gaisberg would already have
known the nautch girls' American song (which would remain popular for
decades), if only because Berliner had recorded it in 1896. The lyrics are
about a village girl, Jane, who goes to New York an innocent maid and returns home with "a naughty twinkle in her eye." Gaisberg's introduction
to music in India was already part of a circuit spanning from New York to
Calcutta.[25] As with Owen in the Trocadero, the sound engineer-explorer
traveled through a clubby world of male sociability; in Calcutta it had the
extra fortification of colonial privilege, which eased his way to the super-
intendent of police and an escort through the city.

   The nautch girls of the Classic Theater gave the most interesting performance he heard in the theater halls that day, but they were not the right
material for the record studio. The same evening, however, the indefatigable Gaisberg and his companions slunk their way through an "unsavory al-
ley," where they were "jostled by fakirs and unwholesome sacred cows," to
a dinner party with dance entertainment at the house of a wealthy Indian.
It was an evening marked by hospitality and colonial divide. Europeans
ate a European dinner at a table separate from that of their Indian guests,
including their host. Then they went into a room with Indians at one end,
some wearing "strings of pearls and diamonds and valuable rings," while
the few Europeans gathered at the other end in evening dress. One of the
performers that night was Gauhar Jaan. Gaisberg's autobiography, published forty years later, identified her as "an Armenian-Jewess who could
sing in twenty languages and dialects. Her great hit that evening was an
adaptation of 'Silver Threads Among the Gold.'"[26] Gauhar Jaan was not
in fact Jewish; the misnomer picks up unpleasantly on Gaisberg's observations in Russia, with Jewishness in both places signifying an unsavory
foreignness.

   By the time Gaisberg met her, Gauhar Jaan's familiarity with Western
culture far surpassed his knowledge of India, for her repertoire already
included this American song about a graying but still romantic couple,
published in 1873 and popular for decades thereafter. It was not recorded
until 1903, so Gauhar Jaan could not have learned it from the gramophone; somehow otherwise, perhaps through sheet music, she had added
it to her repertoire. Gaisberg described her in his diary from the time as

"a Mohammedan, rather fat and covered with masses of gold armlets, anklets, rings, pearl necklaces, masses of heavy earrings hanging about ten piercings in each ear," with a diamond on the side of her nose and teeth red from betel-chewing.[27] Then as later, he responded to foreignness with humorous-revulsive markers of difference. But Gaisberg did not let his racism cloud his musical judgment. After listening to her in his makeshift recording space, he was impressed by her voice's sharpness and brightness. Like Caruso, she had just the vocal qualities to shine on early records.

Gauhar Jaan first recorded for Gaisberg on November 8. Not every famous singer could adapt to this new form of music making. Like their counterparts in Europe and the United States, many performers thought at first that it was beneath their dignity to do so. In addition, they would have to modify their singing; as Edison had observed, celebrity singers might not be ready to adjust to the limitations of the early recording space, which required a new kind of precise positioning. Indian singers would be used to the leisurely rhythms of performance at court or in private celebrations, and would suddenly have to pack their art into the few minutes of an early recording.[28] But Gauhar Jaan was a quick learner and a pragmatist. Moreover, she could cross linguistic barriers: her biographer, Vikram Sampath, writes that she made records in "Hindustani, Bengali, Urdu, Persian, English, Arabic, Pashto, Tamil, Marathi, Peshawari, Gujarati, French," and other languages, and that she did so across the entire range of classical Indian musical genres.[29] Her hundreds of recordings, wrote Gaisberg, were one of the foundations of Gramophone's business in India. On can hear some of her early recordings online now, in which her voice rings out at the end: "My name is Gauhar Jaan!" This was a way of making sure that the factory workers in Hanover, who would often have had trouble identifying singers and titles, would paste on the right label. Her proud identification in English of Indian recordings for German workers was also a testimony to the globalization of the phonograph.

The Fred Gaisberg who met Gauhar Jaan was not an American naif dropped down without any preparation in sophisticated Calcutta. He arrived as a seasoned traveler who had already experienced a panoply of climates, languages, arts, and peoples. If we read his comments about the dirt and splendor of Calcutta and the temperamental Gauhar Jaan with his previous education in mind, his practical transnationalism takes shape. He was used to the strange and the gaudy; he responded to them by claiming male and colonial privilege, but also recognized her greatness as the bearer of a classical tradition and had an impeccable ear for the quality of her voice. Without curiosity and receptiveness, he could not have found her or other Indian artists—she was one of many memorable talents he encountered—and could not have worked with them on the novel art of recording.

Fred Gaisberg's biography fits one kind of modern success story: that of the scrappy kid who has talent and an eye for the main chance, whose good luck and readiness to learn carry him to fame. Gauhar Jaan's life fits a different kind of pattern: that of the social déclassé who lives through years of searing pain, is a natural virtuoso, becomes a master musician, absorbs a treasure trove of musical tradition, takes apart traditional genres, and reinvents them for the modern marketplace. No movie has yet been made of Gauhar Jaan's life, to match the admirable *Ray*, about the life of Ray Charles—but perhaps, now that her biography has been written, an artistically inclined Bollywood or Hollywood director will see the market opportunity. Her life was certainly dramatic enough, from beginning to end.

She started out as Eileen Angelina Yeoward, the name her parents, William Robert Yeoward and Adeline Victoria Hemmings—a Christian father and Hindu mother—gave her when she was born in 1873. Gauhar Jaan's beginnings are a story of her mother's desperate search for survival amid adverse circumstances. The early death of Victoria's father left her family without means, and Victoria went to work in a dry ice factory. There she had a first opportunity to climb out of poverty: Yeoward, an Armenian engineer at the factory, fell in love with her, and married her at the Holy Trinity Church of Allahabad when he was twenty and she was fifteen. Eileen, born a year after the marriage, was baptized two years later at the Allahabad Methodist Episcopal Church. After four more years of marriage, disaster struck: Yeoward, jealous over what he perceived as Victoria's flirtation with another man, walked out on her; they were divorced in 1879. In the same year, a Muslim nobleman took Victoria in as his lover, and together they moved to Vanarasi. At this point mother and daughter, who under different circumstances might have assimilated into British mores, converted to Islam and took new names. Victoria became Malka; her daughter became Gauhar. Mother, daughter, and lover moved in 1888 to Calcutta in order to advance Malka's promising career as a singer-dancer and to open up musical opportunities for her daughter. As Sampath points out, both she and her mother were extraordinarily gifted artists. Her mother became a *tawaif* or courtesan; in contrast to prostitutes, these were supposed to be cultivated women, suitable companions for men of high status. The tawaifs could devote themselves to the arts—and could marry respectable men. A gifted poet as well as a successful dancer and singer, Malka provided her daughter with an artistic education, starting at an early age with language tutors and music gurus while apprenticing her early for her musical career by staging celebrated mother-daughter performances. At the same time, Gauhar's education was enhanced by the half-life of the court traditions of musical patronage. After the Indian Rebellion of 1857, the British deposed the Nawab of Oudh, Wajid Ali Shah. He and his entourage moved their court from Lucknow, where it had been a center for the arts, to Calcutta. They settled in the Chitpur area in the northern part of the city, which was filled with poor natives and immigrants whose houses and shops jostled against temples, mosques, and the houses of the rich. A court musician named Bindadin Majarj offered to teach Gauhar Jaan when she was ten; he became her guru and also furthered her musical education by taking her on trips to Lucknow. Fred Gaisberg was quite correct to regard Gauhar Jaan as a source of Indian musical traditions: even as the old court system fell apart, she took in broad stretches of it.[30]

The meeting of Gaisberg and Gauhar Jaan in 1902 exemplifies a historic moment: the convergence of the old and the new, the culture of the princely courts and the requirements of the early recording studio. Gauhar Jaan's artistic dedication, her desire for wealth and reputation, her ability to adapt to the phonograph; Gaisberg's dedication to turning a profit, but also his musical ear and love of the foreign and new—all of these factors contributed to a refashioned music that could flourish in the commercial markets of the twentieth century. One can observe in this encounter the beginnings of a distinctive Indian pattern of musical modernization. In Japan, traditional court music was hit by the tsunami of bureaucratic reform, which flooded the public schools and left behind melodies adapted to Western harmony. In China, the many-sided conflict over music in the early twentieth century had a devastating effect on elite musical traditions and, as Andrew Jones has chronicled, eventuated in the victory of the simplistic folk music favored by Communist arbiters as the authentic music of the people.[31] During the first half of the twentieth century, Indian musicians had to adapt to multiple challenges, from the end of court patronage to the rise of the phonograph and then of radio and film; it met these challenges with remarkable resilience. Local South Asian musical traditions continued to enjoy wide audiences; so did the Bollywood dance and music that were internationally successful and inimitably Indian.

These varieties of musical experience under the impact of modern technology and politics are only a few examples from the multitude of twentieth-century musical modernizations. On the Western side, the story of Gramophone's global empire, told only in fragmentary and exemplary form here, was in turn just one part of a greater phonographic revolution that involved other big firms like Columbia and Pathé. Even this limited sampling raises general questions about the redefinition of musical cultures in the twentieth century. How was modern technology setting new conditions for cultural production? How did the great political events of the twentieth century, like World War I and decolonization, alter what was once called culture, or even fracture it beyond recognition? Older European conceptions of culture as a unified totality of expressive forms underwent fundamental challenges from exposure to foreign cultures, wartime destruction, mass migration, modern cities, the radicalization of nationalist ideologies, and the overturning of traditional divisions of status and class. New genres of music arose that no longer fit the old cultural molds; instead, they were expressions of transit, modern urban experience, and encounters between classes and peoples long held apart. Debates about the old culture versus the new sprang up at the end of the nineteenth century, and in different forms they have continued until today. These controversies have been inseparable from the more general question of whether culture will be the possession of a hegemonic nationality or a stage for mutual listening and exchange.

10

Commerce versus Culture

Americans and their foreign counterparts competed for markets around the world. They did so with astonishing speed. It had to do not only with the money to be made, but also with the imperial imagination: with the belief that El Dorados were opening up everywhere, that fortunes were awaiting the conquistadors of commerce, and that the profit of the chase was worth the hardships and the risks. Germans caught up quickly with American, British, and French entrepreneurs to become aggressive competitors on world markets. The home of the German industry was Berlin. Like the East Coast metropolises of the United States, Berlin teemed with inventors who made improvements to phonograph and record production. At a time when the city itself was undergoing a tremendous expansion of population, industry, and geographic area and combined wealthy investors with large reserves of craft skill, it had the right ingredients to generate makers and markets of the new medium. They collided with Germany's self-confident, firmly established high culture. More than anyplace else, Germany and its capital, Berlin, became the site of conflict between old and new loyalties: between the classical music culture that Germans regarded as peculiarly their own, and the new technology that threatened to undermine it.

The Global Competitors

Emile Berliner's visit of 1889 may serve as a starting point for the German phonograph industry. In that year he made contact with Kämmerer and Reinhard, a puppet manufacturer in Waltershausen, Thuringia; it made the first gramophones, with record discs of hard rubber, to be produced in Germany. These crude machines, hand-cranked and little more than toys, were a failed experiment that was discontinued after two years.[1] With their next production venture, the Berliner brothers got it right: Deutsche Grammophon went from success to success as a partner in the worldwide Gramophone empire. The pressing plant stayed in Hanover, but in the same year its phonograph division was set up in Berlin. The first director in the capital was Theodore Birnbaum, who came over from London, while Joseph Berliner remained director in Hanover. The pieces were in place for the company's success over the next decade and a half.[2]

Its activities after mid-decade revealed a distinctive feature of the German record industry that set it apart from its American counterpart: its quest for cultural acceptance by Germany's educated elite.[3] In 1907, Leo B. Cohn (who changed his last name to Curt after marrying the lieder singer Elisabeth van Endert) took over the firm's Berlin office and worked to elevate its prestige. This he did with considerable success. It started with the same tactic that had worked for Victor in the United States: in mid-decade, Gramophone brought out phonograph models that hid the unsightly megaphone inside a wooden cabinet. In 1909 a branch firm opened up specially designed, elegantly decorated boutiques in Berlin, Breslau, Düsseldorf, Cologne, Königsberg, Kiel, and Nürnberg; these housed demonstration rooms where customers could listen to records "as in one's own home." The records themselves gained in fidelity, thanks to Bruno Seidler-Winkler, a recording engineer who had a special gift for arranging orchestra members to produce a satisfying balance of instruments. An early moment of triumph came in 1913, when the Berlin Philharmonic Orchestra made its first recording, a rendition of Beethoven's Fifth Symphony, which appeared on four two-sided records. Unlike many artists and connoisseurs, the conductor, Arthur Nikisch, welcomed the phonograph into the world of music, and through this recording made a newsworthy addition to its prestige. The great breakthrough to enthusiasm for the phonograph among cultural elites took place during the Weimar Republic; but even before World War I, Deutsche Grammophon could see the success of its campaign for admission into the world of high culture.[4]

As part of a global enterprise, the Berliner firm pressed records for foreign markets. It was not, however, an active agent in bringing phonographs to foreign music listeners at home or abroad. Instead, newer German start-ups occupied this market space. By the turn of the century, Berlin was the German center for these entrants into the phonograph business, who were soon competing with Gramophone, Victor, Edison, and Columbia for markets at home and abroad.

Two of the newcomers swiftly became leaders of the drive to record in overseas markets. By 1905 the Berlin firm Beka "offered recordings in eleven languages." In the same year one of its owners, Heinrich Bumb, made a world tour with stops in Cairo, Bombay, Calcutta, and Hong Kong; he claimed to have come back with a network of more than 1,500 contacts. The Darmstädter Bank, one of the great banks that not only served as a lender but also played an entrepreneurial role in creating and directing client firms, was the record company's major backer.[5] By 1911 Beka was the second-largest record company in India, with "1,539 titles in a dozen languages, including Bengali, Burmese, Hindustani, Marathi, Punjabi, Tamil and Telugu."[6] For a little more than a half dozen years, the Beka label jolted the established companies with its worldwide recording campaign and stood out for its urbane advertising in the pages of the *Phonographische Zeitschrift*, the industry trade journal. Heinrich Bumb garnered free publicity for his upstart company by furnishing it with an account of his 1905–6 voyage around the world. His reports are a reminder of what a wonder it was that any recording at all got done. On October 5, 1905, an express train took him and his entourage via Vienna and Budapest (an uneventful trip except, he noted drily, for a collision in Belgrade that injured two people and destroyed a freight train) to Constantinople. There he admired the view over the Bosphorus and the Golden Horn, but not much else. Even though they stayed in a side street of the elegant, Europeanized Grand Rue de Pera (today İstiklal Caddesi), wild dogs howling in the streets and night watchmen rapping with metal canes on house doors kept him and his companions awake at night. But they were able to carry out their business in their rooms, where they recorded performances of male and female singers accompanied by Turkish instruments. Bumb continued his journey across Asia, often amateurish and incomprehending as he raced from place to place, but with enough success to worry Gramophone management in London.[7] A second firm, Odeon, introduced the two-sided record in 1904 and opened subsidiaries in Cairo and Calcutta. In the same year, it sent a recording engineer named John

Daniel Smoot to North Africa, Greece, and Turkey; by 1905 it had more than seven thousand titles in Arabic, Greek, and Turkish.

Despite their early successes, Beka and Odeon were unable to maintain their independence amid the crashes and recoveries of the phonograph industry. A third firm, Lindström, bought out Beka and Odeon as well as the German firms Favorite, Lyrophon, and Dacapo. By 1912 Lindström was an international giant with the capital, catalog and contacts to compete with Anglo-American and French firms from Cairo to Shanghai. A Swedish mechanic named Carl Lindström had founded a small company in Berlin that in 1903 went bankrupt. The following year, its assets were bought by a consortium of investors led by Max Straus and his partner, Otto Heinemann; it was incorporated under its previous owner's name. Starting out by making phonographs, over the next seven years it rounded out its business by buying up record companies. With the backing of the Bank für Handel und Industrie, the Lindström firm quickly caught up with American, British, and French manufacturers in market after market.[8]

Imagining High Culture: The *Phonographische Zeitschrift*

The American and German trade journals documented their industries' contrasting visions of the "world" that they wished to saturate with music. *Talking Machine World*, the leading American journal, was all business: its articles on foreign markets considered them simply as opportunities for profit. As in the circus and world's-fair presentations of the imperial era, its comments on foreign cultures purveyed galleries of curiosities, material for comedy and self-satisfaction. Ordinary Germans were little different from Americans in their outlook on non-European cultures. The German trade journal, the *Phonographische Zeitschrift*, could be equally superficial. Yet it also had a dimension virtually absent from its American counterpart: a dedication to cultural refinement that extended to its coverage of non-European music. Serious reviews of music recordings, both Western and non-Western; space for articles on archives; presentations of ethnological research; and an insistence on the value of the phonograph as a medium for the cultural elevation of consumers—all of these recurred in its pages. It did not escape the racism of its era, but it also drew on older European traditions of sympathetic curiosity about foreign cultures, which encouraged receptiveness to unfamiliar instruments and tonalities. Music was never all business in the German trade; its representatives wanted to persuade their social superiors—professors, members of the free professions, and civil servants—that they merited respect for their devotion to scientific and artistic progress.

Cosmopolitanism went hand in hand with German businessmen's seriousness about multiplying profits. The export market took on early and lasting importance; it hovered before the eyes of contemporary business observers like a glittering prize that could rescue German manufacturers from the instability of the domestic market and bring in unlimited wealth. In 1902 the *Phonographische Zeitschrift* reported that the sales of the previous holiday season had been unexpectedly good, but factories needed year-round orders. The solution to the postholiday falloff was the overseas export market—especially in the Southern Hemisphere, where, according to the magazine article's author, the high season began in May, just when sales dropped off in Germany.[9] This orientation was not just a journalist's fantasy; German businessmen went abroad with an energy and persistence that lifted their industry from a latecomer to an industry leader, second only to the United States in its share of the world market.

By 1911, the business correspondent for the *Phonographische Zeitschrift*, Arthur Knoch, could report on German success in the phonograph markets of Great Britain, Austria-Hungary, Russia, Argentina, Brazil, France, India, and China, as well as the Dutch East Indies, Chile, Greece, Romania, Spain, and Japan, and tiny markets like Bermuda, Honduras, Thailand, the Canary Islands, and Liberia.[10] In Argentina, German sales pulled ahead of North American sales in 1910: 11,307 phonograph units valued at $24,610, versus American phonograph sales of 2,073 units valued at $7,053. German records also brought in more money than American records: $199,373 to $173,812. In the Brazilian market, too, Germans beat out American phonographs and records, for combined totals of $175,070 to $134,300. While North America dominated the high end of the phonograph market around the world, Germans in Brazil—and indeed virtually everywhere else, notably India and China—had the edge in cheap phonographs.[11] The practical difficulties of opening and profiting from these markets called for strong nerves. A *Phonographische Zeitschrift* article from 1912, asking how Germany could increase its exports to East Asia, discussed the importance of producing cheap phonographs for ordinary people in China and Japan; of using newspaper inserts for advertising, as the Americans already did; of finding local middlemen and getting around reliance on London export firms; and of sending German products via Siberia, which was faster than overseas.[12]

The case of India provides a sample of German businesses' engagement with foreign markets and their cultures. Bumb's experience was profitable, but frustrating. He was entirely dependent on local businessmen and their estimation of how to deal with him—in anything but a "colonial" situation of Europeans pushing around complacent locals. His Indian contacts had the language skills and time on their side, while he was under pressure to negotiate before traveling on to his next destination, Burma. In Bombay everything went smoothly; but in Calcutta he found himself passed from one "friend" to another until he finally picked out one unimportant businessman who was, presumably, more eager for his business than were the larger entrepreneurs. The Gramophone manager in Calcutta reported to his boss in London that Bumb was relying on hotel employees to bring in recording artists, "so you can imagine what class of stuff they got."[13] This may have been self-protective pooh-poohing by a manager eager to impress his home office. But Bumb's report is maddening to read and does not inspire confidence in his ability to round up outstanding artists. In contrast to Gaisberg, who could be crude but had an ear for music that comes through in his diaries, Bumb's chronicle reads like the letters of a cranky tourist on a package tour. It complains about the poor accommodations (Why was first class worse off than second class on the steamer to Bombay?) and gushes over a side trip to Darjeeling, but has little to say about music and musicians. In Calcutta, to judge from his report, Bumb might as well have been selling shoes.[14] Despite the hard conditions and his indifference to aesthetic content, he did what he was supposed to do, probably because he found the right collaborator. Valabhdas Runchordas, the heir to a music business dating back to at least the mid-nineteenth century, was the critical ally who helped Beka assemble its catalog of hundreds of recordings in multiple South Asian languages. Odeon likewise depended on local businessmen to arrange its recording of hundreds of Indian artists.[15]

According to the US State Department survey of phonograph exports, on the eve of World War I, Germans in India recorded in local languages, which Americans did not do. Also—we have the American consul in Madras to thank for a telling detail—they shipped wooden cabinets that warped in the Indian climate.[16] On a trip to New York in December 1918, Runchordas, the same businessman who had worked with Bumb, still observed that in general, Americans were inclined "to force their standard styles and designs upon the native buyers rather than follow the example of European manufacturers and redesign their products to meet the

wishes and requirements of the export trade." The Americans' unwilling-
ness to make even small accommodations to local taste, he added, forced
Indian dealers to stop handling American products.[17] Between their acute
sense of dependence on foreign markets and their eagerness to show that
they appreciated high culture, German phonograph businessmen were
determined to do better at understanding the mentality of their export
markets.

Phonographs and Cultural Progress

The manifesto that opened the very first issue of the *Phonographische Zeitschrift* in 1900 announced as its aim "to make the invention of the phonograph useful for the progress of culture."[18] While the journal did not often
state its cultural mission so plainly, it did come back to it at the end of a
decade of dramatic increase in exports. Knoch reflected in 1911 on what it
meant for Germans to occupy a large share of the foreign market. Beyond
all the technical developments, the talking machine was finally getting
recognition "not just as a means to entertainment and amusement, but
from the ethical side as an instrument for instruction and cultivation,
for awakening a feel for the arts and elevating the taste of broad popular
circles." There was hardly a better counterweight to the degradation of
the young and the appearance of smut in print, he wrote, than the records of good music and song that could touch the popular heart and soul
and awaken a feel for the works of Germany's great composers, poets, and
lecturers.[19]

The same kind of sentiment seeped into a 1914 report from a German traveler to Latin America, Otto Sperber. Far and wide, he reported,
where no other source of culture existed, the reproduction of good music
ennobled the feelings of listeners. For the Indians on sugar plantations,
he wrote, it provided evening entertainment that was a source of joy, and
steered them away from the rum produced on the grounds. In Mazatlan,
Guatemala, Sperber had heard four marimba players give an astonishing
performance of the opera *Cavalleria rusticana*; in the "primeval" jungles
of the Amazon, at a remote settlement for collecting rubber, the sound of
"Wacht am Rhein" wafted through the air, played by "genuine mulattos"
on guitar, accordion, and drum; in the Chaco region of Argentina he had
heard a servant sing "Du, du, liegst mir im Herzen." It was the phonograph
that had brought these jewels of European culture to remote regions.[20]
Sperber's statements were oblivious to the realities of the regions he

passed through. The Amazon rubber plantations' abuse of their workers was already an international scandal; it was bizarre to suggest that a German nationalist song somehow elevated them. To American wholesalers and retailers, his report, with its praise for the power of the phonograph to lift popular morals and culture, would have sounded absurd. Not so to German ears: popular and elite classes alike believed in the transforming power of high culture.

The links between phonograph and culture were evident in the *Phonographische Zeitschrift*'s numerous articles about phonographic archives. Beginning in 1902, the journal reported on archives in several European metropolises. The Paris Anthropological Society—a group dominated by physical anthropology—stored some four hundred cylinders that one Dr. Alonzet had recorded during the recent world exposition (presumably the Universal Exposition of 1900 in Paris). He had used the gathering, reported the journal, to capture conversation, storytelling, songs, and music of the members of "different races," including samples of Chinese, Indian, Tartar, and Serbian dialects, as well as songs in Arabic, Zulu, Sudanese, Ethiopian, and Malagasy (spoken in Madagascar).[21] As for the phonograph archive in Vienna, it had three goals: to capture languages, music, and the voices of famous personalities on cylinders. By 1902 it had provided phonographs for the expeditions of Professor Richard von Wettstein to Brazil, of Professor Milan Ritter von Resetar to Croatia and Slavonia, and of Professor Paul Kretschmer to Lesbos.[22] Coverage of archival activities abroad was not just a way of adding colorful anecdotes to the journal's pages; it legitimated the phonograph by arguing that it contributed to serious scientific enterprises.

The founding of a state archive in Vienna set off competitive envy in Berlin. In 1904 an unnamed director of Deutsche Grammophon spoke to an unnamed, highly placed statesman about creating a state-sponsored phonograph archive; the statesman responded favorably, but asked for public discussion of the issue. The record firm made a selection of thirty of its best recordings to accompany public forums, including Caruso singing an aria from *Manon Lescaut*, the famous violinist Josef Joachim playing a Hungarian dance, Fritz Kreisler playing a sarabande (composers unnamed), and the celebrated cantor Gershon Sirota singing sacred music; also included were recordings of a Chinese comic routine, a Japanese geisha chorus, and Arab clarinet music. In the same year, Felix von Luschan, from the Berlin Ethnological Museum, delivered a paper to the Berlin Anthropological Society about the importance of the phonograph for ethnology, in the hope that Berlin, like Vienna, would get a phonograph archive.[23] For years, one Baron von Hagen pleaded for the creation of an archive; in 1907 he reported on his sarcastic exchange with a Prussian bureaucrat who refused to take him seriously until he had the backing of the learned world. The University of Berlin already housed several recording archives; the Anthropological Society, the Ethnological Museum, and the Institute for Psychology all had their collections. And there was the Phonogramm Archiv, whose director, Carl Stumpf, was powerful and respected by his colleagues. But the journalist writing for the *Phonographische Zeitschrift* could not take seriously its collection of music by "primitive peoples." As it was, the push for a phonograph archive came mainly from enthusiasts and businessmen, and neither of these counted for much in the eyes of Prussian bureaucrats, who were cautious with their money and with dispensing state prestige.[24] The *Phonographische Zeitschrift* aligned itself with Stumpf, as well as with the nonacademics who were eager to exploit the serious use of the new technology for music, language studies, and historical preservation of voices of the famous. Despite the halting success at getting state funding, the journal's discussions document the eagerness of phonograph adherents to make a show of the technology's cultural attainments.

Hearing Foreign Cultures

The *Phonographische Zeitschrift* took another step that would hardly have been thinkable in the United States: it hired a serious music critic. Max Chop was a true child of Germany's educated elite. His father was a provincial judge, and his mother was the daughter of a builder, a modest occupation; but a great-uncle was a minister of culture in Saxony. Chop married a pianist who, for her part, came from a prominent Dutch family of musicians and ministers of state. With the encouragement of Franz Liszt, Chop broke off his legal studies in 1885 for a career as a music journalist, moving permanently to Berlin in 1902. He started writing reviews for the *Phonographische Zeitschrift* in 1905; by 1912, when the journal celebrated his fiftieth birthday, he had written more than a hundred books. Chop was a popularizer, but at a high level, directing his readers to musical form as well as historical context.[25] He usually reviewed records of Western classical music, but exotic offerings drew his attention to music from the Middle East and Asia.

Chop's initial extra-European review of 1906 is a fascinating document of his first exposure to foreign music. He does not seem to have had any awareness of Stumpf's research, even though it went back twenty years, or of the Phonogram Archive, even though it was a half dozen years old. Instead, he was astonished by the commercial recordings he received, especially the cornucopia resulting from the Beka expedition of 1905–6. But Chop's ignorance makes his reviews all the more interesting. He had no one to guide his listening; with the equipment of a Western connoisseur, he had to puzzle out the unfamiliar music for himself.[26]

The strangeness began with his bafflement over the tempos and rhythms of Turkish music. Establishing the key gave him trouble too. He could discern a prevalent minor mode—but it matched none of the familiar European scales. The Turkish recordings contained microtones, and he tried to appreciate their use for a dramatic heightening of emotion, but could still only think of them as a defect in harmonization.[27] Chinese music impressed him as nothing but noise: he called a Chinese ensemble piece a "masterpiece of cacophony" in which each member of the group seemed to go his own way, with neither style nor rhythm in common—a striking reference to the heterophony that often bewildered Europeans.[28] A year and a half later, in his comments on Indian recordings, he was still stumbling over the use of dissonance.[29] In other words, Chop managed to come on his own to some of the central points of contrast between Western and non-Western systems that had preoccupied comparative musical analysis since the time of Stumpf and Ellis in the mid-1880s; the diversity of scales shook up his fundamental sense of what constituted music.

Chop was not just responding to foreign scales. He realized that contemporary German music was flirting with dangerous extremes of dissonance. "Richard Strauss," he added to his comments on the Indian recordings, "would be delighted to find a confirmation of [one of] his basic principles among the Himalayan children of nature: that affect or passion breaks apart harmonic order and must lead to disharmony." Neither Himalayans nor avant-garde Germans could budge his allegiance to harmony. High culture understood the art of keeping sorrow and pain within prescribed bounds. Chop came back to the same point the next year, this time comparing the cacophony of Tamil or Chinese music to Strauss's operas *Salome* and *Elektra*. It was an arresting comparison. With it, the perception of extra-European music as noise converged with discomfort over the ever bolder European distensions of harmony.

Despite his misgivings about foreign music, Chop also found much to praise. The most intriguing case was Indian music from Bombay, which captivated him with its display of virtuoso coloratura. "It's astonishing!" he exclaimed. "Our best coloratura singers could not match it!" Even though the music as such did not move him, he could value the technical achievement.[30] Chop fell easily into clichés of the early 1900s, clucking over wild Oriental fantasy and the weirdness of nasal intonations.[31] He was not just a sponge for the racial prejudices of his time, however. A recording sung by the chief cantor of Bucharest, Bernhard Wladowsky (who went on to a brilliant singing career in North America), in memory of the Jewish victims of a recent wave of violence in Russia, deeply moved him. This was not an obvious choice for aesthetic respect, since the "sobbing" style of the Eastern European chazzans easily met with scorn from educated Westerners.[32] Despite his sometimes incomprehending remarks, Chop was aware that his own training was inadequate for appreciating non-Western music.[33] He combined irritation over its strange features with thanks for its expansion of his horizons, and hope that the records would find a wide reception in the West.[34]

The scientific and educational value of the recordings was self-evident to Chop. His first review praised them as a revelation: suddenly he could listen to "Eastern" music, not just read about it. With the availability of recordings like these, the phonograph was taking its proper place as a mediator in the service of pedagogy and research.[35] Chop noted the excitement that the Beka records in particular had stirred at a recent Berlin trade fair, where they had won praise in the press for their cultural value; and he pointed out the opportunities they gave the music historian and the ethnographer for serious study.[36] His excitement still ran high in a review of 1908 in which called them documents of "priceless value."[37] Chop himself was an adherent of the theory that humanity had originated in the Himalayas and that the music of Asia had dispersed outward from there; for him, the recordings were an exciting confirmation, allowing him to hear homologous features of different "Asian" traditions, such as the drone, from Istanbul to Calcutta, and to imagine that they came from a common source. Western culture and its music, he thought, had an entirely different origin among the Celts; his reviews drew a radical line between the original cultural forms of Orient and Occident. Contradictory exceptions, such as the often-noted use of the drone in the Scottish bagpipe, escaped his attention, as did the more general need for a disciplined analysis of cultural dissemination. Chop was an inheritor of the kind of racialized speculation that had dominated the evolutionary historical thinking of the nineteenth century but was now giving way to the more skeptical views of modern sociology and anthropology. Despite the amateurish quality of his views, he appreciated the value of recordings for research and study. One review ended with an appeal to the state: the records ought to meet with interest "in all academic circles," and deserved "the attention of the state authorities who are the representatives of our culture."[38] Combating his contemporaries' scoffing, he sought to establish the phonograph's potential for broadening European musical taste.

How much Europeans paid attention to the music newly available for purchase is a difficult question. The simple answer would be: very little. Foreign-language recordings produced by labels like Beka and Odeon were almost entirely made for foreign audiences. Westerners who listened to them were rare, and even a well-meaning trained listener like Chop did not have the intellectual resources to understand very much. Rather, early responses like his belonged to the beginning of a process of cultural transfer that would grow richer over the course of the twentieth century.

The contrast between German and American attitudes, which Germans themselves dwelled on throughout the nineteenth century, disguises complexities in the meaning of culture. Germans admired *high* culture, whether at home or abroad; that was what enticed Chop to review recordings from afar. An appreciation of *popular* music was generally absent from the elite imagination. To be sure, folk music could merit attention as a document of national identity and as a source of classical art, but that was different from valuing popular music in its own right. There, the American recording industry's lack of cultural aspirations became an advantage; the industry leaders had a different kind of multicultural market and were happy to exploit it, recording Yiddish vaudeville and Yom Kippur liturgy, gross ethnic humor and Verdi—whatever the market would reward. An American transformation of the meaning of culture was underway in which the sentimental Victorian songs favored by Edison and Alaskan prospectors would seep into the symphonies of Charles Ives, the twangy tunes of the interior would undergo an elevation in Aaron Copeland, and the syncopations from New Orleans would begin their worldwide journey as ragtime and then jazz. Vulgar, gaudy, commercialized, hit-or-miss—the foreign recordings of the American phonograph companies may look disappointing from the perspective of our time; but, compared to their German counterparts, they worked across class and ethnic lines to change the very definition of musical culture.

Conclusion

After 1918, Europeans had to come to terms with a world in ruins. The irrationality of the war itself challenged their belief in their own rationality; losses on the battlefield brought tragedy into many homes; once secure families formerly able to live from their investments saw their resources depleted, their ability to travel limited, and the luxuries of the past replaced by the shopworn and shabby. But while the war brought demoralization to Europeans, it opened opportunities to many of their colonial subjects. Asians and Africans had fought side by side with Europeans on the battlefields; even if they were not yet emancipated from European empires, their intelligentsia could take heart from the Russian Revolution and imagine a better future for their own nations. Alongside the foundering of long-established colonial relations abroad, there was a shift in class hierarchies at home: the new mood of the 1920s was democratic, scornful of old elites, and tempted by radical agendas in politics and culture. Popular musical forms, many of them hardly noticeable to elites before the war, now blared from cafes and ballrooms. As for the elites themselves, they were not necessarily hostile to the new cultural genres. Leading critics and musicians also admired the improvements in phonograph sound fidelity, and embraced the phonograph as the means to create a new democratic culture.

Postwar Polyglot Music: Caribbean, Hawaiian, Latin, Jazz

Although newly audible, the popular music of the 1920s and beyond was generally the outcome of long histories. Caribbean music burst forth from islands like Trinidad, Jamaica, and Cuba in genres that differed from place to place and made their way to the mainland United States and Europe. The islanders' formative experiences reached back to Columbus and the conquistador invasion of the islands, the decimation of native peoples, the free migration of Europeans, the forced migration of Africans, and the nineteenth-century arrival of indentured laborers from India; Caribbean music embodied century-long experiences of work, sex, religion, and politics, with different histories from place to place. The diverse musical styles of the islands were a reflection on movement around the Atlantic and the longer lines of commerce across the Pacific. By 1938, "Rum and Coca-Cola," a calypso song by Lord Invader attacking the baleful behavior of American soldiers in Trinidad, made the top of the popular music charts in a bowdlerized version sung by the Andrews Sisters.[1] Hawaiian music had a more compact history, but was also a crystallization of colonial encounters. The first missionaries, puritanical New England Protestants, arrived in Oahu in 1820 and considered music a powerful means of touching the souls of native Hawaiians; over the next few decades they shaped a genre of hymns that synthesized Protestant melodies and the Hawaiian language. By the end of the century, native Hawaiians were forging European music into the means of their own cultural renaissance. Queen Lili'uokalani, last monarch of the islands, wrote songs that united missionary melodies to love of the land and the Hawaiian people, as did less talented and exalted composers. The ukulele, brought to the islands in the 1870s by indentured Portuguese laborers from Madeira, was thought of by the end of the century as a Hawaiian instrument. The Hawaiian steel guitar, invented and brought to the US mainland by a Hawaiian aristocrat in the early twentieth century, entered into the quintessentially "American" sound of Southern music. By the early twentieth century, pop Hawaiian music enjoyed a place in the white American repertoire that it kept through the 1920s.[2]

Many of these Atlantic and Pacific musical genres came from entrepôts that for centuries had served as hubs of world commerce. Their music was readily received in port cities where ordinary people enjoyed an unusual freedom of movement, dress, and musical expression. But it also came to life in immigrant cities like New York and London, where Europeans, Africans, and others mingled and borrowed rhythm, movement, and melody from one another. The newly globalized music of the twentieth century was a product of both old patterns of servitude and emancipation and a newly accelerating movement of peoples around the world.[3]

Beginning with tango, Latin American dance music genres, too, captured the ethnic crossings of island entrepôts and immigrant metropolises, and quickly turned from local beats into global favorites. Simon Collier has portrayed how tango took shape in a distinct locale that was also a global setting. Argentina in the 1880s and 1890s conquered the pampas and turned them into a reservoir for world exports of wheat and beef. Buenos Aires attracted a torrent of capital from England, and immigrants from Italy and Spain. The city center developed an architecture and glamor to rival European capitals, while its outlying areas were a shamble of buildings quickly thrown up to house new arrivals, a congeries of small shops and transient labor. The working-class suburbs were also a meeting place for country and city: Collier suggests that the gauchos' aggressively male and free way of life caught fire with the young men in this blurred urban zone. Another element linked tango to jazz: its African antecedents and its emergence from the travail of slavery and post-emancipation freedom. In working-class districts away from the city center, black dances and music captured the fancy of white toughs. They mixed them up with other dances circulating in the city, like the habanera, a Cuban-Spanish dance form that had found its way back from Spain to the New World. As Collier observes, tango was a product of the Atlantic triangle, bringing together African, European, and Argentine styles of movement and melody. It came together by crossing the color line between emancipated slaves and white workers who were themselves a mix of rural and urban, native-born, and immigrant. In the last two decades of the nineteenth century, the steps and beat that had begun with whites mocking black dance crystallized into the new dance.[4]

Tango gathered influences into the working-class neighborhoods that were its birthplace. Almost immediately, it reversed the flow of influence and spread outward. Middle-class young men ventured into the working-class districts of Buenos Aires and took the new dance back to their refined neighborhoods in the city center. Dance masters carried it to Paris, where it turned into a fad by 1910. Two years later, the fad had spilled over to London.[5] In both metropoles it was thrill seekers from the upper classes, already familiar with ragtime-based dances, who took up the Argentine import. Bits and pieces of information suggest how far and wide it spread. By 1906, major record companies were vying for control of the

tango market, with Berlin-based Odeon and Victor the leading contend-
ers.[6] The anthropologist Bronislaw Malinowski encountered the tango in
1914 on his first research trip to Papua New Guinea. He noted in a diary
entry of September 20 that he went dancing at the house of one Dr. Simp-
son: "The music there reminded me of many things: some *Rosenkavalier*,
some tangos, the 'Blue Danube.'"[7] The old and the new, the stately Central
European and the swerving Argentine, rocked in Port Moresby.

During the 1920s, tango was still popular in Europe. In 1919, Odeon,
by then a Lindström label, built a record factory in Buenos Aires. The firm
turned to Max Glücksmann, a prominent Buenos Aires impresario, to
supply it with famous tango artists. Glücksmann himself embodied the
new age of far-reaching connections: before the war he had emigrated as
a poor Jewish child from Romania to Buenos Aires and built up an entertainment empire that managed film as well as phonograph investments.[8]
His locally produced recordings of tango music were shipped back to Europe, where it was synonymous with a new freedom of movement, emancipation of the body, and affirmation of sensuality. Tango's new rhythms
crossed lines of color, class, and national identity.

Finally, there was jazz, emblem of the postwar era. One remarkable
characteristic of jazz that furthered a new global culture was its dialogi-
cal character; it emerged from black historical experience and entered
into original combinations with cultures and classes across continents.
Jazz became the paradigmatic genre of global culture, true to its historical
emergence in a racial regime but inviting variations with non-American
partners. Like tango, it broke down the world typologies inherited from
the eighteenth century that hardened into the nineteenth century's racial
stereotypes.[9]

The proto-form of jazz that first reached audiences outside the United
States was ragtime, a sound that had crystallized by the mid-1890s and
had reached one high point of complexity in a cluster of St. Louis composers. The stage for its transmission to wider audiences was the same one
that for decades had brought unfamiliar music to European and American audiences: the international exposition. At the Chicago World's Fair,
white audiences were captivated by new music that its African-American
creators probably, according to Edward Berliner, performed nearby and
not in the official exhibitions.[10] By the eve of World War I, observers were
startled by ragtime's success in Europe. Frank Damrosch, a German-
American immigrant and one of the guiding forces of New York's classical music institutions in the early twentieth century, commented in 1913

on "the present craze of Europe for American ragtime," judging that "if Europe adopts ragtime, it will deserve all the injury it will receive. 'Ragtime tunes,' he said, 'are like pimples. They come and go. They are impurities in the musical system which must be got rid of before it can be considered clean.'"[11] Other contemporary observers, too, were impressed by the growing presence of ragtime in Europe. Walter Stevens, the Edison record executive, reported after a trip abroad on the strong demand for ragtime in European markets. Max Chop was annoyed to detect hints of it ("cake-walk") in a Chinese recording. Writing from Russia and Mexico, US consuls in 1912 made a point of warning that the markets in those countries did *not* share in the widespread craze.[12]

As James Jackson recounts, jazz probably first arrived in France during the war. Afterward it became one of the signature cultural movements of the time, read by contemporaries in many ways: as an infusion of "primitive" energy and contemporary cultural excitement, as a sign of decadence, as an invasion of American culture, or as a threat to the integrity of French traditions. By the late 1920s jazz became French; musicians managed to persuade the public that it belonged to the national patrimony.[13] Amid the chaos of the immediate postwar years, jazz made its way more slowly in Germany. It embodied the excitement of Germany's first democracy and its collision of elite and popular culture. In the late 1920s, the greatest American attraction in Berlin was the Paul Whiteman orchestra, which assimilated jazz into white orchestral conventions. Ernst Krenek's successful opera from 1927, *Jonny spielt auf*, added to the homegrown definitions of jazz for German audiences.[14] By the late 1920s and early 1930s, Germans could hear more American jazz musicians, too, and listen to their records.[15] Hearing had only a loose connection to perceptions, however. What jazz *meant* to many Germans disoriented by the uncertainties of the Weimar era was Americanization, African culture, and Jewish influence. Recent scholarship has emphasized how strongly these cultural resonances echoed throughout the Nazi years, when the regime condemned jazz as decadent, but admirers clung to it as anti-authoritarian and urbane. Jazz was a placeholder for the cultural oppositions of democracy and dictatorship.

The Phases of Musical Globalization

World War I unleashed worldwide creativity for musical genres made by peoples in motion. Yet this remarkable outburst of musical innovation was only one dimension of a new global culture that reached back to the mid-nineteenth century. Between the 1850s and the 1920s this culture took shape in three stages: a growing understanding of non-European forms of music, a worldwide dissemination of records, and a democratization of musical genres. Each of these processes extended backward in time but had a specific moment of breakthrough, arriving successively in Europe by the mid-1880s, mid-1900s, and mid-1920s.

One dimension of the new global culture was a fresh receptivity: an ability to hear non-Western music *as* music instead of noise. The decisive moment for the introduction of new methods and knowledge was the mid-1880s. The work that gave a decisive formulation to hermeneutic listening was Ellis's essay on the variety of human scales. It is easy today to point out its shortcomings, beginning with its assumptions that the scale was the basic unit of music and that music itself was a constant across cultures. Yet we can only make those criticisms because Ellis and his contemporaries initiated an era of thinking beyond Western musical norms. For its quantification of pitch, the thoroughness of its research, the extent of its coverage of musical traditions around the world, and the radical clarity of its conclusion, his essay was the starting point for rethinking the nature of music. Craft entered into Ellis's analysis through his partnership with Hipkins, who made it possible for him to discriminate between the peculiarities of instruments and tones that otherwise would have been beyond his grasp. Science picked up in Germany where Ellis left off: Stumpf's essay on the Nuxalks was published just a year after Ellis's essay, and complemented its discovery of microtones and announcement of their fundamental importance for rethinking the nature of music in general. German science allied with commerce: Stumpf went on to benefit from the commercial development of the phonograph, for under his direction the Phonogram Archive assembled its world archive of recordings from Edison cylinders. Ellis and Stumpf drew on earlier efforts, going back to the Romantics and the Enlightenment, to approach foreign cultures as the expression of historically and psychologically formed identities. The decisive figure for both of them was Helmholtz. Ellis turned to the German scientist's monograph on pitch as the foundation of his own work, while Stumpf responded more critically as he shifted attention to the listener's consciousness of sound. The general forces of globalization permitted Ellis and Stumpf to carry out their comparative inquiries. Railroads, trains, and trade made possible the movement of instruments and musicians around the world; without them there would have been no Japanese village or Chinese orchestra in London, no Nuxalk lessons in Halle, no Thai orchestra in Berlin.

These spectacles alone would have fallen short for the creation of new forms of musical analysis. The modern research university and museum created the context for moving from impressionistic to scientific and scholarly study. Ellis was a Cambridge-trained mathematician with good contacts in the British scientific establishment and the training to translate Helmholtz's work into English. Stumpf was a leader of the experimental psychology movement who made the scientific laboratory the model for the Phonogram Archive. As a university professor, Stumpf was able to create a cohort dedicated to the comparative study of music, a field that eventually became established in research universities around the world. Quantification and globalization alone, however, do not account for the success of their enterprise. As Carl Engel knew, it also took listener sympathy—and that grew from the late Enlightenment and Romanticism. Without this disposition, no amount of quantification or analysis could have led to a satisfactory reception of unfamiliar musical systems.

A second aspect of the new global culture was a dissemination that crossed oceans and continents. This was a many-sided movement that began with instruments and accelerated with musicians' tours, musical experts' transplantation, and mass migration, followed by the global growth of the phonograph industry. The transition was complete by mid-decade after 1900, when phonographs had gone from being amusement for novelty seekers and saloons to mass entertainment on all continents, in small towns and villages as well as metropolises.

The spread of phonographs around the world depended on scientific research. Emile Berliner could not have developed the flat disc record without his education from a German physics textbook, furthered by his work with scientists from Washington to Boston. Commerce and science required the craft skills of machinists like Eldridge Johnson and the mechanically adept adventurers who turned themselves into recording engineers. The phonograph business complemented the circulation of musicians promoted by impresarios with a global imagination. Another aspect of globalization complemented this mass movement of mechanized sound: immigration. The mass migration of Germans to England included Carl Engel and a generation of cultivated Germans who transplanted their belief in music as a sublime art, historical knowledge, and analytical sophistication. By 1900, immigrant communities in North America and Latin America were ready-made audiences for foreign recordings; so were the businessmen and administrators who swarmed across colonies and markets from Cairo to Calcutta. A newly sophisticated sales culture aided this rapid penetration of entertainment markets: heavy investment in advertising and products like the Victrola and the Red Seal records turned phonographs and records into the symbols of a new middle-class consumer culture.

As for the third aspect of the new global culture, the democratization embodied by new musical genres, upper-class Europeans began appropriating them before 1914 as primitive and exotic; they were outliers of the larger prewar wave of primitivism, garnering the greatest publicity in visual artistic movements like Fauvism in France and Expressionism in Germany. The context was different after 1918. The war resulted in a new self-confidence and visibility of mass culture; it advanced the emancipation of women and, along with it, a new freedom of sensuous expression; it set in motion wartime soldiers, who were followed by mobile musicians from North America, Latin America, and the Caribbean. Scientific improvements in recording technology made the phonograph inviting as never before to Europe's upper classes. Despite their popular stamp, music forms like jazz and Latin dance were no longer viewed as less than artful; they called for their own performance skills, elicited commentary from classically trained critics, and inflected music heard in concert halls.

Many but not all educated Europeans were thrown off by the transformations of musical life in the postwar era. Weimar Germany was home to intellectuals and artists who defined the 1920s with clarity and verve; some approached their moment of political danger as an incentive to think one's way through to a new social democratic culture. Nowhere was this more visible than in the twenty-fifth anniversary volume published by the Lindström firm in 1929. Ten years earlier, the firm had already shown its dedication to making music education a part of schooling in Germany's first democracy by opening an educational division.[16] The anniversary volume celebrated the democratic and cosmopolitan potential of the phonograph. Nowhere was this more striking than in the testimonial by the novelist Thomas Mann, a political conservative before the war who had turned into an ardent defender of the Weimar Republic. The transformation was not just political; along with it came an interest in democratizing the high culture that had once been the possession of a few. Having once approached the phonograph gingerly, he gave it his full embrace in his testimony in the Lindström volume. One can hear the voice of the cultural conservative arguing with his former self and coming out in favor of the mechanical reproduction of sound:

> Technologization of the artistic—to be sure, it sounds terrible; it sounds like the sound of decline and fall of the soul. But what if, at the moment the soul falls prey to technology, technology gains a soul? If for example the phonograph, not long ago a crude item for bars, has unquestionably risen to the level of a musical item that no musician can approach any longer with contempt? I love this invention, it gives me daily use and pleasure, I owe it the greatest thanks. . . .[17]

By the time Mann confessed his adoration for the phonograph, it had gone from being an intruder into the well-ordered living room to a comforter, a friend, and even an icon of style for the exponents of high culture. Another prominent tastemaker called attention to the cosmopolitanism inherent in the new medium: "A culture—therewith a cohesion, collection, comparison of audio-expressions in life and art, once viewed as a utopia— . . . is now a reality on the little turntable, whose script . . . unifies epochs and peoples. [It yields both] amusement and instruction, imagination and history, emancipation from the prejudices of time and place." So wrote Oscar Bie, son of a wealthy manufacturer, cultural critic, and longtime editor of the well-known cultural review, the *Neue Rundschau*.[18] With its pictures of cultural monuments and record stores from around the world, the anniversary volume displayed Lindström's dedication to emancipation from local prejudice and to the unification of peoples.

The volume ended with an essay by one of Germany's best-known musical exponents of comparison between world musical cultures: Curt Sachs. Comparative musicologist, collaborator with the Phonogram Archive, coauthor with Erich von Hornbostel of a classic paper on the classification of musical instruments, and director of the Berlin state instrument collection, Sachs was already a celebrated scholar, teacher, and organizer. His essay on world music in the anniversary volume discussed an exhibition held in Frankfurt am Main in 1927 on music in popular life (called *Musik im Leben der Völker*), for which he assembled the extra-European galleries. Visitors came to gawk at the strange musical instruments of "savages"; they left, wrote Sachs, with a new respect for the instruments' craftsmanship and sound. But the greatest attraction of this part of the exhibition was the phonograph, which visitor requests kept turning from beginning to end of the exhibition day. The faraway tones of Javanese orchestra pieces and the ecstatic heights of Indian song especially drew them in. He added: "Amid the great crisis of contemporary creativity, we here find values in completely realized form that we feel our way toward in the dark. Beyond all the chasms that make the separation between our world and theirs unbridgeable, despite all that is foreign, not understood and not understandable, we sense a commonality and familiarity that elevates and enriches us." It was a reprise of themes going back seven decades. The title of the Frankfurt exhibition echoed the title of Carl Engel's history of national music from 1866. Like Engel and Hipkins, Sachs turned to instruments to convey the craftsmanship and beauty of music from foreign parts of the world; once again, an exhibition offered entertainment and instruction to a mass audience. The phonograph, no more than a novelty in nineteenth-century exhibitions, could now convey a sound-infused voyage around the world.[19]

Culture's Global Theories

A tradition of social theory going back to the beginnings of high globalization and imperialism predicted the dissolution of local cultures in a universal flow of commodities. "All that is solid melts into air," wrote Marx and Engels in *The Communist Manifesto*. These words from 1848 have rung ever since in the ears of intellectuals, and carried over into characterizations of culture in the age of globalization.[20] Max Weber delivered his own more intellectualized version of a related thesis when he envisioned a universal victory of Western rationalization in his essay on science as a vocation. Similar predictions continued in the second half of the twentieth century, though with the value valences reversed from negative to positive. Modernization theorists welcomed the coming triumph of Western rationality as a gain for the democratic and humane values institutionalized in post–World War II America; Soviet intellectuals did the same when they heralded the advances of scientific socialism in their own societies. Since the 1960s, Marxian critics have offered powerful critiques of the universal spread of the American way of life and American capital as well as its collusion with capitalist elites from other countries. Their criticisms need to be taken up by any comprehensive theory of globalization and culture.[21]

From the opposite political point of view, motivated by fear rather than intellectual analysis, right-wing ideologues across the twentieth century and beyond have declared war on human cooperation beyond the nation-state. The recent wave of political nationalism has brought about a widespread repudiation of a perceived homogenization of peoples and cultures resulting from globalization, a call for defiance of it, and an insistence that the nation-state in all its manifestations—political, economic, social, and cultural—should have priority over universal norms. Its advocates presume that national identities were formed at a mythic point in the past with a timeless purity that is now threatened. Their call to hide behind a channel or a wall is a reaction to globalization that recalls earlier moments of anxiety. A comparison with the actual history of globalization, however, leads to different conclusions about the historical refashioning of identities.

The first generation of theorists of globalization in the 1980s should be credited with discarding the back-and-forth paradigm of paired optimistic and pessimistic theories of a universally triumphant globalization emanating from the West. Instead, they shifted to a paradigm of homogenization versus local identity that took issue with the accompanying fears of a leveling of cultural differences. Among the most important early contributions came from Arjun Appadurai, Carol Breckenridge, and Ulf Hannerz.[22] Perhaps it is no accident that all three positioned themselves slightly outside the North American–Western European center stage of academic discourse, Appadurai and Breckenridge through their familiarity with India, Hannerz as a sociologist in Sweden. Abandoning older conceptions of Western hegemony, they wrote in terms of a unified network of global exchanges, uneven in its distribution of power and wealth, but different from colonial influence beaming from a European center. Their models brought nonmetropolitan places into the field of vision of Western intellectuals as a constitutive dimension of the West's own political economies. As these theorists discerned, by the late 1980s the underlying reality had shifted so much that one could discern the outlines of a different kind of world, one in which a transnational class would play an intermediary role between societies long held apart or capable of communicating only on unequal terms. The example of India, long autonomous as part of the nonaligned movement, its intellectuals shielded from the full force of American influence by a socialist ethos that went along with its political independence, was a guarantor to Appadurai and Breckenridge that the "local" had a role to play within the globalizing world. Their comments anticipated the moment when other nations outside the North Atlantic, including Brazil, Turkey, and China, would become prominent powers in international affairs.

Subsequent students of globalization have addressed the question of whether globalization has taken the form of relations between local agents and global forces. At the end of the 1990s, about a decade after the founding essays by Appadurai and his peers, John Tomlinson surveyed the burgeoning literature on globalization and came to similar conclusions about the persistence of local agency. As he understood it, globalization brought about a "rapidly developing and ever-thickening network of interconnections and interdependences"; time and space shrank as technology brought distant parts of the world into greater proximity. Yet globalization amounted to a context or a frame of reference, in his language, for the perceptions of specific actors who maintained their local autonomy. Individual human subjects, he concluded, worked "to make themselves 'at home' in the world of global modernity.'"[23] More recent anthropologists have continued to criticize older models and offer fresh ones in order to articulate how the creation of a global order stimulates self-assertion and requires a mixing and matching of world perspectives. Anna Lowenhaupt Tsing, studying environmental conflicts in Indonesia, has proposed the term "friction" to identify local self-assertion as an inevitable component of any exchange between social actors—including ones who may share a common goal, such as ending the depredations of a region's forests. Stuart Rockefeller has written a critique of the term "flow" in the lexicon of globalization, where it is used as if capital, human beings, and ideas could circulate unchallenged: in his view, the term contains a managerial fiction that elides local actors' powers of resistance and agency.[24]

In the history of music and globalization, the local has been closely identified with craft, which was usually linked to place and involved individual training and experience. It entered the world of music through the creation of fine artifacts in the form of musical instruments. Engel and Hipkins recovered string and keyboard instruments from the European musical past and from cultures around the world. They learned about them in books, but also found them in dealers' shops, country houses, and church basements as well as museums and private collections. Exploring these, they became aware of qualities for music making that could not be replaced by industrially made instruments, above all the Steinway cast-iron-frame piano. Crafted musical objects are today part of a larger economy of artifacts for which there is a worldwide appetite; even as industrialization and mass production grow, so does the yearning and readiness to buy objects that bespeak local culture and individual personality.

Craft applied not just to musical instruments, but also to musical compositions. Modern nationalism was often the political ally of the will to recover a world of crafted particularity. The two were nineteenth-century twins: nationalism was forged after the Napoleonic era precisely through the creation of "invented traditions" that set each nation apart.[25] Music was a prominent ally of this process of national assertion. Hindustani music, as reconstructed by S. M. Tagore, was supposedly a pure Hindu art, and excluded Muslim musicianship by viewing it as a corruption of a culture going back to the age of the Vedas. You didn't have to be a colonial subject to revive a crafted tradition; the Little England movement did the same thing, as Martin Clayton has shown in his essay on the two renaissances, Bengali and English.[26] Halfway around the world, another beleaguered island culture could mobilize musical resources to create a modern political identity; David Kalākaua and Queen Lili'ukalani rescued what they could of ancient Hawaiian culture. Even though artifacts and texts belonged to their campaign, no medium was more potent than music, which was singularly capable of popular diffusion and the creation of a national community. The ongoing creativity of individuals in specific places drawing on specific traditions persisted as a formative feature of modern art and politics.

The relationship between craft and science, too, suggests a more complicated story than the simple opposition of the global and the local. Modern Western science entered into the rediscovery of the local and the crafted as an aid to analyzing the rationality of different musical systems. This was precisely what happened when Ellis measured scales and pitch. The untutored ear, the "natural" ear, is enclosed in its particularities—for example, the Western scale and harmony—and can only make limited sense out of alien forms of music. Ellis's measurements demonstrated the different logic of non-Western musical traditions; they were especially persuasive because he combined them with attention to instruments and performance practices. His collaboration with Hipkins, the master craftsman, exemplified how a rigorous yet sympathetic analysis gave each musical tradition a place of distinction and validity within a world of musical cultures.

Globalization did not dissolve everything solid into the circulation of commodities. Rather, it created a new set of circumstances within which social actors could choose which kind of culture they wished to create. In the context of diplomatic history, Akira Iriye has spoken of a complementarity of internationalism and local interest, opposed but balanced in a functioning system of state relations.[27] A comparable balance took shape in the realm of culture. On the one hand, there can be no question that a dramatic transformation of the circumstances of artistic and intellectual activity took place. Yet science, craft, and commerce were steadily deployed to enable local artistic expression. Island peoples, rural communities and secondary cities, Europeans and non-Europeans alike, have made use of them to challenge, limit, draw on, and transform the incursions of Western culture and to project their own musical cultures into the outside world. Globalization has been not so much a leveling force as an opportunity best grasped with a knowledge of the past and the resources of the present. From the age of exhibitions to the jazz age, a global culture of new freedoms flourished around the world. We have discovered it in old port towns, in the making of music across cultures to places large and small, in the global encounters that began in gentlemanly London, in the phonograph shipments to Curaçao and Fremantle, and in post-1914 clubs from Berlin to Shanghai.

When discussions of globalization began some twenty-five years ago, they anticipated a growing cosmopolitan class, a readiness to encounter the wider world, and a growing generosity in the face of different cultures. This mood continued through the 1990s, when some utopian academics imagined that they might be on the verge of a withering away of the nation-state, and its replacement by a peaceful anarchy regulated by nongovernmental organizations. Instead, that moment has been checked by a sullen neonationalism and a revolt against elites. There has been a rejection of global exchanges and, along with it, a groundswell of fantasies about cultural purity.

Certainly, cultures crystallize into distinctive forms, and these are the labor of generations, cherished, nurtured, and preserved in places large and small around the world, from the literate civilizations that cover empires to the memories and practices of remote islands. But to insist on isolating cultures is to stifle them. There have rarely, if ever, been self-enclosed cultures—certainly not in Europe, with its constant exchange of art and ideas across borders of language, religion, folkways, and politics, and its creative engagement since antiquity with extra-European cultures. Europe's music and other cultural expressions have thrived when they have been flexible, pragmatic, and open to encounters. The same is true of the Americas, whose cultures have taken shape through historical experiences of migration and conquest. Going beyond these continents, one can think of many other examples of this kind of flexibility, starting with the musical traditions studied in this book, embedded in local religious liturgy and worldly entertainment, yet shaped by histories of reception and innovation. The balancing of local tradition and outside influence did not end in the nineteenth century; rather, the age of globalization stimulated new creative forms. The pure cultures of nationalist lore were already an illusion at the inception of the modern nation-state.

Since the mid-nineteenth century, a new global culture has formed. We cannot evade it, but we can decide how to respond: with fear and insularity, or with the confidence of a free and creative society.

ACKNOWLEDGMENTS

Since the late 1980s I have investigated the history of cultural encounters, studying the moments when the members of different cultures have met. Music attracted my attention as an especially dramatic example. During the nineteenth century, musical cultures with little or no contact suddenly collided; how they were transformed is the story told in this book.

I researched and wrote in a series of overlapping milieus, first and last in Berlin. The book's prehistory was my year as a fellow at the Wissenschaftskolleg zu Berlin during the academic year 2006–2007. There I was exposed to the music and lectures of Toshio Hosokawa, an ongoing lesson in translation between Japanese and European sensibilities. A year later, the Max Planck Institute for the History of Science hosted a Berlin stay in May and June 2008, facilitated by Lorraine Daston. During the second half of that stay, Reinhard Meyer-Kalkus, of the Wissenschaftskolleg, and Anja Zenner, archivist of the Ethnological Museum in Berlin, almost simultaneously encouraged me to seek out the Phonogram Archive, which was housed in the Ethnological Museum. After a first look at its holdings, I could begin to imagine a history of how musical cultures met and reimagined themselves under the conditions of globalization. Since then, Lars-Christian Koch—at that time the Phonogram Archive's director, and today director of the

State Museum Collections in the Humboldt Forum in Berlin—has been a generous host. Ricarda Kopal, current director of the Phonogram Archive, has been equally welcoming. Berlin again provided a stimulating setting near the end. During my spring 2017 fellowship semester at the American Academy in Berlin, I completed my draft of the book manuscript under near-perfect conditions of beautiful surroundings, kindness from the academy staff, and stimulating conversation with the other fellows. A Humboldt Research Prize from the Alexander von Humboldt Foundation permitted me to return to Berlin in summer 2018 to complete my revisions of the manuscript and continue my dialogue with Berlin colleagues.

In Champaign-Urbana, conversations with Bruno Nettl over lunch at local eateries and at the ever-welcoming Nettl home have been a seminar in their own right, taking me deep into the learning and lore of ethnomusicology; Bruno has also been unfailingly generous about introducing me to his friends and former students. William Kinderman has shared his musical knowledge and, especially relevant to this book, his expertise on the piano and the politics of nineteenth-century composers. From 2014 to 2016 we codirected the initiative "Dissonance: Music and Globalization since Edison's Phonograph," sponsored by the Center for Advanced Study, University of Illinois; I am indebted to him and to the participants in our 2016 seminar on the Weimar Republic for conversations about the meanings of dissonance in politics and music. Masumi Iriye, deputy director of the Center for Advanced Study, brought imagination to planning the initiative, and efficiency to organizing its special events. During the directorship of Mike Ross, the Krannert Center for the Performing Arts at the University of Illinois has become a model community for music, dance, and theater from the most diverse traditions, and has offered an ongoing lesson in how to push beyond fixed cultural horizons. Supported by a grant from the Mellon Foundation, the Krannert Center and the Krannert Art Museum have for more than ten years hosted an undergraduate course, Exploring Arts and Creativity, that brings the arts into the classroom. My co-teacher in recent years, Philip Johnston from the Department of Dance, has opened my eyes to the connections between dance and the other arts; our students, coming from many different parts of the world, have been enthusiastic conversation partners. Susan Feder, friend and Mellon Foundation administrator, has nurtured the program from its beginnings a decade ago to its current strength as a model for undergraduate education in the arts. Several units at the University of Illinois have provided critical material support for my research and writing. I wish to thank the

Campus Research Board for a Humanities Released Time leave in the fall semester of 2012, the Center for Advanced Study for an associate appointment and leave time in spring 2014, and the Office of the Provost and the College of Liberal Arts and Sciences for Humanities/Arts Scholarship Support. Tom Bedwell, as business manager of the History Department, was the indispensable guide for all questions relating to research assistants, grants, and leaves.

Closely related to Urbana has been my collaboration with colleagues in Chicago and in Madison, Wisconsin. Philip V. Bohlman at the University of Chicago has been a guide to world music past and present, and an organizer of intellectual and artistic events. He took the lead in directing the project "A History of World Music Recording," administered by the Illinois Program for Research in the Humanities at the University of Illinois and supported by the Humanities without Walls consortium as part of its Global Midwest initiative, with financial support from the Mellon Foundation. Along with Philip Bohlman, James Nye (University of Chicago) and Ronald Radano (University of Wisconsin–Madison) as codirectors of the project furthered my thinking about recordings and their global dissemination, as did the graduate students and colleagues at our workshops at the University of Chicago, the University of Wisconsin, and the University of Illinois. Phil and Ron encouraged me to submit my book manuscript to the Big Issues in Music series, thereby adding to our dialogue between history and musicology; this book has benefited at many points from their criticisms.

Another milieu has been transnational. Thanks to support from the Wissenschaftskolleg zu Berlin, Jürgen Osterhammel and I were able to codirect a postdoctoral summer institute sponsored by Some Institutes of Advanced Study (SIAS), "Cultural Encounters: Global Perspectives and Local Exchanges, 1750–1914," financially supported by the Alexander von Humboldt Foundation and the Mellon Foundation, and held under the auspices of the Wissenschaftskolleg zu Berlin in summer 2013 and the National Humanities Center in summer 2014. My conversations with Osterhammel, along with his writings, have been a corrective to my own preference for intensive milieu studies and have drawn my attention to large-scale historical structures and transformations, a reorientation that has widened the scope of this book. His eye for the central questions of modern history impressed me once again during my stay as his guest at the University of Konstanz in summer 2017.

My sons, Ben and Jack, have been my technical experts and indispensable interpreters of data on the global dissemination of phonographs. Ben had the idea of digitizing source materials and continues to make me aware of their uses; Jack turned the information into tables and a chart. My research assistants—Elizabeth Matsushita, Zachary Riebeling, and Christopher Goodwin—were conscientious and spirited aides as they entered data into spreadsheets.

Philip Bohlman, Peter Fritzsche, Bruno Nettl, Mark Pottinger, Ronald Radano, and Martin Rempe read and offered critical commentary on different chapters. The self-identified musicologist who served as one of the anonymous University of Chicago Press referees read the manuscript with unusual engagement. His or her suggestions for revising the final chapters were invaluable; the report's ethos of interdisciplinary conversation helped me imagine how a historian's book would appear to musicologist readers. I am thankful to colleagues who have influenced this book in other ways. A. J. Racy gave an unforgettable concert of classical Middle Eastern music at the University of Illinois's Krannert Center in 2015; in conversations before and since and in his writings, he has introduced me to that music's performative requirements and social meaning. Claudius Torp has been a valued interlocutor for seeking historical paths into the globalization of music; Le Qiliang played a special role in deepening my comprehension of Chinese culture, as did his colleagues in the History Department of Zheziang University; and Carsten Dutt's presentations and writings have exemplified a fruitful dialogue between philosophy and history which continues in my introductory remarks on Reinhart Koselleck and Hans-Georg Gadamer.

At the University of Chicago Press, my editor, Elizabeth Branch Dyson, gave me just the right mixture of encouragement and criticism, directing me to a clear presentation of the big issues I wished to examine. Dylan Montanari has been an able assistant, speedily responding to all my questions. I am deeply grateful to Renaldo Migaldi, who served as manuscript editor; his word-by-word scrutiny of the manuscript has resulted a clarity and precision of expression that I would not otherwise have achieved.

This book was researched and written in an era of declining support for the humanities and social sciences in the United States. The administrators who should be the guardians of these precious national resources have sometimes become the very agents of their diminishment. In this setting I am all the more grateful to those institutions and staff that have persisted in the United States and abroad in supporting scholarship: the American Academy in Berlin, with thanks to Michael Steinberg, Carol Scherer, and Yolanda Korb; the Archive of American Music and Sousa Archive, University of Illinois, with thanks to Scott Schwartz; the Berlin-Brandenburgische Akademie der Wissenschaften; the Berlin Ethnological Museum Archive, with thanks to Anja Zenner; the British Library, London; the EMI Archive Trust, with thanks to Joanna Hughes; the History, Philosophy, and Newspaper Library at the University of Illinois, with thanks to Mary Stuart and Celestina Savonius-Wroth; the Library of Congress, Washington; the Music School Library at the University of Illinois, with thanks to William Buss; the Phonogramm Archiv, Berlin, with thanks to Lars Koch and Ricarda Kopal; the Royal School of Music Library, London, with thanks to Peter Horgon; the Staatsbibliothek, Berlin; the Thomas Edison National Historical Park, in Edison, New Jersey, with thanks to Leonard DeGraaf; the University of London Archive, Senate Building, London; the Victoria and Albert Museum Archive (Blyth House), with thanks to Emma Rogers; and the Asian Department of the Victoria and Albert Museum, with thanks to Nick Bernard.

Audiences between December 2012 and June 2018 discussed and improved the ideas in this book. I wish to thank organizers and listeners at the following institutions where I gave presentations in the course of extended stays: the American Academy in Berlin; Central European University and Eötvös University, Budapest; the Historisches Seminar at the University of Konstanz; and Zhejiang University. I am especially thankful, too, for the comments in response to my lectures in the scholarly commons workshop at the Illinois Program for Research in the Humanities at the University of Illinois; the Department of History at Nanjing University; the Department of History at Shanghai Normal University; the Historisches Seminar and Global History Workshop at the University of Zurich; and the Department of History at Xiamen University. Finally, two sets of events truly functioned as "workshops" and, in the best craft tradition, helped me refine the conceptual tools for the book. The first two "Historicizing Cultural Brokers" workshops, at Gonville and Caius College, Cambridge University, and at the University of Konstanz, broadened my understanding of these mediating figures and their mixtures of idealism and self-interest. A conference on Reinhart Koselleck and Begriffsgeschichte at the Deutsches Literaturarchiv, Marbach, opened fresh philosophical perspectives on Koselleck's methodology and made it freshly useful for my work.

Translations are mine where not otherwise noted. Names present a special problem—especially in a book about communication between cultures—since they can contain a welter of conflicting historical usages and power relationships. I have not followed a uniform rule, but instead have weighed competing claims case by case, generally leaving historical names unchanged but occasionally correcting foreign impositions. Canton is left in place, though I hope one day to visit Guangzhou; Bella Coola is replaced in most contexts by Nuxalk; Bombay is preferable to Mumbai as the historical designation and underlines the city's multilingual character up to the present day.

For my wife and fellow historian, Dorothee Schneider, a book; a fragment from our never-ending conversations.

NOTES

Introduction

1. Ravi Shankar, *My Music, My Life*, 2nd ed. (1968; San Rafael, CA: Mandala, 2007). Cf. the account of this era, and the larger story of his reception in Europe and America, in the remarkably comprehensive book by Peter Lavezzoli, *The Dawn of Indian Music in the West: Bhairavi* (New York: Continuum, 2006). Nalini Ghuman points out that by placing the "dawn" in the 1950s, Lavezzoli overlooks the longer history of Indian music's reception in the West. See Ghuman, *Resonances of the Raj: India in the English Musical Imagination, 1897–1947* (New York: Oxford University Press, 2014), 1, 10.

2. See *Ravi Shankar in Portrait* (BBC/Opus Arte, 2002).

3. On these encounters, see Lavezzoli, *Dawn of Indian Music in the West*. Steven Feld adds a commercial perspective to Lavezzoli's narrative of masters, disciples, and cultural encounters when he observes that the Beatles–Shankar collaboration demonstrated the commercial potential of "world music." See Steven Feld, "A Sweet Lullaby for World Music," in Arjun Appadurai, ed., *Globalization* (Durham, NC: Duke University Press, 2001), 189–216, here 193. Artistic and commercial motives alike informed the twentieth-century globalization of music.

4. I use the word "flow" as a marker of the discourse of the 1990s about the novelty and extent of global circulation. Cf. the critique by Stuart Alexander Rockefeller, "'Flow,'" in *Current Anthropology* 52, no. 4 (August 2011): 557–578. More than Rockefeller acknowledges, Arjun Appadurai and other early writers on globalization appreciated the persistence of local interests

and cultures. Still, his essay is incisive and provides a fruitful starting point for
further discussion.

5. I borrow from the English-language title of André Malraux, *Museum without
Walls*, trans. Stuart Gilbert and Francis Price (1947; Garden City, NY: Doubleday,
1967). The French title merits pondering too: *Le Musée imaginaire* (Geneva: Skira,
1947).

6. The journal *Songlines* and the Rough Guides to world music give overviews
of this contemporary world music scene, with its tremendous variety of products.
They report on many musicians who subordinate the foreignness of foreign music
to a Western beat (and the slick packaging of festivals and tours). But they also demonstrate the explosive creativity of contemporary musicians, whether to cultivate
traditions in their integrity or to open them up to innovation.

7. J. H. Elliott, *The Old World and the New, 1492–1650* (Cambridge: Cambridge
University Press, 1972); Bernard Smith, *European Vision and the South Pacific*, 2nd ed.
(1960; New Haven: Yale University Press, 1985).

8. See Hans-Georg Gadamer, *Truth and Method* (1960, 2nd ed. 1965; New York:
Continuum, 1975), 216–217, 269–274, 340.

9. The classic definition of conceptual history appears in Reinhart Koselleck,
"Einleitung," in Otto Brunner, Werner Conze, and Reinhart Koselleck, eds.,
*Geschichtliche Grundbegriffe: Historisches Lexikon zur politisch-sozialen Sprache
in Deutschland*, 8 vols. (Stuttgart: Klett-Cotta, 1972–1997), 1: xiii–xxvii. See also
Koselleck, *Futures Past: On the Semantics of Historical Time*, trans. Keith Tribe (1979;
Cambridge, MA: MIT Press, 1984).

10. Daniel T. Rodgers, introduction to *Cultures in Motion*, ed. Daniel T. Rodgers,
Bhavani Raman, and Helmut Reimnitz (Princeton, NJ: Princeton University Press,
2014), 1–19; Stephen Greenblatt, "Cultural Mobility: An Introduction," in *Cultural
Mobility: A Manifesto* (Cambridge: Cambridge University Press, 2010), 1–23. Cf. Ruth
Benedict, *Patterns of Culture* (1934; Boston: Houghton Mifflin, 1960). It is difficult to
cite a single book by Boas with the impact of Benedict's; he never wrote a monograph on his most important area of fieldwork, the Pacific Northwest, and in any
case was at his best in short essays. For an initial sampling, see the essays collected
in Franz Boas, *Race, Language and Culture* (1940; Chicago: University of Chicago
Press, 1982). The famous phrase "thick description" comes from Clifford Geertz,
"Thick Description: Toward an Interpretive Theory of Culture," in *The Interpretation
of Cultures* (New York: Basic, 1977), chapter 1. The recent emphasis on mobility does
not "replace" the Boasian tradition so much as it modifies it; sites of thick description are, in the language of networks often used to describe cultures in the global
era, nodes between which communication takes place.

11. H. Glenn Penny, *Objects of Culture: Ethnology and Ethnographic Museums in
Imperial Germany* (Chapel Hill: University of North Carolina Press, 2002); Clare E.
Harris, *The Museum on the Roof of the World: Art, Politics, and the Representation of
Tibet* (Chicago: University of Chicago Press, 2012); C. A. Bayly, *Imperial Meridian: The
British Empire and the World, 1780–1830* (London: Longman, 1989).

12. On eighteenth-century conceptions of race, a challenging beginning is still Arthur O. Lovejoy, *Essays in the History of Ideas* (1948; New York: Capricorn, 1960). In the late twentieth-century heyday of social history, Lovejoy's name was a pejorative equivalent of "out of date," but his choice of subjects and keen critical skills continue to be timely. For more recent treatments of Enlightenment attitudes, see Jürgen Osterhammel, *Unfabling the East: The Enlightenment's Encounter with Asia* (1998; Princeton, NJ: Princeton University Press, 2018); and Harry Liebersohn, *Aristocratic Encounters: European Travelers and North American Indians* (Cambridge: Cambridge University Press, 1998).

13. On Darwin, see Harry Liebersohn, *The Travelers' World: Europe to the Pacific* (Cambridge, MA: Harvard University Press, 2006), 286–288; on Boas's evolving views on race, see Douglas Cole, *Franz Boas: The Early Years, 1858–1906* (Seattle: University of Washington Press, 1999), 168–169, 270–271, and 277–278.

14. Frederick Hoxie, *This Indian Country: American Indian Activists and the Place They Made* (New York: Penguin, 2012); Catarina Krizancic, "Tahiti Royale: Divine Kings Disguised as a Rising French Colonial Elite." Ph.D. dissertation, University of Chicago, Department of Anthropology, 2009.

15. Emily S. Rosenberg, introduction to Akira Iriye and Jürgen Osterhammel, general eds., *A History of the World*, 3: *A World Connecting, 1870–1945*, ed. Emily S. Rosenberg (Cambridge, MA: Harvard University Press, 2012), 3–25, here 6. While trying to articulate the continuities, Rosenberg gives full weight to the shattering effects of World War I.

16. Annegret Fauser, *Musical Encounters at the 1889 Paris World's Fair* (Rochester, NY: University of Rochester Press, 2005). Philippe Albèra makes a broad case for the impact of "exoticism" on European music in the nineteenth and twentieth centuries, with emphasis on Debussy's role as innovator, in "Les leçons de l'exotisme," in *Cahiers de musiques traditionnelles* 9, new series (1996): 53–84. On Debussy, see also Roy Howat, "Debussy and the Orient," in *Recovering the Orient*, ed. Andrew Gerstle and Anthony Milner (Chur, Switzerland: Harwood, 1994), 45–81; Jean-Michel Nectoux, *Harmonie en bleu et or: Debussy, la musique et les arts* (Paris: Fayard, 2005); and the comment on the limits of the composer's appropriations from East and Southeast Asian music in Mark DeVoto, *Debussy and the Veil of Tonality: Essays on His Music* (Hillsdale, NY: Pendragon Press, 2004), 193.

One of the major influences on Debussy's interest in non-European cultures was Victor Segalen, a naval doctor, writer, and music ethnographer. See Charles Forsdick, *Victor Segalen and the Aesthetics of Diversity: Journeys between Cultures* (Oxford: Oxford University Press, 2000); Annie Joly-Segalen and André Schaeffner, eds., *Segalen et Debussy* (Monaco: Rocher, 1961); Claude Debussy, *Correspondance, 1884–1918*, ed. François Lesure (Paris: Hermann, 1993), 224, 229–230; and Rollo Myers, "The Opera That Never Was: Debussy's Collaboration with Victor Segalen in the Preparation of *Orphée*," *Musical Quarterly* 64, no. 4 (October 1978): 495–506.

17. While this paragraph gives an example originating in Europe, comparable careers across borders appeared in other parts of the world. Cf. Seema Alavi,

"'Fugitive Mullahs and Outlawed Fanatics': Indian Muslims in Nineteenth Century Trans-Asiatic Imperial Rivalries,'" *Modern Asian Studies* 45, no. 6 (2011): 1337–1382.

On Idelsohn, see Philip V. Bohlman, *World Music: A Very Short Introduction* (Oxford: Oxford University Press, 2002), 124–125; and *Jewish Music and Modernity* (Oxford: Oxford University Press, 2008), 44–51; Ruth F. Davis, "Music in the Mirror of Multiple Nationalisms: Sound Archives and Ideology in Israel and Palestine," in *The Cambridge History of World Music* (Cambridge: Cambridge University Press, 2013), 498–521, esp. 498–507; and Edith Gerson-Kiwi and Israel J. Katz, "Idelsohn, Abraham Zvi," in *Grove Music Online: Oxford Music Online*, Oxford University Press, http://www .oxfordmusiconline.com/subscriber/article/grove/music/13702, accessed July 20, 2017. The documentary descriptions in Israel Adler and Judith Cohen, *A. Z. Idelsohn Archives at the Jewish National and University Library* (Jerusalem: Magnes Press, 1976) [Yuval Monograph Series, vol. 4] evoke Idelsohn's far-flung treks.

18. Marc Matera, *Black London: The Imperial Metropolis and Decolonization in the Twentieth Century* (Berkeley: University of California Press, 2015); Su Lin Lewis, *Cities in Motion: Urban Life and Cosmopolitanism in Southeast Asia, 1920–1940* (Cambridge: Cambridge University Press, 2016). See also the overview in Michael Denning, *Noise Uprising: The Audiopolitics of a World Musical Revolution* (London: Verso, 2015).

19. Professional historians do not—or at least they should not, according to the tenets of their profession—construct fables, fictions, alt-truths, or "theories" with foregone conclusions in the service of political ideologies; but they do necessarily make selections from a sea of facts in order to shape the past into a meaningful narrative. For a first orientation, see R. G. Collingwood, *The Idea of History* (New York: Oxford University Press, 1946); Arthur C. Danto, *Analytical Philosophy of History* (Cambridge: Cambridge University Press, 1965); Hayden White, *Metahistory: The Historical Imagination in Nineteenth-Century Europe* (Baltimore: Johns Hopkins University Press, 1974); and Lionel Gossman, *Between History and Literature* (Cambridge, MA: Harvard University Press, 1990). The journal *History and Theory* has for many decades served as a forum for discussions of historical narrative.

20. See the articles in Koselleck et. al., eds., *Geschichtliche Grundbegriffe*. Just as Koselleck and the many article coauthors discovered changes in sociopolitical vocabulary in response to domestic causes between the 1780s and 1848, so, I am suggesting here, an analogous transformation took place around mid-century in response to global causes.

21. For overviews of late-nineteenth and early-twentieth-century exhibitions, see Paul Greenhalgh, *Ephemeral Vistas: The Expositions Universelles, Great Exhibitions and World's Fairs, 1851–1939* (Manchester, UK: Manchester University Press, 1988); and Robert W. Rydell, *All the World's a Fair: Visions of Empire at American International Expositions, 1876–1916* (Chicago: University of Chicago Press, 1984). On the Great Exhibition of 1851 as a display of European conceptions of hierarchy, see George W. Stocking, Jr., *Victorian Anthropology* (New York: Free Press, 1987).

22. Scholars from many disciplines have fastened onto spectacles and brought them to the attention of a wide readership—sometimes fruitfully, sometimes turn-

ing them into total ideologies, omnipresent and sufficient to explain the mentality of Western societies. From the perspective of ethnomusicology, Veit Erlmann includes a stimulating discussion of nineteenth-century music as spectacle in *Music, Modernity, and the Global Imagination: South Africa and the West* (New York: Oxford University Press, 1999), chapter 4.

My own discussion of the spectacle owes much to Walter Benjamin. I have been influenced less by famous essays like "The Work of Art in the Age of Mechanical Reproduction" (though I make reference to the title) than by his critique of the modernist retreat from politics into a self-enclosed world of art—which was later succeeded by the aestheticization of politics. See especially Benjamin's attack on the Stefan George circle in "Goethe's Elective Affinities," trans. Stanley Korngold, in Walter Benjamin, *Selected Writings*, vol. 1, 1913–1926, ed. Marcus Bullock and Michael W. Jennings (Cambridge, MA: Harvard University Press, 1996), 297–360. See also Benjamin's praise of Brecht for creating a theater that disrupts the illusions of aesthetic spectacle in "What Is the Epic Theater? (II)," in *Selected Writings* 4 (1938–1940), ed. Howard Eiland and Michael W. Jennings, trans. Harry Zohn (Cambridge, MA: Harvard University Press, 2003), 302–309.

23. Michael Geyer and Charles Bright, "World History in a Global Age," *American Historical Review* 100, no. 4 (October 1995): 1034–1060. Geyer and Bright's article anticipates my distinction between world and global cultures. Cf. Charles Maier's remarks on the mid-nineteenth-century crisis of older polities resolved by European global hegemony in "Leviathan 2.0," *A World Connecting*, ed. Rosenberg, 29–282, here 118–123 and 148–152. On the concept of globalization, see also the important early contribution by Ulf Hannerz, "Notes on the Global Ecumene," *Public Culture* 1, no. 2 (Spring 1989): 66–75.

One can reasonably ask whether "globalization" is not "modernization" slightly refurbished, bringing a concept inherited from the 1950s into the scholarly discourse of the post–Cold War era. A classic statement of modernization theory is Walter W. Rostow, *The Stages of Economic Growth: A Non-Communist Manifesto* (Cambridge: Cambridge University Press, 1960). For the purposes of this book, there are several striking contrasts worth underlining. One is that "globalization" allows more scope for the discontinuities of modern history; as I have used the term, it refers to economic and social processes that took place during a certain epoch but were irregular even then and were radically altered and disrupted by World War I. Second, "globalization" has from the beginning opened up discussion of the relationship between local cultures and global exchanges, a theme central to this book. In other words, as used here, "globalization" is a nonteleological framework containing interactions between macro- and microhistories.

24. On Cook and world voyage accounts, see Liebersohn, *The Travelers' World*. Cf. the famous illustrations accompanying the official account of Cook's first circumnavigation, John Hawkesworth, comp., *An Account of the Voyages undertaken by the Order of His present Majesty for making discoveries in the Southern Hemisphere . . .* , 3 vols. (London: Strahan and Cadell, 1773).

25. A paradigmatic example was the so-called Indian Gallery of George Catlin. See William H. Truettner, *The Natural Man Observed: A Study of Catlin's Indian Gallery* (Washington: Smithsonian, 1979).

26. See Philip V. Bohlman, "Johann Gottfried Herder and the Global Moment of World-Music History," in Philip V. Bohlman, ed., *Cambridge History of World Music*, 255–276; and the collection of Herder's writings on music in Johann Gottfried Herder and Philip V. Bohlman, *Song Loves the Masses: Herder on Music and Nationalism* (Berkeley: University of California Press, 2017). For a broad treatment of Enlightenment conceptions of world music, see Sebastian Klotz, "Tartini the Indian: Perspectives on World Music in the Enlightenment," in Bohlman, *Cambridge History of World Music*, 277–297.

27. A revaluation of Jones has taken place in recent years as his cross-cultural interests have turned him from a marginal figure into an outstanding example of the cosmopolitan or "global" intellectual. See Michael J. Franklin, *Orientalist Jones: Sir William Jones, Poet, Lawyer, and Linguist, 1746–1794* (Oxford: Oxford University Press, 2011); and "Jones, Sir William (1746–1794)," in the *Oxford Dictionary of National Biography*, ed. H. C. G. Matthew and Brian Harrison (Oxford: Oxford University Press, 2004); online edition, ed. David Cannadine, May 2011, http://www.oxforddnb .com.proxy2.library.illinois.edu/view/article/15105 (accessed March 15, 2017). See also the contextualization of Jones in Rosane Rocher, "Weaving Knowledge: Sir William Jones and Indian Pandits," in Garland Cannon and Kevin R. Brine, eds., *Objects of Enquiry: The Life, Contributions, and Influences of Sir William Jones (1746–1794)* (New York: New York University Press, 1995), 51–79, with special attention to music on p. 66.

Sir William Jones, "On the Musical Modes of the Hindoos," is reprinted in Sourindro Mohun Tagore, ed., *Hindu Music from Various Authors*, 2nd ed. (Calcutta: Bose, 1882), 125–160. For the dating of the essay as well as a broader view of its place in Western interpretations of Indian music, see Bennett Zon, "From 'Very Acute and Plausible' to 'Curiously Misinterpreted': Sir William Jones's 'On the Musical Modes of the Hindus' (1792) and its Reception in Later Musical Treatises," in Michael J. Franklin, ed., *Romantic Representations of British India* (London: Routledge, 2006), 197–219, here 199 and 214n20. For other treatments of Jones's essay, see Bennett Zon, *Representing Non-Western Music in Nineteenth-Century Britain* (Rochester, NY: University of Rochester Press, 2007), esp. 5–7 and 51–59; Joep Bor, "The Rise of Ethnomusicology," *Yearbook for Traditional Music* 20 (1988): 51–73, here 55; and Joep Bor (?), introduction to Joep Bor, Françoise 'Nalini' Delvoye, Jane Harvey, and Emmie te Nijenhuis, eds., *Hindustani Music: Thirteenth to Twentieth Centuries* (New Delhi: Manohar, 2010), 11–32, here 12. For the Indian musical context of Jones's essay, see also Gerry Farrell, *Indian Music and the West* (Oxford: Clarendon Press, 1997); on Anglo-Indian sociability, see Ian Woodfield, *Music of the Raj: A Social and Economic History of Music in Late Eighteenth-Century Anglo-Indian Society* (New York: Oxford University Press, 2000). For the aesthetic context of Jones's views, see Maria Semi, *Music as a Science of Mankind in Eighteenth Century Britain* (Farnham, Surrey, UK:

Ashgate, 2012); and Vanessa Agnew, *Enlightenment Orpheus: The Power of Music in Other Worlds* (Oxford: Oxford University Press, 2008).

28. Hendrik Birus, Anne Bohnenkamp, and Wolfgang Bunzel, *Goethes Zeitschrift ueber Kunst und Alterthum: Von den Rhein- und Mayn-Gegenden zur Weltliteratur* (Göttingen: Göttinger Verlag der Kunst, 2016; Hendrik Birus, "Goethes Idee der Weltliteratur: Eine historische Vergegenwärtigung" (19.01.2004), in *Goethezeitportal*, http://www.goethezeitportal.de/db/wiss/goethe/birus_weltliteratur.pdf, accessed February 16, 2017; and Reinhard Meyer-Kalkus, "World Literature beyond Goethe," in Greenblatt, *Cultural Mobility*, 96–121. Goethe's own comments about world literature as well as editorial commentary may be found in Johann Wolfgang von Goethe, *Sämtliche Werke: Briefe, Tagebücher und Gespräche*, vol. 39: Johann Peter Eckermann, *Gespräche mit Goethe in den letzten Jahren seines Lebens*, ed. Christoph Michel with the assistance of Hans Grüters (Frankfurt am Main: Deutscher Klassiker Verlag, 1999), 193–215 and 223–225. See also Fritz Strich, *Goethe und die Weltliteratur*, 2nd ed. (1946; Bern: Francke, 1957); David Damrosch, *What Is World Literature?* (Princeton, NJ: Princeton University Press, 2003); and John Pizer, *The Idea of World Literature: History and Pedagogical Practice* (Baton Rouge: Louisiana State University Press, 2006). A closely contextualized analysis of Goethe's relationship to extra-European cultures is Marcel Lepper, *Goethes Euphrat: Philologie und Politik im West-östlichen Divan* (Göttingen, Germany: Wallstein, 2016).

"World culture" and "global culture" are concepts of the kind that Max Weber called ideal types. They designate schematic abstractions, drawn from empirical phenomena but not identical to them; as heuristic tools they illuminate distinctions within an inexhaustibly complex empirical reality. An important point about Weber's use of these types was that they had no intrinsic relationship to historical change over time. Hence, when Weber proposed three ideal-typical forms of domination—traditional, bureaucratic, and charismatic—they did not correspond to an evolution from the Middle Ages to the modern era. To be sure, bureaucracy underwent a historically unprecedented expansion in the nineteenth century. But Weber detected bureaucracy as a chief feature of ancient Egyptian and traditional Chinese societies; and for its part, tradition continued to be a constitutive modern form of political legitimation. "World culture" and "global culture" present an analogous case of ideal types that do not logically succeed one another over time. In particular, "world culture" continues to define many attempts at presentation of cultural diversity to the present day, whether in the humanitarian form of the world music or literature survey, or in the hostile stereotypes of racial ideology.

29. The famous phrase comes from *The Communist Manifesto* of Marx and Engels. Marshall Berman made it a byword for the transience of modern culture in *All That Is Solid Melts into Air: The Experience of Modernity* (New York: Simon and Schuster, 1982).

30. Geyer and Bright make the case for "the continuing irreducibility of the 'local'" as a defining feature of the global age in "World History in a Global Age," 1044.

31. These accelerating exchanges form one chapter in the history of sound, a

subject of much discussion in recent years and a subset of the interdisciplinary formation of sound studies. A recent overview, as well as a sampling of historically grounded case studies, can be found in Daniel Morat, ed., *Sounds of Modern History: Auditory Cultures in Nineteenth and Twentieth-Century Europe* (New York: Berghahn, 2014; see especially the editor's introduction, 1–9); Stefan Gauß, "Listening to the Horn: On the Cultural History of the Phonograph and the Gramophone," 71–100; and Alexandra E. Hui, "From the Piano Pestilence to the Phonograph Solo: Four Case Studies of Musical Expertise in the Laboratory and on the City Street," 129–152. For sound studies in German society and history, see Florence Feiereisen and Alexandra Merley Hill, *Germany in the Loud Twentieth Century: An Introduction* (New York: Oxford University Press, 2012); and Nora M. Alter and Lutz Koepnick, *Sound Matters: Essays on the Acoustics of Modern German Culture* (New York: Berghahn, 2004). Theoretical approaches are explored in Jonathan Sterne, *The Audible Past: Cultural Origins of Sound Reproduction* (Durham, NC: Duke University Press, 2003); and Richard Leppert, *Aesthetic Technologies of Modernity, Subjectivity, and Nature: Opera–Orchestra–Phonograph–Film* (Berkeley: University of California Press, 2015). The work I have found most valuable is David Suisman, *Selling Sounds: The Commercial Revolution in American Music* (Cambridge, MA: Harvard University Press, 2009), which sets the music industry within the larger history of American capitalism.

32. Friedrich Meinecke, *Cosmopolitanism and the National State*, trans. Robert B. Kimber (1907; Princeton, NJ: Princeton University Press, 1970).

33. For samples of this literature, see Pheng Cheah and Bruce Robbins, eds., *Cosmopolitics: Thinking and Feeling beyond the Nation* (Minneapolis: University of Minnesota Press, 1998); and Martha Nussbaum with respondents, *For Love of Country: Debating the Limits of Patriotism*, ed. Joshua Cohen (Boston: Beacon, 1996). While the contributions to these two collections include a wide range of opinions, some of them skeptical about the withering away of nationalism, overall the writers take for granted the paradigm of nationalism versus cosmopolitanism.

34. I use the word "pure" as an anachronism conveying the flavor of the time: idealistic in the self-perceptions of the moment, but with undercurrents pulling in the direction of of political-ethnic "purity."

35. George Eliot, *Daniel Deronda*, ed. and introd. Barbara Hardy (1876; Harmondsworth/Middlesex: Penguin, 1967), 283–284. While there has been some debate about Klesmer's identity, it would be rather fatuous to dispute that he is supposed to be Jewish, especially in light of his self-description. On this dimension of his personality, see Allan Arkush, "Relativizing Nationalism: The Role of Klesmer in George Eliot's 'Daniel Deronda,'" in Jewish *Social Studies* (new series) 3, no.3 (Spring/Summer 1997): 61–73.

Musical contexts for understanding the concatenation of Jews, music, and cosmopolitanism can be found in Bohlman, *Jewish Music and Modernity*; Michael P. Steinberg, *Judaism Musical and Unmusical* (Chicago: University of Chicago Press, 2007); and Celia Applegate, *Bach in Berlin: Nation and Culture in Mendelssohn's Revival of the "St. Matthew Passion"* (Ithaca, NY: Cornell University Press, 2005). James

Loeffler, *The Most Musical Nation: Jews and Culture in the Late Russian Empire* (New Haven: Yale University Press, 2010), offers general insights into the place of Jews in public life, as well as comments on *Daniel Deronda* identifying Klesmer with the Russian-Jewish musician Anton Rubinstein, emblem of a Jewish generation that balanced national and cosmopolitan identities.

36. Akira Iriye, "Transnational History," in *Contemporary European History* 13, no. 2 (2004): 211–222. The articles in Akira Iriye and Pierre Saunier, *The Palgrave Dictionary of Transnational History* (New York: Palgrave Macmillan, 2009), suggest how widely useful the concept of transnationalism is for historical studies. For a concise definition of transnationalism for historians, see Alex Körner "Transnational History: Identities, Structures, States," in Barbara Haider-Wilson, William D. Godsey, and Wolfgang Mueller, eds., *Internationale Geschichte in Theorie und Praxis/ International History in Theory and Practice* (Vienna: Verlag der Österreichischen Akademie der Wissenschaften, 2017), 265–290. Patricia Clavin introduces the metaphor of "honeycombs"—which, more than "networks," she argues (and, one might add, their nodes), suggests the semiautonomous spaces within which transnational identity formation takes place. See Clavin, "Defining Transnationalism," *Contemporary European History* 14 (2005): 421–439. Doris Bachmann-Medick, ed., *The Trans/ National Study of Culture: A Translational Perspective* (Berlin: DeGruyter, 2014), links transnationalism to the notion of translation, which had its own history reaching back to Wilhelm von Humboldt in the early nineteenth century, but took on new historical implications in the age of globalization. Cf. Roger Langham Brown, *Wilhelm von Humboldt's Conception of Linguistic Relativity* (The Hague and Paris: Mouton 1967).

37. I draw "relative autonomy" from my readings in late-nineteenth-century German social thinkers like Max Weber and Georg Simmel. For some suggestive readings, see Max Weber, "Science as a Vocation," (1917, erroneously dated 1918) in *From Max Weber Essays in Sociology*, ed. Hans Gerth and C. Wright Mills (1946; New York: Oxford University Press, 1958), 129–156; and Georg Simmel, *The Philosophy of Money*, trans. Tom Bottomore and David Frisby (1900; London: Routledge and Kegan Paul, 1978). The phrase suggests a qualified acknowledgment of Marx's grounding of culture in economy and society, but dissent from the reduction of culture to a manifestation of social forces.

Chapter 1

1. Engel's writings were not the only beginning of ethnomusicology, but they were important for his British successors and, by extension, for the movement around the Anglo-German Atlantic that is the main subject of this book. Joep Bor qualifies the originality of late-nineteenth-century appreciation of non-European music in "The Rise of Ethnomusicology," *Yearbook for Traditional Music* 20 (1988): 51–73. Malou Haine, "Concerts historiques dans la seconde moitié du 19e siècle," in Henri Vanhulst and Malou Haine, *Musique et Société: Hommages à Robert Wangermée* (Brussels: Éditions de l'Université de Bruxelles, 1988), 121–142,

reconstructs the history of original instrument performances going back to 1830s; it makes reference to Engel as well as Hipkins.

2. On this receptive moment in England, see Celia Applegate, "Mendelssohn on the Road: Music, Travel, and the Anglo-German Symbiosis," in Jane F. Fulcher, ed., *The Oxford Handbook of the New Cultural History of Music* (New York: Oxford University Press, 2011), 228–244.

Philip Bohlman discusses Engel's idea of national music in *Focus: Music, Nationalism, and the Making of the New Europe*, 2nd ed. (New York: Routledge, 2011); Bennett Zon calls attention to the originality and importance of Engel's ethnomusicology in "The Music of Non-Western Nations and the Evolution of British Ethnomusicology," in *The Cambridge History of World Music*, ed. Philip V. Bohlman (Cambridge: Cambridge University Press, 2013), 298–318, here 308–310; and Bruno Nettl includes an appreciation of him in *Nettl's Elephant: On the History of Ethnomusicology* (Urbana: University of Illinois Press, 2010), 43–44.

Apart from these recent appreciations, little has been written on Engel since the witty and well-informed essay by the younger Carl Engel (the twentieth-century American musicologist, no relation), "Some Letters to a Namesake," *Musical Quarterly* 28, no. 3 (July 1, 1942): 337–379; and Gustave Reese, "More about the Namesake," in *A Birthday Offering to Carl Engel* (New York: Schirmer, 1943), 181–195. Both essays publish original correspondence by Carl Engel. As far as I am able to tell, since the appearance of these essays there has been no published research based on manuscript materials. As the notes below indicate, I have found Engel sources in the University of London and Royal College of Music libraries as well as the Blyth House archive and the South Asia Department of the Victoria and Albert Museum. I have also used four tiny handwritten and bound manuscript volumes at the Library of Congress, Washington, "Materialien National Musik betreffend," that document Engel's wide reading.

3. See the description of the Saxon town of Kaisersaschern in the opening chapters of Thomas Mann, *Doctor Faustus: The Life of the German Composer, Adrian Leverkühn, as Told by a Friend*, trans. H. T. Lowe-Porter (New York: Knopf, 1948). Uncannily relevant to Carl Engel's life work as a collector and scholar of musical instruments is the description of the town's musical instrument shop in the first pages of chapter 7.

4. Royal College of Music, London. Carl Engel, "Autobiographical Preface" in *Musical Antiquities and Studies*, ms. 6858a. On Engel's biography, see A. J. Hipkins, "Engel, Carl," in *A Dictionary of Music and Musicians, A. D. 1450–1889*, vol. 4, ed. George Grove (London: Macmillan, 1900), 627–628, as well as Engel, "Some Letters to a Namesake," and Reese, "More about the Namesake." The brief entry in the current Grove's dictionary does not substantially add to the earlier publications. Cf. Philip Bate and Michael Musgrave. "Engel, Carl (i)," in *Grove Music Online / Oxford Music Online*, Oxford University Press, accessed March 16, 2017, http://www.oxfordmusiconline.com/subscriber/article/grove/music/08797.

5. Friedrich Engels, *The Condition of the Working Class in England*, ed. Victor Kiernan (1845; London: Penguin, 1987).

6. Michael Kennedy. "Manchester," in *Grove Music Online / Oxford Music Online*, Oxford University Press, accessed April 13, 2015, http://www.oxfordmusiconline.com/subscriber/article/grove/music/17587. Cf. Manchester's rising appetite for visual art from the 1820s, recapitulated in John Seed, "'Commerce and the Liberal Arts': The Political Economy of Art in Manchester, 1775–1860," in Janet Wolff and John Seed, eds., *The Culture of Capital: Art, Power and the Nineteenth-Century Middle Class* (Manchester, UK: Manchester University Press, 1988), 45–81.

7. See letters from members of the Bowman family in Engel, "Letters to a Namesake," 357–359 and 374. Information on the Paget family can be found at http://www.anatpro.com/index_files/Carl_Daniel_J_Y_Engel.htm, which gives leads to further sources on the family in print and local archives. See especially the description of the Pagets in William Gardiner, *Music and Friends; or, Pleasant Recollections of a Dilettante*, 2 vols. (London: Longman, Brown, and Green, 1838), 236 and 241–243. See also K. Bryn Thomas, "The Manuscripts of Sir William Bowman," in *Medical History* 10 (1966): 245–256; Alexander Gordon, rev. Giles Hudson, "Bowman, John Eddowes the elder," in *Oxford Dictionary of National Biography* online, accessed February 6, 2015; and D'A. Power, rev. Emilie Savage-Smith, "Bowman, Sir William," in *Oxford Dictionary of National Biography* online, accessed February 6, 2015.

Did the famous eye surgeon and researcher share his brother-in-law's taste for exotic instruments? So it would seem from Engel's later correspondence. On August 26, 1879, Engel wrote to the director of the South Kensington Museum: "I should be obliged if you will kindly permit me to withdraw from my collection of musical instruments in your Museum—

No 212: *Shank, Hindu Conch Trumpet with brass ornamentation.*

The instrument belongs to Mr. W. Bowman, who would like to have it in his house."

Victoria and Albert Archive. MA/1/E/E699 Engel, Carl NF 1869–1882.

8. Reese, "More about the Namesake," 185–186; Carl Engel, *The Pianist's Hand-Book: A Guide for the Right Comprehension and Performance of our Best Pianoforte Music* (London: Hope and Co., 1853).

9. Carl Engel, *The Music of the Most Ancient Nations, Particularly of the Assyrians, Egyptians, and Hebrews; With Special Reference to Discoveries in Western Asia and in Egypt* (1864; London: William Reeves, 1929, facsimile of the 1864 edition), 2–3.

10. Engel was excerpting from Sir John Hawkins, *General History of the Science and Practice of Music*, 2nd ed. (1776; London: Novello, 1853), 1:xiii; cf. Hawkins' disparagement of Chinese civilization on pp. xxiii and xxx.

11. Engel, *Music of the Most Ancient Nations*, 3–4. Cf. Paul Henry Lang, *George Friedrich Handel* (New York: Norton, 1966), 354, which, relying on the musicologist Ernst Bücken, refers to the pastoral portions of the *Messiah* as "so full of Calabrian and Sicilian rhythms, tunes, and echoes."

12. Engel, *Music of the Most Ancient Nations*, 4.

13. Ibid., 8, 21.

14. Bennett Zon emphasizes Engel's departure from the evolutionary paradigm

in "The Music of Non-Western Nations and the Evolution of British Ethnomusicology," 309. George W. Stocking Jr. portrays the emergence of a hegemonic evolutionary paradigm ("socio-cultural evolutionary theory") in *Victorian Anthropology*
(New York: Free Press, 1987). Stocking's historical reconstruction of this paradigm
remains fundamental for understanding the period, and it would be a mistake to
underestimate the pervasiveness of evolutionary ideas in European thought at mid-
century. Yet there was never a time when it went unchallenged, as the example of
Engel indicates.

15. Carl Engel, *An Introduction to the Study of National Music: Comprising Researches into Popular Songs, Traditions, and Customs* [reprint] (London: Longmans,
Green, Reader, and Dyer, 1866), 8.

16. Ibid., 25, 30, 32, 68. Cf. Hermann L. F. Helmholtz, *On the Sensations of Tone as
a Physiological Basis for the Theory of Music*, trans. Alexander J. Ellis, new introd. by
Henry Margenau (1863; New York: Dover, 1954), 235. Engel might have read Helmholtz's book before publishing his own, but he did not list it in his extensive bibliography. It seems more likely that there was a convergence of insights here by two
thinkers equally steeped in the Western musical tradition, with Helmholtz's observations derived from his scientific work and Engel's from his ethnographic research.
At some later point Engel did read Helmholtz, mentioning the Ellis translation of
Helmholtz's book in *The Literature of National Music* (London: Novello, 1879), 77.

I myself have previously placed the break in the hierarchical view of culture
closer to the 1880s. But Engel's writings and their wide reception justify an earlier
date. Cf. George W. Stocking, Jr., "Franz Boas and the Culture Concept in Historical Perspective," in *Race, Culture, and Evolution: Essays in the History of Anthropology*
(Chicago: University of Chicago Press, 1968), 195–233, here 201, which places the
break after 1900.

17. Carl Engel, "Music," in John George Garson and Charles Hercules Reid, eds.,
*Notes and Queries on Anthropology: For the Use of Travellers and Residents in Uncivilized
Lands*, edited for the British Association for the Advancement of Science (London:
Edward Stanford, 1874), quoted from the third edition (London: The Anthropologi-
cal Institute, 1899), 164–170, here 165. Bennett Zon emphasizes the value of Engel's
contribution to *Notes and Queries* in "The Music of Non-Western Nations and the
Evolution of British Ethnomusicology," 308.

18. Engel, *Literature of National Music*, 4, 6, 21–22, 42, 65–68, 93.

19. Engel, "Letters to a Namesake," 341, 363–365, 376–377. Mahillon's family
woodwind manufacturing firm had a branch in London. See William Waterhouse,
"Mahillon" (subject entry), *Grove Music Online / Oxford Music Online*, Oxford University Press, accessed April 17, 2014, http://www.oxfordmusiconline.com/subscriber/
article/grove/music/50043.

20. British Library. Hipkins Papers MS 41636, vol. 1. Carl Engel to Hipkins,
2 March 1870; 4 January 1875; 24 September 1878; 21 February 1882; 2 June 1827 July
1882; 15 July 1882.

21. On Albert, see Stanley Weintraub, "Albert [Prince Albert of Saxe-Coburg and

Gotha] (1819–1861)," in *Oxford Dictionary of National Biography*, ed. H. C. G. Matthew and Brian Harrison (Oxford: OUP, 2004); online edition ed. Lawrence Goldman, May 2012, http://www.oxforddnb.com.proxy2.library.illinois.edu/view/article/274 (accessed June 12, 2015); Winslow Ames, *Prince Albert and Victorian Taste* (New York: Viking Press, 1968), which is strong on the German background; Roger Fulford, *The Prince Consort* (London, Macmillan, 1949), which describes his advocacy of music and friendship with Felix Mendelssohn, pp. 204–206; and Hermione Hobhouse, *Prince Albert: His Life and Work* (London: Hamish Hamilton, 1983), valuable for its descriptions of Albert's role in the Society of Arts, the Great Exhibition, and the South Kensington Museum. Hermione Hobhouse, *The Crystal Palace and the Great Exhibition: Art, Science and Productive Industry—A History of the Royal Commission for the Exhibition of 1851* (London: Athlone Press, 2002), is the definitive history of its subject.

22. Michael Conforti, "The Idealist Enterprise and the Applied Arts," in Malcolm Baker and Brenda Richardson, eds., *A Grand Design: The Art of the Victoria and Albert Museum* (New York: Abrams, 1997), 26.

23. Ibid., 27.

24. Ibid., 33–34.

25. Ibid., 32–33.

26. Victoria and Albert Archive. MA/1/E/E699 Engel, Carl NF 1869–1882.

27. Ibid.

28. Ibid.

29. Carl Engel, *Musical Instruments*, rev. ed. (1874; London: Wyman, 1908).

30. Ibid., 3–5.

31. I capitalize Arts and Crafts to denote the specific movement associated with William Morris, and use lower case for the broader arts and crafts revival since the late eighteenth century.

32. See the obituary articles on Engel in *The Times* (London), November 22 and 23, 1882; and Arne Perras, *Carl Peters and German Imperialism, 1856–1918: A Political Biography* (Oxford: Clarendon Press, 2004), 21–23.

33. Perras, *Carl Peters*, 20–25. Cf. the account in Carl Peters, *Dr. Peters Lebenserinnerungen* (Hamburg: Rüsch'sche Verlagsbuchhandlung, 1918), 58–67.

34. Meirion Hughes and Robert Stradling, *The English Musical Renaissance, 1840–1940* (Manchester, UK: Manchester University Press, 2001), 77–79, quote from 78.

35. On the generational shift, see Sven Oliver Müller, "'A Musical Clash of Civilizations'?: Musical Transfers and Rivalries around 1900," *Wilhelmine Germany and Edwardian Britain: Essays on Cultural Affinity*, ed. Dominik Geppert and Robert Gerwarth (Oxford: Oxford University Press, 2008), 305–329.

36. Michael Short, *Gustav Holst: The Man and His Music* (Oxford: Clarendon Press, 1990), 24, 29–30, 54, 63–64, 115; quote from p.46. I have also profited from Colin Matthews, "Holst, Gustav," in *Grove Music Online / Oxford Music Online*, Oxford University Press, accessed April 12, 2017, http://www.oxfordmusiconline.com/subscriber/article/grove/music/13252.

37. Nalini Ghuman, *Resonances of the Raj*, chapter 3. Holst's special attachment to the religion and music of India comes to life in his daughter's appreciation, Imogen Holst, *Holst* (London: Faber and Faber, 1974); and in Alan Gibbs, *Holst among Friends* (London: Thames, 2000). See also the comments on Holst's interest in India in the larger context of English music life in Martin Clayton, "Musical Renaissance and Its Margins in England and India, 1874–1914," in *Music and Orientalism in the British Empire, 1780s-1940s: Portrayal of the East*, ed. Martin Clayton and Bennett Zon (Aldershot/Hampshire, England: Ashgate, 2007), 76–78.

38. Short, *Holst*, 37–38, 76–78, 113. On Holst's most famous composition, see the interpretation in Richard Greene, *Holst: The Planets* (Cambridge: Cambridge University Press, 1995).

39. Victoria and Albert Archive. ED 84/231: music instruments 1896–1928, minute paper of July 25, 1910. Cf. Conforti, "The Idealist Enterprise," in *A Grand Design*, 45–46.

40. See "Display: Musical Wonders of India," http://www.vam.ac.uk/content/exhibitions/display-musical-wonders-of-india/, accessed March 16, 2017. A related exhibition on a fascinating figure, which reinforces the historical connection between India and the Arts and Crafts movement, is "Lockwood Kipling: Arts and Crafts in the Punjab and London," https://www.vam.ac.uk/exhibitions/lockwood-kipling-arts-and-crafts-in-the-punjab-and-london, accessed March 16, 2017.

Chapter 2

1. Anon., "Alfred J. Hipkins," *The Musical Times and Singing Class Circular*, 39, no. 667 (September 1, 1898): 581–586, here 581. The author was probably his daughter, Edith Hipkins.

2. Johan Huizinga, *The Waning of the Middle Ages: A Study of the Forms of Life, Thought, and Art in France and the Netherlands in the Fourteenth and Fifteenth Centuries* (1919; Garden City, NY: Doubleday, 1954), 10–11. Huizinga's work deserves prominence here as a classic of cultural history that recognizes the prominence of bells for traditional European society—and their significance as a marker of the contrast to our own, temporally mechanized world. Remarks on bells in public life strikingly similar to those of Huizinga appear in Reinhard Strohm, *Music in Late Medieval Bruges* (Oxford: Oxford University Press, 1985), 2–4. Alain Corbin situates bells in French social and political history in *Village Bells: Sound and Meaning in the Nineteenth-Century French Countryside* (New York: Columbia University Press, 1998). On the history of the Westminster Abbey bells, see http://www.westminster-abbey.org/our-history/abbey-bells, accessed April 28, 2017.

3. "Hipkins," *Musical Times*, here 581–582.

4. Ibid., 582.

5. Edith J. Hipkins, *How Chopin Played: From Contemporary Impressions Collected from the Diaries and Note-books of the Late A. J. Hipkins* (London: Dent, 1937), 4. Sigismond Thalberg (1812–1871) was one of the famous piano virtuosos of the nineteenth century. He made several visits to London.

In 1884 a request came to purchase the piano in Hipkins's house for a Chopin museum in Cracow. British Library, add. Ms. 41637, Alfred Hipkins papers vol. 2, [unintelligible] to Hipkins, Berlin, July 31, 1884.

Clara Schumann was another pianist who turned to Hipkins for help in finding the right piano. See British Library, add. Ms. 41636, Alfred Hipkins papers vol. 1, Clara Schumann (writing in execrable English) to Alfred J. Hipkins, March 13, 1871[?] and March 18, 1871[?].

6. "Hipkins," *Musical Times*, 585.

7. Edith Hipkins, *How Chopin Played*, 2.

8. Ibid., 1–2. The German is Edith Hipkins's insertion.

9. Alfred J. Hipkins, "Musical Instruments: Their Construction and Capabilities," Cantor Lectures, Society for the Encouragement of Arts, Manufactures and Commerce, delivered before the Society on January 26 and February 2 and 9, 1991, reprinted in the *Journal of the Society of Arts*, July 31 and August 7 and 14, 1891 (London: Trounce, 1891), 21. Hipkins's writings still have reference value today: his monograph on the history of the piano, *A Description and History of the Pianoforte and of the Older Stringed Keyboard Instruments*, 3rd ed. (1895; London: Novello, 1929), is the first entry in the bibliography to Edwin M. Good, "Piano," in *The Harvard Dictionary of Music*, 4th ed., ed. Don Michael Randel (Cambridge, MA: Harvard University Press, 2003), 652–659, here 658.

10. George Grove, *A Dictionary of Music and Musicians (A.D. 1450–1889)*, appendix ed. J. A. Fuller-Maitland, 4 vols. (London: Macmillan, 1879–1890), 1:vi.

11. Alfred J. Hipkins, "Pianoforte," in Grove, *Dictionary of Music*, 709–723, here 723.

12. Hipkins, "Musical Instruments," Cantor Lectures, 30.

13. Ibid.

14. On the Steinway piano and its competition with Erard and Broadwood, see Cynthia Adams Hoover, "The Steinways and Their Pianos in the Nineteenth Century" [offprint], *Journal of the American Musical Instrument Society* 7 (1981): 47–64. She comes to the same conclusion as do Hipkins and Max Weber (see below): that the ascendancy of the Steinway piano was a triumph of *industrial* efficiency, not *aesthetic* requirements (p. 64).

15. Dorothy De Val, *In Search of Song: The Life and Times of Lucy Broadwood* (Surrey, UK: Ashgate, 2011), 36–37, 39. Lucy Broadwood at first collaborated with Cecil Sharp, but came to dislike him as a self-promoting braggart. See "Lucy Broadwood and Cecil Sharp (1859–1924)" on the website *Exploring Surrey's Past*, http://www .exploringsurreyspast.org.uk/themes/people/musicians/lucy_broadwood/cecil -sharp/, accessed April 28, 2017. By contrast, Hipkins's encouragement deserves note as an exception to the almost entirely masculine cast of characters in this book. That was of a piece with Hipkins's general freedom from social snobbery and his unassuming curiosity about other cultures.

16. Hipkins, "Clavichord," in Grove, *Dictionary of Music* (1879–1890) 1:366–369, quote from p. 368.

17. Malou Haine, "Concerts historiques dans la seconde moitié du 19e siècle," in Henri Vanhulst and Malou Haine, *Musique et Société: Hommages à Robert Wangermée* (Brussels: Éditions de l'Université de Bruxelles, 1988), 121–142, here especially 123–124 and 129–130.

On Salaman, see Christina Bashford, "Salaman, Charles," in *Grove Music Online / Oxford Music Online*, http://www.oxfordmusiconline.com/subscriber/article/grove/music/24355, Oxford University Press, accessed July 24, 2017. Hipkins was friendly with Salaman, whose writings, as well as his performances, addressed the growing British curiosity in the late nineteenth century about music from other times and places. See British Library, Hipkins Papers, add. Ms. 41637, Charles K. Salaman to Alfred J. Hipkins, January 2, 1884. Salaman's article "Music in Connection with Dancing," *Musical Times* 19, no. 423 (May 1, 1878): 262–266, drew on travel literature from the United States, Latin America, Australia, the Caribbean, Africa, the Middle East, and India.

18. J. A. Fuller-Maitland, *A Door-Keeper of Music* (London: John Murray, 1929), 110.

19. On the naming of the movement in 1888, see Peter Stansky, *Redesigning the World: William Morris, the 1880s, and the Arts and Crafts* (Princeton, NJ: Princeton University Press, 1985), 12.

20. George Henschel, *Musings and Memoirs of a Musician*, (1918; New York: Da Capo, 1979), 152–153, 156–157.

21. Sir Lawrence Alma-Tadema, *Portrait of the Singer George Henschel*, 1879, Van Gogh Museum, Amsterdam. Information on the painting, including the Golden Room setting and the dating of Alma-Tadema's and Henschel's friendship, comes from the Van Gogh Museum Journal, 1991, online at http://www.dbnl.org/tekst/_van012199501_01/_van012199501_01_0012.php. This article also points out the imperial eclecticism of the room despite its Old Masters look, "with its wainscoting in Byzantine style," the Chinese silk origins of its curtain, and the use of Mexican onyx for the windowpanes. A color version of the image can be viewed at https://www.wikiart.org/en/sir-lawrence-alma-tadema/portrait-of-the-singer-george-henschel-1879.

22. The artist's first letter to Henschel dates from 1877, the year in which they met, according to the Van Gogh Museum Journal; they frequently wrote back and forth thereafter. Like the picture of Henschel, their friendship is a reminder of the close connections among the arts in the late nineteenth century, bringing music together with poetry and painting.

Hipkins slips into the painter's correspondence a few times: Alma-Tadema wrote to him twice, once in 1876, and another time in 1879, in reply to letters of congratulation. University of Birmingham, Sir Lawrence Alma-Tadema Collection, photographs and correspondence, correspondence with Sir George Henschel, G. Boughton, and A. J. Hipkins; microfiche 212, letters to Henschel October 10, 1877, August 2, 1879, and February 18, 1881; microfiche 215, letters to Hipkins June 21, 1879, and January 27, 1876.

Tadema wrote directly to Hipkins on November 8, 1893 to thank him for his interest in one piano. Lucy Ethel Broadwood Papers, Surrey Historical Centre, reference 2185/LEB/1/217, excerpted and summarized on the National Archives website at http://discovery.nationalarchives.gov.uk/browse/r/h/9249d8eb-80cd-479c-981a-39912aa36700, accessed October 20, 2017.

23. Anon., "Occasional Notes," in *Musical Times* 46, no. 752 (October 1, 1905): 655. This recollection is another source for Hipkins's early introduction to musical traditions from ancient monuments in the heart of London. "Sir Alma Tadema, R.A., O.M., designed the brass, and while making use of suggestions from the Christian catacombs, he has not omitted to introduce the Scotch fir, so dear to Mr. Hipkins by reason of its being the badge of his mother's family, the Grants. It is of special interest that his grandmother Grant lies in that very churchyard, and she it was who taught him as a child to love traditional melodies. Mr. Hipkins, who was christened at St. Margaret's, loved the church; he lived near to and often spoke of it."

On Alma-Tadema, A. J. Hipkins, and the Pre-Raphaelites, see Matthew C. Potter, "Revisiting the Shores of Bohemia: The Sketches of John Alfred Hipkins and the World of the Pre-Raphaelites," *British Art Journal* 5, no. 3 (Winter 2004): 49–55.

24. Alfred J. Hipkins, *Musical Instruments: Historic, Rare and Unique*, with forty-eight plates drawn by William Gibb (1888; London: A. and C. Black, 1921), vii–viii.

25. The description of the set, its display, and its owner comes from the website of the Victoria and Albert Museum, which owns one of the armchairs: http://collections.vam.ac.uk/item/O21544/armchair-alma-tadema-lawrence/. The piano and stools are at the Clark Museum, Williams College. See http://www.clarkart.edu/Collection/10373, accessed October 20, 2017.

26. "Hipkins," *Musical Times*, 585. Also cited in Anne Dzamba Sessa, *Richard Wagner and the English* (London: Associated University Presses, 1979), 26.

27. On this episode, see "Hipkins," *Musical Times*, 585; Sessa, *Richard Wagner and the English*, 25–28; and Michael Allis, "Performance in Private: 'The Working Men's Society' and the Promotion of Progressive Repertoire in Nineteenth-Century Britain," in *Music and Performance Culture in Nineteenth-Century Britain: Essays in Honour of Nicholas Temperley*, ed. Bennett Zon (Burlington, VT: Ashgate, 2012), chapter 7.

28. Jeremy Dibble. "Dannreuther, Edward," *Grove Music Online / Oxford Music Online*, Oxford University Press, http://www.oxfordmusiconline.com/subscriber/article/grove/music/07189, accessed March 28, 2017.

29. Paraphrased from Sessa, *Richard Wagner and the English*, 35.

30. John Warrack and Rosemary Williamson. "Hueffer, Francis," *Grove Music Online / Oxford Music Online*. Oxford University Press, accessed March 28, 2017, http://www.oxfordmusiconline.com/subscriber/article/grove/music/13495.

31. Potter, "Revisiting the Shores of Bohemia," especially 49–51.

32. Debora L. Silverman traces the relationship between arts and traditional crafts in the parallel case of France in *Art Nouveau in Fin-de-Siècle France: Politics, Psychology, and Style* (Berkeley: University of California Press, 1989); it includes a discussion of Japanese crafts, 179–181.

For the contrast between the revolutionary, critical art of Manet and the pretensions of bourgeois art (with reference to French academic painting, not the Pre-Raphaelites), see T. J. Clark, *The Painting of Modern Life: Paris in the Art of Manet and His Followers* (New York: Knopf, 1985), chapter 4 ("Olympia's Choice"), 79–146. Clark's attention to the social reality of prostitution underlying the portrayal of the nude provides a critical context for the Pre-Raphaelites' trawling for lower-class women as models and lovers. Those women also might occasionally become wives, as in the famous case of Jane Burden, wife of William Morris and lover of Dante Gabriel Rossetti.

Roberta Smith, "Blazing a Trail for Hypnotic Hyper-Realism: 'Pre-Raphaelites'" at the National Gallery of Art (*New York Times*, March 28, 2013), is an acute, entertaining attack on the kitsch element in Pre-Raphaelite painting. But kitsch was not everything, especially in a movement that worked in so many media. As we shall see below in Hipkins's discussion of musical instruments in Rossetti's art, "hyper-realism" could be ironically deployed for nonrealist artistic ends. A. S. Byatt, *The Children's Book* (New York: Knopf, 2009), does not ignore the kitsch (or the artists' narcissism), but it also re-creates the Arts and Crafts movement's dedication to craft through the unusual strategy of attention to its pottery. More recently, Byatt has written an appreciation of the Arts and Crafts movement that pairs its founder with an Italian counterpart: *Peacock and Vine: On William Morris and Mariano Fortuny* (New York: Knopf, 2016). For another admiring view of the Pre-Raphaelites, see Fiona MacCarthy, "Why the Pre-Raphaelites were the YBAs of their Day," *The Guardian*, August 31, 2012, https://www.theguardian.com/artanddesign/2012/aug/31/pre -raphaelites-ybas.

33. John Ruskin, "The Nature of the Gothic," in *The Genius of John Ruskin: Selections from his Writings*, ed. John D. Rosenberg (1964; Charlottesville: University of Virginia Press, 1998), 170–196, here 172.

34. For a portrait of Morris as socialist, see E. P. Thompson, *William Morris: Romantic to Revolutionary* (1955; New York: Pantheon, 1976).

35. Fiona MacCarthy, *The Last Pre-Raphaelite: Edward Burne-Jones and the Victorian Imagination* (Cambridge, MA: Harvard University Press, 2012), 305.

36. Elizabeth Helsinger, "Listening: Dante Gabriel Rossetti and the Persistence of Song," *Victorian Studies* 51, no. 3 (Spring 2009): 409–421, here pp. 412, 414. "Georgie and Ned" refer to Georgiana and Edward Burn-Jones.

37. Karen Yuen, "Bound by Sound: Music, Victorian Masculinity and Dante Gabriel Rossetti," *Critical Survey* 20, no. 3 (2008): 79–96, here 82–84.

38. Ibid., 82. On Wagner and debates about the autonomy of music, see Mark Evan Bonds, *Absolute Music: The History of an Idea* (New York: Oxford University Press, 2014).

39. Alfred J. Hipkins, "The Musical Instruments in Rossetti's Pictures," *The Musical Review, A Weekly Musical Journal* [London], January 13, 1883, and February 3, 1883. Cf. Smith, "Blazing a Trail for Hypnotic Hyper-Realism."

40. Hipkins comments on *A Sea-Spell* in his *Musical Review* article of February 3.

On this famous painting, which is now at the Fogg Museum, Harvard University, see Henry Johnson, "Dante Gabriel Rossetti and Japan: The Musical Instrument Depicted in 'The Blue Bower' and 'A Sea-Spell,'" in *Music in Art* 30, no. 1–2 (Spring-Fall 2005): 145–153. Cf. the comments on the related painting "The Blue Bower" in Jan Marsh, *Dante Gabriel Rossetti: Painter and Poet* (London: Weidenfeld and Nicolson, 1999), 288. An online reproduction of *A Sea-Spell*, with commentary and bibliography, can be viewed at https://www.harvardartmuseums.org/art/230614.

41. Mantle Hood, *The Ethnomusicologist* (New York: McGraw Hill, 1971), 90. Hood was especially taken by Hipkins's suggestion that students of non-Western music should learn non-Western notation (pp. 90–91), an issue that will come up in the next chapter of this book in connection with controversies over Indian music.

42. Hipkins, *Musical Instruments: Historic, Rare and Unique*, xxiii.

43. Aviva Briefel, "On the 1886 Colonial and Indian Exhibition," in *BRANCH: Britain, Representation and Nineteenth-Century History*, ed. Dino Franco Felluga, extension of *Romanticism and Victorianism on the Net*, http://www.branchcollective.org/?ps_articles=aviva-briefel-on-the-1886-colonial-and-indian-exhibition, accessed September 24, 2013. On the growing challenges to Britain's status as dominant world power, see Stansky, *Redesigning the World*, 12–13.

44. Eric Hobsbawm and Terence Ranger, eds., *The Invention of Tradition* (Cambridge: Cambridge University Press, 1983).

45. Hipkins, *Musical Instruments: Historic, Rare and Unique*, vii–xiii. Hipkins provided the three shofar musical phrases in Western musical notation. Francis Lyon Cohen was the rabbi of Borough Synagogue in South London, and in addition was appointed Officiating Chaplain to the Forces in 1892, the first Jew to hold this office, which he exercised in the military camp at Aldershot. He had a serious interest in Jewish music and served as music editor of the *Jewish Encyclopaedia*. In 1905 he emigrated to Sydney, Australia, in order to serve as chief minister of the Great Synagogue, Sydney. Raymond Apple, *Oz Torah*, http://www.oztorah.com/2010/09/francis-l-cohen-britains-first-jewish-chaplain/, accessed September 24, 2013.

46. Hipkins's notebooks reveal how his training as a piano tuner facilitated his analysis of the most diverse musical instruments from around the world. He assessed the construction of each one and its formation of pitch. They also show his curiosity not just about the instrument in isolation, but about its physical production and its social and ritual significance. In the case of the shofar, he noted a meeting of November 3, 1886, with Mr. Pollak, reader at the Finsbury Park Synagogue, who played all the notes used for the High Holidays on two shofars. Hipkins also took down what were described to him as the ten reasons given in the Talmud for blowing the shofar on Rosh Hashanah. As practiced by Hipkins, the study of instruments quickly graduated into a grasp of cultural connections. Papers of Alfred James Hipkins, Historic Collections, Senate House, University of London Library, MS 943/1: Research Notebooks, book 5.

47. Hipkins, *Musical Instruments: Historic, Rare and Unique*, xix–xxi.

48. Ibid., viii, xix, xxi.

49. Charles R. Day, *The Music and Musical Instruments of Southern India and the Deccan*, introd. A. J. Hipkins, 1974 reprint (Delhi: B. R. Publishing, 1891). Bennett Zon discusses the wide reception of Day's book and its place in the history of ethnomusicology in *Representing Non-Western Music in Nineteenth-Century Britain* (Rochester: University of Rochester Press, 2007), 255–260.

50. William Dalrymple, *White Mughals: Love and Betrayal in Eighteenth-Century India* (2002; New York: Penguin, 2004).

51. A. J. Hipkins, "Major C. R. Day," *Musical Times* 41, no. 686 (April 1, 1900): 245–246; Day, *Music and Musical Instruments of Southern India*, xvi.

52. Charles Capwell, "South Asia," *Harvard Dictionary of Music*, 812–822, here especially 813–814, 817–819.

53. Day, *Music and Musical Instruments of South India*, 1.

54. Ibid.

55. Ibid., 2.

56. Ibid., 7.

57. As Mantle Hood urged on students and colleagues in *The Ethnomusicologist*, 230–232.

58. Day, *Music and Musical Instruments of South India*, 58.

59. Ibid.

60. Capwell, "South Asia," 814.

61. Day, *Music and Musical Instruments of South India*, 4–5.

62. Ibid., 5.

63. Ibid., 60, 93.

64. Ibid., 92–93.

65. See Martin Rempe, "Cultural Brokers in Uniform: The Global Rise of Military Musicians and Their Music," in *Itinerario* 41, no. 2 (2017): 327–52.

66. Hipkins, introduction to Day, *Music and Musical Instruments of South India*, ix–xii, quote from ix. Hipkins was equally skeptical about other speculative topics: whether music's effects have the same cause as those of poetry (no), whether instrumental or vocal music came first (unclear), and whether Indian music had an ancient link to the music of Asia Minor and ancient Greece (skeptical) (ix, xi).

67. On the development and contents of Boas's conception of culture, see George W. Stocking Jr., "Introduction: The Basic Assumptions of Boasian Anthropology," in Franz Boas, *A Franz Boas Reader: The Shaping of American Anthropology, 1883–1911* (1974; Chicago: University of Chicago Press, 1989), 1–20.

68. Hipkins, introduction to Day, *Music and Musical Instruments of South India*, xi.

69. Ibid., xi–xii.

70. Ibid., xii.

Chapter 3

1. British Library, add. Ms. 41636, Alfred Hipkins papers, vol. 1, Alexander J. Ellis to Alfred Hipkins, October 31, 1876.

2. That meeting took place a few years later. Watson was wounded in July 1880 at the Battle of Maiwand during the Second Anglo-Afghan War. Holmes met him after his convalescence and return to London, which would place their initial encounter sometime in the early 1880s, part of the period in which Hipkins and Ellis were collaborating. Cf. Arthur Conan Doyle, *A Study in Scarlet* (1887; London: Penguin, 2009), chapter 1.

3. See Ellis's testimonies to Hipkins's aid in Alexander J. Ellis, "On the Measurement and Settlement of Musical Pitch," *Journal of the Society of Arts* 25, no. 1279 (May 25, 1877): 664–687, here 674, hereinafter cited as Ellis, "Musical Pitch"; and "On the Musical Scales of Various Nations," *Journal of the Society of Arts* 33, no. 1688 (March 27, 1885): 485–527, here 485, hereinafter cited as Ellis, "Musical Scales of Various Nations." See also Alfred J. Hipkins, supplemented by Edith J. Hipkins, "Ellis (formerly Sharpe), Alexander John," *Grove's Dictionary of Music and Musicians*, 3rd ed., vol. 2 (New York: Macmillan, 1942), 158.

4. Biographical details in the following paragraphs are drawn from British Library, Hipkins papers, vol. 3, add. Ms 41638: Edith J. Hipkins, "A few notes on Mr A. J. Ellis's engaging personality, and the photograph taken within four months of his death." I am also indebted to the account by M. K. C. MacMahon, "Ellis [formerly Sharpe], Alexander John (1814–1890)," in *Oxford Dictionary of National Biography*, ed. H. C. G. Matthew and Brian Harrison (Oxford: Oxford University Press, 2004); online edition ed. David Cannadine, January 2007, http://www.oxforddnb.com.proxy2 .library.illinois.edu/view/article/8683 2017), accessed July 19, 2011. See also W. R. Thomas and J. J. K. Rhodes, "Ellis, Alexander J.," *Grove Music Online / Oxford Music Online*, Oxford University Press, http://www.oxfordmusiconline.com/subscriber/ article/grove/music/08733, accessed October 24, 2017; and Jonathan P. J. Stock, "Alexander J. Ellis and His Place in the History of Ethnomusicology," *Ethnomusicology* 51, no. 2 (Spring/Summer 2007): 306–325.

5. George Bernard Shaw, "Preface" (1916), *Pygmalion* (New York: Penguin, 2003), 3.

6. Ellis's combination of compassion and scientific training comes through in one of the sermons he delivered there, *Auguste Comte's Religion of Humanity: A Discourse Delivered at South Place Chapel*, Sunday, October 31, 1880 (London: South Place Chapel [Library] and Trübner, 1880). Comte's positivism attracted a large international following in the nineteenth century and has lingered on into our own time, though by now it attracts only a small number of cult adherents. See the poignant account from Rio de Janeiro of the Positivist Church of Brazil: Simon Romero, "Nearly in Ruins: The Church Where Sages Dreamed of a Modern Brazil," *New York Times*, December 25, 2016.

7. Edith Hipkins, "A Few Notes on Mr. A. J. Ellis's Engaging Personality."

8. British Library, Hipkins papers, vol. 1 (41636): Ellis to Hipkins, December 9, 1878; May 1, 1880; and December 10 and 12, 1882. Ellis to Hipkins, Hipkins papers, vol. 2 (41637), April 26, 1883; October 5, 1883; August 4 and 23, 1884; February 13, 1885; May 22, 1885; and July 8, 1885.

9. Edith Hipkins, "A few notes on Mr. A. J. Ellis's engaging personality."

10. On the alliance of science and craft, see Myles W. Jackson, *Harmonious Triads: Physicists, Musicians, and Instrument Makers in Nineteenth-Century Germany* (Cambridge, MA: MIT Press, 2006). As Jackson points out on p. 2, science contained a craft dimension in its own right, apart from any assistance that it received from professional craftsmen.

11. Hermann L. F. Helmholtz, *On the Sensations of Tone as a Physiological Basis for the Theory of Music*, trans. Alexander J. Ellis (New York: Dover, 1954). The translation was based on the fourth German edition of 1877. Ellis published the first edition of his translation in 1875, and the second, revised edition (reprinted by Dover) in 1885. The latter was a significant date; in the same year he published his essay on the diversity of musical scales, the culmination of his own musicological research.

12. Henry Cowell, *New Musical Resources*, ed. David Nicholls (1930; Cambridge: Cambridge University Press, 1996); Harry Partch, *Genesis of a Music: Monophony: The Relation of Its Music to Historic and Contemporary Trends; Its Philosophy, Concepts, and Principles; Its Relation to Historic and Proposed Intonations; and Its Application to Musical Instruments*, fwd. by Otto Luening (Madison: University of Wisconsin Press, 1949).

13. See Yonatan I. Fishman, Igor O. Volkov, M. Daniel Noh, P. Charles Garell, Hans Bakken, Joseph C. Arezzo, Matthew A. Howard, and Mitchell Steinschneider, "Consonance and Dissonance of Musical Chords: Neural Correlates in Auditory Cortex of Monkeys and Humans," *Journal of Neurophysiology* 86 (2001): 2761–2788.

14. Helmholtz, *Sensations of Tone*, 1–2, 4, 8, 14–15.

15. Ibid., 14–15, 18.

16. Ibid., 4.

17. Ibid., 49–65.

18. Ibid., 253–255, 315, 326–327, 371.

19. The Cage quote comes from David Nicholls, "Cage and America," in David Nicholls, ed., *The Cambridge Companion to John Cage* (Cambridge: Cambridge University Press, 2002), 3–19, here 16.

20. On Ellis's contact with Müller and Helmholtz, see Benjamin Steege, *Helmholtz and the Modern Listener* (Cambridge: Cambridge University Press, 2012), 193–196.

21. Max Müller to Hermann Helmholtz, March 19, 1863, in Hermann Helmholtz, *Brückenschlag zwischen zwei Kulturen: Helmholtz in der Korrespondenz mit Geisteswissenschaftlern und Künstlern*, ed. Herbert Hörz (Marburg/Lahn: Basilisken-Presse, 1997), 389–390.

22. Berlin-Brandenburgische Akademie der Wissenschaften, Nachlass Helmholtz, nr. 131. The publisher's quote is from (?) [representative of Robert Cocks] to Alexander J. Ellis, July 1863. In addition, see Nachlass Helmholtz nr. 131, Baillière to Ellis, April 10, 1863; Churchill to Ellis, May 22, 1863; [representative of Chapman and Hall] to Ellis, June 20, 1863; and [representative of Henry Bohn] to Ellis, July 14, 1863. On Helmholtz's visit and Ellis's subsequent comments on the progress of the trans-

lation, see Nachlass Helmholtz nr. 131: Alexander J. Ellis to Hermann Helmholtz, April 10, 1864; February 3, 1873; February 20, 1873; December 1, 1873; August 12, 1874; October 10, 1874; and July 5, 1875.

23. Ellis, "On the Measurement and Settlement of Musical Pitch." Cf. Ellis, *The History of Musical Pitch* (London: Trounce, 1880), reprinted with corrections and an appendix from the *Journal of the Society of Art*, March 5 and April 2, 1880.

24. Ellis, "On the Measurement and Settlement of Musical Pitch," 664; cf. Ellis, *History of Musical Pitch*, 313–314, for Ellis's criticism of the Society of Arts committee.

25. Ellis, *History of Musical Pitch*, 293–294.

26. Ellis, "Measurement and Settlement of Musical Pitch," 675–676.

27. Ibid., 677–678, quote from 678.

28. Ellis, *History of Musical Pitch*, 308.

29. Ibid., 302.

30. Ibid., 309.

31. Ibid., 309–310.

32. Ibid., 310. On military bands, see Martin Rempe, "Cultural Brokers in Uniform: The Global Rise of Military Musicians and Their Music," in *Itinerario* 41, no. 2 (2017): 327–352.

33. Ellis, *History of Musical Pitch*, 310.

34. Ibid., 310.

35. Ibid., 312.

36. Ibid., 313.

Chapter 4

1. Alexander J. Ellis, "On the Musical Scales of Various Nations," *Journal of the Society of Arts* 33 (March 27, 1885): 485–527, hereinafter cited as Ellis, "Musical Scales of Various Nations." For a recent assessment of Ellis, see Jonathan P. J. Stock, "Alexander J. Ellis and His Place in the History of Ethnomusicology," *Ethnomusicology* 51, no. 2 (Spring/Summer 2007): 306–325. See also Bruno Nettl's assessment in *Encounters in Ethnomusicology: A Memoir* (Warren, MI: Harmonie Park Press, 2002), 31–32; Volker Kalisch, "A. J. Ellis und sein Beitrag zur Methodologie," in *Die Musikforschung* 46, no.1 (January-March 1993): 45–53, especially 45–46 for the reception of his methodology by Hornbostel and others; and Klaus Wachsmann, "Spencer to Hood: A Changing View of Non-European Music," in *Proceedings of the Royal Anthropological Institute of Great Britain and Ireland*, no. 1973 (1973): 5–13. The larger context of nineteenth-century evolutionary thought is laid out in George W. Stocking, Jr., *Victorian Anthropology* (New York: Free Press, 1991).

2. Mahillon was an important collaborator for Hipkins and Ellis. See Hipkins's biographical entry on him in *Grove's Dictionary of Music and Musicians*, 3rd ed., ed. H. C. Colles, vol. 3 (New York: Macmillan, 1942), 291.

3. Ellis, "Musical Scales of Various Nations," 486. The elusive connection to Hermann Smith—Ellis does not offer any more information about him, in contrast

to his usual effusiveness about his sources—may have come about through their shared interest in organs, a subject on which Smith published two books. A *New York Times* review from September 3, 1904 of Smith's book *The World's Earliest Music Traced to Its Beginnings in Ancient Lands* (New York: Scribner's, 1904) quotes the concluding lines from Ellis's essay about the artificiality of musical scales; it is one bit of documentation to suggest that Ellis's argument was reaching a broad musical public almost two decades after its publication.

4. Thomas Philipp, "Class, Community, and Arab Historiography in the Early Nineteenth Century: The Dawn of a New Era," *International Journal of Middle East Studies* 16, no. 2 (May 1984): 161–175; Fruma Zachs, "Mīkhā'īl Mishāqa: The First Historian of Modern Syria," *British Journal of Middle Eastern Studies* 28, no. 1 (May 2001): 67–87.

5. Scott Marcus, "The Interface between Theory and Practice: Intonation in Arab Music," *Asian Music* 24, no. 2 (Spring-Summer 1993): 39–58; Owen Wright et al., "Arab Music," *Grove Music Online / Oxford Music Online*, Oxford University Press, accessed August 29, 2013, http://www.oxfordmusiconline.com/subscriber/article/grove/music/01139pg1; Shireen Maalouf, "Mīkhā'īl Mishāqā: Virtual Founder of the Twenty-Four Equal Quartertone Scale," *Journal of the American Oriental Society* 123, no. 4 (October-December 2003): 835–840.

6. Eli Smith and Mikh'īl Meshaka [Mīkhā'īl Mishāqa], "A Treatise on Arab Music," *Journal of the American Oriental Society* 1, no. 3 (1849): 173–217, here 173–174.

7. The quote and reference to Mishāqa as "my personal friend and correspondent" are from ibid., 174. "Friendship" was already a category widely used in eighteenth-century travel writing. Its ambiguities and power dynamics are analyzed for Oceania in Vanessa Smith, *Intimate Strangers: Friendship, Exchange and Pacific Encounters* (Cambridge: Cambridge University Press, 2010). The same asymmetries of power, calculations of gain on both sides, and genuinely felt affection pertain to modern anthropology's preferred term, "informant."

8. Smith and Meshaka, "Treatise on Arab Music," 176, 180–182.

9. Ellis, "On the Diversity of Scales," 498. In musical practice, improvisation is not arbitrary, but depends on performer training and audience expectation. See Gabriel Solis and Bruno Nettl, eds., *Improvisation: Art, Education, and Society* (Urbana: University of Illinois Press, 2009).

10. A prominent nineteenth-century example was the London Missionary Society missionary William Ellis. See my essay on the rather sympathetic young Ellis, "The Romance of Hawaii in William Ellis's 'Narrative of a Tour through Hawaii, or, Owhyhee,'" in Ib Friis, Michael Harbsmeier, and Jørgen Bæk Simonsen, *Early Scientific Expeditions and Local Encounters: New Perspectives on Carsten Niebuhr and 'The Arabian Journey'* [Scientia Danica, Series H, Humanistica 4, vol. 2] (Copenhagen: Royal Danish Academy, 2013), 208–221. Cf. the critical view of Ellis and the Hawaiian missionaries (from the ABCFM) in Patrick V. Kirch and Marshall Sahlins, *Anahulu: The Anthropology of History in the Kingdom of Hawaii*, vol.1: Marshall Sahlins, with the assistance of Dorothey B. Barrère, *Historical Ethnography* (Chicago: University of Chicago Press, 1992).

11. On the performative context, see A. J. Racy, *Making Music in the Arab World: The Culture and Artistry of Ṭarab* (Cambridge: Cambridge University Press, 2003), 1–6. Gilbert Rouget, *Music and Trance: A Theory of the Relations between Music and Possession*, rev. trans. Brunhilde Biebuyck (Chicago: University of Chicago Press, 1985), makes the more general case for trance as a feature of music and discusses its especially strong connection to Arab music, chapter 7.

12. On the dating of *Japonisme* in England, see Ayako Ono, *Japonisme in Britain: Whistler, Menpes, Henry, Hornel and Nineteenth-Century Japan* (London: Routledge Curzon, 2003), 14–20. On the movement in France, see the exhibition catalog, Gabriel P. Weisberg ed., *Japonisme: Japanese Influence on French Art, 1854–1910* (Cleveland: Cleveland Museum of Art, 1975).

13. The preceding description of the Japanese Village is drawn from Sir Hugh Cortazzi, *Japan in Late Victorian London: The Japanese Native Village in Knightsbridge and The Mikado, 1885* (Norwich, UK: Sainsbury Institute for the Study of Japanese Arts and Cultures, 2009), 9, 11–17, 39, 43–49; cf. the anonymous article in *The Times*, 10 January 1885, published in *The Dictionary of Victorian London*, http://www .victorianlondon.org/entertainment/japanesevillage.htm; and Ellis, "Musical Scales of Various Nations," 522. On Rottmann Strome, see Yasuko Suga, "'Artistic and Commercial' Japan: Modernity, Authenticity and Japanese Leather Paper," in David Hussey and Margaret Ponsonby, *Buying for the Home: Shopping for the Domestic from the Seventeenth Century to the Present* (Aldershot, UK: Ashgate, 2008), 91–114, here 96–98.

14. Ellis, "Diversity of Musical Scales," 520. Veeder is briefly mentioned in Andrew Cobbing, *The Japanese Discovery of Victorian Britain: Early Travel Encounters in the Far West* (London: Japanese Library/Curzon, 1998), 152. In early 1884—by May 28—Hipkins had taken five pages of detailed notes on an article that Veeder published in *The Transactions of the Asiatic Society of Japan* 7, no. 2 (1879). He quotes Veeder as claiming that he learned "'the three chief methods of tuning [the koto]'" from "'the chief musician of the Emperor's band.'" University of London Senate House, Hipkins papers, research notebooks, MS 943/1/13 (1883), undated entry.

15. "International Health Exhibition, 1884," in *The British Medical Journal* 2, no. 1196 (December 1, 1883): 1092–1093; William Lant Carpenter, "Education at the International Health Exhibition, London," in *Science* 4, no. 88 (October 10 , 1884): 353–356.

16. Ellis, "Diversity of Musical Scales," 520.

17. Ibid., 521.

18. Sondra Wieland Howe, *Luther Whiting Mason: International Music Educator* (Warren, MI: Harmonie Park Press, 1997), 58. On Isawa and Mason, see also Donald P. Berger, "Isawa Shūji and Luther Whiting Mason: Pioneers of Music Education," in *Music Educators Journal* 74, no. 2 (October 1987): 31–36.

19. Howe, *Luther Whiting Mason*, 61.

20. Carl Engel, "Some Letters to a Namesake," *Musical Quarterly* 28, no. 3 (July 1, 1942): 337–379, here 341.

21. Howe, *Luther Whiting Mason*, 101–103.

22. See the fine interpretation in Toru Takenaka, "Isawa Shūji's 'National Music': National Sentiment and Cultural Westernisation in Meiji Japan," *Itinerario* 34, no. 3 (December 2010): 97–118, especially 111–113. Isawa was not the only agent in the westernization of Japanese music. Military bands and court musicians were already introducing Western music into Japanese state life in the decade before Isawa began to initiate his reforms. See Atsuko Watabe-Gross, *Die Einführung der europäischen Musik in Japan (1855–1888): Kulturpolitische Aspekte eines Paradigmenwechsels* (Hamburg: Gesellschaft für Natur- und Völkerkunde Ostasiens, 2007), 38–84.

23. Ellis, "Musical Scales of Various Nations," 522, 524. Cf. William P. Malm, *Traditional Japanese Music and Musical Instruments*, new ed. (Tokyo: Kodansha, 2000), 193.

24. Ellis, "Musical Scales of Various Nations," 522, 525.

25. Ibid., 523.

26. On Isawa's aims, see Takenaka, "Isawa Shūji's 'National Music.'" On the generational context of his work, see Kenneth B. Pyle, *The New Generation in Meiji Japan: Problems of Cultural Identity, 1885–1895* (Stanford, CA: Stanford University Press, 1969), 3–5; and William P. Malm, "The Modern Music of Meiji Japan," in Donald H. Shively, ed., *Tradition and Modernization in Japanese Culture* (Princeton, NJ: Princeton University Press, 1971) 257–300.

27. The preceding description is drawn from Frank H. H. King, "Hart, Sir Robert, first baronet (1835–1911)," in *Oxford Dictionary of National Biography*, ed. H. C. G. Matthew and Brian Harrison (Oxford, UK: Oxford University Press, 2004); online ed., ed. Lawrence Goldman, January 2008, http://www.oxforddnb.com.proxy2 .library.illinois.edu/view/article/33739, accessed February 23, 2014. The documentary starting point in print for the history of Hart and the Customs Service is Robert Hart, *The I. G. in Peking: Letters of Robert Hart, Chinese Maritime Customs, 1868–1907*, ed. John K. Fairbank et. al., introd. L. K. Little (Cambridge, MA: Harvard University Press, 1975). See also Hans Van De Ven, "Robert Hart and the Chinese Maritime Customs Service," in *Modern Asian Studies* 40, no. 3 (2006): 545–548.

28. See the introductory note and the newspaper reports from the *The Standard*, 17 July 1884, and from *The Times*, July 10, 1884, in Inspector General of Customs [Robert Hart], *China: Imperial Maritime Customs*, Miscellaneous Series 13: *Illustrated Catalogue of the Chinese Collection of Exhibits for the International Health Exhibition, London, 1884* (London: Clowes, 1884): 181–183 and 185–186. Hereinafter cited as Hart, *Illustrated Catalogue*.

29. See the descriptions of the restaurant and teahouse in Hart, *Illustrated Catalogue*, 134–137; and of the boutiques in the press reports, 181–186.

30. Hart, *Illustrated Catalogue*, 158–180.

31. British Library, add. Ms. 41637, Alfred Hipkins papers, 1: Alexander J. Ellis to Alfred Hipkins, August 4, 1884.

32. Ellis, "Musical Scales of Various Nations," 515–516.

33. On nineteenth-century Western impressions of Chinese music, see

Andrew F. Jones, *Yellow Music: Media Culture and Colonial Modernity in the Chinese Jazz Age* (Durham, NC: Duke University Press, 2001), 27–28. Ruth HaCohen, *The Music Libel against the Jews* (New Haven: Yale University Press, 2012), is not just about the Christian perception of Jewish vocal expression; it also illustrates how "noise" is a fundamental category of cultural perception. Cf. Ronald Radano and Tejumola Olaniyan, "Introduction: Hearing Empire—Imperial Listening," in their edited volume *Audible Empire: Music, Global Politics, Critique* (Durham, NC: Duke University Press, 2016), 8. Veit Erlmann, *Reason and Resonance: A History of Modern Aurality* (New York: Zone Books, 2010), 271, briefly discusses the public use of "noise" to characterize twentieth-century avant-garde Western music. Erlmann, in turn, refers to Alex Ross, *The Rest Is Noise: Listening to the Twentieth Century* (New York: Farrar, Strauss, and Giroux, 2016), which begins by observing how often twentieth-century listeners refer to one another's music as noise (xi–xii).

34. Ellis, "Musical Scales of Various Nations," 516–520, quote from 520.

35. Hart to Campbell, June 19, 1884, and August 14, 1884, *The I. G. in Peking*, vol. 1, 555–556.

36. J. A. van Aalst, *Chinese Music*, reprint (Shanghai: Inspector General of Customs, 1884; New York: Paragon, 1964). Cf. Aalst's contribution, "Chinese Music," in Hart, *Illustrated Catalogue*, 143–180, hereinafter cited as Aalst, "Chinese Music," in Hart, *Illustrated Catalogue*. The best introduction to the relationship of Aalst and Hart is the material to be found in Hart, *The I. G. in Peking*. On Aalst, see also Han Kuo-huang, "J. A. van Aalst and his Chinese Music," in *Asian Music* 19, no. 2 (Spring-Summer 1988): 127–130.

37. Aalst, *Chinese Music*, iii, 5–6, 36. For a sympathetic account of the difficulties of gaining entrance to a Chinese household, see George Carter Stent, "Chinese Lyrics," in *Journal of the North-China Branch of the Royal Asiatic Society*, new series 7 (1871–72): 93–135, here 93–97. An unusual observer for the time, Stent was fascinated by street music and published English translations of popular songs.

38. Aalst, "Chinese Music," in Hart, *Illustrated Catalogue*, 153–154.

39. Ibid., 143–149.

40. Ellis, "Musical Scales of Various Nations," 515–517.

41. See, for example, the productions of the sound artist Thessia Machado, which make use of "waste" objects like discarded computers to create contemporary music that is specific to our own civilization: http://thessiamachado.com/, accessed August 23, 2017.

42. Ellis, "Musical Scales of Various Nations," 500–502. Sourindro Mohun Tagore, *The Musical Scales of the Hindus: Remarks on the Applicability of Harmony to Hindu Music* (1884; New York: AMS Press, 1979); cf. S. M. Tagore, ed., *Hindu Music from Various Authors*, 2nd ed. (Calcutta: Bose, 1882). S. M. Tagore and Rabindranath Tagore were distant relatives who belonged to different branches of the Tagore family. For biographical studies of S. M. Tagore, see Charles Capwell, "Marginality and Musicology in Nineteenth-Century Calcutta: The Case of Sourindro Mohun Tagore," in Bruno Nettl and Philip V. Bohlman, eds., *Comparative Musicology and Anthropology*

of Music: Essays on the History of Ethnomusicology (Chicago: University of Chicago Press, 1991), 228–243; and Capwell, "Representing 'Hindu' Music to the Colonial and Native Elite of Calcutta," in Joep Bor, Françoise 'Nalini' Delvoye, Jane Harvey and Emmie te Nijenhuis, eds., *Hindustani Music: Thirteenth to Twentieth Centuries* (New Delhi: Manohar, 2010), 285–311.

43. Reports from *The Indian Daily News*, February 3 and March 2, 1874, in Sourindro Mohun Tagore, *Public Opinion and Official Communications, about the Bengali Music School and its President* (Calcutta: Pachanun Mookerjee, 1876), 7–9.

44. *Hindoo Patriot*, August 14, 1876, in Tagore, *Public Opinion and Official Communications*, 40.

45. "Supplement to the Public Opinion" [new pagination] in Tagore, *Public Opinion and Official Communications*, 51–53, 74–78, 181–186. Tagore's objects in the South Kensington Museum are listed in the Registry of Acquisition for 1889–90, South Asia Department, Victoria and Albert Museum. They reached the museum too late for Ellis to have used them for his essay on the diversity of scales, which was published in 1885. Tagore attached the following note to the tuning forks (Box no. w2):

> To his excellency the most honorable Earl of Dufferin . . . dedicated by Tagore.
>
> The tuning forks, forming the contents of this box, represent the twenty-two musical intervals that go to make up the Indian Diapason. The position of the *Srutris* with reference to the seven Notes is indicated by the manner in which the forks have been arranged in this box. This is my first attempt—and I believe it is the first of its kind—at representing the minute intervals by means of tuning forks, and it is to be hoped that the forks will afford a tangible, though rough, idea of the minute sub-divisions of the *Octave*, which in the musical language of India, are known as *Srutris*. S. M. Tagore, Calcutta, March, 1886. V&A IS 77–1890.

Like many of the instruments that Tagore sent to the Victoria and Albert, the tuning forks arrived in damaged condition. They were rusted, which would have made them useless for precise calculation. See the note on p. 90 in the Registry of Acquisition 1889/90, South Asia Department, Victoria and Albert Museum.

On the Metropolitan Museum collection, see Rebecca Lindsey and Allen Roda, "Raja Tagore: Renaissance Man of Indian Music," http://www.metmuseum.org/about-the-museum/museum-departments/curatorial-departments/musical-instruments/of-note/2014/raja-tagore, accessed June 9, 2015, which includes fascinating pictures and biographical information.

46. G. B. Vecchiotti, "Rajah Sourindro Mohun Tagore and Indian Music," extract from *Il Raffaello*, a journal of the Royal Academy of Urbino, trans. Rev. A. E. Medlycott, in Tagore, *Public Opinion and Official Communications*, supplement, 124–135.

47. Ibid., supplement, 89–92. Original in *Jenaer Literaturzeitung* 31 (1877), 487–488.

48. Julius Jolly, "Eine Reise nach Ostindien: IV. Calcutta," *Deutsche Rundschau* 40 (July-Sept. 1884): 107–127, here 120–122. Jolly was famous in his own time, and

continues to be admired today for his studies of classical Indian law and Indian medicine. See the recent appreciation by Ludo Rocher, review of Julius Jolly: Kleine Schriften, in *Journal of the American Oriental Society* 134, no. 3 (July-Sept. 2014): 542–544.

49. Ray Desmond, "Clarke, Charles Baron (1832–1906)," in *Oxford Dictionary of National Biography*, online ed., ed. Lawrence Goldman, Oxford: Oxford University Press, http://www.oxforddnb.com.proxy2.library.illinois.edu/view/article/32425, accessed November 28, 2012.

50. S. M. Tagore, "Hindu Music," reprinted from the *Hindoo Patriot*, September 7, 1874, in S. M. Tagore, ed., *Hindu Music from Various Authors*, 339–397, here 340.

51. Ibid., 364–365.

52. Ibid., 365.

53. Ibid., 366.

54. On the opposing approaches to Indian culture, see Harry Liebersohn, *The Return of the Gift: European History of a Global Idea* (Cambridge: Cambridge University Press, 2011), chap. 1.

55. On the tensions between nationalist and cosmopolitan politics in modern India, see Sunil Khilnani, *The Idea of India* (New York: Farrar, Straus and Giroux, 1999). See also Eric Hobsbawm and Terence Ranger, eds., *The Invention of Tradition* (Cambridge: Cambridge University Press, 1984).

56. Teresa Segura-Garcia, "Baroda, the British Empire and the World, c. 1875–1939" (PhD diss., University of Cambridge, 2015).

57. On the early formation of postcontact Hawaiian music, with references to the wider literature, see Liebersohn, "Romance of Hawaii."

58. Vecchiotti, "Rajah Sourindro Mohun Tagore and Indian Music," in Tagore, *Public Opinion and Official Communications*, 135.

59. Gerry Farrell, *Indian Music and the West* (Oxford: Clarendon Press, 1997), remains the best introduction to the late-nineteenth and early-twentieth-century reception of Indian music in Europe.

60. Ellis, "Musical Scales of Various Nations," 526.

61. On Helmholtz as a representative of the German educated elite, see Robert Brain, "Bürgerliche Intelligenz" (review essay), in *Studies in the History and Philosophy of Science* 26 (1995): 617–635. Cf. the discussion of Helmholtz's aesthetic preferences in Gary Hatfield, "Helmholtz and Classicism: The Science of Aesthetics and the Aesthetics of Science," in David Cahan, ed., *Hermann von Helmholtz and the Foundations of Nineteenth-Century Science* (Berkeley: University of California Press, 1993), 522–558.

Chapter 5

1. On the mood of German elites between 1848, see Reinhart Koselleck, *Preussen zwischen Reform und Revolution: Allgemeines Landrecht, Verwaltung und soziale Bewegung von 1791 bis 1848* (Stuttgart: Klett-Cotta, 1975); and Werner Conze, "Vom 'Pöbel' zum 'Proletariat.' Sozialgeschichtliche Voraussetzungen für den Sozialismus in

Deutschland," in *Moderne deutsche Sozialgeschichte*, ed. Hans-Ulrich Wehler (Cologne: Kiepenheuer and Witsch, 1973), 111–136.

2. Sebastian Conrad, *German Colonialism: A Short History* (Cambridge: Cambridge University Press, 2012), 12.

3. On the role of German scientists in the British Empire, see Moritz von Brescius, *German Science in the Age of Empire: Enterprise, Opportunity and the Schlagintweit Brothers* (Cambridge: Cambridge University Press, 2018).

4. From the large literature on the German educated elite and its universities, see Charles E. McClelland, *State, Society and University in Germany, 1700–1914* (Cambridge, 1980); and Werner Conze and Jürgen Kocka, eds., *Bildungsbürgertum im 19. Jahrhundert*, vol. 1: *Bildungssystem und Professionalisierung in internationalen Vergleichen* (Stuttgart: Klett, 1985). Alexander Honold and Klaus R. Scherpe, eds., *Mit Deutschland um die Welt: Eine Kulturgeschichte des Fremden in der Kolonialzeit* (Stuttgart: Metzler, 2004), contains useful short sketches of colonial encounters and reports from 1869 to 1918; Sebastian Conrad and Jürgen Osterhammel, eds., *Das Kaiserreich transnational: Deutschland in der Welt 1871–1914* (Göttingen, Germany: Vandenhoeck und Ruprecht, 2006) is a collection of secondary literature on Germany in the world.

5. On Weber's global cosmopolitanism, see Guenther Roth, "Global Capitalism and Multi-Ethnicity: Max Weber Then and Now," in *The Cambridge Companion to Weber*, ed. Stephen Turner (Cambridge: Cambridge University Press, 2000), 117–130. To be sure, individual German scholars turned outward to the extra-European world as early as the opening decades of the nineteenth century, when August von Schlegel helped to initiate the professional study of Indian civilization; but this work was on a modest scale compared to the German universities' global scholarly industry by 1900.

6. On Boas and German higher learning, see Harry Liebersohn, "'Culture' Crosses the Atlantic: The German Sources of 'The Mind of Primitive Man,'" in *Indigenous Visions: Rediscovering the World of Franz Boas*, ed. Isaiah L. Wilner and Ned Blackhawk (New Haven: Yale University Press, 2018), 91–108.

7. The use of the word "Indian" raises troubling questions of entangled histories that can no longer be completely disentangled. This is a book that deals with both South Asians and Native Americans. Each group deserves to be named in its own right (and furthermore, these broad denominations in turn encompass large numbers of distinctive groups of people). Sometimes, as in this case, historical context requires retaining the term "Indian" for native peoples of North America.

8. Carl Stumpf, "Lieder der Bellakula-Indianer," *Vierteljahrsschrift für Musikwissenschaft* 2 (1886): 405–426. "Bella Coola" is retained here only as a term of historical usage. On Stumpf's meeting with the Nuxalk performers, cf. Liebersohn, "'Culture' Crosses the Atlantic," 100–101.

The journal as a place of publication was significant in its own right. In its founding issue of the preceding year, the musicologist Guido Adler, one of its coeditors, published a manifesto for the newly emerging discipline of musicology that included a call for a comparative approach widening it to a global scope: Guido Adler, "Umfang, Methode und Ziel der Musikwissenschaft," in *Vierteljahrsschrift für Musikwissenschaft* 1 (1885): 5–20. Bruno Nettl considers Adler's essay to be the centerpiece of the "seminal 1880s," as he names this critical moment for the creation of a cosmopolitan musical science. See *Encounters in Ethnomusicology: A Memoir* (Warren, MI: Harmonie Park Press, 2002), 20–22.

9. For a brief biography in English, see Helga Sprung and Lothar Sprung, *Portraits of Pioneers in Psychology*, vol. 4, ed. Gregory A. Kimble and Michael Wertheimer (Washington: American Psychological Association, 2000), 50–69.

10. Stumpf, "Lieder der Bellakula-Indianer," 406, 426.

11. Ibid., 406–407.

12. The following account of Hagenbeck's business empire is drawn from Eric Ames, *Carl Hagenbeck's Empire of Entertainments* (Seattle: University of Washington Press, 2008), which emphasizes how Hagenbeck's business functioned through a worldwide network for collecting and distributing animals, people, and objects.

13. Quoted in ibid., 24.

14. Ibid., 12, 27–28. On the worldwide market and German competition for indigenous artifacts, see H. Glenn Penny, *Objects of Culture: Ethnology and Ethnographic Museums in Imperial Germany* (Chapel Hill: University of North Carolina Press, 2002).

15. Ames, *Carl Hagenbeck's Empire of Entertainments*, 33–38, quotes from 35 and 38.

16. The documents of Franz Boas's stay on Baffin Island vividly demonstrate the kind of tug-of-war that could take place between a European visitor and local parties in the extreme north. See Franz Boas, *Franz Boas among the Inuit of Baffin Island, 1883–1884: Journals and Letters*, trans. William Barr and ed. Ludger Müller-Wille (Toronto: University of Toronto Press, 1998).

17. Stumpf, "Lieder der Bellakula-Indianer," 406–407.

18. Ibid., 405–406. The phrase about writing it down draws on Clifford Geertz, *The Interpretation of Cultures* (New York: Basic, 1977), 19.

19. Theodore Baker, *Über die Musik der Nordamerikanischen Wilden* (Leipzig: Breitkopf und Härtel, 1882), iii–iv.

20. Ibid., 19–23.

21. Susan Neylan, *The Heavens Are Changing : Nineteenth-Century Protestant Missions and Tsimshian Christianity* (Montreal: McGill-Queen's University Press, 2003).

22. Stumpf, "Lieder der Bellakula-Indianer," 411, 417.

23. Ibid., 408, 413–414, 420. On Boas and the Nuxalks, see Douglas Cole, *Franz Boas: The Early Years, 1858–1906* (Seattle: University of Washington Press, 1999), 97, 149 and 267.

24. Carl Stumpf, review of Alexander J. Ellis, "On the Musical Scales of Various Nations," in *Vierteljahrsschrift für Musikwissenschaft* 2 (1886): 511–524, here 511. Stumpf heard the singers in November 1885 and published his account of their music the following year. Ellis's paper "On the Musical Scales of Various Nations" was

read to the Society of Arts in March 1885, and was probably printed in the society's journal during the summer of that year.

25. Stumpf, "Lieder der Bellakula-Indianer," 410.

26. Paraphrased from Franz Boas, *Publications of the Jesup North Pacific Expedition* 1 (1898), reprinted in *A Franz Boas Reader: The Shaping of American Anthropology, 1883–1911*, ed. George W. Stocking Jr., reprint ed. (1974; Chicago: University of Chicago Press, 1982), 107–116, here 114.

27. Editors' introduction to T. F. McIlwraith, *At Home with the Bella Coola Indians: T. F. McIlwraith's Field Letters, 1922–4*, ed. John Barker and Douglas Cole (Vancouver: University of British Columbia Press, 2003), 3–27, here 9–10.

28. Ibid., 10–11; Anton F. Kolstee, *Bella Coola Indian Music: A Study of the Interaction between Northwest Coast Indian Structures and their Functional Context*, Canadian Ethnology service paper no. 83, National Museum of Man, Mercury Series (Ottawa: National Museums of Canada, 1982), 6–20.

29. Carl Stumpf, "Carl Stumpf: A Self-Portrait (1924)," in *The Origins of Music*, trans. and ed. David Trippett (1911; Oxford: Oxford University Press, 2012), 189–190.

30. Ibid., 191–192.

31. Ibid., 193–197.

32. Sebastian Klotz, "Tonpsychologie und Musikforschung als Katalysatoren wissenschaftlich-experimenteller Praxis und der Methodenlehre im Kreis von Carl Stumpf, *Berichte zur Wissenschaftsgeschichte* 31 (2008): 195–210, here 197–198.

33. Helmut Böhme, *Deutschlands Weg zur Grossmacht: Studien zum Verhältnis von Wirtschaft und Staat während der Reichsgründungszeit, 1848–1881* (Cologne: Kiepenheuer und Witsch, 1966).

34. Carl E. Schorske, *Fin-de-siècle Vienna: Politics and Culture* (New York: Knopf, 1980).

35. Carl Stumpf, *Tonpsychologie*, vol. 1 (Leipzig: Hirzel, 1893); Mitchell G. Ash, *Gestalt Psychology in German Culture, 1890–1967: Holism and the Quest for Objectivity* (Cambridge: Cambridge University Press, 1995), 30, 39–40.

36. See Julia Kursell, "Hermann von Helmholtz und Carl Stumpf über Konsonanz und Dissonanz," *Berichte zur Wissenschaftsgeschichte* 31 (2008): 130–143, especially 134, 137–139; Klotz, "Tonpsychologie und Musikforschung," 199–200.

37. Ash, *Gestalt Psychology in German Culture*, 3, 8, 28–41.

38. Stumpf, Review of Ellis, "On the Musical Scales of Various Nations," 511–513.

39. Ibid., 523.

40. Ibid., 524.

41. Nic Leonhardt, editorial, special issue, "Negotiating the Entertainment Business: Theatrical Brokers around 1900," in *Popular Entertainment Studies* 6, no. 2 (2015): 1–3, quotes from 1–2.

42. Christopher Balme, "Managing Theatre and Cinema in Colonial India: Maurice E. Bandmann, J. F. Madan and the War Films Controversy," in ibid., 9–12.

43. meLê yamomo, "Brokering Sonic Modernities: Migrant Manila Musicians in the Asia Pacific, 1881–1948," in ibid., 22–37.

44. Carl Bock, *Temples and Elephants: The Narrative of a Journey of Exploration through Upper Siam and Laos* (London: Sampson Low, Marston, Searle and Rivington, 1884), 47; Ernst von Hesse-Wartegg, *Siam, das Reich des weissen Elefanten* (Leipzig: Weber, 1899), 127–130.

45. Hesse-Wartegg, *Reich des weissen Elephanten*, 128.

46. Nic Leonhardt, "'From the Land of the White Elephant through the Gay Cities of Europe and America': Re-routing the World Tour of the Boosra Mahin Siamese Theatre Troupe (1900)," in *Theatre Research International* 40, no. 2 (July 2015): 140–155, quote from 147.

47. Carl Stumpf, "Tonsystem und Musik der Siamesen," in *Beiträge zur Akustik und Musikwissenschaft*, 3 (1901): 69–138, here 69–70.

48. Ibid., 70.

49. Alfred J. Hipkins, *Musical Instruments: Historic, Rare and Unique*, with forty-eight plates drawn by William Gibb (1888; London: A. and C. Black, 1921).

50. Stumpf, "Tonsystem und Musik der Siamesen," 73–77.

51. Ibid., 81.

52. Ibid., 82.

53. Ibid., 81–85.

54. Ibid., 132–133.

55. Ibid., 133.

56. Ibid., 133–138.

57. Ibid., 105–107, quote from 107.

58. Ibid., 132. "Heterophony" is widely used today in descriptions of music from the Middle East to East Asia. See, for example, the precise ethnographic references in Jim Samson, *Music in the Balkans* (Leiden, Netherlands: Brill, 2013), 53, 99, 188. It is also used to describe a technique of many twentieth- and twenty-first-century composers. Today's definition of the term is rather widely inclusive; it often seems to describe ornamental variations on a main melody rather than radically different melodies. The simultaneous performance of different melodies was what struck Stumpf and his contemporaries as a challenge to their notions of harmony, which went beyond the familiar, acceptable limits of dissonance.

59. A. J. Ellis, "On the Musical Scales of Various Nations," *Journal of the Society of Arts* 33 (27 March 1885): 485–527, here 509.

60. Stumpf, "Music der Siamesen," 131.

61. Ibid., 131–132, quote from 132. Stumpf is referring to a passage from Plato, *Laws*, book 7, 812b–812e.

62. August Wilhelm Ambros, *Geschichte der Musik*, 3rd ed., 5 vols., 1: *Die Musik des griechischen Altertums und des Orients*, ed. B. von Sokolovsky (Leipzig: Leuckart, 1887), 510–529. The forces of order still contend today with the "noise" of the Chinese street. See Chris Buckley and Adam Wu, "Toning Down Rowdy Retirees at the 'Noisiest Park in the World,'" *New York Times*, July 4, 2016 [Midwestern print edition p. A4].

63. J. A. van Aalst, *Chinese Music*, reprint (Shanghai: Inspector General of Customs, 1884; New York: Paragon, 1964), iii, 6, 36–37.

64. Guido Adler, "Heterophony (1908)," translated in Mitchell, *Mahler: Songs and Symphonies of Life and Death*, 624–634, quote from 624. Cf. Mitchell's discussion of Adler's article, p. 127.

65. Was there also a connection between Adler's essay and the music of Gustav Mahler? Personal friendship linked the musicologist and the composer, and at the same time Mahler had personal and thematic affinities with the Secession artists. Mahler composed *Das Lied von der Erde* in 1908–1909, overlapping with the publication of Adler's essay; it made use of heterophony and turned to the Tang Dynasty (eighth-century CE) Chinese poet for verses despairing over life's finitude. But there is no evidence that Adler and Mahler ever discussed the concept, nor that Mahler was inspired by Chinese music, although he may have heard recordings of it. Cf. the discussions in Donald Mitchell, *Gustav Mahler: Songs and Symphonies of Life and Death—Interpretations and Annotations* (Berkeley: University of California Press, 1985), 62–63, 125–127; Stephen E. Hefling, *Mahler: Das Lied von der Erde (The Song of the Earth)* (Cambridge: Cambridge University Press, 2000), 36–37; Martin Stelzle, *Das Eigene im Fremden: Gustav Mahler und der ferne Osten* (Hildesheim, Germany: Georg Olms Verlag, 2014), 205–282; Peter Revers, "Aspekte der Ostasienrezeption in Gustav Mahlers *Das Lied von der Erde*" [Freie Referate 13: Mahler/Schönberg], in Hermann Danuser and Tobias Plebuch, eds., *Musik als Text: Bericht über den internationalen Kongress der Gesellschaft für Musikforschung, Freiburg im Breisgau*, vol. 2: Freie Referate (Kassel, Germany: Bärenreiter, 1998), 376–383; Robert T. Mok, "Heterophony in Chinese Folk Music," in *Journal of the International Folk Music Council* 18 (1966): 14–23; Mahler Archive, "Das Lied von der Erde: The Literary Changes," http://www.mahlerarchives.net/Archive%20documents/DLvDE/DLvDE.htm, accessed June 29, 2016; and Teng-Leong Chew, "Tracking the Literary Metamorphosis in 'Das Lied von der Erde,'" http://www.mahlerarchives.net/Archive%20documents/daslied_lit.pdf," accessed June 29, 2016.

Chapter 6

1. For an introduction to the Phonogram Archive, see Artur Simon, ed., *Das Berliner Phonogramm-Archiv 1900–2000: Sammlungen der traditionellen Musik der Welt* (Berlin: Verlag für Wissenschaft und Bildung, 2000); and Susanne Ziegler, *Die Wachszylinder des Berliner Phonogramm-Archivs* (Berlin: Staatliche Museen zu Berlin, 2006). An authoritative introduction to the aims of the archive's founders is Lars-Christian Koch, "Images of Sound: Erich M. von Hornbostel and the Berlin Phonogram Archive," in Philip V. Bohlman, *The Cambridge History of World Music* (Cambridge: Cambridge University Press, 2013), 475–497. The figure for the number of recordings at the outbreak of the war comes from Ziegler, "Die Walzenbestände des Berliner Phonogramm-Archivs und die Geschichte ihrer Erschliessung," in *Wachszylinder des Berliner Phonogramm-Archivs*, 23.

The Berlin Phonogram Archive was not the first sound archive; the Vienna Phonogram Archive was established in 1899 by the Imperial Academy of Sciences. The Viennese archive had as its main goal human voice recordings. It did include musical recordings from around the world in its collections; A. Z. Idelsohn, mentioned in the introduction above, and Rudolf Pöch, discussed below, were among the contributors to its music collection. In contrast to the Berlin archive, however, it did not develop a systematic program for gathering or understanding the significance of music. On the Vienna Phonogram Archive, see Gerda Lechleitner, "Zukunftsvisionen retrospektiv betrachtet: Die Frühzeit des Phonogrammarchivs," *Das Audiovisuelle Archive* 45 (September 1999), http://www.phonogrammarchiv.at/wwwnew/literatur/lechleitner_g.pdf, accessed 20 July 2017; and Helmut Kowar, "Die musikethnologischen Bestände des Phonogrammarchivs," in *Das Audiovisuelle Archiv* 45 (September 1999), http://www.phonogrammarchiv.at/wwwnew/literatur/kowar2.pdf, accessed July 20, 2017.

2. Folk song and work song provided rich fields for investigation that educated Europeans could pursue at home. Some did. Herder was the great pioneer here, the first of a succession of nineteenth-century collectors. On Herder's originality—and indeed, on his coining of the term "folk song"—see Philip V. Bohlman, prologue to J. G. Herder and Philip Bohlman, *Song Loves the Masses: Herder on Music and Nationalism* (Berkeley: University of California Press, 2017), 5. On labor and work, an original nineteenth-century treatment was Karl Bücher, *Arbeit und Rhythmus* (Leipzig: Hirzel, 1896). See my discussion of this book in *The Return of the Gift: European History of a Global Idea* (Cambridge: Cambridge University Press, 2011), 125.

3. Multiple perspectives on Hornbostel's life and work can be found in Sebastian Klotz, ed., *Vom tönenden Wirbel menschlichen Tuns: Erich M. von Hornbostel als Gestaltpsychologe, Archivar und Musikwissenschaftler* (Berlin: Schibri-Verlag, 1998).

4. Susanne Ziegler, "The Wax Cylinder Project in Rescue of the Largest Collection of Old Sound Documents of Traditional Music from Around the World: Wax Cylinders and Shellac Records of the Berlin Phonogramm-Archiv," in Simon, *Berliner Phonogramm-Archiv*, 189–202; Albrecht Wiedmann, "A Few Technical Remarks on the Digital Conservation of the Old Inventory of the Berlin Phonogramm-Archiv," in ibid., 203–208. See also Susanne Ziegler, "Walzenbestände des Berliner Phonogramm-Archivs," in Ziegler, *Wachszylinder des Berliner Phonogramm-Archivs*, 19–34; and Albrecht Wiedmann, "Restaurierung und Digitalisierung der Bestände des Berliner Phonogramm-Archivs," in ibid., 35–38.

5. Carl Stumpf, "Das Berliner Phonogramm Archiv," *Wissenschaftliche Wochenschrift für Wissenschaft, Kunst und Technik*, February 22, 1908, reprinted in Simon, *Berliner Phonogramm-Archiv*, 65–84, here 69; Anon., "Exotische Musik," *Phonographische Zeitschrift* 12, no. 22 (June 1, 1911): 485.

6. See the tables in Ziegler, "Wax Cylinder Project," 190–191. More evidence of the breadth of the collection can be found in Simon, *Berliner Phonogramm-Archiv*, 230–252, and Ziegler, *Wachszylinder*, 467–474.

7. The National Library of Israel, Music Department, archives of Robert Lachmann, Mus26/C12: Jaap Kunst, Zum Tode Erich von Hornbostel's. Kunst published an admiring obituary for Hornbostel as "guru" of ethnomusicology that left out these details. See "On the Death of Erich von Hornbostel" (1937), reprinted in Simon, *Berliner Phonogramm-Archiv*, 121–129.

8. On the scientific goals of Hornbostel's research, see Koch, "Images of Sound," 484–496.

9. Erich von Hornbostel, "Über ein akustisches Kriterium für Kulturzusammenhänge," *Zeitschrift für Ethnologie*, 43 (1911): 601–615. By the standards of the nineteenth century, Hornbostel's search for analogies across great distances of time and place *was* scientific. One could have pointed at the time to the success of historical linguistics at constructing linguistic family trees reaching back into prehistory. Darwin's writings, too, contributed to the acceptance of this kind of inquiry as a cultural analogue to evolutionary theory. Franz Boas's critique of precisely this kind of "comparative method" was one of his major contributions to social scientific methodology, disputing decontextualized schemas and replacing them with empirically grounded research and direct causal connections. Boas's trenchant comments in *The Mind of Primitive Man* (New York: Macmillan, 1911) 174–196, were the outcome of a long process of reflection, and they continue to make for valuable methodological reading.

10. [Erich von Hornbostel, contributor, in] Felix von Luschan, *Anleitung für ethnographische Beobachtungen und Sammlungen in Afrika und Oceanien*, 5th ed., Abschnitt L, "Musik," (Berlin: Königliches Museum für Völkerkunde in Berlin, 1908), 1. Luschan thanked Hornbostel for his contribution in a letter of August 31, 1908, file Luschan, Phonogramm-Archiv, Berlin.

11. Hornbostel, "Musik," *Anleitung für ethnographische Beobachtungen*, 1.

12. Ibid., 14.

13. Luschan had an early and lasting fascination with skin color. As a visitor to the Paris Exposition of 1878, he counted among its foremost wonders the first woman from India he had ever seen. Writing to his parents, he called her gracious and refined (*vornehm*)—but almost the only detail he mentioned was her marvelous golden "patina." Berlin Staatsbibliothek, Nachlass Felix von Luschan, Karten 3. I. Konvolut "Briefe aus Paris 1878," Felix von Luschan an seine Eltern, S. 22–24v. On Luschan, see Andreas E. Furtwängler, "Luschan, Felix Ritter von," in *Neue Deutsche Biographie* 15 (1987), 528–529 (online edition), http://www.deutsche-biographie.de/pnd117319813.html, accessed June 17, 2016; and Peter Ruggendorfer and Hubert D. Szemethy, eds., *Felix von Luschan (1854–1924): Leben und Wirken eines Universalgelehrten* (Vienna: Böhlau, 2009).

14. The quote is from the general director to the Minister der geistlichen Angelegenheiten, May 11, 1904; see the archival volume housed in the Phonogram Archive, Berlin Ethnological Museum, Acta betreffend phonographisches Material, vol. 1, June 20, 1903 to December 31, 1908, Pars I B C1: Luschan to Stumpf, November 27, 1903; Stumpf to Luschan, November 30, 1903; Hornbostel to Luschan, December 21, 1905; Hornbostel to Luschan, January 5, 1906. Stumpf enumerated the archive's funding sources in "Das Berliner Phonogramm Archiv," reprinted in Simon, *Das Berliner Phonogramm-Archiv*, 68.

15. See the mention of the Kwakiutl recordings in Artur Simon, "The Musical Traditions of Mankind in the Berlin Phonogramm-Archiv 1900–2000: Collecting,

Preserving, Researching and Communicating," in idem., *Berliner Phonogramm-Archiv*, 50. On the Thompson River recordings, see Phonogramm-Archiv, Boas Thompson River 1897 file. Bruno Nettl gives a portrait of George Herzog in *Becoming an Ethnomusicologist: A Miscellany of Influences* (Lanham, MD: Scarecrow Press, 2013), 27–84.

16. On the related subject of Boas's intellectual affinities with Stumpf, see Harry Liebersohn, "'Culture' Crosses the Atlantic: The German Sources of 'The Mind of Primitive Man,'" in Ned Blackhawk and Isaiah L. Wilner, *Indigenous Visions: Rediscovering the World of Franz Boas* (New Haven: Yale University Press, 2018), 91–108. On Boas's scientific principles, see Douglas Cole, *Franz Boas: The Early Years, 1858–1906* (Seattle: University of Washington Press, 1999), 261–267.

17. Berlin Ethnological Museum, Acta betreffend die von dem Dr. Dorsey erworbenen [und] angebotenen Sammlungen aus Amerika. Vom 1. Mai 1903 bis [not filled in, should read 1907, H. L.], Vorgangsnummer: von 1903/0723 bis 1907/1440. Pars I.B.56. Dorsey to Karl von den Steinen, May 11, 1903 (E 723/1903), Karl von den Steinen to Dorsey, June 17,1903; Dorsey to von den Steinen, August 3, 1903 (E 1071/1903); von den Steinen to Dorsey, August 31, 1903 (Zu 1071/1903); and Dorsey to von den Steinen, September 15, 1903 (Zu 1071/1903).

18. Berlin Ethnological Museum, Pars I B.19: Die Reise des Professors Dr. Neuhauss nach der Südsee.

19. Phonogramm Archiv, Hornbostel Pawnee Nordamerika 1906 folder.

20. On Pöch, see Richard Thurnwald, "Rudolf Pöch," *Archiv für Anthropologie*, n.F., 19 (1923): 1–7; Don Niles, biographical sketch "Rudolf Pöch (1870–1921)," pp. 23–29 of the booklet included in Dietrich Schüller, general ed., *Tondokumente aus dem Phonogrammarchiv der Österreichischen Akademie der Wissenschaften: Gesamtausgabe der Historischen Bestände 1899–1950*, series 3: *Papua New Guinea (1904–1909)—The Collections of Rudolf Pöch, Wilhelm Schmidt, und Josef Winthuis*. Comments by Don Niles, music transcriptions by Erna Mack, ed. Gerda Lechleitner (Vienna: Verlag der Österreichischen Akademie der Wissenschaften, 2000); and Thomas Theye, ed., *Der geraubte Schatten: Eine Weltreise im Spiegel der ethnographischen Photographie* (Munich: Bucher, 1989), 374–376, 521–522.

21. Rudolf Pöch, "Reisen in Neu-Guinea in den Jahren 1904–1906," *Zeitschrift für Ethnologie* 39 (1907): 382–400, here 392–394, quotes from 394; idem., "Beobachtungen über Sprache, Gesänge und Tänze der Monumbo anlässlich phonographischer Aufnahmen in Deutsch-Neu-Guinea (in der Zeit vom 28. Juli bis zum 24. November 1904)," in *Mitteilungen und Sitzungsberichte der Anthropologischen Gesellschaft in Wien* 30 (1905): 230–237.

22. On Bartók's early fieldwork and its fin de siècle setting, see Judit Frigyesi, *Béla Bartók and Turn-of-the-Century Budapest* (Berkeley: University of California Press, 1998); and Malcolm Gillies, "Bartók, Béla," *Grove Music Online/ Oxford Music Online*. Oxford University Press, accessed April 21, 2017, http://www.oxfordmusiconline.com/subscriber/article/grove/music/40686pg2.fs. Bartók conveyed his excitement over his fieldwork experience in his letter to Martha and

Hermina Ziegler, February 3, 1909, in Béla Bartók, *Briefe*, ed. János Demény, trans. Klára L. Brüll et. al. (Budapest: Corvina Verlag, 1973), 104–108, esp. 105–106. Katie Trumpener offers a critical perspective in "Béla Bartók and the Rise of Comparative Ethnomusicology: Nationalism, Race Purity, and the Legacy of the Austro-Hungarian Empire," in Ronald Radano and Philip V. Bohlman, eds., *Music and the Racial Imagination* (Chicago: University of Chicago Press, 2000), 403–434. Cf. the judicious remarks in Timothy J. Cooley, "Folk Music in Eastern Europe," in Bohlman, *Cambridge History of World Music*, 352–370, here 355–357.

23. Vera Lampert, "Bartók and the Berlin School of Ethnomusicology," *Studia Musicologica: Academiae Scientiarum Hungaricae* 49, no. 3–4 (September 2008): 383–405.

24. Béla Bartók, "Comparative Music Folklore (1912)," in *Essays*, ed. Benjamin Suchoff (London: Faber and Faber, 1976), 155–158, here 158.

25. Bartók, "Music Folklore (1919)," in *Essays*, 159–163, here 159–160.

26. In this context what matters is place of residence, not place of birth or education. Boas settled in the United States and became a correspondent. Thurnwald settled in Germany and functioned as part of German institutions, in contrast to Pöch, who stayed in Vienna.

27. Phonogramm Archiv, Originalkorrespondenz Phonogrammarchiv, Korrespondenz des Phonogrammarchivs aus den Jahren 1903–1909, Luschan to Hornbostel, March 2, 1906; Luschan to Stumpf, June 18, 1906; Luschan to Hornbostel, July 27, 1906; and Luschan to Stumpf, October 19, 1906.

28. Harry Liebersohn, "Coming of Age in the Pacific: German Ethnography from Chamisso to Krämer," in *Worldly Provincialism: German Anthropology in the Age of Empire*, ed. H. Glenn Penny and Matti Bunzl (Ann Arbor: University of Michigan Press, 2003), 31–46; "Smend, Julius," entry in Ziegler, *Wachszylinder des Berliner Phonogramm-Archivs*, 377; https://de.wikipedia.org/wiki/Max_Girschner; https://de.wikipedia.org/wiki/Georg_August_Zenker; entry Georg Zenker in Ziegler, *Wachszylinder*, 391.

29. Berlin Ethnological Museum, Acta betreffend die Reise des Dr Koch nach Amerika 1903/1905. Pars I.B.44. Karl von den Steinen to the directorship of the Ethnological Museum / Ethnologisches Hilfscomité, February 20, 1903 (Zu E 190/1903); Theodor Koch to Karl von den Steinen, August 28, 1903 (E 1418/1903); von den Steinen to General-Verwaltung der Koniglichen Museen, December 22, 1904 (E 1679/1903); von den Steinen to Koch, January 12, 1904 (Zu E 1679/1903); von den Steinen to Koch, June 13, 1904 (E 323/1904); and Koch to General-Verwaltung der Koniglichen Museen, July 1, 1905 (copy). See also Ziegler, *Wachszylinder*, 167–169, 350–351.

For an introduction to the violent history of the rubber industry in South America and its immediate precursor in the Congo Free State, see Michael Taussig, *Shamanism, Colonialism, and the Wild Man: A Study in Terror and Healing* (Chicago: University of Chicago Press, 1986); and Adam Hochschild, *King Leopold's Ghost: A Story of Greed, Terror, and Heroism in Colonial Africa* (Boston: Houghton Mifflin, 1998).

30. On Thurnwald's biography, see Marion Melk-Koch's detailed but uncritical

monograph, *Auf der Suche nach der menschlichen Gesellschaft: Richard Thurnwald* (Berlin: Museum für Völkerkunde Berlin, 1989). Cf. Melville Herskovits on the racial cast of his work by the 1930s in his review of Thurnwald, "Black and White in East Africa," in *American Anthropologist* 39, no. 4 (October-December 1937), 690–692. On his anthropology before 1933, see Liebersohn, *Return of the Gift*, 104–122. .

31. Phonogramm Archiv, Thurnwald Melanesien, Richard Thurnwald to Erich von Hornbostel, March 5, 1908.

32. Ibid.

33. Phonogramm Archiv, Thurnwald Melanesien, Richard Thurnwald to Erich von Hornbostel, May 20, 1908.

34. Richard Thurnwald, "Im Bismarckarchipel und auf den Salomoinseln 1906–1909," *Zeitschrift für Ethnologie* 42, no. 1 (1910): 98–147.

35. On the expedition, see the online description on the Bundesarchiv website, https://www.bundesarchiv.de/oeffentlichkeitsarbeit/bilder_dokumente/00929/index.html.de, accessed June 3, 2016. See also Rainer F. Buschmann, *Anthropology's Global Histories: The Ethnographic Frontier in German New Guinea, 1870–1935* (Honolulu: University of Hawaii Press, 2009), on this and other German expeditions.

36. Phonogramm Archiv, Kaiserin Augusta Expedition 1912–13, Thurnwald to Hornbostel, March 23, 1913.

37. Ibid., September 1, 1913, March 24, 1914.

38. "Stumpf, "Das Berlin Phonogramm Archiv," 65–72.

39. Ibid., 72; my translation, but cf. the text translation by Rosee Riggs.

40. Ibid., 72–73.

41. Ibid., 73–82.

42. Carl Stumpf, *The Origins of Music*, trans. and ed. David Trippett (1911; Oxford: Oxford University Press, 2012).

43. Carl Lumholtz, *Among Cannibals: An Account of Four Years' Travels in Australia and of Camp Life with the Aborigines of Queensland* (London: Murray, 1889); Georg Schweinfurth, *The Heart of Africa: Three Years' Travels and Adventures in the Unexplored Regions of Central Africa, from 1868 to 1871*, trans. Ellen E. Frewer (New York: Harper, 1874).

44. Stumpf, *Origins of Music*, 72–74. He mentions his dislike of Wundt in the autobiography included in "Carl Stumpf: A Self-Portrait (1924)," 204.

45. Stumpf, *Origins of Music*, 74–76.

46. Ibid., 35–37, 43–50.

47. Ibid., 105.

48. Ibid., 106.

49. Guenther Roth, *Max Webers deutsch-englische Familiengeschichte 1800–1950, mit Briefen und Dokumenten* (Tübingen, Germany: J. C. B. Mohr [Paul Siebeck], 2001), 136–137, 144–145.

50. Max Weber, *Zur Musiksoziologie: Nachlass 1921*, ed. Christoph Braun and Ludwig Finscher, *Max Weber Gesamtausgabe*, section 1, vol. 14 (Tübingen, Germany: J. C. B. Mohr [Paul Siebeck], 2004).

51. Ibid., editors' introduction, 42–51, editors' footnote, 158n32; on Weber's appreciation of the phonograph, see Weber's text, 162, 179–180. Weber discusses the unexpected complexity of the music of the Patagonians on p. 183.

52. Weber, *Musiksoziologie*, 187–191.

53. Ibid., editor's introduction, 108, and Weber's text, 159–160.

54. Ibid., 106–107, 110–111. The student was Paul Honigsheim.

Chapter 7

1. The global expansion of European music is surveyed in Jürgen Osterhammel, "Globale Horizonte europäischer Kunstmusik, 1860–1930," in *Geschichte und Gesellschaft* 38, no. 1 (2012): 1–47. On Rimbaud, see the biography and analysis of his poetry in "Arthur Rimbaud," Poetry Foundation website, https://www.poetry foundation.org/poets/arthur-rimbaud, accessed December 13, 2017.

2. On the history of the phonograph industry, Peter Martland, *Recording History: The British Record Industry, 1888–1931* (Lanham: Scarecrow, 2013), includes valuable accounts of American, German, French, and British businesses. Pekka Gronow, "The Record Industry Comes to the Orient," *Ethnomusicology* 25, no. 2 (May 1981): 251–284, is a remarkable survey of the spread of the phonograph in the early twentieth century. Pekka Gronow and Ilpo Saunio, *An International History of the Recording Industry*, trans. Christopher Moseley (London: Cassell, 1999), follows the industry from its beginnings to the digital age. Roland Gelatt, *The Fabulous Phonograph: From Edison to Stereo*, rev. ed. (New York: Appleton-Century, 1965), continues to be a source of much valuable information. See also Peter Tschmuck, *Creativity and Innovation in the Music Industry* (Dordrecht, Netherlands: Springer, 2006). The distinction between Edison's "phonograph" and Berliner's "gramophone" was never consistently applied; unless context requires otherwise, I have used "phonograph" to refer to both.

3. Gelatt, *Fabulous Phonograph*, 39, cf. 100–101; Annegret Fauser, *Musical Encounters at the 1889 Paris World's Fair* (Rochester: University of Rochester Press, 2005), 279; Andreas Steen, *Zwischen Unterhaltung und Revolution: Grammophone, Schallplatten und die Anfänge der Musikindustrie in Shanghai, 1878–1937* (Wiesbaden, Germany: Harrassowitz Verlag, 2006), 33.

4. Amitabha Ghosh, "The Pre-Commercial Era of Wax Cylinder Recordings in India," in Amal Das Gupta, *Music and Modernity: North Indian Classical Music in an Age of Mechanical Reproduction* (Calcutta: Thema, 2007), 27.

5. On Gramophone in Australia, see EMI Archive, India, to May 1906; anonymous to Theodore Birnbaum, January 13, 1900; and Australia, 1900 to 1906, [London] Board Minutes of February 14, 1900 (penned copy). On the Victor-Gramophone division of world markets, see Gronow and Saunio, *International History*, 11. On Gaisberg in Russia, see Gronow, "Record Industry Comes to the Orient," 255, and Frederick W. Gaisberg, *The Music Goes Round* (1942; New York: Arno Press, 1977), 26–34.

6. On the Asian trip, see Gaisberg, *The Music Goes Round*, 48 ff.; and Fred Gaisberg, "Diaries, Part II: Going East (1902–1903)," ed. Hugo Strötbaum, 2010, at http://

www.recordingpioneers.com/docs/GAISBERG_DIARIES_2.pdf; Suresh Chandvankar, "Centenary of Indian Gramophone Records," in Gupta, *Music and Modernity*,
5. On Columbia's Charles J. Hopkins in Asia, see Steen, *Zwischen Unterhaltung und
Revolution*, 52, 124. On the early history of the phonograph in India, see Gerry Farrell,
Indian Music and the West (Oxford, UK: Clarendon Press, 1997).

7. On the spread of recorded music in Latin America, see Gronow and Saunio,
International History, 30; on Cairo and the Middle East, see A. J. Racy, "Record Industry and Egyptian Traditional Music, 1904–1932," *Ethnomusicology* 20, no. 1 (January
1976): 23–48, here 25.

8. "Afraid of Talking Machines: The Russian Government Prohibit Their Use
When Polish Patriotic Airs Are Used," *Talking Machine World* 3, no. 1 (January 1907):
1; "Columbia Co. Entertain [*sic*] Newsboys," *Talking Machine World* 3, no. 1 (January
1907): 1–2.

9. "Talking Machines in Africa,"*Talking Machine World* 3, no. 1 (January 1907): 51.

10. "Trade Booming in Mexico," *Talking Machine World* 3, no. 3 (March 1907): 25;
"Stevens' Mexican Trip," *Talking Machine World* 3, no. 6, 35–37.

11. "Japanese Will Bear Watching," *Talking Machine World* 3, no. 7 (July 1907): 4;
"Pays to Use Foreign Records," 3, no. 7, 28.

12. "Yankee 'Push' in the South Seas," *Talking Machine World* 3, no. 10 (October
1907): 9.

13. Advertisement, *Talking Machine World* 3, no. 10 (October 1907): 42.

14. "To Explore Philippines," *Talking Machine World* 3, no. 2 (February 1907): 33;
"'Talker' among Savages," 3, no. 12 (December 1907), 4.

15. "Truthful propaganda" was the phrase sometimes used to describe the Jesuit
Relations, the reports that Jesuits sent from their overseas missionary statements to
readers in Europe. The ambiguous description also fits the trade journal reports of
the early phonograph industry.

16. *Talking Machine World* 1, no. 4 (April 15, 1905): 23.

17. Source: *Talking Machine World*, 1905–1914. Spreadsheets were prepared with
the use of an Abbyy FineReader at the University of Illinois Library by Zachary Riebeling, and were converted into the tables and pie chart by Carl J. Liebersohn. In the
boom year, 1907, London shipments totaled 29,725, more than four times the figure
for Sydney, the second-largest market. The total export figures for 1914 show a steep
decline to 3,574 packages, probably because of wartime disruptions in the second
half of the year. There is no indication of the contents of the "packages," which may
have contained phonographs, disc records, cylinders, needles, or other machine
parts.

18. On the sharing arrangement, see Martland, *Recording History*, 149.

19. US Department of Commerce and Labor, Bureau of Foreign and Domestic
Commerce, *Foreign Trade in Musical Instruments* [Special Consular Reports, no. 55]
(Washington: Government Printing Office, 1912), 84, 86–87. According to the consul,
part of the 12 percent of the trade attributed to Hong Kong for the same year was
"really American" (84).

20. Cf. *Foreign Trade in Musical Instruments*, 88.

21. On the gold rush in Western Australia, see R. T. Appleyard, "Western Australia: Economic and Demographic Growth, 1850–1914," in C. T. Stannage, ed., *A New History of Western Australia* (Nedlands: University of Western Australia Press, 1981), 211–236, especially 212–227.

22. Johan Hartog, *History of the Netherlands Antilles*, vol. 3: *Curaçao: From Colonial Dependence to Autonomy* (Aruba: De Wit, 1968), 265–268, 278, and 304.

23. *Foreign Trade in Musical Instruments*, 68. The *Talking Machine World* figure for 1910 includes exports to two places in Argentina, Buenos Aires and Rosario, whose figures are aggregated above.

24. *Foreign Trade in Musical Instruments*, 63, 65, 68, 87, 88, 90.

25. For an introduction to the large literature on British and American polar expeditions, see Fergus Fleming, *Barrow's Boys* (New York: Grove Press, 1998); and David Crane, *Scott of the Antarctic: A Life of Courage and Tragedy in the Extreme South* (London: HarperCollins, 2005). On the German expeditions, see Herbert Abel und Hans Jessen, *Kein Weg durch das Packeis: Anfänge der deutschen Polarforschung (1868–1889)* (Bremen, Germany: Schünemann, 1954). On Boas, see Douglas Cole and Ludger Müller-Wille, "Franz Boas' Expedition to Baffin Island, 1883–1884," in *Études Inuit / Inuit Studies* 8, no. 1 (1984): 37–63; and Laurel Kendall and Igor Krupnik, eds., *Constructing Cultures Then and Now: Celebrating Franz Boas and the Jesup North Pacific Expedition* (Washington: Arctic Studies Center, National Museum of Natural History, Smithsonian Institution, 2003).

26. "The Talking Machine Excites Interest among the Aleutian Islanders," *Talking Machine World* 1, no. 1 (January 1905): 6. Contemporaries in the early nineteenth century were eloquent critics of the Russian subjugation of the Aleuts. See, for example, Adelbert von Chamisso, *A Voyage around the World with the Romanzov Exploring Expedition in the Years 1815–1818 in the Brig 'Rurik,' Captain Otto von Kotzebue*, trans. and ed. Henry Kratz (Honolulu: University of Hawai'i Press, 1986), 95–96. On the civilizing mission, see Jürgen Osterhammel, *Europe, the "West" and the Civilizing Mission* (London: German Historical Institute, 2006); Michael Adas, "'Contested Hegemony: The Great War and the Afro-Asian Assault on the Civilizing Mission Ideology,'" *Journal of World History* 15, no. 1 (2004): 31–63; and Stefan Hübner and Diego Olstein, eds., Special Issue on Preaching the Civilizing Mission and Modern Cultural Encounters, *Journal of World History* 27, no. 3 (September 2016), including Harry Liebersohn, "Introduction: The Civilizing Mission": 383–387.

27. "Music at the North Pole: Proof of the Civilizing Influence of the Talking Machine Submitted by Mr. Hutchinson," *Talking Machine World* 1, no. 2 (February 15, 1905): 10. Among the bizarre features of this report is its extension of the word "Indian" to the extreme north. On Hutchinson, see the biographical sketch by Edith Hayes in *Idaho State Historical Society Reference Series* 854 (1987), http://www.history .idaho.gov/sites/default/files/uploads/reference-series/0854.pdf , accessed September 7, 2015. The Wikipedia entry and YouTube playlist for "The Holy City," written by Michael Maybrick with lyrics by Fredric Weatherly, document its enduring fame.

28. William R. Hunt, "Stefansson, Vilhjalmur," *American National Biography Online*, http://www.anb.org.proxy2.library.illinois.edu/articles/20/20–00985.html?a=1&f=Stefansson&ia=-at&ib=-bib&d=10&ss=3&q=4, accessed August 15, 2017.

29. The EMI Archive still has it. See Adam Sherwin, "Revealed: The Secret of Captain Scott's Playlist," reprinted from *The Independent*, May 9, 2012, on the EMI blog, The Sound of the Hound, May 11, 2012, https://soundofthehound.com/2012/05/11/revealed-the-secrets-of-captain-scotts-playlist/, accessed September 7, 2015.

30. Raymond Sooy, "Memoirs of my Recording and Traveling Experiences for the Victor Talking Machine Company, 1898–1925," David Sarnoff Library, http://www.davidsarnoff.org/soo.html, accessed November 12, 2013.

31. Edward N. Burns, "Developing Our Export Trade," *Talking Machine World* 4, no. 2 (February 1908): 18–21.

Chapter 8

1. For a general account of Edison's invention and promotion of the phonograph in the context of his skills at creating a laboratory and a corporate structure to promote his inventions, see Leonard DeGraaf, *Edison and the Rise of Innovation* (New York: Sterling, 2013), chapter 3. On the late-nineteenth-century beginnings of the phonograph industry, see Pekka Gronow and Ilpo Saunio, *International History of the Recording Industry* (London: Cassell, 1998), 3–5.

2. Thomas Edison, "The Phonograph and its Future," *North American Review* 126 (May-June 1878): 527–536.

3. Edison National Historic Site Archives, Primary Printed–Edison Companies, Phonograph Division, box 26, EDIS-54100, National Phonograph Co., Foreign Record Catalogues, 1902–1904, *Edison Gem Phonograph: Directions for Setting Up and Operating*; *How to Make Records at Home with an Edison Phonograph*. Hereinafter Edison Archives. These two instruction manuals were not dated. The archival copies have the dates 1912 and 1908 penciled on them respectively, which I have accepted as valid.

4. DeGraaf, *Edison and the Rise of Innovation*, 110–112.

5. Edison Archives, Recording Division and Related Records, Phonograph Artists Files, box 2 (A–Bar), Alfredo; Allessios; De Filippis Mandolin Orchestra. There is a photocopied handwritten version of this memorandum, plus a typed copy to the London office bearing the date December 20, 1911.

6. Edison Archives, Recording Division and Related Records, Phonograph Artists Files, box 12 (Ke–Laz), Kingsman, Tracy. Tracy J. Kingman to W. H. Meadowcroft, November 19, 1912; unsigned to Kingman, November 21, 1912.

7. Edison Archives, Recording Division and Related Records, Phonograph Artists Files, box 14 (Mars–Mun), Morgan, Maud. My thanks to Leonard de Graaf for discussing Edison's recording criteria with me.

8. David Suisman discusses the contrast between Edison and Eldridge Johnson at Victor in *Selling Sounds: The Commercial Revolution in American Music* (Cambridge, MA: Harvard University Press, 2009), 104.

9. Edison Archives, Recording Division and Related Records, Phonograph Artists Files, box 2 (A–Bar): Eva Abbey–Irwin Abrams file, letter from [?] Cronkhite [sic], June 17, 1906, to William E. Gilmore and W. H. Miller.

10. Ibid., box 14 (Mars–Mun): Frederic Martin file, William H. Miller to Frank L. Dyer, February 26, 1909.

11. Ibid., box 2: Agostinelli file [Unsigned], Recording Department, to Adelina Agostinelli Quiroli, April 3, 1912. The file includes both correspondence and the signed contract.

12. Ibid., box 12 (Ke–Laz): Fritz Kreisler file, C. F. Coffin to Frank L. Dyer, October 26, 1909.

13. Edison Archives, Edison Laboratory Notebooks, N-12–00–00–2, 1912. The notebooks are not paginated and the entries are not dated.

14. Edison Archives, Primary Printed–Edison Companies, Phonograph Division, box 26, EDIS-54100, National Phonograph Co., Foreign Record Catalogues, 1902–1904, "Edison Gold Moulded Records: British, European, Asiatic, Canadian, Mexican," December 15, 1904.

15. Ibid., 1908–1910, "Edison Gold Moulded Records: Foreign Selections" (pencil: 1908); "Edison Records: Belgian, Bohemian, Chinese, Danish, Dutch, Japanese, Hebrew, Hungarian, Italian, Norwegian, Polish, Swedish" (1910); "Edison Records: Spanish, Mexican, Argentine, Cuban, Porto Rican [sic], Portuguese & Filipino Selections" (1910); "Edison Records: German Selections" (1910); "Edison Records: French Selections" (1910).

16. *Voice of the Victor* 8, no. 6 (June 1913): 14. Victor's trade magazine was actually slower than its Edison counterpart to promote its recordings for the immigrant American market.

17. *Edison Phonograph Monthly* 1, no. 1 (March 1903): 2; and 2, no., 3 (May 1904): 2, 8. The German song title parodied the popular "Du, du, liegst mir im Herzen." For descriptions of the different cylinders, see the UCSB (University of California, Santa Barbara, Library) Cylinder Audio Archive, with a description of the gold-moulded cylinders at http://cylinders.library.ucsb.edu/history-goldmoulded.php, accessed July 29, 2018.

18. *Edison Phonograph Monthly* 1, no. 1 (March 1903): 2.

19. *Edison Phonograph Monthly* 1, no. 3 (May 1903): 2.

20. Ibid.; Wikipédia France, http://fr.wikipedia.org/wiki/Frank_Seiden.

21. *Edison Phonograph Monthly* 1, no. 1: 6.

22. *Edison Phonograph Monthly* 1, no. 7 (September 1903): 3.

23. *Edison Phonograph Monthly* 1, no. 2 April 1903): 2; and 2, no. 3 (May 1904), 2.

24. Leonard C. McChesney to Thomas Edison, January 7, 1909, Thomas A. Edison, *Thomas A. Edison Papers : A Selective Microfilm Edition*, ed. Thomas E. Jeffrey (Frederick, MD: University Publications of America, 1985–), reel 217, COM-35, National Phonograph Company Records, correspondence, domestic, 1909, pp. 1 ff. Hereinafter cited as Edison Papers.

25. *Edison Phonograph Monthly* 1, no. 2 (April 1903): 3.

26. *Edison Phonograph Monthly* 1, no. 7 (August 1903): 1.

27. Joseph H. White, European sales manager, to W. E. Gilmore, Orange, NJ, president, National Phonograph Co., January 20, 1904, Edison Papers, part 4, 1899–1910, Company Records: National Phonograph Co., reel 216, COM-34, p. 2.

28. Walter Stevens to W. E. Gilmore, April 11, 1907, Edison Papers, part 4, 1899–1910, Company Records: National Phonograph Co., reel 216, COM-34, pp. 811 ff.

29. Walter Stevens to Frank Dyer, December 8, 1908, Edison Papers, part 4, 1899–1910, Company Records: National Phonograph Co., Reel 216, COM-34, 1153 ff.; Edison Archives, C. C. Squire to William E. Gilmore, December 13, 1907, National Phonograph Company, William E. Gilmore files (1907: advertising–foreign–general), box 12, NPS Cat # EDIS-58066.

30. Department of Commerce and Labor, Bureau of Foreign and Domestic Commerce, *Foreign Trade in Musical Instruments* [Special Consular Reports, no. 55] (Washington: Government Printing Office, 1912), 63.

31. Edison Archives, Walter Stevens, Mexico City, May 2, 1907, to Gilmore, National Phonograph Company, William E. Gilmore files (1907: advertising–foreign–general), March-April 1907, box 12, NPS Cat# EDIS-58066.

32. Walter L. Stevens to W. E. Gilmore, June 11, 1907, Edison Papers, part 4, 1899–1910, Company Records: National Phonograph Co., reel 216, COM-34, pp. 818 ff.

33. Ibid.

34. Walter L. Stevens to W. E. Gilmore, June 17, 1907, Edison Papers, part 4, 1899–1910, Company Records: National Phonograph Co., reel 216, COM-34, 826 ff.

35. Walter L. Stevens to W. E. Gilmore, May 8, 1908, Edison Papers, part 4, 1899–1910, Company Records: National Phonograph Co., reel 216, COM-34, pp. 1059 ff.; "Personal," *Edison Phonograph Monthly* 6, no. 6 (June 1908): 13.

36. Edison Archives, letter from Joseph Beaudry, music dealer and publisher, Quebec, 263 rue St.-Jean, January 12, 1907, to the National Phonograph Company, forwarded by W. McChesney to Gilmore, January 14, 1907, William E. Gilmore files (1907: advertising–foreign–general), March-April 1907, box 12, NPS Cat# EDIS-58066.

37. Joseph L. McKay (?) to Frank L. Dyer, January 31, 1909, Edison Papers, reel 217, COM-35, National Phonograph Company Records, correspondence, domestic, 1909, pp. 33 ff.

38. [Frank L. Dyer] to Thomas Graf, February 9, 1910, Edison Papers, reel 217, COM-35, National Phonograph Company Records Correspondence, foreign, 1910; Graf to Dyer, May 10, 1910; Graf to Dyer, November 14, 1910.

39. Walter Stevens to Frank Dyer, February 16, 1909, Report of orders received by the foreign department for the month of December 1908, Edison Papers, reel 217, COM-35, National Phonograph Company Records, correspondence, foreign, 1909, pp. 151 ff..

40. Edison Papers, Foreign Department, letterbook I, Walter L. Stevens to Messrs Ramsey and Company, Hong Kong, May 21, 1908, p. 601; to Mesara Y. Narayan and

Bros., Madras, India, May 29, 1908, p. 604; to Mr. John G. Hoamer, American Board of Commissioners for Foreign Missions, Boston, MA, May 28, 1908, p. 630. Letterbook II, Stevens to Oxan Ourfalian, Adana, Turkey, January 7, 1909, p. 652.

41. Library of Congress. Emile Berliner Collection, Recorded Sound Reference Center, Motion Picture, Broadcasting and Recorded Sound Division. Diaries and journals, miscellaneous notes and papers, box 13 / RPA 00843, folder 1: Journal of Cora A. Berliner and copies, 1889–1890. The journal is not paginated. The collection is cited hereinafter as Library of Congress, Berliner Collection.

Emile Berliner had made a previous return trip to Germany in 1881. See Frederic William Wile, *Emile Berliner: Maker of the Microphone* (Indianapolis, IN: Bobbs-Merrill, 1926), 162.

42. Library of Congress, Berliner Collection, journal of Cora Berliner. On Samoa, see Paul M. Kennedy, *The Samoan Tangle: A Study in Anglo-German-American Relations, 1878–1900* (New York: Barnes and Noble, 1974), 1–50, 122, 133–134, 239, 240, 257, 263–264; and Harry Liebersohn, "Coming of Age in the Pacific: German Ethnography from Chamisso to Krämer," in *Worldly Provincialism: German Anthropology in the Age of Empire*, ed. H. Glenn Penny and Matti Bunzl (Ann Arbor: University of Michigan Press, 2003), 31–46.

43. Library of Congress, Emile Berliner Collection, journal of Cora A. Berliner.

44. Wile, *Berliner*, dedication page, preface, and foreword (unpaginated).

45. On the synthesis of German, Jewish, and American influences in the making of the modern music industry, see David Suisman, *Selling Sounds: The Commercial Revolution in American Music* (Cambridge, MA: Harvard University Press, 2009), 34–35.

46. Peter Schulze, "Die Berliners: Eine jüdische Familie in Hannover (1773–1943)," in Peter Becker et al., *100 Jahre Schallplatte: Von Hannover in die Welt* [Beiträge und Katalog zur Ausstellung vom 29. September 1987 bis 10. Januar 1988 im Historischen Museum Am Hohen Ufer, Hannover] (Hamburg: Polygram, 1987), 75–81.

In Berliner's papers at the Library of Congress is a memorial volume of the Jewish charitable association, *Gedenkblätter zu Erinnerung an den 105: Stiftungstag des Wohltätigkeitsvereins der Synagogengemeinde Hannover, 1762–1912* (Hannover, Germany: Druck der Vereinsbücherei zu Hannover, 1912). On the cover, Emile Berliner wrote: "On p. 52 account of my grandfathers [sic] 42 years service in Jewish charity work also p.13 & p.77 etc." Library of Congress, Berliner Collection, box 6, folder 2: Books–Gedenkblätter, 1879–1928. As for Emile Berliner himself, he worked for decades in philanthropic causes. He led the drive for pasteurization of milk in Washington, and in 1908 he created the first major postdoctoral fellowship for women in the United States, the Sarah Berliner Research Fellowship. See Wile, *Berliner*, 234–250, 302; and the obituary in the *New York Herald Tribune*, August 4, 1929, in Library of Congress, Berliner collection online, Digital ID berl 02010810.

47. On the Samson School and the social mobility of its students, see Simone Lässig, *Jüdische Wege ins Bürgertum: Kulturelles Kapital und sozialer Aufstieg im 19. Jahrhundert* (Göttingen, Germany: Vandenhoeck und Ruprecht, 2014), 607–608. Cf. Wile, *Emile Berliner*, 9–10.

48. Wile, *Emile Berliner*, 15–41, quotes from 38 and 40.

49. Ibid., 40; Gottlob Kirschmer, "Müller, Johann Heinrich" in *Neue Deutsche Biographie* 18 (1997): 329–330 [online edition], http://www.deutsche-biographie.de/pnd117592803.html. Wile calls the book *Synopsis of Physics and Meteorology*, a name that leaves unclear which work Berliner actually read. "Synopsis" does not match the title of the one-volume American edition, Johann Muller [sic], *Principles of Physics and Meteorology* (Philadelphia: Lea and Blanchard, 1848), which in any case was an abbreviated version, with its section of some 45 pages on acoustics and 130 on electricity. It more nearly matches the title of one of the German editions, which was designed for pre-university studies, Johann Müller, *Grundriss der Physik und Meteorologie: Für Lyceen, Gymnasium, Gewerbe- und Realschulen, so wie zum Selbstunterrichte*, 2nd ed. (Braunschweig, Germany: Viewig, 1850), but this work lacks a section on electricity and would have been too elementary for Berliner's needs. The German version of the full-length university textbook, Johannes Müller, *Lehrbuch der Physik und Meteorologie*, 7th ed., 2 vols. (Braunschweig, Germany: Vieweg, 1868), contains 1,798 woodcut illustrations. Volume 1 has an entire section of some 130 pages on acoustics; volume 2 has almost 500 pages on electricity. It seems most likely that Berliner used this demanding but pedagogically conceived introduction.

50. Wile, *Emile Berliner*, 71, 107–112, 117–129, 156–159. Berliner also had some contact with Joseph Henry, director of the Smithsonian Institution until 1878, thanks to the mediation of Adolphus Simeon Solomons, a prominent Jewish businessman and philanthropist whom Wile describes as a "book dealer," one of his many occupations. The connection to Solomons offers a glimpse into the kind of social networks that furthered Berliner's scientific and social success in the United States. Solomons came from a well-established Sephardic Jewish family (his father had emigrated from London) and he moved freely in upper-class political and philanthropic circles in the United States. He was prominent in aiding Russian Jews in Russia, and also in the United States after their immigration. In later years, Berliner remained grateful to Solomons as one of his earliest patrons; his family and theirs were still linked by friendship in the 1920s. The social networks were Jewish, but not exclusively so, and—for Western European Jews—they overlapped rather easily with Protestant elites. Wile, *Emile Berliner*, 120; Marvin Rusinek, "Guide to the Papers of Adolphus Simeon Solomons (1826–1910), undated, 1841–1966," American Jewish Historical Society, Center for Jewish History, P-28, http://digifindingaids.cjh.org/?pID=364847.

51. Wile, *Emile Berliner*, 119–120, 156–157, 162–165; Dieter Tasch, "Die 'Grammophon' in Hannover: 100 Jahre Schallplattengeschichte," in *100 Jahre Schallplatte*, 41–74, here 44–45.

52. Wile, *Emile Berliner*, 171–201.

53. Ibid., 171, 202–215.

54. Tasch, "Die 'Grammophon' in Hannover," *100 Jahre Schallplatte*, 52–53.

55. Ibid., 53–54.

56. On the early history of Berliner's business, see Benjamin L. Aldridge, *The*

Victor Talking Machine Company, ed. Frederic Bayh (Camden, NJ: RCA Sales Corporation, 1964), available on the Sarnoff Library website at http://www.davidsarnoff.org/vtm.html.

57. "The Berliner Gram-o-phone Company of Canada," Libraries and Archives of Canada, https://www.collectionscanada.gc.ca/gramophone/028011-3005-e.html.

58. Peter Martland, *Since Recordings Began: EMI–The First 100 Years*, consultant ed. Ruth Edge (London: EMI, 1997), 13.

59. Ibid., 38; Peter Martland, *Recording History: The British Record Industry, 1888–1931* (Lanham, MD: Scarecrow, 2013), 47–48.

60. Martland, *Since Recordings Began*, 32; Geoffrey Jones, "The Gramophone Company: An Anglo-American Multinational, 1898–1931," *Business History Review* 59, no. 1 (Spring, 1985): 76–100, here 79.

61. Martland, *Since Recordings Began*, 41–43; and *Recording History*, 54.

62. Martland, *Since Recordings Began*, 49.

63. E. R. Fenimore Johnson, *His Master's Voice Was Eldridge R. Johnson*, 2nd ed. (Milford, DE: n.p., 1974), 42–43.

Chapter 9

1. On Owen, see Peter Martland, *Since Recordings Began: EMI–The First 100 Years*, consultant ed. Ruth Edge (London: EMI, 1997), 36–37. For a more detailed history of the Gramophone Company, see Peter Martland, *Recording History: The British Record Industry, 1888–1931* (Lanham, MD: Scarecrow, 2013).

2. The EMI Group Archive Trust, Australia, 1900–1906: box 1, Australia/NZ, especially the board meeting minutes of September 13, 1905. Box 2, Australia/NZ 1900, Peter Bohanna to Gramophone, March 27, 1900; Bohanna to William Barry Owen, November 26, 1901; A/F. for Gramophone to Bohanna, June 25, 1901; Bohanna [to Owen], April 23, 1901. Box 3, Australia 1902, Bohanna to Owen, May 16, 1903. Hereinafter EMI Archive.

3. EMI Archive, Registrator Sammelband, Von Herrn Direktor N. M. Rodkinson erledigte Korrespondenz . . . 1904/05: Norbert Rodkinson to Theodore Birnbaum, October 29, 1904; Rodkinson to Joseph Berliner, December 7, 1904. Russian general correspondence, 1903/1 of 2: Rodkinson to William Barry Owen, April 2, 1903. Russian general correspondence, 1904/2 of 2: Owen to Rodkinson, June 9, 1904; Rodkinson to Birnbaum, 27/10 May [sic] 1904. Russian General Correspondence, 1905: Gramophone, London to Cie Française du Gramophone Brussels, December 18, 1905.

4. EMI Archive, India to May 1906: unsigned [William Barry Owen] to Jack Watson Hawd, January 13, 1900; unsigned [Owen] to Theodore B. Birnbaum, January 13, 1900; Hawd to unnamed recipient, December 19, 1901. India 1906: Norbert Rodkinson to Theodore Birnbaum, December 7, [1906?]; unsigned [Rodkinson] to James Muir, July 17, 1907; Rodkinson to Birnbaum, March 25, 1907.

The name of The Gramophone Company changed several times. For the sake of clarity, I refer to it in the text continuously under its original name, to which it returned until its absorption into EMI in 1931.

5. EMI Archive, India to May 1906: Charles E. Gilpin to Gramophone, May 13, 1906.

6. EMI Archive, India 1907: Norbert Rodkinson to Birnbaum, March 25, 1907; Gramophone (penciled: P. J. O.) to Charles E. Gilpin, March 27, 1907. On Rodkinson, see Martland, *Since Records Began*, 70–71.

7. EMI Archive, minutes of the board of directors, report of William Barry Owen to the chairman and directors of Gramophone, October 8, 1902.

8. EMI Archive, China to 1915: T. D. Addis to Gramophone, October 1903. On Moutrie, which was critical to selling in the Chinese market, see Andreas Steen, *Zwischen Unterhaltung und Revolution. Grammophone, Schallplatten und die Anfänge der Musikindustrie in Shanghai, 1878–1937* (Wiesbaden, Germany: Harrassowitz Verlag, 2006), 118–121.

9. EMI Archive, India to May 1906: Gilpin to Gramophone, May 13, 1906. On William Gaisberg's recording tour, see Michael S. Kinnear, *The Gramophone Company's First Indian Recordings, 1899–1908* (Bombay: Popular Prakashan, 1994), 27–33.

10. EMI Archive, minutes of the board of directors, meeting of January 10, 1906.

11. EMI Archive, meeting of March 14, 1906. Joseph Berliner was not present at the March meeting.

12. EMI Archive, minutes of the board, June 23, 1906. The hiring of Siegfried Sanders is mentioned in Kinnear, *The Gramophone Company in India*, 30.

13. On India, see Kinnear, *The Gramophone Company's First Indian Recordings*, 30–32; and Pekka Gronow, "The Record Industry Comes to the Orient," *Ethnomusicology* 25, no. 2 (May 1981): 251–284, here 257–258.

14. The above biographical account closely follows Jerrold Northrop Moore, *A Voice in Time: The Gramophone of Fred Gaisberg, 1873–1951* (London: Hamish Hamilton, 1976), 1–10, quote from 7. The first names of Gaisberg and his father point to Prussian family origins, not Bavarian as Moore reports. On Tainter, see Steven E. Schoenherr, "Charles Sumner Tainter and the Graphophone," http://history.sandiego.edu/gen/recording/graphophone.html, accessed January 20, 2018. There is a helpful chronology of these early years of the phonograph industry on the website of the Library and Archives Canada, https://www.collectionscanada.gc.ca/gramophone/028011-3009-e.html.

15. Frederick W. Gaisberg, *The Music Goes Round: An Autobiography* (1942; New York: Arno Press, 1977), 18.

16. Ibid., 17. On Giannini's recording career, which began with Berlin in 1896, see "Ferruccio Giannini (vocalist: tenor vocal)," in *Discography of American Historical Recordings*, http://adp.library.ucsb.edu/index.php/talent/detail/40759/Giannini_Ferruccio_vocalist_tenor_vocal, accessed December 4, 2015.

17. Gaisberg, *Autobiography*, 24.

18. Ibid., 26.

19. Ibid., 45–48. Cf. David Suisman, *Selling Sounds: The Commercial Revolution in American Music* (Cambridge, MA: Harvard University Press, 2009), 104.

20. Gaisberg, *Autobiography*, 26–27.

21. Ibid., 29–32.

22. Ibid., 33–34.

23. Ibid., 34.

24. Ibid., 49.

25. Ibid., 55; Fred Gaisberg, "Diaries, Part II: Going East (1902–1903), ed. Hugo Strötbaum 2010, in Hugo Strötbaum, *Recording Pioneers*, http://www.recording pioneers.com/docs/GAISBERG_DIARIES_2.pdf, 14.

Maud Foster (performer), "Her Golden Hair Was Hanging Down Her Back," lyrics and music by Felix McGlennon and Monroe Rosenfeld, Library of Congress Audio, http://www.loc.gov/item/berl.13563, accessed December 9, 2013. The complete lyrics, longer than the recording medium would then have permitted, can be found online at *American Old Time Song Lyrics*: theater, music-hall, nostalgic, Irish & historic old songs, vol. 44, "And Her Golden Hair Was Hanging Down Her Back," http://www.traditionalmusic.co.uk/songster/44-and-her-golden-hair-was-hanging -down-her-back.htm, accessed December 9, 2013.

26. Gaisberg, *Autobiography*, 55–56. For information and recordings, see the National Jukebox project of the Library of Congress, http://www.loc.gov/jukebox/ recordings/detail/id/2730/, accessed December 10, 2013.

27. Gaisberg, "Diaries, Part 2," 16–17.

28. Vikram Sampath, *"My Name is Gauhar Jaan!": The Life and Times of a Musician* (New Delhi: Rupa, 2010), 109.

29. Ibid., 99.

30. Sampath brings to life the rich musical culture assimilated by Gaujar Jaan in ibid., 34–39.

31. See Andrew F. Jones, *Yellow Music: Media Culture and Colonial Modernity in the Chinese Jazz Age* (Durham, NC: Duke University Press, 2001).

Chapter 10

1. Edwin Hein, *65 Jahre Deutsche Grammophon Gesellschaft 1898–1963* (n.p.: Deutsche Grammophon Gesellschaft, 1963), 8.

2. Hein, *Deutsche Grammophon*, 10–11.

3. To be sure, recording classical singers was an important part of Victor's marketing strategy. As we have seen above, the Victrola had the attraction of a stately piece of furniture for middle-class living rooms, and Victor's high-end line, the Red Seal records, set it apart from its competitors. But there was a fundamental contrast between the American middle-class yearning for social respectability and the established status of German elites, especially when it came to music. As for Britain, Peter Martland gives a valuable account of Gramophone's marketing of prestige performers to British consumers, beginning with Caruso; they seem to have been a middling case between the American and German positions on the spectrum of connoisseurship and educationally defined status consciousness. See Martland, *Recording History: The British Record Industry, 1888–1931* (Lanham, MD: Scarecrow, 2013), chapter 7.

4. Hein, *Deutsche Grammophon*, 16–17.

5. In 1908, Joseph Berliner negotiated with bank representatives over purchasing the heavily indebted record firm for Gramophone. Joseph Berliner to Theodore Birnbaum, March 23, 1908, letter from the EMI archive in Hayes cited in Hugo Strötbaum, "Director Dies, Beka Record Company Up for Grabs," *Recording Pioneers* (online), http://www.recordingpioneers.com/docs/BEKA_Director_Dies_1908.pdf, translation in text, original as Document E, accessed December 10, 2015.

6. Pekka Gronow, "Beka Records: A Brief History," in Pekka Gronow, Christiane Hofer, and Frank Wonneberg, eds., *Contributions to the History of the Record Industry / Beiträge zur Geschichte der Schallplattenindustrie: "Our Trip Around the World / Unsere Reise um die Erde: The Oriental Expedition of Beka Records in 1905–1906,"* Lindström Project 6 (Vienna: Gesellschaft für Historische Tonträger, 2015), 48–53, here 51, drawing on research by Michael Kinnear.

7. For Bumb's text and commentaries on the recordings from different countries, see Gronow et. al., *Contributions to the History of the Record Industry*, Lindström Project, vol. 6.

8. Christiane Hofer, Pekka Gronow and Frank Wonneberg, foreword to *Contributions to the History of the Record Industry*, Lindström Project, vol. 6, 5–6; Hugo Strötbaum, "The Beka Recording Trips to Turkey and Egypt," Lindström Project, vol. 6, 66–69; Peter Tschmuck, *Creativity and Innovation in the Music Industry*, trans. Marco Abel (Dordrecht, Netherlands: Springer, 2006), 22; Peter Martland, *Recording History: The British Record Industry, 1888–1931* (Lanham, MD: Scarecrow, 2013), 112–114; Alfred Gutmann, ed., *25 Jahre Lindström 1904–1929* (Berlin: Carl Lindström, 1929), 12; Paul Vernon, "Odeon Records: Their 'Ethnic' Output," , in *Musical Traditions: The Magazine for Traditional Music throughout the World*, http://www.mustrad.org.uk/index.htm (home page), Article MT003, accessed February 28, 2018. Dietrich Schulz-Köhn, *Die Schallplatte auf dem Weltmarkt* (Berlin: Reher, 1940) contains useful information but is tainted by Nazi ideology and must be used with caution.

9. "Die bevorstehende neue Saison," *Phonographische Zeitschrift* 3, no. 15 (July 16, 1902): 179–180; "Der Beginn der Hochsaison," *Phonographische Zeitschrift* 3, no. 24 (October 22, 1902): 269–270.

10. For a sampling of some of the more important business reports, see Arthur Knoch, "Die Geschäftsaussichten am Jahresbeginn," *Phonographische Zeitschrift* 12, no. 1 (January 5, 1911): 3–4; Knoch, "Die Sprechmaschine als Exportartikel," *Phonographische Zeitschrift* 12, no. 6 (February 9, 1911): 93–95; Knoch, "Fortentwicklung des deutschen Sprechmaschinen-Export," *Phonographische Zeitschrift* 12, no. 14 (April 6, 1911): 345–347; Knoch, "Sprechmaschinen-Export—Handelsbeziehungen Deutschlands im Jahre 1911," *Phonographische Zeitschrift* 13, no. 5 (February 1, 1912): 81–83; Ludwig W. Schmidt, "Deutsche Phonographen für Südamerika," *Phonographische Zeitschrift*, 13, no.18 (May 2, 1912): 399–401.

11. Department of Commerce and Labor, *Foreign Trade in Musical Instruments* [Special Consular Reports, no. 55] (Washington: Government Printing Office, 1912), 68.

12. G. S., "Wie kann die deutsche Phonographen-Industrie ihren Export nach Ostasien erhöhen?" *Phonographische Zeitschrift* 13, no. 38 (September 19, 1912): 877–978.

13. The EMI Group Archive Trust, India to May 1906, Charles Gilpin to Theodore Birnbaum, March 8, 1906.

14. The texts are now available in Gronow et al., *Contributions to the History of the Record Industry*, Lindström Project, vol. 6, but I have used the original serialized articles: Heinrich Bumb, "Unsere Reise um die Erde," *Phonographische Zeitschrift* 7, no. 27 (July 5, 1906): 561–563; 7, no. 28 (July 12, 1906): 582–584; 7, no. 29 (July 19, 1906): 602–604; 7, no. 30 (July 26, 1906): 622–23; 7, no. 31 (August 2, 1906): 643–645; 7, no. 32 (August 9, 1906): 662–663; 7, no. 33 (August 16, 1906): 692; 7, no. 34 (August 23, 1906): 718–720; 7, no. 35 (August 30, 1906): 759–760; 7, no. 36 (September 6, 1906): 788–789; and 7, no. 37 (September 13, 1906): 808–809. Details about the steamer to Bombay and Darjeeling are from 7, no. 27: 563, and 7, no. 29: 602.

15. Suresh Chandvankar, "Lindström Labels in India," in Pekka Gronow and Christiane Hofer, eds., *The Lindström Project* 2 (Vienna: Gesellschaft für Historische Tonträger, 2011), 88–94, quote from 88; and from Paul Vernon, "Odeon Records." See also Suresh Chandvankar, "Centenary of Indian Gramophone Record," 1–18, and Amitabha Ghosh, "The Pre-Commercial Era of Wax Cylinder Recordings in India," 19–29, in Amlan Das Gupta, *Music and Modernity: North Indian Classical Music in an Age of Mechanical Reproduction* (Calcutta: Thema, 2007). Runchordas began a phonograph business at the end of 1902, marketing Columbia, Edison, and Pathé phonographs and records. See Paul Vernon, *Ethnic and Vernacular Music, 1898–1960: A Resource and Guide to Recordings* (Westport, CT: Greenwood, 1995), 53.

16. *Foreign Trade in Musical Instruments*, 87.

17. "India from the Viewpoint of the Business Man," *Music Trade Review* 67, no. 24 (December 14, 1918): 45, accessed at mbsi.org, arcade-museum.com.

18. *Phonographische Zeitschrift* 1, no. 1 (August 15, 1900): 1.

19. *Phonographische Zeitschrift* 12, no. 2 (January 12, 1911): 19–21, here 19.

20. Otto Sperber, "Musikautomaten als Kulturträger," *Phonographische Zeitschrift* 15, no. 30 (July 23, 1914): 588–589.

21. "Ein phonographisches Archiv in Paris," *Phonographische Zeitschrift* 3, no. 7 (March 26, 1902): 80.

22. "Vom Wiener Phonographischen Archiv," *Phonographische Zeitschrift* 3, no. 22 (October 8, 1902): 258–259.

23. "Ein staatliches Phonogramm-Archiv in Deutschland," *Phonographische Zeitschrift* 5, no. 8 (February 24, 1904): 111–114, here 112.

24. "Das preussische Kultusministerium und das Phonogramm-Archiv," *Phonographische Zeitschrift* 8, no. 51 (December 19, 1907): 1472–1473.

25. "Max Chop," *Phonographische Zeitschrift* 13, no. 20 (May 16, 1912): 435; Karl Lenzen, "Chop, Friedrich Johann Theodor Maximilian," in *Neue Deutsche Biographie* 3 (1957): 214 [online edition], http://www.deutsche-biographie.de/pnd116506946.html, accessed February 28, 2018.

26. Chop comments on the difficulty of listening to "Eastern, Asiatic music" in "Phono-Kritik: Morgenländische Musik," *Phonographische Zeitschrift* 7, no. 25 (June 21, 1906): 531–535, here 531; and *Phonographische Zeitschrift* 7, no. 26 (June 28, 1906): 547–549. On the impact of the Beka recordings, see Max Chop, "Phono-Kritik: Neue Asiatische Beka-Aufnahmen," *Phonographische Zeitschrift* 10, no. 26 (June 30, 1909): 624–630, here 624.

27. Chop, "Morgenländische Musik," *Phonographische Zeitschrift* 7, no. 25, 531–532.

28. Ibid., 532.

29. Max Chop, "Phonokritik: Orientalische Beka-Aufnahmen," *Phonographische Zeitschrift* 9, no. 3 (January 16, 1908): 61–63, here 63; and *Phonographische Zeitschrift* 9, no. 4 (January 23, 1908): 91–93.

30. Chop, "Morgenländische Musik," *Phonographische Zeitschrift* 7, no. 25 (June 21, 1906): 532.

31. Chop, "Morgenländische Musik," *Phonographische Zeitschrift* 7, no. 26 (June 28, 1906): 547–548, with reference to Turkish, Arabic, and Indian music.

32. Chop, "Morgenländische Musik," *Phonographische Zeitschrift* 7, no. 25 (June 21, 1906): 533. A Wladowsky recording can be found on YouTube at http://www.youtube.com/watch?v=ssdq3bgQyzM, accessed on February 28, 2018.

33. Chop, "Morgenländische Musik," *Phonographische Zeitschrift* 7, no. 25 (June 21, 1906): 532.

34. Chop, "Morgenländische Musik," *Phonographische Zeitschrift* 7, no. 26 (June 28, 1906): 549.

35. Chop, "Morgenländische Musik," *Phonographische Zeitschrift* 7, no. 25 (June 21, 1906): 532.

36. Chop, "Morgenländische Musik," *Phonographische Zeitschrift* 7, no. 26 (June 28, 1906): 547.

37. Chop, "Phonokritik: Orientalische Beka-Aufnahmen," *Phonographische Zeitschrift* 9, no. 3 (January 16, 1908): 61.

38. Chop, "Phonokritik: Orientalische Beka-Aufnahmen," *Phonographische Zeitschrift* 9, no. 4 (January 23, 1908): 93.

Conclusion

1. On the emergence of Caribbean music from the meeting of diverse peoples on the islands, see Timothy Rommen, "Landscapes of Diaspora," in Philip V. Bohlman, ed., *The Cambridge History of World Music* (Cambridge: Cambridge University Press, 2013), 557–583; Peter Manuel, "Afro-Caribbean Music," in *Grove Music Online / Oxford Music Online*, http:////www.oxfordmusiconline.com/grovemusic/view/10.1093/gmo/9781561592630.001.0001/omo-9781561592630-e-1002087149, accessed August 1, 2018; and Nancy Morris, "Cultural Interaction in Latin American and Caribbean Music," *Latin American Research Review* 34, no. 1 (1999): 187–200.

2. On world capitalism and the Hawaiian Kingdom, see Marshall Sahlins and Patrick V. Kirch, *Anahulu: The Anthropology of History in the Kingdom of Hawaii,*

vol. 1, Marshall Sahlins, *Historical Ethnography* (Chicago: University of Chicago Press, 1992). On the early missionaries in Hawaii, see George S. Kanahele, "Hīmeni, History of," in Kanahele, ed., *Hawaiian Music and Musicians: An Illustrated History* (Honolulu: University of Hawai'i Press, 1979), 129–141. On the musical instruments, see Jim Tranquada and John King, *The 'Ukulele: A History* (Honolulu: University of Hawai'i Press, 2012); and John Troutman, *Kīka Kila: How the Hawaiian Steel Guitar Changed the Sound of Modern Music* (Chapel Hill: University of North Carolina Press, 2016).

3. Michael Denning sketches the role of port cities in *Noise Uprising: The Audiopolitics of a World Musical Revolution* (London: Verso, 2015). Marc Matera portrays London as a meeting place for African intellectuals and the new popular music in *Black London: The Imperial Metropolis and Decolonization in the Twentieth Century* (Berkeley: University of California Press, 2015), 145–199; see especially his discussion of calypso music, 183–185.

4. Simon Collier, "The Popular Roots of the Argentine Tango," in *History Workshop Journal* 34 (1992): 92–100. For an overview of the development of tango, see Gerard Béhague, "Tango," in *Grove Music Online / Oxford Music Online*, Oxford University Press, accessed January 13, 2017, http://www.oxfordmusiconline.com/subscriber/article/grove/music/27473. For contemporary global and gender perspectives, see Kathy Davis, *Dancing Tango: Passionate Encounters in a Globalizing World* (New York: New York University Press, 2015).

It is a historical illusion to heap praise on democratic musical genres as inevitable allies of political democracy. The same kinds of folk music that gave expression to political emancipation can be taken up by dictators creating their own variation on populist culture. For a sample of this kind of appropriation of the new music, see Lisa Shaw, "São Coisas Nossas: Samba and Identity in the Vargas Era (1930–45)," *Portuguese Studies* 14 (1998): 152–69.

5. Simon Collier, "'Hullo Tango': The English Tango Craze and Its After-Echoes," in *The Land That England Lost: Argentina and Britain—a Special Relationship*, ed. Alistair Hennessy and John King (London: British Academic Press, 1992), 215.

6. Marina Cañardo, "Max Glücksmann and Odeon Records in Argentina," in Pekka Gronow and Christiane Hofer, eds., *The Lindström Project* 3 (Vienna: Gesellschaft für Historische Tonträger, 2010), 41.

7. Bronislaw Malinowski, *A Diary in the Strict Sense of the Term*, trans. Norbert Guterman (New York: Harcourt, Brace and World, 1967), 12.

8. Cañardo, "Max Glücksmann," 40.

9. The global reach of jazz is sampled in Atkins E. Taylor, "Toward a Global History of Jazz," in Taylor, ed., *Jazz Planet* (Jackson: University Press of Missouri, 2003), xi–xxvii. Robert W. Rydell and Rob Kroes discuss jazz within a general history of the spread of mass culture in *Buffalo Bill in Bologna: The Americanization of the World, 1869–1922* (Chicago: University of Chicago Press, 2005), 91–94. For a general appreciation of jazz with special attention to Germany, see Berndt Ostendorf, "Subversive Reeducation? Jazz as a Liberating Force in Germany and Europe," *Revue Française*

d'études américaines (2001): 53–71. Ann Douglas discusses the spread of jazz to Europe in the context of black/white cultural confrontations in *Terrible Honesty: Mongrel Manhattan in the 1920s* (New York: Farrar, Straus and Giroux, 1995). Ronald Radano criticizes ahistorical appropriations of jazz in "On Ownership and Value," *Black Music Research Journal* 30, no. 2 (Fall 2010): 363–370, and in Ronald Radano and Samuel A. Floyd Jr., "Interpreting the African-American Musical Past: A Dialogue," *Black Music Research Journal* 29, no. 1 (Spring 2009): 1–10.

10. The preceding description is drawn from Edward A. Berlin, "Ragtime," in *Grove Music Online / Oxford Music Online*, Oxford University Press, http://www.oxfordmusiconline.com/subscriber/article/grove/music/A2252241, accessed February 22, 2017.

11. "Musical Gossip Which Will Be of Interest to Your Customers," *Voice of the Victor* 8, no. 10 (October 1913): 14. Debussy and Stravinsky offered playful musical responses to the fashion for ragtime. See Ann McKinley, "Debussy and American Minstrelsy," *The Black Perspective in Music* 14, no. 3 (Autumn 1986): 249–258; and Barbara B. Heyman, "Stravinsky and Ragtime," *Musical Quarterly* 68, no. 4 (October 1982): 543–562.

12. Walter Stevens, "Home from Europe," *Talking Machine World* 5, no. 5 (1914): 1; Max Chop, "Phonokritik: Beka," *Phonographische Zeitschrift* 13, no. 21 (May 22, 1913): 458; US Department of Commerce and Labor, *Foreign Trade in Musical Instruments* [Special Consular Reports, no. 55] (Washington: Government Printing Office, 1912), 62 and 82.

13. Jeffrey H. Jackson, "Making Jazz French: The Reception of Jazz Music in Paris, 1927–1934," in *French Historical Studies* 25, no. 1 (Winter 2002): 149–170, here especially 159–168.

14. See Ostendorf, "Subversive Reeducation?"; and J. Bradford Robinson, "The Jazz Essays of Theodor Adorno: Some Thoughts on Jazz Reception in Weimar Germany," *Popular Music* 13, no. 1 (1994): 1–25.

15. In contrast to Ostendorf and Bradford, Michael Kater argues for an earlier diffusion and vibrant jazz culture in Berlin in *Different Drummers: Jazz in the Culture of Nazi Germany* (New York: Oxford University Press, 1992). See also Cornelius Partsch, "That Weimar Jazz," *New England Review* 23, no. 4 (Fall 2002): 179–194, on the affinity between jazz and a German stylistic development, *Neue Sachlichkeit* (the New Objectivity); and Michael H. Kater, "Forbidden Fruit? Jazz in the Third Reich," *American Historical Review* 94, no. 1 (February 1989): 11–43.

John Willett captures the spirit of *Neue Sachlichkeit*—and therewith a context for German jazz—in *Art and Politics in the Weimar Period: The New Sobriety, 1917–1933* (New York: Pantheon, 1980). Willett's book analyzes the culture of the Weimar Republic as the midpoint of a force field between the United States and Soviet Russia; it is worth reading for this approach, worked out with more skill than in many subsequent cultural histories that advertise themselves as transnational.

16. This was a commercial venture to rival the prewar establishment of a school pedagogy division by Victor; but Ludwig Koch, the director of the Lindström

division, had utopian ambitions of bringing high culture to the masses. See Ludwig Koch, "Was wir wollen," in *Kultur und Schallplatte* 1, no. 1 (July 1919): 1. On Koch and the educational division, see Christiane Hofer, "'Die Schallplatte als Wegweiser zum Wissen': Ludwig Koch und die Kulturabteilung der Lindström AG," in *Lindström Project* 3, 6–13.

17. Thomas Mann in *25 Jahre Lindström, 1904–1929*, ed. Alfred Gutman (Berlin: Carl Lindström, 1929), 144.

18. Oscar Bie, "Kultur und Schallplatte," in *25 Jahre Lindström*, 140. On Bie, see Walther Vetter, "Bie, Oskar" in *Neue Deutsche Biographie* 2 (1955): 219–220 [Online-fassung], http://www.deutsche-biographie.de/pnd116161795.html. The anniversary volume *25 Jahre Lindström* can now be viewed online at http://grammophon-platten .de/page.php?479.6.

19. Curt Sachs, "Exotische Musik," in *25 Jahre Lindström*, 196–199, quote from 199.

20. Marshall Berman, *All That Is Solid Melts into Air: The Experience of Modernity* (New York: Simon and Schuster, 1982).

21. Max Weber, "Science as a Vocation," in *From Max Weber: Essays in Sociology*, ed. Hans Gerth and C. Wright Mills (1919; Oxford University Press, 1946), 129–156. The case for a Marxian interpretation of modern society and culture has been renewed by Thomas Piketty, *Capital in the Twenty-First Century* (Cambridge, MA: Harvard University Press, 2014). While Piketty's theoretical claims must be evaluated by economists, his book makes an independent and massively documented historical argument that since the late eighteenth century, with the exception of the three decades after 1945, wealth in capitalist societies has accumulated in tiny elites. His discussions of Jane Austen's *Sense and Sensibility* and Balzac's *Père Goriot* challenge historians to give closer attention to property relations and oligarchic domination in modern societies.

22. Arjun Appadurai and Carol A. Breckenridge, "Editors' Comments," *Public Culture* 1, no. 1 (Fall 1988): 1–4; Appadurai and Breckenridge, "Why Public Culture?" *Public Culture* 1, no. 1 (Fall 1988): 5–9; Ulf Hannerz, "Notes on the Global Ecumene," *Public Culture* 1, no. 2 (Spring 1989): 66–75.

23. John Tomlinson, *Globalization and Culture* (Chicago: University of Chicago Press, 1999), 2–3, 7, 11, 148.

24. Anna Lowenhaupt Tsing, *Friction: An Ethnography of Global Connection* (Princeton, NJ: Princeton University Press, 2005), ix–xiv, 4; Stuart Alexander Rockefeller, "'Flow,'" in *Current Anthropology* 52, no. 4 (August 2011): 557–578.

25. Eric Hobsbawm and Terence Ranger, eds., *The Invention of Tradition* (Cambridge: Cambridge University Press, 1983).

26. Martin Clayton, "Musical Renaissance and Its Margins in England and India, 1874–1914," in *Music and Orientalism in the British Empire, 1780s–1940s: Portrayal of the East*, ed. Martin Clayton and Bennett Zon (Aldershot/Hampshire, UK: Ashgate, 2007), 71–93.

27. Akira Iriye, *Cultural Internationalism and World Order* (Baltimore: Johns Hopkins University Press, 1997).

FURTHER READING

This select bibliography is intended as an introduction to the subjects of this book. It attempts to further a critical understanding of topics like globalization and the changing meanings of music in modern societies by including a wide range of sources. Outstanding older works of scholarship and a few original sources take their place alongside recent scholarly literature; a wide variety of viewpoints and methods is represented. Not all scholarly wisdom is contained in the English language, and a few foreign-language entries are included. Fuller documentation of the book's source material can be found in the notes to the text.

General

Albèra, Philippe. "Les leçons de l'exotisme." *Cahiers de musiques traditionnelles* 9, new series (1996): 53–84.

Appadurai, Arjun, and Carol Breckenridge. "Why Public Culture?" *Public Culture* 1, no. 1 (Fall 1988): 5–9.

Bayly, C. A. *The Birth of the Modern World, 1780–1914*. Oxford, UK: Blackwell, 2004.

Bohlman, Philip V., ed. *The Cambridge History of World Music*. Cambridge: Cambridge University Press, 2013.

Broughton, Simon, and Mark Ellingham. *The Rough Guide to World Music*, new ed., 3 vols. London: Rough Guides, 2006–2009.

Fulcher, Jane E., ed. *The Oxford Handbook of the New Cultural History of Music*. New York: Oxford University Press, 2011.

Geyer, Michael, and Charles Bright. "World History in a Global Age." *American Historical Review* 100, no. 4 (October 1995): 1034–1060.

Iriye, Akira, and Jürgen Osterhammel, general eds. *A History of the World, 3: A World Connecting, 1870–1945*, ed. Emily S. Rosenberg. Cambridge, MA: Harvard University Press, 2012.

Nettl, Bruno. *Encounters in Ethnomusicology: A Memoir*. Warren, MI: Harmonie Park Press, 2002.

Osterhammel, Jürgen. *The Transformation of the World: A Global History of the Nineteenth Century*, trans. Patrick Camiller. Princeton, NJ: Princeton University Press, 2014.

Rockefeller, Stuart A. "'Flow.'" *Current Anthropology* 52, no. 4 (August 2011): 557–578. *Songlines* (1999–).

Part 1. Craft

Baker, Malcolm, and Brenda Richardson, eds. *A Grand Design: The Art of the Victoria and Albert Museum*. New York: Harry Abrams, 1997.

Byatt, A. S. *The Children's Book*. New York: Alfred A. Knopf, 2009.

Clayton, Martin, and Bennett Zon, eds. *Music and Orientalism in the British Empire, 1780s–1940s: Portrayal of the East*. Aldershot/Hampshire, UK: Ashgate, 2007.

Hughes, Meirion, and Robert Stradling. *The English Musical Renaissance, 1840–1940: Constructing a National Music*, 2nd ed. Manchester, UK: University of Manchester Press, 2001.

Jackson, Myles W. *Harmonious Triads: Physicists, Musicians, and Instrument Makers in Nineteenth-Century Germany*. Cambridge, MA: MIT Press, 2006.

Ruskin, John. *The Genius of John Ruskin: Selections from His Writings*, ed. John D. Rosenberg. Charlottesville: University of Virginia Press, 1998.

Stansky, Peter. *Redesigning the World: William Morris, the 1880s and the Arts and Crafts*. Princeton, NJ: Princeton University Press, 1985.

Part 2. Science

Asch, Mitchell G. *Gestalt Psychology in German Culture, 1890–1967: Holism and the Quest for Objectivity*. Cambridge: Cambridge University Press, 1995.

Cole, Douglas. *Franz Boas: The Early Years, 1858–1906*. Seattle: University of Washington Press, 1999.

Ellis, Alexander J. "On the Musical Scales of Various Nations." *Journal of the Society of Arts* 38 (March 27, 1885): 485–527.

Farrell, Gerry. *Indian Music and the West*. Oxford, UK: Clarendon Press, 1997.

Ghuman, Nalini. *Resonances of the Raj: India in the English Musical Imagination, 1897–1947*. New York: Oxford University Press, 2014.

HaCohen, Ruth. *The Music Libel against the Jews*. New Haven: Yale University Press, 2012.

Hart, Robert. *The I. G. in Peking: Letters of Robert Hart, Chinese Maritime Customs, 1868–1907*, ed. John K. Fairbank et al. Cambridge, MA: Harvard University Press, 1975.

Helmholtz, Hermann. *On the Sensations of Tone as a Physiological Basis for the Theory of Music*, trans. Alexander J. Ellis. New York: Dover, 1954.

Lavezzoli, Peter. *The Dawn of Indian Music in the West: Bhairavi*. New York: Continuum, 2006.

Malm, William P. *Traditional Japanese Music and Musical Instruments*, new ed. Tokyo: Kodansha, 2000.

Penny, H. Glenn. *Objects of Culture: Ethnology and Ethnographic Museums in Imperial Germany*. Chapel Hill: University of North Carolina Press, 2002.

Racy, A. J. *Making Music in the Arab World: The Culture and Artistry of Ṭarab*. Cambridge: Cambridge University Press, 2003.

Simon, Artur, ed. *Das Berliner Phonogramm-Archiv 1900–2000: Sammlungen der traditionellen Musik der Welt*. Berlin: Verlag für Wissenschaft und Bildung, 2000.

Stocking, George W., Jr. *Victorian Anthropology*. New York: Free Press, 1987.

Stumpf, Carl. *The Origins of Music*, trans. and ed. David Trippett. Oxford, UK: Oxford University Press, 2012.

Tagore, Sourindro Mohun, ed. *Hindu Music from Various Authors*, 2nd ed. Calcutta: Bose, 1882.

Takenaka, Toru. "Isawa Shūji's 'National Music': National Sentiment and Cultural Westernisation in Meiji Japan." *Itinerario* 34, no. 3 (December 2010): 97–118.

Ziegler, Susanna. *Die Wachszylinder des Berliner Phonogramm-Archivs*. Berlin: Staatliche Museen zu Berlin, 2006.

Part 3. Commerce

Becker, Peter, et al. *100 Jahre Schallplatte: Von Hannover in die Welt*. Hamburg: Polygram, 1987.

DeGraaf, Leonard. *Edison and the Rise of Innovation*. New York: Sterling, 2015.

Gaisberg, Frederick W. *The Music Goes Round: An Autobiography*. New York: Arno Press, 1977.

Gronow, Pekka. "The Record Industry Comes to the Orient." *Ethnomusicology* 25, no. 2 (May 1981): 251–284.

Gronow, Pekka, and Christiane Hofer. *The Lindström Project: Contributions to the History of the Record*. Vienna: Gesellschaft für Historische Tonträger, 2009.

Gutmann, Alfred, ed. *25 Jahre Lindström 1904–1929*. Berlin: Lindström, 1929.

Martland, Peter. *Recording History: The British Record Industry, 1888–1931*. Lanham, MD: Scarecrow, 2013.

———. *Since Recordings Began: EMI–The First 100 Years*. London: EMI, 1997.

Osterhammel, Jürgen. "Globale Horizonte europäischer Kunstmusik, 1860–1930." *Geschichte und Gesellschaft* 38, no. 1 (2012): 1–47.

Racy, A. J. "Record Industry and Egyptian Traditional Music, 1904–1932." *Ethnomusicology* 20, no. 1 (January 1976): 23–48.

Sampath, Vikram. "*My Name is Gauhar Jaan!*": The Life and Times of a Musician. New Delhi: Rupa, 2010.

Steen, Andreas. *Zwischen Unterhaltung und Revolution: Grammophone, Schallplatten und die Anfänge der Musikindustrie in Shanghai, 1878–1937.* Wiesbaden: Harrassowitz, 2006.

Suisman, David. *Selling Sounds: The Commercial Revolution in American Music.* Cambridge, MA: Harvard University Press, 2009.

Conclusion

Collier, Simon. "The Popular Roots of the Argentine Tango." *History Workshop Journal* 34 (1992): 92–100.

Cowell, Henry. *New Musical Resources,* ed. David Nicholls. Cambridge: Cambridge University Press, 1996.

Denning, Michael. *Noise Uprising: The Audiopolitics of a World Musical Revolution.* London: Verso, 2015.

Douglas, Ann. *Terrible Honesty: Mongrel Manhattan in the 1920s.* New York: Farrar, Straus and Giroux, 1995.

Jones, Andrew F. *Yellow Music: Media Culture and Colonial Modernity in the Chinese Jazz Age.* Durham, NC: Duke University Press, 2001.

Lewis, Su Lin. *Cities in Motion: Urban Life and Cosmopolitanism in Southeast Asia, 1920–1940.* Cambridge: Cambridge University Press, 2016.

Matera, Marc. *Black London: The Imperial Metropolis and Decolonization in the Twentieth Century.* Berkeley: University of California Press, 2015.

Radano, Ronald. *Lying Up a Nation: Race and Black Music.* Chicago: University of Chicago Press, 2003.

Shaw, Lisa. "São Coisas Nossas: Samba and Identity in the Vargas Era (1930–45)." *Portuguese Studies* 14 (1998): 152–69.

Troutman, John. *Kīka Kila: How the Hawaiian Steel Guitar Changed the Sound of Modern Music.* Chapel Hill: University of North Carolina Press, 2016.

INDEX

Exposition Universelle of 1889. *See* Paris World's Fair of 1889

fado, 3
Fauser, Annegret, 12
Fétis, François-Joseph, 138
Field Museum, 161
Fiji, 41
Fischer, Erich, 155
flat disc records, 178, 208, 215–216; shellac material, 215
"flow," 271n4
folk music, 31, 37, 52, 103. *See also* Engel, Carl; English Musical Renaissance
Folk-Song Society, 52
Forster, Georg, criticized as utopian, 19
France, 15, 85, 140, 178, 253, 256; musical responses to globalization, 12. *See also* Paris; Pathé Frères
Frankenstein (Shelley), 188
Fremantle, 185, 186
French culture, universalism, 20
French Revolution, 19
Fuller-Maitland, J. A., 53
fusion music, 3, 18

Gadamer, Hans-Georg, 6–7
Gaisberg, Fred, 179, 191, 202, 221, 225–235, 242; Emile Berliner and, 227; discovers Caruso, 228–229; early biography, 226; European tour, 228–229; Indian tour, 222–225; in London, 228; racism, 233; Russian tour, 229–231; transnationalism, 233
Gaisberg, Will, 224, 225
gallery of types, 64; definition, 16; national music types as, 36; static images of peoples in, 15. *See also* Herder, Johann Gottfried; Jones, William; philosophes
General History of the Science and Practice of Music (Hawkins), 33–34
Genesis of a Music (Partch), 79

German East Africa, 44
German immigration: to England, 11, 45; to Manchester, 31–32, 45; to the United States, 11
German phonograph industry, 237–248; dedication to exports, 241; in India, 242–243; sales figures, 241
German South West Africa, 180
German universities, 124, 126–127, 166; University of Berlin, 113, 143, 245; University of Bonn, 39; University of Freiburg, 213; University of Göttingen, 135; University of Leipzig, 130, 136; University of Würzburg, 135
Germany: importance for creation of scientific ethnomusicology, 154; overseas empire and, 124–126; Samoan colony, 209–210; surpasses Austria as cultural center, 12–13
Geyer, Michael, 15
Ghuman, Nalini, 45–56
Gilbert, W. S., 98
Gilmore, W. E., 202, 203
Gilpin, Charles, 223, 224
Girschner, Max, 165
global culture, 14–19; definition of, 18. *See also* new global culture
global encounters, 4–8; historical approach to, 4; specificity of, 4–5. *See also* cultural encounters
globalization, 8, 24; communications transformed in, 134, 152, 254; compared to modernization, 275n23; craft revival and, 18; definition, 15; diversity of culture and, 4; homogenization of culture and, 3–4, 169; networks of knowledge and, 151–153; persistence of culture and, 10–11; theories of, 258–263. *See also* global encounters; localism; new global culture
globalized music, 250–253

Smith, Eli, 95–97
Smith, Hermann, 99, 107
Society of Arts, 51, 84, 85, 93, 98. *See also*
    Ellis, Alexander J. (John Alexander
    Sharpe); Hipkins, A. J.
Sooy, Raymond, 191
sound, history of, 277n31
South Asia. *See* India
South Kensington Museum. *See* Victoria
    and Albert Museum
Stefansson, Vilhjalmur, 189–190
Steinen, Karl von den, 161–162, 166–167
Steinway and Sons, 52
Stevens, Walter, 180, 202, 204, 205, 207,
    253
Stones of Venice, The (Ruskin), 59
St. Petersburg, 142, 143, 230
Stradling, Robert, 44–45
Straus, Max, 240
Stravinsky, Igor, 325n11
Stumpf, Carl, 127–171, 245, 246, 254–
    255; evaluation of Ellis's scale
    measurements, 145; evaluation of
    Ellis's written work, 138–139, 144;
    evolutionary thinking, 139, 146;
    Thai performers and, 139–146.
    See also Boas, Franz; Phonogram
    Archive, Berlin (Phonogramm
    Archiv)
Sullivan, Arthur, 98
Sydney, 184, 221

Tagore, S. M., 111–118, 130, 261
Tahiti, 10
Tainter, Charles Sumner, 226
Talking Machine World, 240; polar
    exploration and phonographs, 188–
    190; stories from around the world,
    179–181
tango, 251–252; post-1918 popularity, 19;
    pre-1914 beginnings, 18
Tanjore, 67
Tartar music, 230–231

technology, globalization of music and,
    24–25
Thai music, 139–146, 152, 255; popular
    and high dance traditions, 140–143.
    See also musical scales
Thai musical instruments, 63–64,
    143–145
Thai performers, world tour, 139–146
"thick description," 7
Thurnwald, Richard, 12; complaints
    about cylinder phonograph,
    167–168
Tlingit Indians, 161
Togo, 165
Tomlinson, John, 260
Tonga, 41
transatlantic triad, 11–14, 217–219
transnationalism, 22–23, 140–142, 233,
    255; Emile Berliner as founder of
    transnational business, 208–219.
    See also Iriye, Akira
Travancore, 67
travel accounts: Europeanization of
    music in, 3, 107; music in, 2–3; net-
    works of knowledge and, 151; world
    voyage accounts as genre, 15–16
Traviata, La (Verdi), 232
Trinidad, 179
Truth and Method (Gadamer), 6–7
tuning forks, 76; Japanese, 99, 102, 144
tuning systems, 70; equal temperament,
    49; mean temperament, 49
Turkish music, 239, 246

universities. *See* Cambridge Univer-
    sity; German universities; Harvard
    University; University of Calcutta;
    University of Vienna
University of Calcutta, 114
University of Vienna, 126, 149, 162

Vecchiotti, G. B., 113, 118
Veeder, P. V., 99